TRAUMA PSYCHOLOGY

TRAUMA PSYCHOLOGY

Issues in Violence, Disaster, Health, and Illness

VOLUME 2: HEALTH AND ILLNESS

Edited by Elizabeth K. Carll

Praeger Perspectives

Contemporary Psychology
Chris E. Stout, Series Editor

Westport, Connecticut
London

Library of Congress Cataloging-in-Publication Data

Trauma psychology : issues in violence, disaster, health, and illness/ edited by
Elizabeth K. Carll ; foreword by H. E. Khunying Laxanachantorn Laohaphan.
   v. ; cm. — (Praeger perspectives) (Contemporary psychology, ISSN 1546–668X)
   Includes bibliographical references and index.
   ISBN-13: 978–0–275–98525–7 (set : alk. paper)
   ISBN-13: 978–0–275–98531–8 (v. 1 : alk. paper)
   ISBN-13: 978–0–275–98532–5 (v. 2 : alk. paper)
  1. Post-traumatic stress disorder.   2. Psychic trauma.   3. Violence—
Psychological aspects.   4. Disasters—Psychological aspects.   I. Carll,
Elizabeth K.   II. Series.   III. Series: Contemporary psychology (Praeger
Publishers)
  [DNLM: 1. Stress Disorders, Traumatic.   2. Crime Victims—
psychology.   3. Disasters.   4. Violence. WM 172 T77755 2007]
  RC552.P67T552   2007
  616.85'21—dc22   2007009459

British Library Cataloguing in Publication Data is available.

Library of Congress Catalog Card Number: 2007009459
ISBN-13: 978–0–275–98525–7 (set)
ISBN-13: 978–0–275–98531–8 (vol 1)
ISBN-13: 978–0–275–98532–5 (vol 2)
ISSN: 1546–668X

First published in 2007

Praeger Publishers, 88 Post Road West, Westport, CT 06881
An imprint of Greenwood Publishing Group, Inc.
www.praeger.com

Printed in the United States of America

The paper used in this book complies with the
Permanent Paper Standard issued by the National
Information Standards Organization (Z39.48–1984).

10 9 8 7 6 5 4 3 2 1

CONTENTS

Introduction

Elizabeth K. Carll

Across the last 15 years, there has been a mushrooming interest in the effects of traumatic events on people and societies. The news media report daily occurrences of war atrocities, disasters, violence, and mayhem. Simultaneously, more attention and research is now focused on examining the psychological effects, particularly stress and trauma, of disaster and violence. Close attention is also being paid to psychological responses to chronic and acute health conditions and disease, and how stress and trauma may affect the course of recovery.

The Evolution of Trauma Psychology

Attention has always been focused on various aspects of trauma, whether the traumas were large scale or individual or occurring as a single event or as a series of ongoing repeated events, as for instance, war, domestic violence, or a catastrophic health condition. The study of these various types of events, though, was generally compartmentalized. In the early 1990s, however, a series of large-scale stressful events—the Persian Gulf Crisis, the first World Trade Center bombing, the Long Island Railroad shooting, and finally, in the mid-1990s, the Oklahoma City bombing—shook the security of our nation.

As a result of these high-profile events, the news media began to increasingly cover the human side of disasters, paying special attention to the trauma experienced by both the survivors and the public. This attention at first appeared specific to each event that occurred; yet it soon became obvious that for mental health professionals and the public a broader understanding was necessary to put the events in context and to understand the relationship of short-term intervention to longer-term treatment. Because of the short life of news stories, for example, the global audience gained the impression that a few months after any disaster everyone had recovered and moved on. This was far from reality, however, especially if the trauma involved the loss of one's home or friends and family. It was also important to recognize that trauma is related not only to violence and disaster, but may have a broad range of causes and precipitating events.

This became especially apparent when I was developing the training course for the Disaster/Crisis Response Network (DRN) that I had established in 1990 for the New York State Psychological Association. The DRN was the first state-wide volunteer disaster mental health network in the nation, and it focused, in particular, on the needs of the public and the community. Training for volunteers was a priority. Training included a compilation of modalities, including Critical Incident Stress Intervention, which was an adaptation of Jeffrey Mitchell's Critical Incident Stress Management Model, as well as psychological first aid, and the distinction between crisis intervention, onsite intervention services, and long term psychotherapy. In addition, it was important for mental health professionals to put these events in context with longer-term traumatic events as well as relate them to trauma issues presented by clients in their practice.

Since a training course or training manual that included all of these facets did not appear to exist in 1990, I began to develop training modules—including one on *Trauma Psychology*—that were sponsored by the state psychological association and to which experienced volunteer members of the Network contributed information. These training modules covered not only crisis intervention and immediate onsite response, but also looked at the continuum of services necessary to help individuals and communities recover. In addition, the training took into consideration preexisting psychological conditions, both recent and longstanding, and the distinction between the use of emergency psychological first aid, short term psychotherapy, and long term psychotherapy as effective interventions.

These training sessions were attended not only by psychologists but also by other mental health professionals and by first responders from the community, including EMS, law enforcement, criminal justice system personnel, clergy, and various hospital staff. By the mid- to late 1990s, other organizations and hospitals were developing various training courses for their own staffs. Universities began looking into developing courses as the demand for trauma training increased.

In the early 1990s, I was often asked to define the term *trauma psychology*. The term was not familiar to mental health professionals, although some were familiar with terms such as psychological trauma, PTSD, and psychotraumatology. Trauma psychology focuses on studying trauma victims and examining intervention modes for immediate, short-term, and long-term trauma caused by a single episode or by ongoing, longer-term events. It also encompasses possible trauma related to the diversity of individual, family, and community events and experiences. The description or definition of trauma psychology, from my perspective, included a broad spectrum of events, that could range from interpersonal violence, sexual assault, war, motor vehicle accidents, workplace violence, and catastrophic illness to trauma relating to acute and chronic health conditions (e.g., cancer, heart disease, spinal cord injury, and paralysis), as well as other types of accidents violence, and illness. Thus, the concept for the two volumes of *Trauma Psychology: Issues in Violence, Disaster, Health, and Illness* grew out of the need for a reference compendium that reflected a wide variety of trauma-related issues. The need for a recognized body or specialty area of trauma research and knowledge within the discipline of psychology had been growing significantly. For example, the International Society for Traumatic Stress Studies was formed in 1985 and has since grown into the largest international organization devoted to the study of trauma-related issues. In addition, the rapidly growing interest in trauma psychology is evidenced by the recent formation, in 2006, of the new Division of Trauma Psychology of the American Psychological Association.

Given this evolution of trauma psychology, it was important that the volumes include not only the typical types of events associated with trauma but also those underrecognized areas that nonetheless have significant traumatic components. Having such a cross section of trauma issues reflects the broad and diverse field of trauma psychology. The two volumes of *Trauma Psychology: Issues in Violence, Disaster, Health, and Illness (Volume 1* and *Volume 2*) are unique, as both volumes include chapters that discuss recognized trauma-related events as well as those underrecognized important areas that reflect the evolving diversity of areas within the specialty of trauma psychology. Volume 1 covers violence and disaster, whereas Volume 2 covers health and medical illness. The chapters in the volumes include a discussion of trauma-related issues and background, along with real-life vignettes and case examples, with recommendations for intervention, treatment, and public policies. The book includes pragmatic information on a broad range of areas related to trauma. *Trauma Psychology: Issues in Violence, Disaster, Health, and Illness* offers chapters discussing well-recognized disasters such as tsunami and fires; accidental disasters such as explosions and transportation accidents; terrorism and violence such as 9/11 and the Madrid terrorist attacks; workplace violence; interpersonal violence; motor vehicle accidents; violence against women; violence and the media; trauma and first responders; the impact of ongoing armed conflict and war on children's development; integrating psychopharmacology into the treatment of PTSD; and the impact of medical illness on children and families.

The volumes also contain often underrecognized trauma-related topics. Included are chapters discussing the impact and effects of politically motivated torture; stalking; kidnapping; the impact of killing on the perpetrator; xenophobia; the effects of homelessness on families and youth; spinal cord injury; burns; AIDS; pain; the difficulty of disclosing trauma in a medical setting; and anesthesia awareness.

The topic of anesthesia awareness, for example, is relatively unknown to many professionals, but it is estimated to occur in one or two of every 1,000 patients who have received general anesthesia and who wake up during surgery because they are underanesthetized. It is estimated that about 50 percent of these patients can hear or feel what is going on but are unable to communicate what is happening because they are temporarily paralyzed, and approximately 30 percent of these patients experience pain. As a result, half of these awareness patients develop significant psychological problems including PTSD.

Defining Trauma

It is important to note, that many people may experience traumatic stress symptoms in the immediate aftermath of crises, but that most do not go on to develop posttraumatic stress disorder. Some people may recover, while others may have lingering and ongoing symptoms, and a still smaller percentage may develop the full syndrome, which can last months, years, and, for a small minority, a lifetime. It is also helpful to keep in mind that individuals may experience a wide variety of traumatic events, but the intensity of a person's responses is a combination of many factors; for instance, the nature of the trauma, its severity, its duration, and, of course, the existence of prior traumatic experiences, as well as what resources and supports are available for dealing with the trauma.

Because the terms *acute stress disorder, posttraumatic stress disorder*, and *complex trauma* are mentioned in the various chapters, the following definitions will assist the reader. *Posttraumatic stress disorder (PTSD)* is considered one of the more extreme forms of anxiety disorders. It is distinguished from all other anxiety disorders in that it is caused by an external event. PTSD is often described as a normal response to an abnormal event. Whether the diagnostic label of acute stress disorder (ASD) or PTSD is used is generally determined by the duration of the symptoms. Essentially they are a set of similar symptoms (as defined below). However, ASD describes the experiencing of symptoms of up to one month's duration. If the symptoms continue past one month, the diagnostic label of PTSD applies. PTSD may develop months or even years after having experienced or witnessed a traumatic event.

A traumatic event can lead to PTSD if it threatens one's physical or mental well-being or results in feelings of intense fear, helplessness, or horror. The major symptoms of PTSD include reexperiencing of the traumatic event (i.e., nightmares, intrusive thoughts, or flashbacks); avoiding reminders of the event and numbing (i.e., avoiding thoughts, people, and activities related to the trauma or an inability to recall aspects of the trauma); and also increased arousal (i.e., difficulty concentrating, trouble falling or staying asleep, hypervigilance, and anger outbursts).

When an individual perceives a danger or threat, a biological alarm is raised, adrenalin increases, heart rate increases, breathing becomes rapid, and the body sets itself up for a fight or flight response. In the majority of individuals, this response returns to equilibrium in a relatively short period of time. For the individual with PTSD, the response may endure. One of my clients described his PTSD as being similar to a car being revved up, where the gas pedal is being pressed but the brakes are on and there is nowhere to go, so the motor just continues to spin and churn.

The terms *Complex PTSD* or *Disorders of Extreme Stress Not Otherwise Specified (DESNOS)* have been suggested to describe a set of symptoms associated with prolonged experiences of severe trauma or interpersonal abuse. This term developed because some experts see PTSD as insufficient to describe the experience and impact of ongoing pervasive trauma. This type of trauma may result from experiences such as chronic child sexual or physical abuse, domestic violence, or ongoing war and torture. Ongoing severe trauma may lead to significant impairment in regulating emotions and behavior, and may have an impact on how survivors perceive themselves and their view of the world.

It is also important to keep in mind that the way people experience, perceive, and display distress is culturally determined, as culture cannot be separated from the worldview of an individual. Definitions of trauma and designations of posttraumatic stress need to be sensitive to the cultural context in which traumatic events occur. For example, for those living in a chronic war zone, the issue of "post" as it relates to stress may not be viewed as meaningful. The chapter on children and war highlights the importance of culture and context, and also gives an overview of the controversy about how differently PTSD may be viewed in different parts of the world.

Interventions also need to take into consideration culture and context because what is considered pathological may vary widely across cultures. Culture also influences peoples' styles of coping, and therefore interventions must address the strengths, rituals, and supports within a community. This was evident in the aftermath of the tsunami, where interventions based on Western values of individualism and open talk may not be viewed as effective in an Eastern culture that values community and interconnectedness and a stoic acceptance of life's adversities. Therefore appropriate interventions need to be tailored to the culture and context in which the traumatic events occur.

These two volumes reflect and highlight a cross section of both recognized and often underrecognized areas within trauma psychology, with a variety of descriptive examples, interventions, recommendations, and suggestions for public policy included. As a result of perusing the volumes, it is hoped the reader will gain a better understanding of the diversity and complexity of issues, as well as the diversity of intervention strategies within trauma psychology.

CHAPTER 1

MOTOR VEHICLE ACCIDENTS AND PSYCHOLOGICAL TRAUMA

Edward J. Hickling and Edward B. Blanchard

MICHELLE'S STORY

The day seemed so ordinary. She'd driven the road hundreds of times. The kids were in their car seats in the back seat, and the radio was playing one of her favorite songs. As she entered the intersection, for just an instant she knew something was wrong! The other car came out of nowhere. Just a black blur to her left and then that horrible sound of the crash. Metal crunching and glass shattering. Oh my God!! This can't be happening! The next thing Michelle remembered was yelling for her kids. "Are you all right? Answer me! Please!" Her son Johnny said, "Yes, mommy, but I'm scared!" but Kelly didn't answer. Not a sound. "Kelly!" As Michelle tried to turn around, she found her left leg was twisted at an unnatural angle, and she was pinned in the seat. She couldn't move, and she felt this sickening feeling take over. Something wet was dripping down her face. As she looked up she saw there was some-one at the door. "Don't move!" he said. "We've called 911. You had an ac-cident." She felt in a daze, and everything seemed unreal. So this is how I'm going to die! Oh no, not now!

After a while, there was a voice saying, "We've got to cover you with this blan-ket, so we can cut you out of the car." Then the air became filled with the sound of the saw cutting her out. How could anyone have survived the crash? Where were her kids? What had happened to them?

Motor vehicle accidents (MVAs) are the most common trauma that occurs in westernized countries. The occurrence of MVAs is so widespread that it is likely that most adults will have been in a car crash by the age of 30. While precise data are not available, the U.S. Department of Transportation has collected data on the number of fatalities and personal injuries. In the United States, the numbers of injuries and fatalities have remained fairly high, albeit with a slow decline in the number of personal injury accidents and the total number of crashes reported over the past decade. There continue to be over 6,000,000 motor vehicle accidents per year in the United States, with over 42,000 fatalities and 2,700,000 personal injuries (United States Department of Transportation, 2004).

Our research, clinical practice and the focus of this chapter will be on people who have suffered a serious injury. While there are a number of less severe, fender bender–type accidents that occur daily, our interest and the focus of this review will be on individuals who suffered an injury serious enough in the MVA to seek medical attention, even though we know that in some instances individuals will suffer psychological injuries in the less severe crashes.

Motor vehicle accidents obviously occur with great frequency. Most people in their life will, unfortunately, have a motor vehicle accident. The seriousness of an accident is hard to define. We could not judge in our research an accident's seriousness by the degree of property damage, as this value varies a great deal dependent upon the year, the make, and the model of each automobile involved. If we tried to judge seriousness by the extent of physical injuries, which can be objectively assessed, we would again have difficulty. As we already know, not all physically injured individuals will have psychological injuries, and those without physical injuries should not be excluded from consideration of having psychological injuries. One solution to this concern, and the one we chose for our investigation, was to look at the individuals who had an MVA that led them to seek some medical attention.

Most of the physical injuries people suffer during MVAs are easy to see. These injuries can force us to take time off from work, to take time out of our personal life, and to use time to heal. Employers and family understand and accept this. The accident, and the injuries caused by the accident, affect our loved ones, and how they now deal with us. They may need to provide care, to get medicines, to act as drivers for children who were usually driven by the MVA survivor, and to accommodate to all the other changes that uniquely affect everyone who is impacted by the MVA. Work may be missed, and meetings with doctors, therapists, and lawyers all need to take place. Children and partners are sometimes forced to adjust to a radical change in a loved one, and often that someone is the person the family depended on in a number of critical and important ways. We take for granted the laundry, the food preparation, and the trips to the store. These can all be instantly affected by an injury to the person who was in a motor vehicle accident.

The overall cost of MVAs is exorbitant. If one considers the time lost from work, the cost of the medical injury, and the impact on a particular individual's life, the overall cost is estimated to be in the tens of billions of dollars each year.

The Center for Stress and Anxiety Disorders at the University at Albany has investigated the psychological aftermath of motor vehicle accidents (MVAs) since 1989, with the development of the Albany Motor Vehicle Accident Project. This project began in the late 1980s, investigating the impact of motor vehicle

accidents psychologically when individuals seen in a private psychological practice seemed to present with symptoms of anxiety and posttraumatic stress disorder (PTSD). However at that time, the diagnostic criteria for PTSD typically
required that the trauma be "outside the range of usual experience." By definition, since most people will in fact experience an MVA in their lifetime, MVAs
were not thought to warrant such a diagnosis. In the early 1990s we were able to
secure funding from the National Institute of Mental Health (NIMH), which
allowed us to begin a systematic investigation of the psychological impact of
MVAs. Since 1995, with continued NIMH funding, we have investigated treatment methods for dealing with PTSD and some of the other frequent psychological consequences of car crashes.

This review will include two major sources of information: a selected review
of the major assessment and treatment findings from available studies and a
summary of the major findings of the Albany MVA Project. Interested readers
are referred to our books if more detailed information is desired (Blanchard &
Hickling, 1997, 2004; Hickling & Blanchard, 1999, 2006a, 2006b). This review
will include the following: a look at MVAs and the traumatic experience that can
follow them, epidemiological studies of MVAs and PTSD, risk factors in the
development of PTSD following MVAs, the natural history of PTSD in MVA
survivors, acute stress disorder, travel anxiety and delayed onset PTSD in MVA
survivors, some of the assessment instruments used for MVA-related PTSD, and
current treatments for the psychological disorders including PTSD that can
follow an MVA.

MVAs and Trauma

What do we mean by trauma? A trauma can be any painful experience, physical
and/or emotional, that can pose a threat of injury or death to oneself or others.
Traumas can make an individual feel terrified and helpless. This means that there
can be at least two parts to the trauma. One is what actually happened, the
physical effects of the trauma; the other is the experience that takes place inside
an individual, the psychological experience. Any powerful event such as an MVA
may or may not turn out to be a traumatic experience for any individual. If an
accident disrupts the person's life and causes a significant physical and/or
emotional reaction, then it can be called traumatic.

It is important to keep in mind that what is traumatic for one person may not
be traumatic for another. How each individual perceives and reacts to an event
determines whether an event turns out to be seen as traumatic or not. For example, people who drive professionally may consider car accidents a natural and
expected part of their life. They may, therefore, not see the circumstances of
some automobile accidents as terribly traumatic. However, watching someone
else's car accident, or even worse, the accident of a family member, may turn out
to be traumatic to the witness. In some examples, even hearing or learning about
a disaster has proven to be traumatic and can cause PTSD. These powerful events

carry the threat of death or personal injury, and can leave the individual feeling powerless and terrified at what occurs.

Epidemiological Studies

Estimates of the incidence and prevalence of PTSD in the U.S. population have varied a great deal. Several studies have looked at the occurrence, or epidemiology, of PTSD using very large surveys. Norris (1992) conducted a telephone survey of 1,000 adults in each of four southern cities. Half the people sampled were male and half were female. Half were Caucasians and half were African Americans. The survey assessed the lifetime occurrence of nine different traumatic events, followed by a series of questions to determine if these individuals met the PTSD criteria for that particular trauma. Norris found that there was a lifetime prevalence of 7.4 per 100 for PTSD from all causes. Important for this chapter was the finding that 23.4 percent of those individuals had experienced an MVA during their lifetime, including 2.6 percent in the past year. Overall, 69 percent of the participants had experienced some traumatic event in their lifetime, 21 percent in the past year. Of those individuals who had a serious MVA, 11.5 percent met the criteria for PTSD, and 9.5 percent of the people who had been in an accident within the past year had PTSD. Norris commented that the high rate of PTSD from MVAs was approximately 2.7 per 100 over the lifetime.

In a similar study, Breslau, Davis, Andreski, and Peterson (1991) assessed 1,007 young adults, aged 21 to 50, who were members in a health maintenance organization in Detroit. The assessors were trained to assess the occurrence of eight specific stressors including serious MVAs. Breslau et al. found that 39.1 percent of those sampled had at least one traumatic event and 3.6 percent had three or more traumatic events in their lifetime. Over 9 percent of the sample had developed PTSD. In addition, 9.4 percent had been involved in serious MVAs, with 11.6 percent of those developing PTSD.

Kessler and colleagues (1994) conducted a large national epidemiological study of psychiatric disorders in the United States. In a sample of 8,098 individuals aged 15–54, trained interviewers again asked about mental health and the impact of specific traumatic events. Of interest to us, Kessler, Sonnega, Bromet, Hughes, and Nelson (1995) asked each individual to select the most upsetting traumatic event in his or her life and then asked about the development of PTSD as a result of that event. A large number of individuals acknowledged being in a life-threatening accident (25% of the men and 13.8% of the women). We do not know how many of these life-threatening accidents were MVAs, but we do know most were. For life-threatening accidents, 44.6 percent of the men and 44.5 percent of the women selected these accidents as the most traumatic events that they had ever experienced. About 6.3 percent of the men who had been in a life-threatening accident developed PTSD while 6.8 percent of the women did. However, these values may underestimate the actual numbers because the possibility of developing PTSD from a serious MVA was not assessed if the respondent identified some other trauma as being more serious.

Overall, women who were exposed to any trauma were twice as likely as men to develop PTSD (20.4% for women vs. 8.2% for men). The researchers found that there was a significant advantage in having received mental health treatment for up to about 6 years posttrauma. Beyond that period of time, about 40 percent of the sample continued to have PTSD for as long as 10 years after the trauma.

We believe that the lifetime prevalence values multiplied by the population in the United States for these three studies give us some estimate of the problem. We estimate that there are between 2,500,000 and 7,000,000 cases of PTSD following MVAs in the United States alone. We believe this is a very sizable mental health problem that has been ignored by all too many American researchers and health care providers.

What Portion of MVA Survivors Develop PTSD?

Another way to ask the question is: "What percentage of MVA survivors develop PTSD?" According to the earlier epidemiological studies, about 19.4 percent of Americans (Kessler, 1995) or up to 23.4 percent (Norris, 1992) are involved in a MVA that is described as a serious trauma. We also found that a sizable portion of the individuals in our studies on MVAs developed PTSD.

As part of the Albany Motor Vehicle Accident Project we initially assessed 158 MVA survivors of serious car accidents with a very comprehensive psychological evaluation (Blanchard, Hickling, Taylor, & Loos, 1995; Blanchard, Hickling, Barton, Taylor, et al., 1996). The evaluation included the Clinician Administered PTSD Scale (CAPS; Blake, et al., 1995b) from which the diagnosis for PTSD was strictly determined. We found that 39.2 percent of the survivors of serious MVAs met the criteria for PTSD one to four months following their accident. Another 45 (28.5%) developed what we termed subsyndromal PTSD. We developed the term subsyndromal PTSD to recognize individuals who had symptoms of PTSD following their accident, but not quite enough to reach the full criteria for PTSD (Criterion B was met, and either Criterion C or D). We also found several individuals who were identified as having subsyndromal PTSD initially but who later developed full PTSD, or delayed onset PTSD. Our rate for developing PTSD is higher than that given by several other studies. We believe this is because we sampled people who were injured seriously enough to seek medical attention, not just anyone who was in an accident. Our sample is also somewhat different in that we waited at least one month to speak to people, because of the need for symptoms to persist for 30 days following the MVA to qualify for a diagnosis for PTSD.

Several other studies have investigated the occurrence of MVA-related PTSD. The largest study to date was conducted in Oxford, England, by Ehlers, Mayou, and Bryant (1998). In their study of 888 emergency room attendees who had been in a MVA, they found that about 23 percent had PTSD when they were reassessed at 3 months, while 16.5 percent continued to have PTSD when reassessed at one year.

Based on the studies to date, we estimate that somewhere between 10 and 45 percent of the survivors of personal injury MVAs develop PTSD. We have analyzed the available data and determined that the percentage of PTSD is affected by the number of males in the sample (the more males, the lower the incidence of PTSD), and by whether some of the patients were more seriously injured and admitted to the hospital. Our best estimate is that about a quarter of the people who are in a serious MVA will develop PTSD (Blanchard & Hickling, 2004).

Predictors/Risk Factors in the Development of PTSD

Our studies have found four independent predictors to the question, "Who develops PTSD from an MVA?" (Blanchard, Hickling, Taylor, Loos, & Forneris, 1996). The first was the history of clinical (or major) depression at some point prior to the MVA. The second was the extent of the physical injury. Third, we found that the degree to which individuals feared dying in their MVA predicted whether they developed PTSD or not. Fourth, we also found that whether or not the survivor had initiated litigation was a strong predictor of later PTSD. We are unsure as to why this last-mentioned variable is a predictor. It may be that if you were injured enough to seek litigation (especially in a "No Fault" insurance state such as New York), then you were probably hurt badly enough to need a lawyer. This could mean that the physical symptoms were not remitting, and that the accident tended to be more severe, more fear provoking, and thus more likely to produce PTSD.

Researchers around the world have replicated each of these predictors (e.g., Ehlers et al., 1998). There are other variables that we also found to be predictive of later PTSD. These variables included the occurrence of dissociative symptoms, reexperiencing symptoms, strong avoidance of thoughts or behavioral reminders of the MVA, history of prior PTSD, gender (female gender was a predictor), and whether or not someone had been killed in the MVA. Other researchers have found that horrific and intrusive memories shortly after the accident predicted later PTSD, as did the presence of initial acute stress disorder (ASD; see, e.g., Harvey & Bryant, 1998).

Several studies have also replicated the finding that being female puts one at greater risk for developing PTSD following a serious MVA, and some have focused on the persistence of ongoing pain or anger (e.g., Mayou, Ehlers, & Bryant, 2002). Interestingly, whom one blames for the accident is a significant predictor of both who develops PTSD and how readily the PTSD remits (Hickling, Blanchard, Buckley, & Taylor, 1999). If one blames oneself for the accident, one tends to fare better. However, if one sees someone else as responsible for the accident, then one is more likely to develop PTSD, and one is less likely to improve spontaneously. Risk factors for the development of PTSD can be found in Table 1.1.

Table 1.1 Risk Factors That Increase the Likelihood of Developing PTSD Following an MVA

Risk Variable	Yes	No
Were there dissociative symptoms (out of body experiences, things seemed unreal, time alteration) at the time of the accident or continuing?		
Are there reexperiencing symptoms (intrusive recollections, nightmares, flashbacks or distress) when reminded of the MVA?		
Are there efforts to try to avoid thoughts or real life reminders of the accident?		
Were the physical injuries serious?		
Was extreme fright or terror caused by the prospect of dying during the MVA?		
Was there a history of depression prior to the MVA?		

MVA-Related PTSD or What You Can Expect over Time

Anyone who has a significant reaction to a trauma wants to know how and when he or she will get better. *Remission* (in our definition) means an individual no longer would meet a full diagnostic criterion for PTSD or subsyndromal PTSD. In many studies the reporting of symptoms that have decreased even by one might still be called remission, although the individual is still plagued with symptoms of PTSD. *Recovery* perhaps is an even more important concept; for us it indicates that an individual no longer falls into the category of still having PTSD or subsyndromal PTSD, and feels much as he or she did before the accident.

The Albany MVA Project first studied a large number of individuals who had developed PTSD following their car accident. The initial group of studies followed individuals who had PTSD at a period 1–4 months after the MVA, and then reassessed these same individuals at 6-month periods for up to a year after their accident and some for even longer. These individuals did not receive any specific psychological treatment and represent, we believe, the natural history of recovery following an MVA (see Blanchard & Hickling, 2004, for a more comprehensive review).

The Albany MVA Project conducted two extensive follow-up assessments after the initial assessment, one at 6 months post-MVA and one at 12 months post-MVA (with a more limited assessment at an 18-month assessment of individuals who had initially had PTSD). We retained 91.8 percent of our sample at 6 months, and 84.6 percent at one year. By a 6-month period of time, 54.5 percent had shown some remission of symptoms, 17 of the 55 showed full recovery, while

13 (23.9%) showed improvement to a subsyndromal level of PTSD. Forty-five percent showed no change in symptoms, retaining the diagnosis of full PTSD over the first 6-month period of time.

Individuals who were originally diagnosed with subsyndromal PTSD showed more rapid remission of symptoms than those who had been diagnosed with full PTSD. By the first month of follow-up, the proportion that remitted was significantly more than that of those in the PTSD group (9.3%). At 3 months, 46.5 percent had remitted and by 6 months, 67.4 percent showed noticeable improvement in their symptoms. However, two participants had, in fact, worsened and now met the criterion for delayed onset PTSD.

The one-year follow-up of the MVA survivors was completed on 83.5 percent of our initial group of MVA survivors. The month-by-month diagnostic status for the 48 MVA survivors who were initially diagnosed with PTSD showed that by 6 months the degree of remission had essentially plateaued, showing little change over the next 6 months. The number of people who still met the criteria for full PTSD ranged from 42 percent for months 10, 11, and 12 to 50 percent for month 7. We were also able to follow 35 of those who had initial PTSD out to 18 months. A plateau-like response remained, with very little change occurring. In months 12 to 18, the proportion of the sample that remained at full PTSD ranged from 34.3 percent for months 17 and 18 to 40 percent for months 14 and 15.

Our data show that the majority of MVA survivors who initially develop PTSD do show noticeable spontaneous improvement over the first 6 to 8 months. Approximately one-third will show complete recovery with no intervention. Thereafter, there is a very gradual remission rate, with a 12-month remission rate of about 65 percent showing some improvement. Kessler et al.'s (1995) study noted there was continued gradual improvement as far as 6 years posttrauma in their retrospective study of a large sample of mixed trauma survivors with PTSD.

It is important to remember that improvement in PTSD symptoms is not equal to absence of symptoms. Improvement means that the symptoms decrease, not that the symptoms go away totally. If you are still bothered by nightmares, or startlement, or intrusive thoughts, or difficulty driving, your life can still be quite severely affected by the accident, even though you know you are better than you were in the weeks right after it.

Who Gets Better?

One of the questions we tried to address was whether or not we could predict who would show improvement at the 6- and 12-month period of time. Using regression analyses we were able to predict, with some degree of success, who would continue to have difficulty and who would show improvement.

One of the criteria we used for prediction was the Clinician Administered PTSD Scale (CAPS) score. The CAPS is a structured interview scoring method that measures both the intensity and the frequency of each PTSD symptom. The higher the score on the CAPS, the more frequent and intense were the symptoms of PTSD. We found we could predict the 6-month CAPS score if we knew the following: (1) the degree of physical recovery; (2) whether the individual had major depression at the time of the initial assessment (about 2 months after the MVA); (3) whether there had been pre-MVA major depression or alcohol abuse; (4) how vulnerable the individual felt at the time of the accident; and (5) the quality of the family relationships after the MVA. The better the family relationships, the better the recovery. Looking at PTSD symptoms at one year, we found that the more severe the symptoms of PTSD, the greater the sense of vulnerability in the MVA, and that the presence of alcohol abuse predicted long-term difficulty.

What became clear was that the initial severity of the PTSD symptoms was a major predictor of both short- and longer-term remission. The more severely affected individuals were more likely to continue to be symptomatic at both 6 and 12 months. We also found that the severity of the physical injury and whether the injury healed well or not predicted short-term psychological symptoms (6 months) but did not seem to predict the recovery from PTSD symptoms at a 12-month period of time. Finally, the indicators of chronic psychological problems before the MVA were also associated with a poor recovery. It became apparent that individuals who had not improved by 6 to 8 months after the MVA on their own were unlikely to show much improvement up to 18 months after the accident.

We also examined whether or not symptoms of PTSD remitted over a longer period of time (18–24 months) by using a mail survey. Here, instead of interviewing each MVA survivor, we used the PTSD Check List, the PCL. We also had the MVA survivors fill out other questionnaires, including mood inventories, anxiety inventories, and measures of the impact of the trauma. We received 100 replies from the original 158 survivors, and found that at 24 months after their initial assessment, 23.5 percent of those initially diagnosed with PTSD were still noticeably symptomatic more than two years after their MVA.

In summary, while we found that almost half of those originally diagnosed with PTSD showed remission over the first 6 months, with some slow, gradual improvement over the next 6 months (12-month follow-up), there was almost no remission of symptoms thereafter.

Delayed Onset PTSD

It has long been recognized that some individuals who apparently do fine with the initial reaction to the trauma develop delayed onset PTSD at a later period of time. Unfortunately, very few studies have been able to investigate prospectively why some people develop delayed onset PTSD whereas others will improve over time and recover from their symptoms. Finding out why these cases occur and learning to identify who is at later risk for PTSD has been a concern for a number of years

The MVA Project in Albany identified seven cases (4.4%), out of the initial 158 participants in our study, who appeared to have delayed onset PTSD (Buckley,

Blanchard, & Hickling, 1996). We did note several findings that were consistent among these seven individuals. All had been initially diagnosed with subsyndromal PTSD. This is important to recognize because it means that none, in fact, had been symptom free. Each individual who subsequently came to be diagnosed with PTSD had symptoms that had been less than sufficient to reach the diagnosis criteria for PTSD but nevertheless reflected an emotional reaction to the accident.

These seven individuals, on average, tended to have had less social support before the MVA and were more alone in dealing with the accident than other MVA survivors who had also been diagnosed to have a subsyndromal version of PTSD. The seven participants who developed delayed onset PTSD also had relatively more psychological distress than those with subsyndromal PTSD who did not develop delayed onset PTSD.

Finally, an additional stressor, whether another accident, a change in job, a worsening of physical health, or some other factor, was identified in three of the seven cases as a precipitant of the onset of delayed PTSD. It is conjectured that the occurrence of another major stressor "could push the individual over the edge," worsening the symptoms to the point of full PTSD.

The primary lesson from our research is that individuals with some symptoms of PTSD after the MVA, but not enough symptoms to reach diagnosis for a full-blown case of PTSD, are at risk to develop PTSD at a later time. In fact, 15 percent of such subsyndromal PTSD cases do develop PTSD at a later time. Thus, while 65 percent of those with initial subsyndromal PTSD have remitted by six months later, another 15%, almost half of those who have not remitted at six months worsen over the next six months.

Acute Stress Disorder (ASD) and MVAs

In 1980, the American Psychiatric Association reintroduced PTSD as a diagnostic category (American Psychiatric Association, 1980). This allowed professionals to diagnose and code individuals who had been exposed to a traumatic event and who had psychological difficulty with avoidance, numbing, hyperarousal, and reexperiencing of symptoms related to the trauma. In order for PTSD to be diagnosed, it was necessary that the symptoms persisted for at least one month. Prior to that time a trauma victim would only be able to be diagnosed and coded with what was termed an adjustment disorder. This diagnosis was deemed an understatement for rape survivors and others who had been seriously traumatized.

However, in 1994 the fourth edition of the *Diagnostic and Statistical Manual* (American Psychiatric Association, 1994) saw the introduction of the new diagnostic category called acute stress disorder (ASD). This diagnosis, in part, was an attempt to remedy the past diagnostic situation and provide a more meaningful label for the distress trauma survivors were experiencing in the days immediately following a trauma.

Two prominent Australian researchers, Richard Bryant and Allison Harvey, have done a great deal of the work on ASD, especially as it relates to MVAs. Bryant and Harvey (1996) assessed 171 MVA survivors who were acute admissions to a trauma center. Among the 171 MVA survivors, 92 individuals had no head injury and 79 had suffered a head injury resulting in posttraumatic amnesia (ranging from five minutes to 48 hours). Even in those who had amnesia, some were still found to have symptoms of diagnosable ASD. In the non-head-injured group, 13 percent met the full *DSM–IV* criteria for ASD while another 20.7 percent met all but one of the criteria and would therefore be deemed to have subclinical ASD.

For the head-injured group only, 5.1% (4) met the full criteria for ASD while 12.7 percent met the criteria for subclinical ASD. This was an important finding, in that it was once believed that if you were unconscious, then you would not be able to develop PTSD or ASD, as there should not be memories that would haunt you. The work of Bryant and Harvey (1996) and our own work (Hickling, Gillen, Blanchard, Buckley, & Taylor, 1998) has shown that posttraumatic symptoms can occur in a number of different groups, including those with head injuries and amnesia. It is conjectured that there are many levels of consciousness, that memories can be stored in a variety of ways, and that events following the period of unconsciousness can also be traumatic, as can the memories and incidents that may follow the recovery of an MVA survivor. All may be possible paths to the presence of PTSD.

What Do We Know about the Occurrence of ASD?

Harvey and Bryant (1999) followed up on their research participants and reassessed 56 of the original 92 participants (61%) two years later. Seven of the 9 with ASD who met the criteria for PTSD at 6 months were still positive for PTSD at two years, while 7 of the 10 sub-ASD participants were positive for PTSD at two years. Of the 38 who had no diagnosis originally, 4 met the criteria for PTSD two years later, after being without a diagnosis during the 6-month evaluation.

Thus it seems that developing ASD in the month following the MVA puts a person at very high risk to have PTSD at 6 months post-MVA and even two years after the accident. Those with this acute pattern of symptoms clearly need early treatment to prevent later psychological problems. Interested readers are strongly encouraged to read Bryant and Harvey's excellent text on ASD (Bryant and Harvey, 2000).

Travel Anxiety—A Common Aftereffect of MVAs

Following motor vehicle accidents, there are often varying degrees of hesitation or reluctance to drive again. If this hesitation leads to significant avoidance, the terms "driving phobia" or "specific phobia" may be applied. A phobia is a fear that is excessive or unreasonable, brought on by the presence of a specific object or situation. Many survivors of MVAs begin to fear driving.

In the United States and Canada, perhaps more than in any other Western nation, we rely upon our automobiles. Studies in our lab and elsewhere have found very high levels of driving fear and phobia. We have found that up to 77 percent of the individuals who had been in accidents had what could be termed a "driving phobia." Kuch, Swinson, and Kirby (1985) found that 60 percent of the survivors of MVAs studied had a driving phobia. This interference with driving and riding in automobiles on a daily basis can pose significant problems in one's life.

Mayou and Bryant (1994) conducted one of the most detailed examinations of driving phobia. In their one-year prospective study of MVA survivors, 65 percent of the individuals who had been drivers in their accident and 44 percent of the people who had been passengers reported lingering effects of the MVA on their travel behavior. Approximately 19 percent of the survivors at one year still showed phobic avoidance of certain travel behaviors (avoiding certain routes or traveling conditions such as driving at night, or on high speed highways) and would show extreme distress if they had to endure those situations. Mayou and Bryant also found that 42 percent of motorcyclists had stopped riding their motorcycles since their accident. Individuals who had been passengers in the accident experienced greater effects with regard to travel difficulty, with 84 percent having difficulty when riding as passengers one year later. Mayou and Bryant (1994) further found that experiencing phobic travel anxiety was associated with having comorbid diagnoses, being female, and having horrific initial memories of the MVA.

Kuch, Cox, Evans, and Shulan (1994) studied 55 MVA survivors who had very minimal physical injuries but did have persistent, lingering pain. They found that 21 participants met the DSM–IV criteria at the time for simple phobia, with regard to driving. Kuch defined "accident phobia" as an intensification of symptoms associated with exposure to driving, fear-related reduction of miles normally traveled, driving restrictions related to certain roads or weather conditions, and excessive cautioning of the driver when the patient was a passenger. Of those individuals with driving phobia, more than one-third met the criteria for PTSD.

Our Albany MVA Project results have also supported the finding of driving phobia and anxiety related to traveling in a car (Blanchard & Hickling, 2004). Technically, it is incorrect to apply a diagnosis of driving phobia to an individual who has PTSD or ASD. The fear of driving is attributed to the MVA and the trauma. However, in the interest of explaining the impact of the accident on an individual, we used the term driving reluctance, which included avoidance of the MVA site, avoidance of MVA-related weather conditions (e.g., snow and rain), avoidance of particular roads, avoidance of particular traffic conditions (e.g., on highways), and avoidance of travel for pleasure when either a driver or a passenger. Individuals that we worked with frequently avoided the trauma situation: some said they had driven miles out of their way and endured all sorts of hardships in terms of extra cost and inconvenience for the sole purpose of avoiding anxiety-provoking situations. Thus, while they were able to drive, they were certainly reluctant and limited as to how or when they drove. We have found this to be very common and important in illustrating how the MVA impacts a survivor's life. A questionnaire entitled "The Travel Anxiety Questionnaire" was subsequently developed to assess these factors, and will be discussed below.

In our sample of individuals who have had PTSD, 93.2 percent of our subjects were found to have travel-limiting anxiety. Seventy-nine percent of those in the subsyndromal PTSD category and even 18 percent of those who did not have a PTSD diagnosis had accident-related driving reluctance. Without question, this change in travel behavior can dramatically affect one's life. This driving difficulty makes it hard to get to a doctor's appointment or to get to work. It becomes hard to live the life that you had prior to your accident if you can't travel as freely as you did before the MVA.

Comorbid Diagnoses

Our own findings on comorbid mood disorders support the frequency of depression for MVA survivors. We found that among MVA survivors who had PTSD, approximately 53.2 percent also had major depression. As mentioned earlier when we discussed risk factors, we also found that MVA survivors who developed PTSD had a more frequent history of major depression than any other group we compared them with. This finding was not surprising to us. We believe that PTSD and depression commonly follow a traumatic injury-producing event. This has been well documented for years in the psychological literature. Breslau et al. (1991) found that 36 percent of the individuals they found to have PTSD also had major depression, while Kessler et al. (1995) found that 48 percent of the individuals they studied had comorbid major depression and PTSD. These values are very similar to ours.

Assessment of PTSD and Related Conditions

A number of instruments have been developed to measure the presence of PTSD. For a comprehensive review, readers are referred to William Koch's excellent book, *Psychological Injuries: Forensic Assessment, Treatment and Law* (2005). Our more limited review here will be on the techniques and instruments we have used and believe are the most relevant to practicing clinicians and researchers in the area of MVAs and trauma.

The Motor Vehicle Accident Interview

The Albany MVA Interview is a structured interview developed to assess the details of an MVA (Blanchard & Hickling, 2004). The interview systematically inquires about immediate physical and medical consequences of the MVA, any treatments undergone as a result of the MVA, subjective reactions to the accident, and impact on subsequent travel behavior. The interview is structured after the fashion of a clinical interview and progresses in a logical fashion, beginning with the survivor of the MVA recounting the details of the MVA, including the circumstances that led up to it. Special attention is paid to the thoughts and feelings related to the MVA in addition to the facts of the accident, in order to obtain information that may be used in later cognitive and exposure-based interventions. Several items from the interview turned out to be important predictors of PTSD, including avoidance of post-MVA travel, fear and belief that the individual involved might die during the MVA, and responsibility for the accident. A copy of the interview can be found in the second edition of *After the Crash* (Blanchard & Hickling, 2004).

In addition to the interview, we believed that a comprehensive evaluation should include a psychosocial history, alcohol and drug history, psychiatric history, and when possible an interview with a collateral source of information.

CAPS: The Clinician Administered PTSD Scale

The Clinician Administered PTSD Scale (CAPS) is a structured interview developed by Blake and colleagues (1995a, 1995b) at the National Center for PTSD to assess the symptoms of PTSD. The test has very good interrater reliability and diagnostic agreement when used for MVA survivors with PTSD (Blanchard, Hickling, Taylor, Forneris, Loos & Jaccard, 1995).

The CAPS is administered with the clinician rating all 17 symptoms of PTSD over the past month (or week) for both frequency (0 = not present; 1 = once or twice, or less than 10% of the time; 2 = once or twice per week, 20–30%; 3 = several times per week, 50–60%; and 4 = daily or almost daily, more than 80%). The severity of each symptom is also rated from 0 to 4. Each symptom has a possible score of 8. A rule of 3 has been determined so that a symptom must have a combined score of 3, composed of at least 1 on either the frequency or severity scale. The use of different scoring rules has been investigated (e.g., Blanchard, Hickling, Taylor, Forneris, Loos, & Jaccard, 1995), and it has been found that those who met the criterion using more stringent CAPS criteria were more distressed on psychological tests.

The SCID

The Structured Clinical Interview for the *DSM–IV* (SCID) is a comprehensive, semistructured interview using *DSM–IV* criteria for diagnosing psychopathology (Spitzer, 1990a). The SCID uses a hierarchical logic to allow the clinician to inquire about a broad range, but not all, of possible *DSM* diagnoses. Interrater reliability for specific diagnoses varies (see Rogers, 2001) and the interview has been found to have moderate test-retest reliability (Williams, et al., 1992). The SCID allows the clinician to assess current and lifetime *DSM–IV* disorders, and a SCID-II version is available to assess Axis II personality disorders (Spitzer et al., 1990b).

The PTSD Check List (PCL)

The PTSD Check List is a self-report measure of PTSD symptoms developed by Weathers, Litz, Herman, Huska, and Keane (1993, 1994). It was restandardized by the Albany MVA Project, and high correlations ($r = 0.929$, $p < .0001$) were found with total CAPS scores and total PCL scores. A score of 44 had the greatest predictive power, yielding a sensitivity of .944 and a specificity of 0.864, and a diagnostic efficiency of 0.900. The PCL provides a useful self-report inventory that complements the information gained by an interview, CAPS, and collateral sources.

The Travel Anxiety Questionnaire (TAQ)

The Travel Anxiety Questionnaire (TAQ) is a self-report questionnaire that looks at specific areas of driving behavior that may have been negatively impacted by an MVA (see Table 1.2). The scores derived on the TAQ are obtained for both the degree of avoidance and the amount of anxiety experienced. There are no critical levels that indicate the presence or absence of travel anxiety. In fact, some items are geographically dependent (e.g., driving in snow), as some areas never or only rarely have certain weather conditions. So, while the score does not produce a critical level, the more items endorsed and the higher the level at which they produce avoidance and anxiety, the more they show problem areas and show how negatively driving has been impacted. The areas of difficulty may suggest specific areas for targeted intervention as well as an indication of how strongly the travel anxiety is expressed.

Additional Inventories

Comorbid conditions and areas of interest may need to be assessed. Additional inventories have included measures of depression and anxiety. Our studies have utilized the Beck Depression Inventory (BDI or BDI-II) for a measure of depression (Beck, Ward, Mendelson, Mock, & Erbaugh, 1961), and the State Trait Anxiety Inventory (Spielberger, Gorsuch, & Lushene, 1970) for a measure of anxiety. While these measures have been used in the prediction of malingering (see Hickling, Blanchard, & Hickling, 2006; Hickling, Blanchard, Mundy, & Galovski, 2002) and correct identification of PTSD (Hickling, Taylor, Blanchard, & Devineni, 1999), it is our opinion, given our current state of knowledge, that clinicians should be advised to use instruments they are comfortable and familiar with to provide self-report information from an MVA survivor.

Psychological Treatment for the Psychological Aftermath of Motor Vehicle Accidents: An Overview of the Psychological Literature

Psychologists have tried for a number of years to treat the emotional aftermath of motor vehicle accidents. The earliest intervention was attributed to

Table 1.2 Travel Anxiety Questionnaire

Name: _____   Date: _____

1. Are you driving at the **present** time? (circle **one**)   1. YES—go to question 3

                                                    2. NO—continue to question 2

2. If you are **not** driving presently, why not?
(check **all** that apply)

                                               ❐ driving makes me anxious

                                               ❐ physically unable

                                               ❐ no car

                                               ❐ no license

                                               ❐ none of the above

3. Here are 8 driving situations. Use the two scales below to **rate how anxious** you are about each situation currently, as well as **how much you avoid** each of these situations **currently**. If the situation does not apply to you, please circle "NA" next to the situation.

Anxiety Rating Scale

——— 0 ——————— 1 ——————— 2 ——————— 3 ——————— 4 ———

	Very Little		Moderate	
No Anxiety	Anxiety	Some Anxiety	Anxiety	Severe Anxiety

Avoidance Rating Scale

——— 0 ——————— 1 ——————— 2 ——————— 3 ——————— 4 ———

None of the	Less than Half	About Half of	More than Half	
Time	of the Time	the Time	of the Time	All of the Time

Nighttime Driving

  Anxiety Rating   NA

  Avoidance Rating   NA

Driving in Snow

  Anxiety Rating   NA

  Avoidance Rating   NA

Driving in Rain

  Anxiety Rating   NA

  Avoidance Rating   NA

Highway Driving

  Anxiety Rating   NA

  Avoidance Rating   NA

Heavy Traffic

  Anxiety Rating   NA

  Avoidance Rating   NA

Table 1.2 *(continued)*

Location of MVA

Anxiety Rating		NA
Avoidance Rating		NA

Pleasure Trips

Anxiety Rating		NA
Avoidance Rating		NA

Being the Passenger

Anxiety Rating		NA
Avoidance Rating		NA

Please circle either yes or no:

4. **Currently,** do you restrict your driving speed?	YES	NO
5. **Currently,** do you only drive to work?	YES	NO

Note: The more risk variables found following the MVA, the greater the chance of subsequent PTSD.

Joseph Wolpe, who, in 1962, utilized systematic desensitization to treat accident-related phobia. Most of the early research was in the form of case studies. Initial treatment efforts were reported over several decades. A summary of these studies can be found in Blanchard and Hickling (2004).

Earlier case studies included treatments that described and made use of the following: relaxation techniques, cognitive techniques, in vivo exposure techniques and imaginal exposure, and stress inoculation training (SIT) in which the feared situations are presented a little at a time to allow the individual to gain control over smaller elements of the situation and thereby gain a greater ability to deal with fuller aspects of the feared situations. Treatments have also included more traditional psychotherapy, supportive psychotherapy, and existential therapy in which the individual dealt with issues of mortality and surviving a near-death experience. Work was also described on how to help people deal with the issues of chronic pain and chronic physical injuries that result from the motor vehicle accident. These studies were very helpful in guiding the development of more comprehensive enquiries into treatments that address the psychological effects of the MVAs.

Controlled Treatment Studies

This section will briefly summarize selected controlled studies that have been done, and then will summarize the Albany MVA Project's treatment studies. We will try to summarize the major findings by examining those treatments that were very brief, those that dealt with early symptoms, and those that treated symptoms once they were present long enough to reach the diagnosis of PTSD.

Single-Session Treatments

The earliest interventions for MVA victims generally involved treating trauma victims shortly after they had their MVA. This could involve either speaking to victims while at the hospital or within a week after they had been seen at the hospital. This type of intervention has generally involved provision of a venue for the victim to review the traumatic event, encouragement to express emotions related to the MVA, information about normal reactions to trauma, and encouragement about a gradual return to normal driving behavior. These early intervention studies were disappointing in that they failed to show any benefit of treatment over no treatment. In fact, they seemed to show that the early intervention may actually may have made the participants worse, or at best, delayed their recovery from the MVA in comparison to that of individuals who did not receive the intervention. Later studies with MVA victims who were not admitted to a hospital did not show a worsening for those who received a brief intervention, but no benefit was found for those who were given the brief, one-session treatment (for a detailed summary, see Blanchard & Hickling, 2004).

Multiple-Session Studies

A number of researchers have examined the effect of multiple sessions for the treatment of emotional disorders/reactions following MVAs. These treatments have used a number of different techniques. The first group of studies we will summarize dealt with early intervention (in the first month after the MVA). These early treatments were trying to help individuals so that they would not develop PTSD or later psychological difficulties following their accidents.

Probably the strongest studies have come out of Bryant and Harvey's work in Australia with acute stress disorder. In their first study (Bryant, Harvey, Dang, Sackville, & Basten, 1998), 12 patients were given cognitive behavioral therapy (CBT) while 12 others were given supportive psychotherapy. Each participant in the study had been evaluated within 10 days of his or her MVA. The CBT treatment condition consisted of five individually provided counseling sessions, which each lasted about 90 minutes. The sessions were spread over a six-week period of time. The supportive psychotherapy condition consisted of education about trauma and training in general problem-solving skills and provided the same amount of treatment. At the end of treatment only one of the CBT-treated participants (8%) met the criteria for PTSD while at six months two met the criteria for having PTSD. In contrast, 10 of the participants (83%) in the supportive treatment condition met the criteria for PTSD at the end of treatment while 8 out of 12 did so at six months. In their second study, Bryant, Sackville, Dang, Moulds, and Guthrie (1999) again showed that intense, early intervention, utilizing combinations of cognitive, exposure, and relaxation techniques, worked better than supportive psychotherapy treatment. It can be concluded at this time that intense, focused, early intervention has been shown to offer a great deal of help to high-risk individuals following MVAs. There is a hint in this research that supportive psychotherapy alone is not helpful and may even hinder spontaneous recovery.

Treatment for Those Diagnosed with PTSD:
The Albany MVA Controlled Treatment Study

The Albany MVA Treatment Project began in 1994 and continued through 2002. The earliest studies were uncontrolled treatment investigations, which allowed us to examine how to best provide differing combinations of psychological treatments. Once an established treatment protocol was in place, we were able write a specific treatment manual and obtain the federal funding to test the effectiveness of a comprehensive psychological intervention for PTSD following MVAs.

This large-scale study involved gathering initial assessment data on 161 individuals (Blanchard et al., 2003). It turned out that 107 of these people were eligible for entry into our study, and 98 of them ultimately attended at least one treatment session. Seventy-eight of these 98 people completed either our cognitive behavioral treatment package or the supportive psychotherapy treatment or a waiting list condition before being given treatment. Twenty of the 98 dropped out of treatment: 9 who had been placed in the CBT condition, 10 who had been placed in the support condition, and 1 who had been on our waiting list condition. Participants were assessed prior to entry into the study, right after they completed treatment, and then at 3, 12 and 24 months afterward to assess the long-term benefits of the treatment.

Treatment consisted of 10 sessions on average. There was some flexibility for the therapist to decide if treatment could be ended at 8 sessions or if it needed to be extended to 12 sessions.

In general, the CBT treatment combined education about PTSD, a review of each patient's particular symptoms, training in relaxation techniques, a written narrative description of the MVA generated by the patient and instructions to read this narrative description three times each day, graded in vivo exposure to feared situations, cognitive therapy to correct dysfunctional self-talk and distorted cognitive fallacies, and initiation of pleasant-events scheduling. The therapist was able to introduce, as needed, anger management techniques and issues related to mortality and near-death experiences.

The support condition also included education about PTSD and the patient's particular symptoms described in such a way as to "normalize" the experience, followed by a detailed review of the patient's past life history with an emphasis on losses and traumas and on how the patient had dealt with these difficulties. The last six sessions were devoted to a discussion of other patient issues (other than the MVA), in a supportive, reflective fashion.

The initial results obtained at the conclusion of treatment were very encouraging: participants in the CBT condition improved significantly more than those in the support condition with regard to symptoms of PTSD. Moreover, those receiving CBT (75%) showed a greater likelihood than those receiving support (50%) of improving sufficiently that they no longer met the criteria for PTSD. The ones receiving CBT also improved more on measures of general psychological distress and overall functioning. Both treated groups improved more than those who went through the assessment but then had to wait three months for a treatment slot.

Three months later only 4 of the 21 participants who had been diagnosed with PTSD and who received CBT treatment still met the criteria for PTSD, as compared with the support condition where 12 of 21 still met the criteria for PTSD. At one-year follow-up, the treatment gains held up very well, with no instances of relapse to PTSD for those who had received CBT treatment. Interestingly, those who received support also continued to show gains in treatment, although they were also significantly more likely to have sought out additional mental health services.

In summary, those who received CBT were able to show significantly greater treatment gains than those in the supportive psychotherapy condition. These treatment gains continued over the first year, despite the finding that those in the supportive psychotherapy condition sought out additional mental health treatment. By the end of two years, both treatment groups were able to show significant improvement.

Guidelines and Policies for the Psychological Treatment of MVA Survivors

The growing knowledge of the psychological impact of MVAs and the ability to treat the disorders that can follow this trauma have led some countries to propose guidelines and recommendations for insurers and practitioners. Two model programs were found in the United Kingdom and Australia.

In England, the International Underwriting Association of London (IUA) and the Association of British Insurers (ABI) have published a guideline entitled *Psychology, Personal Injury and Rehabilitation* (International Underwriting Association of London, 2004). This report was part of a series that addressed the often underestimated and misunderstood psychological aspects of rehabilitation. As described in the foreword to the report, the conclusions and recommendations were based on a series of discussions between industry leaders from the legal, employment, and insurance sectors and leading academics from psychology and liaison psychiatry. The report was designed to provide a common source of present-day knowledge to be used in making practical changes to injury management systems. The report concluded that by their very nature, psychological and social influences must be considered in the broad context of postinjury services and experiences. The report sought to provide information and guidance on "understanding the diversity of outcomes that are found in practice identifying obstacles to recovery in systems and in individuals identifying opportunities for improvement, and [to] recommend changes in current practices, strategic and tactical changes and future research" (p. 4).

There are a number of clinical guidelines for the treatment of PTSD, one being from the National Collaborating Centre for Mental Health in England, put out by the National Institute for Clinical Excellence (NICE) in March 2005. The guidelines include recognition of the problem of PTSD in adults and children in primary and secondary care, screening and assessment, and treatment recommendations (National Institute for Clinical Excellence, 2005). The literature also includes consensus guidelines for the treatment of PTSD, such as that of Foa, Davidson, and Frances (1999). While not solely for MVA survivors with PTSD, they do provide a much-needed resource for treatment of the disorder.

In Australia, the Motor Accidents Authority of New South Wales (2003) has issued guidelines for anxiety, PTSD, and whiplash following MVAs. The target audience for the guidelines was health care practitioners in New South Wales, with companion documents developed for consumers, general medical practitioners, and compulsory third party insurers. The primary guidelines were developed to share current and optimum treatment for the anxiety disorders that follow MVAs. They were not intended to be mandatory or prescribed practice, but were intended for application according to individual need. The guidelines covered recommendations for ASD and PTSD, but did not include other common sequelae such as depression, driving anxiety, or substance abuse, which were identified as common and warranting their own needs. Family and social needs were also acknowledged to be absent from these particular guidelines.

These two sets of guidelines, the International Underwriting Association of London report (2004) and the Motor Accidents Authority guidelines (2003), reflect a model of the collaboration that can occur between practitioners and insurers. These collaborative efforts designed to address the needs of insurers, practitioners, and survivors of MVAs illustrate a growing appreciation of the substantial specialized needs that exist for this population of trauma survivors.

Future Directions

The controlled treatment studies at the Albany MVA Project have continued in several new directions. One frustration has been to see how difficult it has been to train enough psychologists in empirically derived methods that have shown promise to help individuals suffering from PTSD and related psychological disorders following their MVAs. There are just too many MVA victims and too few psychologists to treat them. This has led to our effort to provide a self-directed treatment and a treatment manual for interested psychologists in the Oxford University Press's Treatments That Work Series. These books, a patient workbook, and a therapist treatment manual, were written based on our empirically demonstrated CBT treatment (Hickling & Blanchard, 2006a, 2006b). It is hoped they will reach a wider audience than our earlier work has seemed to.

Our second direction has been to try to extract the most critical components of treatment and provide them in as brief a treatment for early PTSD as possible. A very brief (two and a half sessions) treatment has been developed and piloted

(Hickling, Blanchard, & Kuhn, 2005). While the initial data is encouraging, a more rigorous investigation is needed to determine if this brief intervention is in fact a beneficial intervention for those willing to engage in a largely self-directed treatment.

The third area of current investigation is the use of the Internet for psychological treatment. An ongoing dissertation is investigating the use of an online, Internet-based intervention, which, based on the treatment manual that has been shown to be effective in face-to-face treatment, might have some benefit when provided over the Internet. While it is anticipated that the potential audience for an Internet-based treatment is quite limited, given the extremely large population of potential users of the intervention, even a 1–3 percentuse by victims of MVA survivors would reach a significant portion of suffering individuals (Lerner, 2006).

Finally, we have been pleased to learn of replications of our treatment procedures in other settings. A group in Germany (A. Karl, 2005, personal communication) has experienced very good results with a German translation of our treatment manual (Zollner, Karl, Maercker, Hickling, & Blanchard, 2004). Furthermore, Holzapfel, Blanchard, Hickling, and Malta (2005) were able to replicate our results with a very chronic (2 to 6 year post-MVA) population, most of whom had lingering physical problems. A preliminary investigation is also starting in Italy, and we are encouraged by the continued interest in the application of the assessment and treatment of MVA survivors internationally (Elena Rebulla, personal communication, December 2006). It is hoped that the continued empirical and clinical findings will further guide the development of policies and recommendations of care for survivors of MVAs, insurers, and health care providers.

Acknowledgments

The authors would like to acknowledge with thanks the help of Mr. Bernie Rowe and Dr. Richard Bryant in the locating of information on international policies and guidelines for the treatment of MVA survivors.

References

American Psychiatric Association. (1980). *Diagnostic and statistical manual of mental disorders* (3rd ed.). Washington, DC: Author.

American Psychiatric Association. (1994). *Diagnostic and statistical manual of mental disorders* (4th ed.). Washington, DC: Author.

Beck, A. T., Ward, C. H., Mendelson, M., Mock, J., & Erbaugh, J. (1961). An inventory for measuring depression. *Archives of General Psychiatry, 5*, 561–571.

Blake, D. D., Weathers, F. W., Nagy, L. M., Kaloupek, D. G., Gusman, D. G., Charney, D. S., & Keane, T. M. (1995a). The development of a Clinician Administered PTSD Scale. *Journal of Traumatic Stress, 8*, 75–90.

Blake, D. D., Weathers, F. W., Nagy, L. M., Kaloupek, D. G, Charney, D. S., & Keane, T. (1995b). *Clinician Administered PTSD Scale for DSM–IV (CAPS–DX)*. Boston:

National Center for Posttraumatic Stress Disorder, Behavioral Science Division, Boston VA Medical Center.

Blanchard, E. B., & Hickling, E. J. (1997). *After the crash: Assessment and treatment of motor vehicle accident survivors.* Washington, DC: American Psychological Association.

Blanchard, E. B., & Hickling, E. J. (2004). *After the crash: Assessment and treatment of motor vehicle accident survivors* (2nd ed.). Washington, DC: American Psychological Association.

Blanchard, E. B., Hickling, E. J., Devineni, T., Veazey, C. H., Galovski, T. E., Mundy, E., Malta, L. S., & Buckley, T. C. (2003). A controlled evaluation of cognitive behavioral therapy for posttraumatic stress disorder in motor vehicle accident survivors. *Behaviour Research and Therapy, 41,* 79–96.

Blanchard, E. B., Hickling, E. J., Barton, K. A., Taylor, A. E., Loos, W. R., & Jones-Alexander, J. (1996). One year prospective follow up of motor vehicle accident victims. *Behavior Research and Therapy, 34,* 775–786.

Blanchard, E. B., Hickling, E. J., Taylor, A. E., Forneris, C. A., Loos, W., & Jaccard, J. (1995). Effects of varying scoring rules of the Clinician Administered PTSD Scale (CAPS) for the diagnosis of posttraumatic stress disorder in motor vehicle accident victims. *Behavior Research and Therapy, 33,* 471–475.

Blanchard, E. B., Hickling, E. J., Taylor, A. E., & Loos, W. (1995). Psychiatric comorbidity associated with motor vehicle accidents. *Journal of Nervous and Mental Disease, 183,* 495–504.

Blanchard, E. B., Hickling, E. J., Taylor, A. E., Loos, W. R., & Forneris, C. A. (1996). Who develops PTSD from motor vehicle accidents? *Behavior Research and Therapy, 34,* 1–10.

Breslau, N., Davis, G. C., Andreski, P., & Peterson, E. (1991). Traumatic events and post-traumatic stress disorder in an urban population of young adults. *Archives of General Psychiatry, 48,* 216–222.

Bryant, R. A., & Harvey, A. G. (1996). Initial posttraumatic stress responses following motor vehicle accidents. *Journal of Traumatic Stress, 9,* 223–234.

Bryant, R. A., & Harvey, A. G. (2000). *Acute stress disorder: A handbook of theory, assessment and treatment.* Washington, DC: American Psychological Association.

Bryant, R. A., Harvey, A. G., Dang, S. T., Sackville, T., & Basten, C. (1998). Treatment of acute stress disorder: A comparison of cognitive-behavioral therapy and supportive counseling. *Journal of Consulting and Clinical Psychology, 66,* 862–866.

Bryant, R. A., Sackville, T., Dang, S. T., Moulds, M., & Guthrie, R. (1999). Treating acute stress disorder: An evaluation of cognitive behavior therapy and supportive counseling techniques. *American Journal of Psychiatry, 156,* 1780–1786.

Buckley, T. C., Blanchard, E. B., & Hickling, E. J. (1996). A prospective examination of delayed onset PTSD secondary to motor vehicle accidents. *Journal of Abnormal Psychology, 105,* 617–625.

Ehlers, A., Mayou, R. A., & Bryant, B. (1998). Psychological predictors of chronic post-traumatic stress disorder after motor vehicle accidents. *Journal of Abnormal Psychology, 107,* 508–519.

Foa, E. B., Davidson, J.R.T., & Frances, A. (Eds.). (1999). The expert consensus guide-line series. Treatment of posttraumatic stress disorder. *Journal of Clinical Psychiatry, 60*(Suppl. 16), 1–76.

Harvey, A. G., & Bryant, A. G. (1998). The relationship between acute stress disorder and posttraumatic stress disorder: A prospective evaluation of motor vehicle accident survivors. *Journal of Consulting and Clinical Psychology, 66,* 507–512.

Harvey, A. G., & Bryant, A. G. (1999). The relationship between acute stress disorder and posttraumatic stress disorder. A 2-year prospective evaluation. *Journal of Consulting and Clinical Psychology, 67*, 985–988.

Hickling, E. J., & Blanchard, E. B. (Eds.). (1999). *The international handbook of road traffic accidents: Psychological trauma, treatment and law.* London: Elsevier Science.

Hickling, E. J., & Blanchard, E. B. (2006a). *Overcoming the trauma of your motor vehicle accident: A cognitive behavioral treatment program. Workbook.* New York: Oxford University Press.

Hickling, E. J., & Blanchard, E. B. (2006b). *Overcoming the trauma of your motor vehicle accident: A cognitive behavioral treatment program. Therapist guide.* New York: Oxford University Press.

Hickling, E. J., Blanchard, E. B., Buckley, T. C., & Taylor, A. E. (1999). Effects of attribution of responsibility for motor vehicle accidents on severity of PTSD symptoms. *Journal of Traumatic Stress, 12*(2), 345–353.

Hickling, E. J., Blanchard, E. B., & Hickling, M. T. (2006). The psychological impact of litigation: Compensation neurosis, malingering, PTSD and secondary traumatization and other lessons from MVAs. *DePaul Law Review, 55*, 617–634.

Hickling, E. J., Blanchard, E. B., & Kuhn, E. (2005). Brief treatment for ASD/PTSD following motor vehicle accidents. *Cognitive and Behavioral Practice, 12*, 461–467.

Hickling, E. J., Blanchard, E. B., Mundy, E., & Galovski, T. E. (2002). Detection of malingered MVA related posttraumatic stress disorder: An investigation of the ability to detect professional actors by experienced clinicians, psychological tests and psychophysiological assessment. *Journal of Forensic Psychology Practice, 2*, 33–53.

Hickling, E. J., Gillen, R., Blanchard, E. B., Buckley, T., & Taylor, A. (1998). Traumatic brain injury and posttraumatic stress disorder: A preliminary investigation of neuropsychological test results in PTSD secondary to motor vehicle accidents. *Brain Injury, 12*, 265–274.

Hickling, E. J., Taylor, A. E., Blanchard, E. B., & Devineni, T. (1999). Simulation of motor vehicle accident related PTSD: Effects of coaching with DSM–IV criteria. In E. J. Hickling & E. B. Blanchard (Eds.), *International handbook of road traffic accidents: Psychological trauma, treatment and law* (pp. 305–320). London: Elsevier Science.

Holzapfel, S., Blanchard, E. B., Hickling, E. J., & Malta, L. S. (2005). A crossover evaluation of supportive psychotherapy and cognitive behavioral therapy for chronic PTSD in motor vehicle accident survivors. In M. E. Abelian (Ed.), *Focus on psychotherapy research* (pp. 207–218). Hauppage, NY: Nova Science Publishers.

International Underwriting Association of London. (2004). *Psychology, personal injury and rehabilitation: The IUA/ABI rehabilitation working party.* London: Author.

Kessler, R. C., McGonagle, K. A., Zhao, S., Nelson, C. B., Hughes, M., et al. (1994). Lifetime and 12 month prevalence of DSM–III–R psychiatric disorders in the United States. *Archives of General Psychiatry, 51*, 8–19.

Kessler, R. C., Sonnega, A., Bromet, E., Hughes, M., & Nelson, C. B. (1995). Post-traumatic stress disorder in the national Comorbidity Survey. *Archives of General Psychiatry, 52*, 1048–1060.

Koch, W. (2005). *Psychological injuries: Forensic assessment, treatment and law.* New York: Oxford University Press.

Kuch, K., Cox, B. J., Evans, R. J., & Shulan, I. (1994). Phobias, panic and pain in 55 survivors of road accidents. *Journal of Anxiety Disorders, 8*, 181–187.

Kuch, K., Swinson, R. P., & Kirby, M. (1985). Posttraumatic stress disorder after car accidents. *Canadian Journal of Psychiatry, 30*, 426–427.

Lerner, J. A. (2006). *Internet based assessment and treatment for posttraumatic stress disorder among motor vehicle accident survivors.* Unpublished doctoral dissertation, University at Albany, State University of New York.

Mayou, R. A., & Bryant, B. M. (1994). Effects of road traffic accidents on travel. *International Journal of the Care of the Injured, 25,* 457–460.

Mayou, R. A., Ehlers, A., & Bryant, B. (2002). Posttraumatic stress disorder after motor vehicle accidents: 3-year follow up of a prospective longitudinal study. *Behavior Research and Therapy, 40,* 665–675.

Motor Accidents Authority of New South Wales. (2003). *Guidelines for the management of anxiety following motor vehicle accidents: Technical report.* Motor Accidents Authority of NSW, Sydney, Australia, available at www.maa.nsw.gov.au

National Institute for Clinical Excellence (2005). *Quick reference guide. Post-traumatic stress disorder: The management of PTSD in adults and children in primary and secondary care.* Clinical guideline 26. National Institute for Excellence, London, England, available at www.nice.org.uk

Norris, F. H. (1992). Epidemiology of trauma; Frequency and impact of different potentially traumatic events on different demographic groups. *Journal of Consulting and Clinical Psychology, 60,* 409–418.

Rogers, R. (2001). *Handbook of diagnostic and structured interviewing.* New York: Guilford Press.

Spielberger, C. D., Gorsuch, R. L., & Lushene, R. E. (1970). *STAI manual for the State-Trait Anxiety Inventory.* Palo Alto, CA: Consulting Psychologists Press.

Spitzer, R. L., Williams, J.B.W., Gibbon, M., & First, M. D. (1990a). *Structured clinical interview for DSM–III–R, non-patient edition (SCID–NP) (Version 1.0).* Washington, DC: American Psychiatric Association.

Spitzer, R. L., Williams, J.B.W., Gibbon, M. & First, M. D. (1990b). *Structured clinical interview for DSM–III–R, Personality Disorders (SCID–II) (Version 1.0).* Washington, DC: American Psychiatric Association.

United States Department of Transportation. (2004). *Traffic safety facts 2004: A compilation of motor vehicle crash data from the fatality analysis reporting system and the general estimates system.* Washington, DC: National Highway Safety Administration, U.S. Department of Transportation.

Weathers, F. W., Litz, B. T., Herman, D. S., Huska, J. A., & Keane, T. M. (1993). *The TSD Checklist: Reliability, validity and diagnostic utility.* Paper presented at the annual meeting of the International Society for Traumatic Stress Studies, San Antonio, TX.

Weathers, F., Litz, B., Huska, J. A., & Keane, T. M. (1994). *PCL-C for DSM–IV (PTSD Checklist).* Boston: National Center for PTSD, Behavioral Science Division, Boston, VA Medical Center.

Williams, J. B.W., Gibbon, M., First, M. B., Spitzer, R. L., Davies, M., Borus, J., et al. (1992). The structured clinical Interview for DSM–III–R (SCID): II. Multisite test-retest reliability. *Archives of General Psychiatry, 49,* 630–636.

Wolpe, J. (1962). Isolation of a conditioning procedure as the crucial psychotherapeutic factor: A case study. *Journal of Nervous and Mental Disease, 134,* 316–329.

Zollner, T., Karl, A., Maercker, A., Hickling, E. J., & Blanchard, E. B. (2004). *Manual zur kognitiven Verhaltenstherapie von posttraumatischen Belastungsstorungen bei Verkehrs-unfallopfern.* Dresden, Germany: Pabst Science Publishers.

CHAPTER 2

TRAUMATIC STRESS RESPONSES TO MEDICAL ILLNESS IN CHILDREN AND PARENTS

Margaret L. Stuber

Although few would argue about whether going through diagnosis and treatment for cancer or an organ transplant is extremely stressful for a child and his or her parents, the examination of traumatic stress responses to medical illness is relatively recent. This has to do with the way in which traumatic stress has been understood and defined. The constellation of symptoms known as posttraumatic stress disorder (PTSD) was originally conceptualized as a psychological and physiological response to an overwhelming event, outside the realm of normal human experience. The symptoms of reexperiencing, avoidance, and hypervigilance were initially based on the experiences of adults exposed to events such as combat or torture. Much of the early research about the symptoms, biology, and treatment of posttraumatic stress was done with war veterans and victims of rape. The same types of symptoms were reported in studies of adults exposed to life threats from other types of events, such as fires, earthquakes, and hurricanes. Children and adolescents also began to be studied, and were found to have similar types of responses to life-threatening events, although the symptoms were expressed in different ways according to the child's developmental stage (Terr, 1985; Terr, 1991). Because researchers believed that traumatic events were qualitatively different (not just more severe) in their impact on people than ordinary stressful events, the precipitating events for posttraumatic stress symptoms continued to be defined as external threats to life or body integrity. Medical illnesses were not considered to be events severe enough to precipitate a full posttraumatic stress response.

This was the case until the definition of posttraumatic stress disorder was significantly revised in 1994, when the American Psychiatric Association published its fourth edition of the *Diagnostic and Statistical Manual* (American Psychiatric Association, 1994). Although the description of the symptom clusters remained very similar, the definition of what was considered a potential precipitating event was broadened. One could have a traumatic response to an event that was a threat to one's own life or body integrity, but also to witnessing or even hearing about an event that involved a loved one. A new criterion was added, emphasizing the emotional response of the individual to the event, rather than simply requiring exposure to an event. Chronic medical illness as a potential precipitating factor was specifically mentioned in the text describing posttraumatic stress. This was the result of the preliminary studies, or field trials, that were done as a part of the preparation of the *DSM–IV* (Alter et al., 1996; Pelcovitz et al., 1996). Since the publication of the *DSM–IV* guidelines in 1994, there has been significant interest and research into the prevalence, predictors, course, and types of posttraumatic stress symptoms in adults and children with a variety of medical conditions.

Research in Medical Traumatic Stress

The *DSM–IV* field trials, which led to the inclusion of medical illness in the definition of posttraumatic stress, examined symptoms in a small group of childhood cancer survivors and their mothers. In the study of childhood cancer survivors, three groups were compared: 23 adolescent cancer survivors, 27 adolescents who had been physically abused, and 23 healthy, nonabused adolescents. The results were even more dramatic than had been hypothesized. The cancer survivors reported more symptoms than the healthy, nonabused teens, but they also reported more symptoms than adolescents who had been physically abused. Only 7 percent of the abused adolescents reported having a history of symptoms of PTSD, compared to 35 percent of the cancer survivors (Alter et al., 1996). The study of 24 mothers of pediatric cancer survivors compared with 23 mothers of healthy children also found that significantly more mothers of pediatric cancer survivors reported symptoms consistent with a diagnosis of PTSD at some time in their lives. The surprise in the mothers' study was that the severity of the child's illness did not predict which mothers would have PTSD (Pelcovitz et al., 1996).

Subsequent larger studies have confirmed some, but not all, of these findings. A study of 309 childhood cancer survivors, compared to 219 age-matched healthy control children, found no difference in the prevalence of symptoms reported. Only 2.6 percent of the cancer survivors reported severe PTSD symptoms, compared to 3.4 percent of the healthy comparison group, with 12 percent of both groups reporting symptoms in the moderate range. As has been the case in most studies of posttraumatic stress responses, baseline or trait anxiety was the major predictor as to who would go on to develop persistent posttraumatic stress response symptoms. Severity of illness as judged by the oncologist was not a predictor of which child reported symptoms. However, the child's report of how severe the treatment was, and whether or not the child thought he or she could die, was significantly correlated with symptoms of PTSD. This suggested that the child's perception of the event was what determined whether or not the child developed posttraumatic stress symptoms (Stuber et al., 1997). The survivors' perceptions of treatment intensity and degree of life threat were not correlated with the judgment of the treating oncologist.

The parents in this study were more symptomatic than the cancer survivors, but showed the same disconnect between symptoms and severity of illness. Of the 309 mothers of childhood survivors, 10.1 percent reported severe levels of current posttraumatic stress symptoms and 27 percent reported moderate levels of symptoms. Only 3.0 percent of the 211 mothers in the comparison group reported severe posttraumatic stress symptoms, with 18.2 percent reporting moderate levels of symptoms. The same type of difference was seen in fathers, with 7.1 percent of the 213 fathers of childhood cancer survivors reporting severe symptoms, compared to none of the 114 fathers of a healthy control group. Moderate symptoms were reported by 28.3 percent of the fathers of survivors, compared to 17.3 percent of the fathers in the comparison group (Kazak et al., 1997; Barakat et al., 1997). As had been the case with the child survivors, trait anxiety and perceptions of life threat and treatment intensity were the most significant predictors as to which mothers and fathers went on to develop chronic symptoms of posttraumatic stress.

When members of a subset of the childhood cancer survivors and parents in this study were asked about the worst part of the experience, the survivors usually referred to some aversive or painful aspect of the treatment, while parents referred to the diagnosis or moments in treatment when they felt their child's life was in immediate danger. Younger children often described separation from parents as worse for them than the actual diagnosis. Parents and children appeared to experience different aspects of the cancer experience as traumatic. However, the perceptions of life threat and treatment intensity of the children were significantly associated with those of their mothers, and it was these perceptions that were stronger predictors of posttraumatic stress symptoms than the medical estimate of life threat and treatment severity. Perception appears to be the key to understanding who will be traumatized by an event, and children appear to share (or perhaps be influenced by) their mothers' perceptions, even if the specific worst moment they cite is different.

These studies offered support for the hypothesis that parents of childhood cancer survivors experienced the diagnosis and treatment of their children as traumatic events, capable of producing posttraumatic stress symptoms that could last for years. The children in this study had completed their treatment at least two years before these surveys, with an average of five years. Symptoms were slightly less prevalent in parents whose children had been off treatment longer, but it appeared most of the symptoms were chronic. The fact that parents reported so many symptoms and for such a long period of time was new and useful information for clinicians as well as traumatic stress researchers.

However, the survivors themselves were not reporting symptoms. This raised the question as to whether posttraumatic stress response is really a problem for children with serious medical illnesses, despite the initial field trial. One possible explanation for the discrepancy between parental symptoms and child symptoms in response to the same events is that the parents are somehow protecting the children from trauma. A second possible hypothesis is that children and adults have different responses to traumatic events, and that the discrepancy between parents and childhood cancer survivors is due to developmental differences in understanding and processing the threat.

The parental protection hypothesis would suggest that childhood cancer survivors would continue to report few symptoms as they grew older, as the assumption is that the parent kept them from being traumatized at all, and thus from developing symptoms. However, if the issue is developmental, childhood cancer survivors would be expected to report more posttraumatic stress symptoms when they became adults. In a subsequent study of 78 childhood cancer survivors, now aged 18 to 40 years, the developmental hypothesis appeared to hold. Symptoms consistent with a full diagnosis of PTSD were reported by 20.5 percent of these survivors. The survivors' perceptions of current life threat and more intense treatment histories were associated with symptoms of posttraumatic stress, but the oncologists' estimate of life threat and treatment intensity was not. Higher levels of overall psychological distress were seen in survivors reporting symptoms diagnostic of PTSD (Hobbie et al., 2000). This suggests that children are not protected from the trauma, but that symptoms may simply have been delayed until the survivors are exposed to the developmental expectations of young adulthood. This makes intuitive sense, since completing school, getting a job, finding a life companion, and having children are more difficult for survivors who are likely to have cognitive difficulties, be uninsurable, have scars or disabilities, and be infertile secondary to cancer treatment. The full reality of the impact of cancer may not be felt until they encounter these recurrent reminders of the traumatic events in their past.

To test this interpretation, the evaluation of pediatric medical traumatic stress responses has been expanded to groups beyond childhood cancer survivors. Unfortunately, cancer is not the only life-threatening medical illness with intrusive treatment that children and adolescents experience. But how bad does the illness or treatment have to be to lead to a traumatic stress response in a child? The research to date suggests that simply being sick enough to be in a hospital, stressful as it is for children and families, is generally not enough to produce traumatic stress symptoms. Relatively serious illness and intrusive treatment, at least as perceived by the child, are required to generate this type of response. This is supported by a study comparing the prevalence of symptoms of posttraumatic stress in 35 children hospitalized in a pediatric intensive care unit to 33 children hospitalized on general pediatric wards. None of the children on the wards reported symptoms consistent with a diagnosis of PTSD, compared to 21 percent of children who had been in an intensive care unit. Irritability and persistent avoidance of reminders of the admission were more common in the children from the intensive care unit than in those from the wards (Rees, Gledhill,

Garralda, & Nadel, 2004). A similar prevalence of symptoms is reported by another group of children who clearly undergo intensive intervention, pediatric organ transplant recipients. In a study of 104 adolescent heart, liver, or kidney transplant recipients, more than 16 percent reported symptoms meeting criteria for PTSD (Mintzer et al., 2005).

These studies give further support for the idea that medically ill children are not totally protected from traumatic stress response by their parents. However, when we go beyond childhood cancer, we also confirm that parents appear more symptomatic than their children, even though one could argue that the parents are merely witnesses to the traumatic events.

Of 164 mothers of children who had undergone kidney, heart, or liver transplantation (Young et al., 2003), 26.8 percent met the full diagnostic criteria for PTSD. Similar results were seen in a study of 49 mothers of children with diabetes, with 20.4 percent of the mothers reporting symptoms consistent with a diagnosis of PTSD 12 months after their children were diagnosed. As was seen in the fathers of childhood cancer survivors, the fathers of children with diabetes reported fewer symptoms than the mothers. Of the 48 fathers, 8.3 percent reported symptoms consistent with a diagnosis of PTSD 12 months after the diagnosis of their children (Landolt, Vollrath, Ribi, Gnehm, & Sennhauser, 2003). In parents of children undergoing serious burns, the number endorsing posttraumatic stress symptoms is even higher, with approximately 47 percent reporting significant symptoms three months after the burn (Kenardy, Spence, & Macleod, 2006).

A longitudinal study of parents of infants and children admitted to the pediatric intensive care unit examined the relationship between parental perceptions of illness severity, objective measures of severity, acute traumatic stress responses, and PTSD two months after discharge. Of the 272 parents in the initial assessment, 32 percent (87) met the criteria for a diagnosis of acute stress disorder. Of the 161 parents who also completed the two-month follow-up, 21 percent (33) met the criteria for PTSD. The PTSD symptoms at follow-up were correlated with the ASD symptoms and with the parent's degree of worry that the child might die, but were not correlated with objective measures of the child's severity of illness (Balluffi et al., 2004).

Although there is a common theme as to risk factors, it should be noted that some of the variability in prevalence of children or parents reporting symptoms has to do with the threshold used by researchers. Some researchers considered people to be positive for posttraumatic stress symptoms only if all the *DSM–IV* criteria were met for PTSD, while others included people who had clinically significant levels of symptoms but did not meet the specific diagnosis criteria of the DSM. This will be discussed further in the consideration of future directions.

Why Is This Important?

Any research has to answer the "so what" question. Why is it important to know that life-threatening medical illness leads to chronic symptoms of posttraumatic stress in children and parents? If this had not been noticed prior to 1991, when the first paper on this was published (Stuber, Nader, Yasuda, Pynoos, & Cohen, 1991), is it really clinically important? A partial answer to this was seen in a study of 51 young adult survivors of childhood cancer (18–37 years old), with an average of 11 years post successful treatment. The 11 survivors who met criteria for a diagnosis of PTSD were compared to the 40 who did not on standard measures of quality of life and psychological distress. Those survivors who reported symptoms consistent with a full diagnosis of PTSD reported clinically significant levels of psychological distress and significantly lower quality of life on 17 of the 18 variables measured. The survivors who did not report PTSD fell well within population norms for psychological distress (Meeske, Ruccione, Globe, & Stuber, 2001). This suggests that posttraumatic stress responses are a part of a larger picture of chronic emotional distress and disturbances in quality of life in people exposed to life-threatening medical illness and intrusive, albeit life-saving, treatment.

In addition to concern over the psychological distress of posttraumatic stress symptoms, interest in intervention has been spurred by some recent suggestions that posttraumatic stress responses may affect adherence to medical instructions. A small study of pediatric liver transplant recipients found that nonadherent patients demonstrated improved adherence with immunosuppressive medications after a trauma-focused cognitive therapy intervention that did not directly address the nonadherence (Shemesh et al., 2000). One interpretation of these findings is that the medication is serving as a traumatic reminder, bringing up aversive thoughts and feelings that are avoided by not taking the medication.

There is also a growing body of literature suggesting that there are adverse physiological consequences to chronic posttraumatic stress response. A recent study compared mothers of childhood cancer survivors to mothers of healthy children, using a composite index of biological risk factors that have been associated with chronic stress responses (blood pressure, cholesterol, glycosylated hemoglobin, cortisol, norepinephrine, and epinephrine) known as allostatic load. The results indicated that the survivors' mothers with PTSD had a higher allostatic load than the survivors' mothers who did not have PTSD, who in turn had a higher allostatic load than the mothers of healthy children. This suggests that the traumatic stress response was putting these mothers at greater risk of illness and disability (Glover, Steele, Stuber, & Fahey, 2005). Changes in immune response have also been suggested, with mothers with symptoms of posttraumatic stress having a higher percentage of CD4+ and lower CD8+ levels and demonstrating blunted natural killer cell reactivity to a stress challenge, compared to nonsymptomatic women (Glover & Poland, 2002).

A recent article reviewed all of the published studies on structural abnormalities of the hippocampus and other brain regions in persons with PTSD compared to trauma-exposed and nonexposed control groups. Significantly smaller hippocampal, anterior cingulated cortex, and left amygdala volumes have been reported in adults with PTSD but not in children. Children and adolescents with

PTSD have been found to have significantly smaller corpus callosum and frontal lobe volumes compared to controls. The authors of this meta-analysis suggest a resulting model in which there are abnormalities of multiple frontal-limbic structures, but that hippocampal volumetric differences do not become apparent until adulthood, and then are related to PTSD severity (Karl et al., 2006). Indeed, there is some evidence that hippocampal volume is actually increased in children with PTSD (Tupler & De Bellis, 2006). A specific study of pituitary volume did not show any consistent change in volume between children with PTSD and those who without PTSD (Thomas & De Bellis, 2004). The impact of posttraumatic stress on the anatomy and physiology of the brain and immune systems is a rapidly expanding area of investigation, with many implications for understanding the prevention and treatment of posttraumatic stress.

Of more immediate practical concern is one potential result of these brain changes, which is an impact on memory in children. Children and adolescents with symptoms of posttraumatic stress demonstrate impairments in general memory and in verbal memory, compared to nonsymptomatic trauma-exposed children and adolescents, or to nontraumatized controls (Yasik, Saigh, Oberfield, & Halamandaris, 2006).

CASE EXAMPLE: TRAUMA SYMPTOMS

Terry had undergone a bone marrow transplant as treatment after her second relapse of leukemia, when she was seven years old. Her treatment required her to be in an isolation room in the hospital for almost two months. Visitors were limited, and all those who visited had to be careful to wash their hands. Food, toys, and clothing had to be treated to remove all bacteria or viruses, as her chemotherapy and radiation treatment caused her to be immunosuppressed and very vulnerable to infection. The treatments also made her mouth sore and bleeding, as well as causing her to feel tired and nauseated most of the time.

In the hospital Terry became withdrawn, rarely talking or laughing after the first two weeks. She became anxious if her mother was not in the room, and fought with the nurses who brought her medications. After she got home, she appeared jumpy and irritable. She hated to go to the doctor for follow-up, and would scream in the car on the way to the clinic until she threw up. She had recurrent nightmares of monsters climbing in the windows of her room at the hospital.

Terry's mother wept as she spoke about Terry's hospitalization. She worried about what the radiation would mean for Terry's ability to do well in school, and mourned Terry's likely infertility. She found herself unable to sleep before she took Terry in for a medical visit, terrified that there would be an indication that the leukemia was back. However, she never discussed any of this with her husband or with Terry. She commented that he seemed to be working longer hours and drinking more than he did before Terry's illness and transplant. Both mother and father were reluctant to think too far into the future and preferred to live one day at a time in thinking about Terry.

Psychological Interventions

In the studies of medical traumatic stress responses summarized above, chronic medical illness is conceptualized as a series of potentially traumatic events, including diagnosis, treatment, and aftereffects of treatment. Helplessness, horror, or intense fear may or may not be experienced in response to any of these components of illness. The physiological response to threat is an activation of the "fight-flight" response, most immediately evident in an autonomic system activation causing a rise in heart rate. Pain appears to amplify the biological response, as well as the experience of helplessness. Perceptions of life threat are better predictors of traumatic stress responses than is statistical likelihood of death from a given illness.

Thus it would appear that interventions to decrease helplessness, horror, intense fear, pain, and perceived threat would be helpful in preventing or reducing posttraumatic stress responses and symptoms. This is the underlying assumption of most pharmacological and behavioral interventions for medical posttraumatic stress.

Three basic types of psychological interventions have been reported in the literature for treatment of symptomatic children and parents exposed to medical life threat. The earliest reported in the literature uses play, drawings, and retelling of the event to help the children to process the experience they went through, and to feel more in control (Pynoos et al., 1987; Terr et al., 1999). This approach is based on the pioneering work of Robert Pynoos and Lenore Terr with children exposed to interpersonal violence and natural disasters (Pynoos et al., 1987; Terr et al.,1999; Pynoos & Nader, 1988; Terr, 1985). A second approach is work using a cognitive behavioral approach, called trauma-focused CBT, to help a child become more able to control the fear and to better assess threat (Shemesh et al., 2000). This is based on the extensive work of Edna Foa with women who had been exposed to interpersonal violence (Foa, 2006) and Judy Cohen with children exposed to abuse (Cohen, 2005). The third approach uses a family systems approach to work with families of medically traumatized children to help them understand their differing perspectives and better support one another. Anne Kazak and her group have been the pioneers in this area (Pai & Kazak, 2006). Only this last intervention approach has been tested and found to be feasible and effective in a large sample of medically ill children and their families (Kazak et al., 2005). The cognitive behavioral approaches have a significant amount of supporting data in other childhood trauma and are now manualized, and have been adapted for children with medical traumatic stress symptoms (Shemesh et al., 2000).

The common strategies in each of the psychological interventions include age-appropriate activities, individually or in a group, which allow the following:

(1) experience of a safe place, with a safe person
(2) help in relaxing or modulating distress responses
(3) retelling or reliving aspects of the traumatic event

(4) reassessing the thoughts and feelings associated with the event
(5) reconsidering catastrophic thinking or distortions
(6) recognition of reminders that trigger traumatic distress
(7) reconstructing a sense of what is dangerous and what is safe
(8) dealing with guilt and blame

These treatments are usually time limited and can be as brief as one two-hour session, or as lengthy as a series of 10 sessions. Studies with medical illness are small and nonrandomized at this point. However, a similar approach has been tested and found to be useful in a randomized, controlled trial of group cognitive behavioral treatment within the schools for children exposed to interpersonal violence (Stein et al., 2003).

Identification and early interventions for those who have not yet developed chronic symptoms have also been developed and are available for general use by those caring for medically ill children and their parents. Screening forms for use by clinicians working in emergency departments and intensive care units allow identification of those with symptoms of acute stress disorder, which is seen as a significant risk factor for later development of posttraumatic stress symptoms. Intervention can then be targeted to those most at risk. Educational materials are also available: these can be given to parents to help them identify symptoms that indicate a need for early intervention. These can be used as a part of the "anticipatory guidance" that pediatricians routinely provide for families of children. These tools are available in the Medical Traumatic Stress Toolkit through the National Child Traumatic Stress Network (NCTSN) website, nctsnet.org. Sponsored by the Substance Abuse and Mental Health Services Administration (SAMHSA) of the federal government in the United States, the NCTSN has used a partnership of university centers and community-based service providers to develop and implement interventions for children and families exposed to a variety of traumatic stressors (Stuber, Schneider, Kassam-Adams, Kazak, & Saxe, 2006).

Preventative efforts for all children and parents exposed to medical life threat are also available through the NCTSN website, developed by hospital-based researchers and clinicians based on clinical experience with hospitalized children and children with acute injuries. The general format of these interventions is psycho-educational, utilizing written materials as well as individual and group meetings with clinicians. Basic components include strategies to reduce helplessness, fear, and horror by better understanding what is happening in the treatment, and what kinds of reactions parents can expect from their children. Concrete efforts to restore some of the normal parenting role are also very helpful, for example, allowing parents to feed or bathe their children in the hospital. Parents are helped to adjust their expectations in light of expectable stress-related regression, without removing the entire structure upon which the child relies.

Preventative group interventions, which may help prevent significant posttraumatic stress symptoms by reducing helplessness and the sense of isolation that contributes to fear, have also been used. Support and mutual problem-solving types of groups appear to be more useful for parents than for adolescent cancer survivors in one study (Stuber, Gonzalez, Benjamin, & Golant, 1995). Specific training in problem solving appears to be helpful for mothers (Sahler et al., 2005). However, settings that allow medically ill children to feel less alone and to regain a sense of being "regular kids" appear to be quite successful A popular and informal format for these types of groups is the specialty camp, such as the Ronald McDonald Camp Good Times for childhood cancer survivors, and the Paul Newman Hole in the Wall camps for children with a variety of medical problems, including organ transplant recipients. At this point the data supporting the utility of these camps are limited (Martiniuk, 2003), but the number of camps continues to grow.

With the increasing availability of the Internet, virtual support groups have also been created, with apparent success. A Web site at experiencejournal.com allows children and parents dealing with cancer, heart disease, and organ transplants to read or hear the stories of other patients and families, as well as learn from the experts (DeMaso, Gonzalez-Heydrich, Erickson, Grimes, & Strohecker, 2000). Another Web site, sponsored by the Children's Oncology Group, a national association of pediatric oncologists, offers support and education for adolescents dealing with cancer at http://www.teenslivingwithcancer.org.

Pharmacological Interventions

Pharmacological interventions have also been targeted either at prevention or at treatment of symptoms. Preventative pharmacological interventions have focused on reduction of the fight-flight response, known as autonomic arousal. This approach has been based on two different types of studies. The first type of studies examined heart rate in the immediate posttrauma period as a predictor for later posttraumatic stress symptoms. These studies have been done primarily with children brought into the emergency department after traffic injuries. In one such study, 190 children, aged 8 to 17 years, were assessed for symptoms of posttraumatic stress approximately six months after their injuries. Those children who had a higher heart rate at the time of triage in the emergency department were more likely to report symptoms consistent with a diagnosis of PTSD or "partial PTSD" (Kassam-Adams, Garcai-Espana, Fein, & Winston, 2005). This type of study has led to a number of medication trials with drugs designed to reduce heart rate. Although a number of small trials of such medications have been successful, none have been sufficiently impressive to convince physicians to give medications that could be dangerous to an ill or injured child at the time of hospitalization.

The second type of medication study has been more influential in clinical and research thinking about preventative interventions for posttraumatic stress responses. In 2001, Glenn Saxe and Frederick Stoddard (Saxe et al., 2001) examined the relationship between posttraumatic stress symptoms in children who had sustained major burns and the amount of morphine they had received during the hospitalization. The severity of symptoms of posttraumatic stress reported six months after the burn was negatively associated with the amount of morphine they had received. This was counterintuitive, since one would assume that the amount of morphine should be proportional to the size and severity of the burn, and that the size and severity of the burn would be related to the likelihood of posttraumatic stress symptoms. However, the posttraumatic stress symptoms were not greater in those with more severe burns. Morphine for pain during hospitalization for burns appeared to reduce the likelihood of later posttraumatic stress symptoms. This was hypothesized as a result of pain control and sedation reducing both autonomic arousal and perception of threat, and thus reducing the psycho-physiological process that leads to chronic posttraumatic stress symptoms. At the least, this finding reinforces the need for excellent pain control for ill or injured children. In addition, it raises some interesting questions about the prevention of posttraumatic stress symptoms.

Pharmacological treatments of symptoms are also theoretically based on addressing autonomic arousal and the physiological stress response. For example, persistent increases in cortisol releasing factor (CRF) concentration have been associated with trauma exposure in early life and with PTSD. This increase in CRF may be reversed with the use of paroxetine, a serotonin reuptake inhibitor (Nemeroff et al., 2006). However, most of the pharmacological treatments have been empirical, addressing specific symptoms. Randomized, controlled trials are needed. In the meantime, the literature suggests starting with selective serotonin reuptake inhibitors, known as SSRIs. These have been found to be effective for many of the symptoms associated with posttraumatic stress responses, such as anxiety and withdrawal, and found to improve quality of life. However, SSRIs are not always sufficient to address all of the symptoms. Adrenergic agents such as clonidine may be used alone or in conjunction with an SSRI to treat impulsivity and hyperarousal. In some cases a mood stabilizer, such as lithium, or even an antipsychotic medication may be needed. Each of these agents has been found to be useful in some situations, so clinicians are advised to address targeted symptoms, rather than expecting there to be a PTSD-specific medication for children and adolescents (Donnelly, 2003). One type of medication that is generally not recommended is the benzodiazepines. Although these may be useful short-term medications for sleep disturbances, they may increase a sense of helplessness in acute situations, by causing disinhibition or grogginess without any real reduction in anxiety.

CASE EXAMPLE: INTERVENTION

Rosa is referred for a consultation with the hospital based pediatric psychologist because the liver transplant team is worried that she does not seem to be consistently taking her immunosuppressive medications, and she is starting to reject her liver. Rosa acquired hepatitis on a visit to her extended family in Mexico when she was 10 years old. She had previously been well and very athletic, enjoying playing soccer with her school team. Rosa had a liver transplant four months after her diagnosis, and had a rocky course for the first year after the transplant, with frequent hospitalizations for infections and acute rejection episodes. Rosa is now 12 years old and two years post-transplant, and has been stable. However, over the past few months her liver tests have been less good, and her medication blood levels have been more variable.

On interview, Rosa describes vomiting blood during a soccer game, and the horror she saw on her mother's face. She admits she tries to avoid seeing herself in the mirror when she is undressed, as her scar reminds her of seeing her father crying at her bedside when she woke up after the transplant. She had never seen him cry before, and it terrified her. She had been sure she was dying. She still has nightmares about both of these events.

In the therapy she becomes more able to remember what happened, and gains a sense that she can control the resulting feelings. She learns how to respond when she encounters things that remind her of the transplant. She practices relaxation techniques, and challenges her fears and catastrophic thinking. Over a few weeks she finds that she can get up the courage to try out for the track team, despite her mother's apprehension about her being involved in sports again. Rosa appears more able to concentrate, is doing better in school, and is more social. Her mother reports that Rosa does not seem to "forget" to take her medication as often, and is much less upset now when her mother offers it to her. Rosa's mother is also more relaxed, now that her daughter seems to be back to being a normal, healthy girl.

Best Practices

As described above, clinical research has suggested that children with life-threatening illness and their parents are at risk for the development of chronic symptoms of posttraumatic stress. This has been found in childhood cancer survivors, organ transplant recipients, diabetics, and children with serious burns, among others. The actual prevalence of posttraumatic stress in children with life-threatening illness is still not entirely clear, with a range of 3–35 percent in studies of childhood cancer survivors, with most studies finding reports of significant symptoms in approximately 15–20 percent of child survivors. For perspective, the prevalence of PTSD in a general urban population has been estimated to be 5 percent for men, 10.4 percent for women, and 3.7 percent for 12- to 17-year-old boys and 6.3 percent among 12- to 17-year-old girls (Seng, Graham-Bermann, Clark, McCarthy, & Ronis, 2005).

As has been described above, parental reports of posttraumatic stress in response to the medical illness or injury of their children have been higher than those of the children, ranging between 8 and 45%, with most studies finding more severe symptoms reported by mothers than by fathers. This may be simply a gender difference, as women usually report more symptoms than men (Nemeroff et al., 2006). However, this also may be a reflection of the relative exposure of mothers to traumatic episodes during treatment, since mothers are more likely to accompany their children to the clinic and hospital.

Individuals who are more anxious at baseline are at higher risk to develop post-traumatic stress symptoms in response to medical life threat and intrusive treatment. This applies to both children and parents. A certain threshold of severity of illness appears to be required to develop posttraumatic stress symptoms, as children admitted to the intensive care unit appear to be at much greater risk than those general pediatric wards. However, beyond that threshold, the actual severity of the illness or injury is less important than the child's perception of life threat or treatment intensity in predicting who will go on to develop posttraumatic stress symptoms. Children's perception of threat appears to be influenced by that of the parent, whose posttraumatic stress symptoms are also related to their perception of life threat and treatment intensity. Thus, although the posttraumatic stress symptoms of mothers and children are not directly related, they are indirectly related through the apparent sharing of the perception of life threat and treatment intensity.

Interventions are best conceptualized as either preventative strategies or treatment of symptoms. Prevention of posttraumatic stress symptoms appears to require the following:

(1) Effective pain management
(2) Screening for signs of autonomic arousal, such as increased heart rate
(3) Psychoeducational interventions with parents
(4) Care to avoid additional trauma, such as separation from parents
(5) Efforts to decrease helplessness for child and parent

Examples of successful preventative approaches would be the use of the Medical Traumatic Stress Toolkit from the National Child Traumatic Stress Network, or the camps offered to children with a variety of illnesses that would preclude them from participating in other camps. Support and psycho-educational groups offered for parents are also useful as general preventative approaches.

Treatment approaches should include interventions with both child and parents, and should address feelings of pervasive fear and helplessness. The approaches with the best evidence base are trauma-focused CBT (tested with other types of childhood trauma) and family systems approaches (specifically tested for children with cancer and their families). Both use time-limited approaches, which can be followed individually or in groups.

Medications may be indicated to address specific symptoms, or when the anxiety or concurrent depression is disabling. The class of SSRIs is generally the best first step, with the most research having been done with sertraline and paroxetine (Gothelf et al., 2005). Benzodiazepines should be used sparingly, as they can turn an alert and frightened child into a disinhibited and groggy frightened child, who is even more difficult to comfort.

Helping the parents to be calm and supportive for the children is one of the best investments in preventative and treatment intervention that a clinician can offer. Parents who are out of control emotionally are even more distressing to children in a treatment setting than absent parents. Well-meaning parents can easily increase distress in their children by being apologetic or overly reassuring to the child. Providing information to the parents is usually the single best way to help them to overcome their own helplessness and intense fear, and to enable them to support their children.

Public Policy

Academic medical centers are working all the time to reduce the actual life threat of childhood illnesses. Obviously, reducing the threat would be very helpful in reducing the fear and helplessness of children and parents. However, much of the improvement in survival has been purchased at the cost of increases in treatment intensity. Children diagnosed with cancer often go through years of chemotherapy and radiation treatment, with many painful procedures and separations from their families. Organ transplants require lengthy operations and hospital stays, as well as a lifetime of medication and blood tests. Many successful treatments have become a source of horror and helplessness. Although this cannot be eliminated, hospitals and medical care providers can reduce the traumatic impact by becoming aware of the types of things that are traumatic for children and parents.

A recent survey suggests we have a long way to go to educate physicians about posttraumatic responses in children. Although studies of children after motor vehicle–related injury suggest that up to 80 percent will develop symptoms of acute stress response, only 20 of 287 board-eligible or board-certified pediatric emergency physicians reported that they believed children were likely to develop these types of symptoms. These physicians were aware that an associated parental injury increased the risk of traumatic stress symptoms, but 86 percent incorrectly believed that severity of the injury was associated with future development of PTSD. Only 11 percent of the physicians were aware of the available tools to assess the risk for PTSD, and only 18 percent provided any verbal guidance about PTSD to the parents (Ziegler, Greenwald, DeGuzman, & Simon, 2005). Further education is clearly indicated to address this and the needs of the parents.

Only a generation ago, it was common for children in the hospital to be separated from their parents for all but a few hours a day. This was justified on the basis of space, infection control, and how upset the children became when the parents left. Today parents are able to stay with their children throughout a hospital stay, even sleeping in their rooms except in intensive care or isolation settings. This reflects a shift in the understanding of the needs of hospitalized children. Current debates now center on the presence of parents as a child prepares for anesthesia preoperatively, with similar arguments made on both sides. Once again, however, the wrong question is being asked. Rather than asking whether children will do better or worse if their parents are present, the question is how to make the parents as helpful as they can be to the child. A supportive, calm adult is what the child needs. If that person can be the parent or close relative, it is much more effective for the child than any other adult. However, because the child will tend to interpret the danger of a situation from the parent's response, an anxious parent will be worse than a calm staff person. Pediatric hospitals now help prepare children for surgery with tours, photographs, and coloring books. Psychoeducational and support services should be offered to their parents as well, so that parents can be with their children in a supportive way throughout the hospital experience.

Pain control has already been recognized as a major health concern. However, control of pain in children continues to be difficult. Children are not as good reporters of pain as adults, and are less able to localize or describe types of pain. As pain is better understood, anticipation of pain should allow us to premedicate surgical patients. Pain medication should be regularly titrated and given around the clock, rather than using "prn" or "as needed" dosing. This prevents the buildup of pain to an unacceptable level before the next medication is given, and reduces the delay between the onset of pain and the distribution of pain medication in the blood stream, thus reducing physiological and psychological stress on the child and parents. Education of physicians, nurses, and other hospital staff is needed to change the way that we think about pain medication.

Prevention of traumatic stress responses requires changes in what is done acutely in the hospital and over time in treatment. Communication is the key ingredient to reducing helplessness in these settings. Parents need to have good education and communication about their child's illness and treatment from the beginning. They also need to know that they will not get differing opinions and information from the variety of medical teams who see their child. This requires good communication between the different teams.

Current research is rapidly increasing the understanding of the neurobiology of posttraumatic stress responses. This will ultimately be the key to understanding both prevention and treatment. In the meantime, however, better treatment studies are needed. To do these properly, investigators will have to better understand the constellation of symptoms of posttraumatic stress responses in children and adolescents and to find out whether symptoms are the same in people exposed to medical life threat as they are to natural disasters or interpersonal violence. It may be that the prolonged experience of intrusive and painful procedures that are performed with parental permission and by seemingly well-meaning people has a very different impact on children than one-time episodes of violence, much as sustained abuse by a parent has a different impact from a single disaster (Terr, 1991). Although we now know that children can be traumatized even if physicians are doing things "for their own good," we still have much to learn about the full significance of these symptoms for the lifetime that has been restored to them.

CASE EXAMPLE: TRAUMA PREVENTION IN A HOSPITAL

Toby is brought in to the hospital after collapsing at school. His parents have been called and have come to the emergency room, but have not been able to locate where he is or get any information on his status. They are frantic by the time they find a nurse who knows where he is, and even then they are told to wait before they can see him. When they are brought in to see him, he is hooked up to a number of beeping machines. He does not respond to their voices, and his mother begins to cry. His heart rate begins to climb, and the machines start making shrill noises. His parents are told they must leave now, and wait until he is admitted to the hospital. They meet with several doctors, who all seem to ask the same questions. Is there anyone in the family with heart disease or diabetes? They are told that Toby has had a syncopal episode, that his glucose level is over 300, and that he may have diabetes. They are stunned and confused, not really understanding anything except that last word. Yes, mother had a relative with diabetes, an aunt. She became blind, had to go on dialysis, and died of an infection when she was only 34. Is that what will happen to Toby?

When they join Toby in his room in the pediatric intensive care unit (PICU), he is fighting with a nurse who is trying to draw his blood. His mother runs over to comfort him, happy to see him awake. His father looks around at the PICU. It reminds him of Las Vegas. The lights are on as if it is day, although it is now almost midnight, and everyone is busy, with machines humming. Toby asks his parents what happened, and when he can go home. He is eight years old and has never slept away from home without his parents.

One of the nurses introduces herself to the family. She explains that there will be an opportunity for them to meet with the doctor and the team who will care for Toby in the morning. There is a room in which they can sleep that night if they want. Toby is likely to be moved to a regular pediatric bed in the morning, and there will be a bed there in the room with him for one of them to stay with him. They will meet with the nutritionist and be taught whatever they will need to know about Toby's care before he goes home. In the meantime, they need to know that diabetes care is much better than when mother's aunt was a girl. Toby is finally sleeping comfortably, and they decide to have dad stay in the hospital, while mother goes home to collect some things to make Toby feel more at home—and to finally eat something for the first time in over 12 hours.

References

Alter, C. L., Pelcovitz, D., Axelrod, A., Goldenberg, B., Harris, H., Meyers, B., et al. (1996). Identification of PTSD in cancer survivors. *Psychosomatics, 37*(2), 137–143.

American Psychiatric Association. (1994). *Diagnostic and statistical manual of mental disorders* (4th ed.). Washington, DC: Author.

Balluffi, A., Kassam-Adams, N., Kazak, A., Tucker, M., Dominguez, T., & Helfaer, M. (2004). Traumatic stress in parents of children admitted to the pediatric intensive care unit. *Pediatric Critical Care Medicine, 5*(6), 547–553

Barakat, L. P., Kazak, A. E., Meadows, A. T., Casey, R., Meeske, K. & Stuber, M. L. (1997). Families surviving childhood cancer: A comparison of posttraumatic stress symptoms with families of healthy children. *Journal of Pediatric Psychology, 22*(6), 843–859.

Cohen, J. A. (2005). Treating traumatized children: Current status and future directions. *Journal of Trauma and Dissociation, 6*(2), 109–121,

DeMaso, D. R., Gonzalez-Heydrich, J., Erickson, J. D., Grimes, V. P., & Strohecker, C. (2000). The Experience Journal: A computer-based intervention for families facing congenital heart disease. *Journal of the American Academy of Child and Adolescent Psychiatry, 39*(6), 727–734.

Donnelly, C. L. (2003). Pharmacologic treatment approaches for children and adolescents with posttraumatic stress disorder. *Child and Adolescent Psychiatric Clinics of North America, 12*(2), 251–269.

Foa, E. B. (2006). Psychosocial therapy for posttraumatic stress disorder. *Journal of Clinical Psychiatry, 67*(Suppl. 2), 40–45.

Glover, D. A., & Poland, R. E. (2002). Urinary cortisol and catecholamines in mothers of child cancer survivors with and without PTSD. *Psychoneuroendocrinology, 27*(7), 805–819.

Glover, D. A., Steele, A. C., Stuber, M. L., & Fahey, J. L. (2005). Preliminary evidence for lymphocyte distribution differences at rest and after acute psychological stress in PTSD-symptomatic women. *Brain and Behavior Immunology, 9*(3), 243–251.

Gothelf, D., Rubinstein, M., Shemesh, E., Miller, O., Farbstein, I., Klein, A., et al. (2005). Pilot study: Fluvoxamine treatment for depression and anxiety disorders in children and adolescents with cancer. *Journal of the American Academy of Child and Adolescent Psychiatry, 44*(12), 1258–1262.

Hobbie, W. L., Stuber, M., Meeske, K., Wissler, K., Rourke, M. T., Ruccione, K., et al. (2000). Symptoms of posttraumatic stress in young adult survivors of childhood cancer. *Journal of Clinical Oncology, 15;18, 24,* 4060–4066.

Karl, A., Schaefer, M., Malta, L. S., Dorfel, D., Rohleder, N., & Werner, A. (2006, May). A meta-analysis of structural brain abnormalities in PTSD [Electronic version]. *Neuroscience and Biobehavioral Review, 30*(7), 1004–1031.

Kassam-Adams, N., Garcai-Espana, J. F., Fein, J. A., & Winston, F. K. (2005). Heart rate and posttraumatic stress in injured children. *Archives of General Psychiatry, 62*(3), 335–340.

Kazak, A. E., Barakat, L. P., Meeske, K., Christakis, D., Meadows, A. T., Casey, R., et al. (1997). Posttraumatic stress, family functioning, and social support in survivors of childhood leukemia and their mothers and fathers. *Journal of Consulting and Clinical Psychology, 65*(1), 120–129.

Kazak, A. E., Simms, S., Alderfer, M. A., Rourke, M. T., Crump, T., McClure, K., et al. (2005). Feasibility and preliminary outcomes from a pilot study of a brief psychological intervention for families of children newly diagnosed with cancer. *Journal of Pediatric Psychology, 30*(8), 644–655.

Kenardy, J. A., Spence, S. H., & Macleod, A. C. (2006). Screening for posttraumatic stress disorder in children after accidental injury. *Pediatrics, 118*(3), 1002–1009.

Landolt, M. A., Vollrath, M., Ribi, K., Gnehm, H. E., & Sennhauser, F. H. (2003). Incidence and associations of parental and child posttraumatic stress symptoms in pediatric patients. *Journal of Child Psychology and Psychiatry, 44*(8), 1199–1207.

Martiniuk, A. L. (2003, October 1). Camping programs for children with cancer and their families [Electronic version]. *Support Care Cancer, 11*(12), 749–757.

Meeske, K. A., Ruccione, K., Globe, D. R., & Stuber, M. L. (2001). Posttraumatic stress, quality of life, and psychological distress in young adult survivors of childhood cancer. *Oncology Nurses Forum, 28*(3), 481–489.

Mintzer, L. L., Stuber, M. L., Seacord, D., Castaneda, M., Mesrkhani, V., & Glover, D. (2005). Traumatic stress symptoms in adolescent organ transplant recipients. *Pediatrics, 115*(6), 1640–1644.

Nemeroff, C. B., Bremner, J. D., Foa, E. B., Mayberg, H. S., North, C. S., & Stein, M. B. (2006, October 18). Posttraumatic stress disorder: a state-of-the-science review [Electronic version]. *Journal of Psychiatric Research, 40*(1), 1–21.

Pai, A. L., & Kazak, A. E. (2006). Pediatric medical traumatic stress in pediatric oncology: Family systems interventions. *Current Opinions in Pediatrics, 18*(5), 558–562.

Pelcovitz, D., Goldenberg, B., Kaplan, S., Weinblatt, M., Mandel, F., Meyers, B., et al. (1996). Posttraumatic stress disorder in mothers of pediatric cancer survivors. *Psychosomatics, 37*(2), 116–126.

Pynoos, R. S., Frederick, C., Nader, K., Arroyo, W., Steinberg, A., Eth, S., et al. (1987). Life threat and posttraumatic stress in school-age children. *Archives of General Psychiatry, 44*(12), 1057–1063.

Pynoos, R. S., & Nader, K. (1988). Children who witness the sexual assaults of their mothers. *Journal of the American Academy of Child and Adolescent Psychiatry, 27*(5), 567–572.

Rees, G., Gledhill, J., Garralda, M. E., & Nadel, S. (2004). Psychiatric outcome following pediatric intensive care unit (PICU) admission: A cohort study. *Intensive Care Medicine, 30*(8), 1607–1614.

Sahler, O. J., Fairclough, D. L., Phipps, S., Mulhern, R. K., Dolgin, M. J., Noll, R. B., et al. (2005). Using problem-solving skills training to reduce negative affectivity in mother of children with newly diagnosed cancer: Report of a multisite randomized trial. *Journal of Consulting and Clinical Psychology, 73*(2), 272–283.

Saxe, G., Stoddard, F., Courtney, D., Cunningham, K., Chawla, N., Sheridan, R., et al. (2001). Relationship between acute morphine and the course of PTSD in children with burns. *Journal of the American Academy of Child and Adolescent Psychiatry, 40*(8), 915–921.

Seng, J. S., Graham-Bermann, S. A., Clark, M. K., McCarthy, A. M., & Ronis, D. L. (2005). Posttraumatic stress disorder and physical comorbidity among female children and adolescents: Results from service-use data. *Pediatrics, 116*(6), e767–e776.

Shemesh, E., Lurie, S., Stuber, M. L., Emre, S., Patel, Y., Vohra, P., et al. (2000). A pilot study of posttraumatic stress and nonadherence in pediatric liver transplant recipients. *Pediatrics, 105*(2), E29.

Stein, B. D., Jaycox, L. H., Kataoka, S. H., Wong, M., Tu, W., Elliott, M. N., et al. (2003, August 6). A mental health intervention for school children exposed to violence: A randomized controlled trial. *Journal of the American Medical Association, 290*(5), 603–611.

Stuber, M., Gonzalez, S., Benjamin, H., & Golant, M. (1995). Fighting for recovery: Group interventions for adolescent with cancer patients and their parents. *Journal of Psychotherapy Practice and Research, 4*, 286–296.

Stuber, M. L., Kazak, A. E., Meeske, K., Barakat, L., Guthrie, D., Garnier, H., et al. (1997). Predictors of posttraumatic stress symptoms in childhood cancer survivors. *Pediatrics, 100*(6), 958–964.

Stuber, M. L., Nader, K., Yasuda, P., Pynoos, R. S., & Cohen, S. (1991). Stress responses after pediatric bone marrow transplantation: Preliminary results of a prospective longitudinal study. *Journal of the American Academy of Child and Adolescent Psychiatry, 30*(6), 952–957

Stuber, M. L., Schneider, S., Kassam-Adams, N., Kazak, A. E., & Saxe, G. (2006). The medical traumatic stress toolkit. *CNS Spectrum, 11*(2), 137–142.

Terr, L. C. (1985). Psychic trauma in children and adolescents. *Psychiatric Clinics of North America, 8*(4), 815–835.

Terr, L. C. (1991). Childhood traumas: An outline and overview. *American Journal of Psychiatry, 148*(1), 10–20.

Terr, L. C., Bloch, D. A., Michel, B. A., Shi, H., Reinhardt, J. A., & Metayer, S. (1999). Children's symptoms in the wake of Challenger: A field study of distant-traumatic effects and an outline of related conditions. *American Journal of Psychiatry, 156*(10), 1536–1544.

Thomas, L. A., & De Bellis, M. D. (2004, April 1). Pituitary volumes in pediatric maltreatment-related posttraumatic stress disorder. *Biological Psychiatry, 55*(7), 752–758.

Tupler, L. A., & De Bellis, M. D. (2006, March 15). Segmented hippocampal volume in children and adolescents with posttraumatic stress disorder [Electronic version]. *Biological Psychiatry, 59*(6), 523–529.

Yasik, A. E., Saigh, P. A., Oberfield, R. A., & Halamandaris, P. V. (2006). Posttraumatic stress disorder: Memory and learning performance in children and adolescents [Electronic version]. *Biological Psychiatry, 18*.

Young, G. S., Mintzer, L. L., Seacord, D., Castaneda, M., Mesrkhani, V., & Stuber, M. L. (2003). Symptoms of posttraumatic stress disorder in parents of transplant recipients: Incidence, severity, and related factors. *Pediatrics, 111*(6, part 1), e725–e731.

Ziegler, M. F., Greenwald, M. H., DeGuzman, M. A., & Simon, H. K. (2005). Posttraumatic stress response in children: Awareness and practice among a sample of pediatric emergency care providers. *Pediatrics, 115*(5), 1261–1267.

CHAPTER 3

Trauma and the Treatment of Pain

Allen Lebovits

Pain is one of the most complex of human experiences. It is the most common reason for which patients seek medical care. Over 80 percent of all physician visits are due to pain. Pain accounts for over $70 billion annually in health care costs and lost productivity (Gatchel & Turk, 1996). It is defined by the International Association for the Study of Pain as "an unpleasant sensory and emotional experience associated with actual or potential tissue damage." Accordingly, the perception of pain is not only a sensory experience but also an emotional experience. Sensory information and affective state play interactive roles. Pain is reacted to with varying levels of emotional distress that can mitigate the perception of pain. Heightened levels of anxiety in reaction to the pain often exacerbate the very sensation of pain.

It is important to distinguish between acute and chronic pain. The distinction between the two is not simply a matter of duration: (1) Acute pain is biologically useful; it serves as the body's alarm warning of an underlying medical condition, while chronic pain has lost its biological usefulness. (2) The etiology of acute pain is almost always identifiable, while the complex interaction of physical and emotional factors in chronic pain makes the etiology often unclear. (3) Cure and relief are almost always attainable in acute pain but are often not possible with chronic pain. The goal in chronic pain treatment is to improve functionality, for example, increasing activities of daily living, interacting more with people, and/or returning to work. (4) Acute pain may lead to anxiety while chronic pain is often associated with depression. These distinctions between acute and chronic pain have important therapeutic implications. The treatment approaches for each are very different.

The first psychological model of chronic pain was the psychodynamic approach, which emphasized the psychological etiology of pain. Freud viewed pain as a symptomatic expression of an unconscious conflict seeking awareness. In 1965, Melzack and Wall revolutionized the way we think about pain with their "gate control" theory. For the first time, pain theory incorporated higher brain functions such as cognition and affect. The theory postulated the existence of a "spinal gate," in the dorsal horn of the spinal column, that modulates transmission cells influenced by inhibitory and facilitative fibers. Quite significantly, the theory postulated that cognitive and affective states can help open or close the gate. Although the theory has been revised due to new physiological discoveries, its basic premises still remain.

Behavioral models, particularly operant conditioning, proposed by William Fordyce in the 1970s, became popular. Fordyce proposed that the behavioral expression of pain, pain behavior, is the result of positive and negative reinforcers from the patient's environment, such as social reinforcement from family and friends, medications from physicians, financial incentives, or avoidance of activities. Subsequently, cognitive behavioral models of pain became more popular and remain the prevailing theory with regard to the assessment and treatment of chronic pain today. The cognitive behavioral model theorizes that the experience of pain is a reciprocal interaction of thoughts, feelings, physiology, and behavior (Bradley, 1996).

The traditional medical model of chronic pain was that pain had either a physical basis or a psychological one. It is now well accepted that chronic pain is a complex interplay of physiologic, psychologic, and social processes (Turk & Okifuji, 1996). These biopsychosocial determinants of chronic pain interact with one another: Neurophysiologic responses to noxious stimuli such as pain can trigger psychological responses, while psychological states such as depression or anxiety can affect the neurophysiologic system by enhancing or inhibiting the transmission of noxious signals. Social factors such as stress, trauma, environmental reinforcers of pain (for example, an overly attentive spouse), or financial compensation (through disability or litigation, for example), can significantly influence a patient's perception of pain. Many patients with chronic pain, particularly if the pain resulted from an accident at work, will go on disability because they cannot or will not return to work. The disability system, however, often works against the best interests of the patient and the goals of pain management: (1) by offering compensation comparable to work: in effect, paying the patient to have pain; (2) by promoting activity restrictiveness, which works against the goal of returning patients to a more optimal level of function; (3) by extensive delays in authorizations for medical and psychological evaluations and treatments—many pain syndromes have a much better prognosis if treated earlier rather than later; and (4) by the lack of light-duty work or trial return-to-work periods. This can lead to fear on the part of the patient to return to work and lose his or her disability. Another potential problem is the definition of "light duty," which can be inappropriate. For example, a bus driver returning from disability may be assigned to cleaning buses rather than driving them.

The most prevalent psychological characteristic of chronic pain patients is depression (Romano & Turner, 1985). Depression and chronic pain occur together so frequently that it is often difficult to determine whether the depression is a precipitant of the pain or a consequence of living with intractable pain. Levels of depression can range from minor mood-state disturbances to major clinical depressions with active suicidal ideation. Other characteristics of patients with chronic pain include increased dependency on others; increased illness behaviors such as grimacing; overreliance on medications; increased health care utilization; and family dysfunction; for example, spouses of pain patients may display clinically significant levels of emotional distress.

Psychological Assessment of Chronic Pain

The multidisciplinary evaluation and treatment approach to the patient suffering with chronic pain is widely practiced today and considered to be the standard of care (AAPM Council on Ethics, 2005). The psychological evaluation and assessment of chronic pain patients has evolved from unidimensional to multidimensional models. Since the formation of the first multidisciplinary pain center in 1961 by John Bonica at the University of Washington, there has been a proliferation of such centers. A multidisciplinary pain center is a facility in which a comprehensive evaluation and treatment are provided by a team of health care professionals including physicians, psychologists, physical therapists, occupational therapists, and nurses. A major advantage of the team approach is that a broad base of knowledge and expertise is available, and this can facilitate a team analysis of the appropriate diagnosis of pain and the appropriate treatment approach.

Despite the increasing recognition of the importance of appropriate pain control, as evidenced by the formation of national professional societies such as the American Pain Society and the recently revised accreditation criteria of the Joint Commission on Accreditation of Hospitals, mandating pain evaluations of every hospitalized patient, pain is often undertreated. Lack of knowledge on the part of health care professionals regarding the appropriate evaluation and treatment of pain and poor attitudes, particularly the unwarranted fear of addiction on the part of both patient and provider, hamper proper pain control efforts (Lebovits et al., 1997). Appropriate pain control therefore continues to be a significant challenge for the patient, the patient's family, and health care providers.

It is important to assess for the occurrence of trauma, as its contribution to the complexity of the pain diagnosis may not always be evident. Some patients may avoid discussing trauma due to fearfulness. In other cases, people may be unaware of their trauma. Additionally, some of the symptoms of posttraumatic stress disorder (PTSD), such as affective disturbance, hyperarousal, or sleep problems, could be seen by the health care provider as being due to the patient's pain. Alternatively, severe, unrelenting pain could be the source of the trauma itself: Many patients with chronic pain fear that it is life threatening; they anticipate further medical interventions, such as surgeries, which can be a threat to their physical integrity. The sudden onset and life-altering nature of chronic pain often lead to feelings of helplessness and intense fear.

Measures of Pain

A useful assessment measure for patients with chronic pain and trauma is the Posttraumatic Chronic Pain Test (PCPT) (Muse & Frigola, 1986). The PCPT contains six true-false items that screen for the presence of PTSD related to the accident that caused the patient's pain. The PCPT has good reliability (.90), split half reliability (.59), and interrater reliability (.93). An important area of investigation in the clinical interview with the patient with chronic pain, particularly with women presenting with chronic pelvic pain, is a history of childhood physical, emotional, or sexual abuse. There appears to be a relationship between childhood abuse and physical pain in adulthood (Schofferman, Anderson, Hines, Smith, & White, 1992).

Although the treatment of a patient with chronic pain mandates a comprehensive evaluation of the medical as well as psychological contributors to the etiology, maintenance, and exacerbation of pain, evaluating and treating chronic pain patients with a unimodal, strictly medical approach still occurs. Relying solely on radiographic results, which have been shown to be unreliable indices of pain, to explain a patient's pain, can lead to failed surgical interventions. Additionally, significant spinal abnormalities are found in patients who do not experience back pain. Jensen et al. (1994) found that 64 percent of 98 individuals who did not have any pain had a disk bulge, protrusion, or extrusion on MRI. Thirty-eight percent had an abnormality of more than one intervertebral disk.

Other detrimental effects of a strictly medical approach to chronic pain includes not evaluating chronic pain patients for PTSD, which can lead to failed medical interventions and subsequent significant psychological morbidity as a result of another failed treatment approach. In fact, the depression often experienced by PTSD patients can be exacerbated by the failure of treatment based on a unimodal medical approach, as they get increasingly frustrated by the failures of treatment and as their depression does not get addressed. Physical pain is often accompanied by emotional pain, particularly when the circumstances of onset are traumatic. The early and accurate identification of individuals who are at risk of developing PTSD could lead to psychological interventions that can potentially lessen the severity of PTSD symptoms.

CASE REPORT 1

A 28-year-old three-time karate champion from a South American country, married with two small children, was crossing the street in Manhattan when his life changed suddenly forever. He awoke in a hospital bed in excruciating pain to discover that his right leg had been amputated above his knee after he was hit by a car. I saw him six months later for the first time. He was trying to adjust to a prosthesis and had florid symptoms of posttraumatic stress disorder and severe chronic pain.

Pharmacologic interventions took the edge off his physical pain but didn't touch his emotional pain. He told me he had gone to the roof of his apartment building three times to jump off but "hasn't had the courage" to do it yet. Pain drugs weren't enough for him. No one in the busy medical system thought it worthwhile to address his significant depression, his constant nightmares, and his enormous rage at the doctors who amputated his leg. No one asked him about his failing marriage and the growing distance between him and his children.

Psychological treatments for pain are often overlooked by doctors as well as insurance companies. Doctors may resort to more invasive and expensive pain interventions, such as spinal cord stimulators and implantable pumps, that are more likely to be reimbursed by insurance companies but offer minimal evidence of being useful, especially when compared to less costly and less invasive psychological treatments. Cognitive behavioral methods, such as biofeedback and relaxation training, have proven effective for specific pain syndromes yet are thought of as "alternative" or "complementary." In this case example, had the young man had more immediate psychological attention, his emotional as well as physical pain would probably not have been so far out of control.

Another example of the psychological issues that can be overlooked without a comprehensive psychological evaluation is patterns of somatization, which can lead to repeated medical interventions and further contribute to medical and psychological morbidity. Therefore, the Commission on Accreditation of Rehabilitation Facilities (CARF) accredits only chronic pain programs that are interdisciplinary in both their evaluation and their treatment of patients and require a psychologist or psychiatrist as part of the core pain team.

The psychologist needs to take the results from pain questionnaires, clinical interviews, and psychological assessment measures, and with sound clinical judgment formulate a diagnosis and treatment plan that is individually geared to each patient. These results need to be evaluated together with the medical findings and be part of the interdisciplinary overall treatment plan. To paraphrase Sir William Osler, "It is not the type of disease that a patient has that is as important as the type of patient that has the disease."

Psychological Management of Pain

Psychological intervention with the patient who has chronic pain is an integral part of a multidisciplinary approach to pain management. The overall goal of pain management centers today is to return the patient to a more optimal level of functioning. Improved functionality rather than cure of pain is often the focus of pain management. Many pain patients have difficulty accepting that the primary treatment goal is improved functionality rather than pain relief. Frequently, behavioral functioning is the primary goal, followed by emotional functioning. Family members can be very helpful to the therapist in supporting patients' "wellness" behaviors rather than reinforcing "pain" behaviors. Decreased reliance on medications and utilization of the health care system as well as reduced level of subjective pain sensation are important but secondary treatment goals. The simultaneous engagement of physical therapy as part of the patient's recovery is essential as it mitigates the negative influence of deconditioning that many patients experience. Activity and physical therapy are often the focus of the psychological therapy and need to be continually inquired about and reinforced.

The most commonly utilized psychological approach is the cognitive behavioral modality. The general objective of cognitive behavioral treatment strategies is to assist the patient in reconceptualizing his/her belief about pain as an uncontrollable medical symptom to a belief that the patient's response to pain can to an extent be under his/her control. The initial step is educating the patient about the mind-body relationship. The effectiveness of this step depends on the patient's defensiveness, level of knowledge about the mechanism of pain, and attitudes about the mind-body relationship. The mainstay of this approach is relaxation training, which helps patients to redirect their focus away from pain, reduce autonomic reactivity, and enhance a sense of self-control. Relaxation training can be accomplished through guided imagery, progressive muscular relaxation, biofeedback, and hypnosis. Relaxation seems to work through reduction of muscle tension, distraction of the patients from their pain and bodies, and creation of a feeling of enhanced control over their bodies.

Guided imagery has the patient focus on a multisensory imaginary scene. Typically, the image is elicited from the patient, and the psychotherapist guides the patient through the image, substituting sensations such as warmth or numbness for pain. Diaphragmatic breathing (inhaling and exhaling more deeply by using diaphragmatic muscles as opposed to more superficial breathing using primarily chest muscles) is an important part of the relaxation experience, distracting the patient even further.

In progressive muscular relaxation, patients are taught to alternately tense and relax individual muscle groups throughout the body. Only nonpainful muscle groups and body locations are used. Patients learn to recognize and differentiate feelings of tension and relaxation.

Biofeedback is a particularly effective modality for teaching chronic pain patients relaxation as well as self-regulation of physiological processes. Biofeedback monitors ongoing physiological processes such as muscle tension, heart rate, temperature, and even brain waves (called EEG neurofeedback) and provides the patient with visual and auditory feedback. Body sensors attached to a computer enable the patient to achieve relaxation, which can increase pain tolerance, decrease emotional distress, and even relax specific muscle spasms. Physiological self-control leads to a sense of control, better coping skills, and hopefulness. Pain syndromes with which biofeedback is most effective include headaches, transmandibular joint dysfunction (TMD), myofascial pain syndrome, fibromyalgia, and pain exacerbated by stress or anxiety.

Hypnosis is another particularly effective therapeutic technique with pain patients. It not only teaches patients relaxation but also enables them to experience an analgesic reinterpretation of their pain, experiencing numbness, for example, instead of pain. In one study, women with metastatic breast carcinoma pain undergoing weekly group therapy with self-hypnosis had significantly lower pain ratings over one year than a control group (Spiegel & Bloom, 1983).

In addition to education and relaxation training, an essential part of the cognitive behavioral approach is cognitive restructuring. With this technique, patients are taught to identify maladaptive negative thoughts that pervade their thinking and to replace them with more constructive and adaptive positive thoughts. The maladaptive thoughts often take the form of statements about oneself or one's illness that are negative and can include overgeneralizing or catastrophizing. Typical maladaptive thoughts of patients with chronic pain include the following: "Pain signifies something is terribly wrong," "Pain means I need more surgery," and "No one can help me. It's hopeless."

A National Institutes of Health (NIH) technology assessment conference on the efficacy of mind-body approaches for the treatment of chronic pain and insomnia found "strong" to "moderate" evidence to support the use of relaxation techniques, hypnosis, cognitive behavioral therapy, and biofeedback in reducing chronic pain (NIH Technology Assessment Panel, 1996). The American Psychological Association has specified that the psychological treatment of chronic pain is one of 25 areas for which there is empirical validation for psychological intervention.

Psychotherapy also plays an essential role in psychological intervention with pain patients. This can include supportive psychotherapy, group therapy, psychoanalytic (dynamic) psychotherapy, and/or family therapeutic interventions.

Nevertheless, there are barriers to the integration of these psychological therapies into chronic pain management practice. These barriers include a continued overemphasis on the biomedical model, a lack of standardization of psychological techniques, physician reluctance to refer (due to lack of awareness of benefits and concern regarding patient feeling that the physician perceives patients' pain as imaginary or "in their head"), and poor insurance reimbursement.

Trauma and Pain

Medical advances have increased the rates of survival subsequent to major trauma, and these, in turn, have increased the prevalence of chronic pain as a sequela of trauma. Thus, patients with chronic pain often have a traumatic onset etiology. A significant number of patients seen by chronic pain specialists may experience considerable amounts of psychological distress and some may have PTSD. Motor vehicle accidents, a frequent precipitating event for the onset of pain, has been estimated to produce approximately 28 individuals with significant PTSD symptoms in every 1,000 adults in the United States (Norris, 1992). Studies have reported between 29 percent and 43 percent of patients with temperomandibular disorders (TMD) as having had a trauma as the precipitating cause (Greco, Rudy, Turk, Herlich, & Zaki, 1997; Harkins & Martenay 1985).

The complexity of the mind-body relationship in patients who have chronic pain is amplified when they also have PTSD. PTSD has been estimated to occur in about 10 percent of chronic pain patients (Benedikt & Kolb, 1986; Muse, 1985). When patients with pain as a result of an accident are referred for psychological treatment, the reported PTSD rates increases from 50 percent (Hickling & Blanchard, 1992) to 100 percent (Kuch, 1987). One study evaluating Vietnam veterans with PTSD found a rate of pain of 77 percent, though the chronicity of the pain was not specified. Fibromyalgia patients whose pain developed as a result of an MVA compared to fibromyalgia patients whose pain was not related to an MVA had a threefold increase in PTSD or phobia. The reexperiencing and intrusive recollections of the traumatic event are associated with an increase in muscle tension as well as anxiety, which exacerbates pain (Blanchard et al., 1983). PTSD has been theorized to decrease the pain threshold due to neurobiologic changes such as changes in the release of norepinephrine or decreased hippocampal volume. It is unclear whether the decreased pain tolerance observed in posttrauma victims is due to changes in physiology resulting in hypersensitivity to pain or due to changes in selective attention and sensory appraisal. Hypervigilance to bodily sensations is commonly reported by post-MVA victims. Heightened body awareness and anticipation of pain due to having a trauma may lead to an increased focus on physical sensations and misinterpretation of benign sensory input as pain. The failure to diagnose and treat PTSD properly in chronic pain patients can lead to minimal or inadequate pain relief (Benedikt & Kolb 1986; Muse, 1985).

Unresolved traumatic stress can help maintain chronic pain for many years or actually activate physical pain many years later. In a study of 100 spinal surgery patients, 95 percent of patients who recalled no developmental traumas (physical, sexual, or emotional abuse, alcohol/drug abuse in caregiver, or abandonment) had a successful postsurgical outcome (Schofferman, Anderson, Hines, Smith, & White, 1992). Only 15 percent of patients who recalled three or more of these traumas/risk factors had a successful postsurgical outcome. The authors of this study theorized that for those patients with a history of abuse, surgery is another traumatic event that reactivates the childhood template of abuse. Patients who can be consoled are likely to improve; those who have been psychologically traumatized and are not readily consolable may not improve.

Clinically, it has often been noted that patients presenting with chronic pain with a traumatic onset, such as an accident, are frequently more difficult to treat than patients presenting with chronic pain with idiopathic onset (pain not originating as a result of traumatic onset) (Turk & Okifuji, 1996). Posttraumatic pain patients report significantly higher levels of pain severity, disability, life interference, and affective distress, as well as lower levels of activity, than do idiopathic onset pain patients. Additionally, significantly more traumatic onset pain patients receive opioid medications and are treated with nerve blocks, physical therapy, and TENS (transcutaneous electrical nerve stimulation) than nontraumatic onset pain patients. Traumatic onset pain patients who also have significant levels of posttraumatic stress disorder (PTSD) report higher levels of pain and affective disturbance than do traumatic onset pain patients with low levels of PTSD and nontraumatic onset pain patients. Patients with accident onset pain, regardless of the presence of PTSD, report greater disability than do patients whose pain is not accident related (Geisser, Roth, Bachman, & Eckert, 1996).

The treatment of both pain and PTSD have had mixed results. Systematic desensitization, used successfully to reduce PTSD symptoms, has had marginal effects on pain. However, imaginal exposure therapy to the accident scene did lead to pain improvement in one study (Kuch et al., 1985). In a comparison of patients suffering from traumatic onset of temporomandibular disorders (TMD) with those reporting symptoms of unknown origin, Greco et al. (1997) showed that both traumatic and nontraumatic onset groups had positive outcomes following treatment that included biofeedback. The authors acknowledge that the lack of differences may be due to their very broad definition of traumatic onset ("specific onset event") as compared to that of others who used a more limited definition of trauma, such as overt trauma. Nevertheless, they did find that a significantly higher percentage of trauma patients used pain medication at follow-up, similar to previous findings that traumatic onset pain patients required more treatment modalities. Several studies, however, have reported less improvement due to treatment in patients with traumatic onset of pain, with treatment success rates doubling in nontraumatic onset pain patients. Waylonis and Perkins (1994), however, found that the symptoms of traumatically induced fibromyalgia were similar to those of spontaneous fibromyalgia.

Traumatic onset pain patients appear to have greater difficulty in adapting to their chronic pain than do patients whose pain onset was gradual and nontraumatic. This situation is exacerbated when traumatic onset pain patients also have symptoms of PTSD. Sudden changes in lifestyle may have an adverse effect and be more difficult to cope with. When an event is sudden and catastrophic, adaptation is slower than when the individual has an opportunity to adapt to change over time. Additionally, perception of fault is a potential mediator of pain severity; having a target to blame interferes with a healthy recovery and adaptation to pain. In fact, feeling victimized may increase the likelihood of developing PTSD. This might be why individuals with pain who are also involved in litigation tend to cope less well than others. Traditional modalities of chronic pain management (pharmacologic interventions, nerve blocks) do not address the special needs of accident victims.

A confounding variable is that many traumatic onset pain patients are in litigation (Romanelli, Mock, & Tenenbaum, 1992), which in of itself could account for many of the obtained findings, such as increased affective distress and the need for more treatments. Litigating traumatic onset pain patients tend to remain in treatment longer and have less treatment success than nonlitigating traumatic onset pain patients (Burgess & Dworkin, 1993). Similarly, studies have suggested that individuals with pain receiving Workers' Compensation tend to respond poorly to treatment, due to secondary gain issues involved. Because Worker's

Compensation is based on the occurrence of an accident, PTSD symptoms may play a mediating role in explaining the poor treatment outcome for pain patients receiving Workers' Compensation compared to patients whose pain is not accident related. An additional confounding variable when comparing studies of type of onset pain is the duration of pain of the patients, with the longer the duration the less the impact of onset type.

Report on a Study of the Relationship between Trauma and Pain

A study was undertaken to determine whether the circumstances of onset of pain are related in a significant manner to pain variables such as number of pain locations, pain intensity ratings, constancy of pain, interference with sleep, litigation and financial compensation, frequency of analgesic intake, health care utilization, work status, interference with activities and relationships, physical activity, health perception, and mood state disturbance. Additionally, we were interested in determining to what extent these variables could predict onset type.

The participants in this study were 1094 patients with chronic pain (of mixed noncancer diagnoses), referred to the NYU Pain Management Center, who completed a questionnaire about their pain as well as standardized psychological measures on their initial visit. The NYU Pain Management Center is a multidisciplinary pain program housed within the Department of Anesthesiology of the NYU Medical Center. After a multidisciplinary evaluation, patients can receive a wide array of medical and psychological interventions. Participants were grouped into two categories based on their response on the initial questionnaire to the question regarding the circumstances of their pain onset:

Patients completed a specially devised pain questionnaire that assesses areas of clinical relevance. The pain questionnaire, designed to yield objective clinical outcome measures as recommended by the Commission on Accreditation of Rehabilitation Facilities, evaluated the following: (a) demographic characteristics (age, gender, education, marital status, race, and living situation); (b) pain variables (locations, 0–10 scales rating worst, least, and average intensity, constancy, duration, sleep interference, and intensity variation since onset); (c) circumstances related to the onset of pain; (d) litigation and compensation status; (e) analgesic intake and relief; (f) use of health care resources (hospitalizations for pain, pain visits to doctors, previous pain interventions and their efficacy); (g) functionality (work status, job satisfaction, household functions, volunteer work, occupational/vocational rehabilitation enrollment, 0–10 rating scales of degree of pain interference in seven areas, hours spent resting, and blocks able to walk); and (h) a health perception rating scale.

Patients also completed two standardized measures of mood state: the Beck Depression Inventory (BDI) (Beck et al., 1961; Beck, Steer, & Garbin, 1988) is one of the most widely used tests with chronic pain patients because it is a relatively quick measure of depression—a mood state closely linked with chronic pain. The BDI consists of 21 items that evaluate both the cognitive/affective and vegetative symptoms of depression. Patients endorse various symptoms of depression, and this produces a total score of depression ranging from 0 to 63. Scores above 10 reflect minor depressive states, while scores above 17 are indicative of a moderate to severe state. The BDI is able to distinguish between depressed and nondepressed chronic pain patients. Alpha coefficients for the BDI range from .73 to .95. Patients also completed the Spielberger State Anxiety Inventory (STAI), a 20-item self-report measure that is one of the most widely used measures of state anxiety (Spielberger, 1983) and has demonstrated good validity and reliability. Patients are asked to rate statements on a four-point scale regarding how they feel right now, which evaluates "state" anxiety, transitory feelings of anxiety usually in response to specific situations. Scores range from 20 to 80, with each item rated by the patient from 1 ("not at all") to 4 ("very much so"). Total scores can then be converted to normative percentiles, based on medically ill populations.

Analyses show many statistically significant differences between the two groups. Demographically, traumatic onset patients are significantly younger (44.2 vs. 60.1), are significantly more likely to be male (53% vs. 43%), and are significantly more likely to be involved in litigation (42% vs. 0%) and receiving Workers' Compensation (34% vs. 3%). Their pain intensity levels are significantly worse, and they have significantly more pain locations. With regard to health care utilization, they report significantly more pain visits to doctors in the past month, and have tried significantly more pain interventions. Trauma onset patients as opposed to nontrauma onset patients perceive their health as significantly worse. They are also more dysfunctional, spending significantly more time resting, and perceiving their pain as interfering significantly more with life's activities. There were no differences, however, with regard to the number of household tasks done. Trauma onset patients are significantly more depressed and anxious than nontrauma onset patients.

These results point to the importance of the trauma onset variable in any pain assessment and as a determinant of pain, health behaviors, functional level, and mood state. Traumatic onset patients have greater difficulty in adapting to their chronic pain than nontraumatic onset patients. The sudden change in life as a result of an accident, as well as posttraumatic reactions, appears to adversely affect the ability to cope. Traditional modalities of pain management (such as pharmacologic interventions and nerve blocks) may not address the special needs of accident victims.

CASE REPORT 2

A 15-year-old girl was in her usual state of health until two months prior to her presentation to the multidisciplinary pain clinic for right arm pain. She was with her boyfriend and two other persons when an assailant burst into the apartment and sprayed bullets around, fatally shooting her boyfriend and one other person. The patient received five gunshot wounds (one on the right side of her neck, three in the right upper extremity, and one to her abdomen); she was awake and alert when rushed to the hospital but complained of right-handed numbness and abdominal pain. She suffered numerous thoracic and abdominal injuries that required extensive surgery as well as through and through bullet wounds to her right arm. Throughout the hospitalization she was given opioids for pain. She was discharged on day six of hospitalization.

The patient presented to the Pain Service two months later with a constant dull burning pain of her right arm that she rated as 9 out of 10 where 0 = no pain at all and 10 = the worst imaginable pain. She was very protective of her arm and verbally abused a physician who attempted to touch it. She would wear a warm damp towel around her arm and would continually get up to wet the towel even during the interview. The skin was shiny, the muscles were atrophic, and there was a slight bluish discoloration of her fingers. Her hand was hyperesthetic and she described a feeling of coolness in that arm. She was able to move her hand and arm by herself and appeared to have a normal range of motion. She stated that she could not close her hand. Her past medical history was noncontributory; she denied any history of drug or alcohol abuse. Her symptoms were consistent with a diagnosis of complex regional pain syndrome (CRPS).

The patient presented with a strongly anxious affect, accompanied by a vigorous shaking of both legs such that the chair rattled and her heels made a loud tapping sound. She held her right hand bent upward at the elbow, and also clutched a damp rag in the palm of her left hand. She would moan whenever her hand moved.

She was appropriately oriented to all three spheres but displayed a constricted range of affect—predominantly anxiety and anger. There was a mild loosening of thought associations. Since the traumatic event and as was evident in the sessions she would continually and intrusively recollect the traumatic event in minute detail. She also reported experiencing recurrent dreams of the event as well as sleep disturbance. She focused in an obsessive style on the now idealized six-month intense relationship that she had had with her boyfriend, and on his death rather than her near fatal wounds. She had strong feelings of guilt for having survived and not having saved her boyfriend. She readily acknowledged a strong relationship between stress now and exacerbations in her pain intensity levels. She also had insight into the fact that she did not want her pain to go away, in order not to forget her boyfriend. Her physical pain was a reminder to her of him and her way of holding onto him.

A significant functional limitation was that she would not go outside by herself for fear of being shot. She had withdrawn socially from her friends and had a diminished interest in all activities.

Significant premorbid history included her parents' separation five years earlier and their recent divorce. She denied any history of physical or sexual abuse. Her mother appeared to have a very close relationship with her but had great difficulty in setting limits. The patient herself, a bright adolescent, was a freshman in high school who, due to her relationship, had not been attending classes regularly prior to the shooting. She was diagnosed as having posttraumatic stress disorder.

The pain management intervention was multidisciplinary, based on three therapeutic modalities: nerve blocks and pharmacologic interventions, physical rehabilitation, and cognitive behavioral interventions. The three treatment modalities were intertwined, supportive and facilitative of each other to produce a synergistic effect. The goal was to achieve a physically and psychologically functional adolescent with minimal residual pain.

Over the course of 15 weeks she received 13 stellate ganglion blocks as well as pharmacologic management: she was put on ibuprofen 400 mg qid and 25 mg amitryptiline, which was gradually increased to 50 mg daily. Only after the nerve blocks did she become less protective of her hand and agree to physical therapy. The pain-free arm mobility that she experienced after each nerve block enabled her to tolerate physical therapy. She was seen in psychological treatment over a 20-week period. Her mother was seen conjointly for three of the sessions and treated separately by a social worker. The objectives of psychological treatment were as follows: (1) to have her vent feelings, among which anger and guilt predominated; (2) to increase her age-appropriate behaviors, such as return to school, peer socialization, and shopping, behaviors that served the pain management objective of distraction and adoption of wellness behaviors; (3) to support health promotive behaviors, such as compliance with her medical appointments as well as physical therapy; and (4) to decrease her illness behaviors, such as wearing and watering the towel and the number of hours spent in the house and bed.

Her physical pain improved significantly with the nerve blocks, which enabled aggressive physical therapy as well as facilitated her engagement in cognitive behavioral therapy. The intensity of her feelings lessened, and her PTSD symptoms improved remarkably, characterized by significantly fewer intrusive recollections. She became noticeably calmer and less distressed, and displayed a wider range of affect. She went shopping with her mother and significantly increased her socialization activities with her friends. Follow-up nine months after her treatment had ended revealed a marked improvement in her pain intensity and frequency. She could write with her hand, and, although she still had not returned to school, she was seeing a home tutor. Her PTSD symptoms continued to improve but still were not completely resolved. She increased her peer activities and relationships and would go out of her house by herself.

This individual initially presented as a distraught, difficult-to-manage young adolescent with intense physical and emotional pain, but a patient multidisciplinary approach to her pain proved efficacious. Continued pain improvement and increased arm mobility were greatly facilitated through the process of her venting of emotions, which replaced her communication through pain symptoms. Physical pain had been her method of communicating her emotional pain, her unresolved grief and anger, rather than direct emotional expression. She had great difficulty in letting go of her pain and illness behavior, which meant accepting the finality of her boyfriend's death. Improved range of motion and greater mobility accomplished through physical therapy facilitated the accomplishment of the psychological-behavioral goals of having her dress herself, shop, and socialize.

Conclusions

The simultaneous presentation of physical pain and emotional pain such as PTSD requires a multidisciplinary approach based on the conjoint utilization of interconnected specialties. The patient whose pain started as a result of trauma demonstrates the complex biopsychosocial interplay that is characteristic of chronic pain. Better, more individualized assessment of patients who have pain and PTSD can only lead to more effective treatment of this very difficult-to-treat population. Targeting PTSD symptoms as a primary therapeutic focus may help chronic pain programs improve the treatment outcome for the multitude of issues that these patients have.

References

AAPM Council on Ethics. (2005). Ethics charter from American Academy of Pain Medicine. *Pain Medicine, 6,* 203–212.

Beck A. T., Steer R. A., & Garbin, M. G. (1988). Psychometric properties of the Beck Depression Inventory: Twenty-five years of evaluation. *Clinical Psychology Review, 8,* 77–100.

Beck, A. T, Ward, C. H., Mendelson, M., Mock, J. & Erbaugh, J. (1961) An inventory for measuring depression. *Archives of General Psychiatry, 4,* 461–471.

Benedikt, R. A., & Kolb, L. C. (1986). Preliminary findings on chronic pain and pttraumatic stress disorder. *American Journal of Psychiatry, 143,* 908–910.

Blanchard, E. B., Kolb, L. C., Pallmeyer, T. P., & Gerardi, R. J. (1983). A psychophysiologic study of posttraumatic stress disorder in Vietnam veterans. *Psychiatry Quarterly, 54,* 220–228.

Bradley, L. A. (1996). Cognitive-behavioral therapy for chronic pain. In R. J. Gatchel and D. C. Turk (Eds.), *Psychological approaches to pain management* (pp. 131–147). New York: Guilford Press.

Burgess, J. A., & Dworkin, S. F. (1993), Litigation and post-traumatic TMD: How patients report treatment outcome. *Journal of the American Dental Association, 124,* 105–110.

Gatchel, R. J., & Turk, D. C. (1996). Preface. In R. J. Gatchel & D. C. Turk (Eds.), *Psychological approaches to pain management.* New York: Guilford Press.

Geisser, M. E., Roth, R. S., Bachman, J. E., & Eckert, T. A. (1996). The relationship between symptoms of post-traumatic stress disorder and pain, affective disturbance and disability among patients with accident and non-accident related pain. *Pain, 66,* 207–214.

Greco, C. M., Rudy, T., Turk, D. C., Herlich, A., & Zaki H. H. (1997). Traumatic onset of temporomandibular disorders: Positive effects of a standardized conservative treatment program. *Clinical Journal of Pain, 13,* 337–347.

Harkins, S. J., & Martenay, J. L. (1985). Extrinsic trauma: A significant precipitating factor in temporomandibular dysfunction. *Journal of Prosthetic Dentistry, 54*, 271–272.

Hickling, E. J., & Blanchard, E. B. (1992). Post-traumatic stress disorder and motor vehicle accidents. *Journal of Anxiety Disorders, 6*, 285–291.

Jensen, M. C., Brant-Zawadzki, M. N., Obuchowski, N., Modic, M. T., Malkasian, D., & Ross, J. S. (1994). Magnetic resonance imaging of the lumbar spine in people without back pain. *New England Journal of Medicine, 331*, 69–73.

Kuch, K. (1987). Treatment of posttraumatic stress disorder following automobile accidents. *Behavior Therapy, 10*, 224–225.

Kuch, K., Swinson, R. P., & Kirby, M. (1985). Post-traumatic stress disorder after car accidents. *Canadian Journal of Psychiatry, 30*, 426–427.

Lebovits, A. H. (2004, December 27). More than mind matters: Mental and physical ailments deserve equal health care coverage. *Washington Post*, p. A29.

Lebovits, A. H., Florence, I., Bathina, R., Hunko, V., Fox, M., & Bramble, C. (1997). Pain knowledge and attitudes of health care providers: Practice characteristic differences. *Clinical Journal of Pain, 13*, 237–243.

Lebovits, A. H., Yarmush, J., & Lefkowitz, M. (1990). Reflex sympathetic dystrophy and posttraumatic stress disorder: Multidisciplinary evaluation and treatment. *Clinical Journal of Pain, 6*, 153–157.

Melzack, R. & Wall, P. (1965). Pain mechanisms: A new theory. *Science, 150*, 171–179.

Muse, M. (1985). Stress-related posttraumatic chronic pain syndrome: Criteria for diagnosis, and preliminary report on prevalence. *Pain, 23*, 295–300.

Muse, M., and Frigola, G. (1986). Development of a quick screening instrument for detecting posttraumatic stress disorder in the chronic pain patient: Construction of the Posttraumatic Chronic Pain Test (PCPT). *Clinical Journal of Pain, 2*, 151–153.

NIH Technology Assessment Panel on Integration of Behavioral and Relaxation Approaches into the Treatment of Chronic Pain and Insomnia. (1996). Integration of behavioral and relaxation approaches into the treatment of chronic pain and insomnia. *Journal of the American Medical Association, 276*, 313–318.

Norris, F. (1992). Epidemiology of trauma: Frequency and impact of different potentially traumatic events on different demographic groups. *Journal of Consulting and Clinical Psychology, 60*, 409–418.

Romanelli, G. G., Mock, D., & Tenenbaum, H. C. (1992). Characteristics and response to treatment of posttraumatic temporomandibular disorder: a retrospective study. *Clinical Journal of Pain, 8*, 6–17.

Romano, J. M., & Turner, J. A. (1985). Chronic pain and depression: Does the evidence support a relationship? *Psychology Bulletin, 97*, 18–34.

Schofferman, J., Anderson, D., Hines, R., Smith, G., & White, A. (1992). Childhood psychological trauma correlates with unsuccessful lumbar spines surgery. *Spine, 17*, S138–S144.

Spiegel, D., & Bloom, J. (1983). Group therapy and hypnosis reduce metastatic breast carcinoma pain. *Psychosomatic Medicine, 45*, 333–339.

Spielberger, C. D. (1983). *Manual for the State-Trait Anxiety Inventory*. Palo Alto, CA: Consulting Psychologists Press.

Turk, D. C. (1996). Biopsychosocial perspective on chronic pain. In R. J. Gatchel & D. C. Turk (Eds.), *Psychological approaches to pain management* (pp. 3–32). New York: Guilford Press.

Turk, D. C., & Okifuji, A. (1996). Perception of traumatic onset, compensation status, and physical findings: Impact on pain severity, emotional distress, and disability in chronic pain patients. *Journal of Behavioral Medicine, 19*, 435–453.

Waylonis, G. W., & Perkins, R. H. (1994). Post-traumatic fibromyalgia. A long term follow-up. *American Journal of Physical Medicine and Rehabilitation, 73*, 403–412.

CHAPTER 4

ANESTHESIA AWARENESS AND TRAUMA

Donald M. Mathews and Michael Wang

Patients who undergo general anesthesia expect to be placed in a state of oblivion and have no memory of the surgical experience. Anesthesia providers also intend to render their patients unconscious and maintain such conditions throughout the surgical procedure. Current information from the United States (Sebel et al., 2004) and Europe (Sandin, Enlund, Samuelsson, & Lennmarken, 2000) reveals, however, that at some point following routine surgery and anesthesia care, one to two patients per thousand are able to recall events of their operation. In the United States this is estimated to result in 100 cases per workday. The incidence during procedures recognized to be at "high risk" may be 10 times greater. There is a spectrum of psychological outcomes following postoperative recall of intraoperative consciousness (or more colloquially, "anesthesia awareness"), which ranges from relatively minor outcomes to a severe and persistent posttraumatic stress disorder (PTSD). This chapter will discuss the current state of understanding of this phenomenon, present case studies, and discuss treatment and prevention strategies.

General Anesthesia

General anesthesia (GA) is a state of unresponsiveness to the stimulation of surgery. In a well-delivered general anesthetic the patient is unconscious, his or her autonomic nervous system is either not responding or responding only minimally to surgical stimulation, and the patient is quiescent, or not moving, during stimulation. Unconsciousness is usually induced and maintained through the use of hypnotic drugs. Examples of hypnotic drugs include volatile inhalation agents such as isoflurane, desflurane and sevoflurane, benzodiazepines, barbiturates, and propofol. It is possible to create a state of GA by utilizing only a hypnotic drug, but this requires very large doses of the mono-agent and can result in very prolonged wake up times from anesthesia and undesirable side effects; all these agents, for example, cause depression of heart function. More typically the anesthesiologist creates a state of GA by administering several agents, each intended to achieve individual goals: hypnotic drugs to create a state of unconsciousness, opioids and/or nitrous oxide to limit transmission of noxious stimulation to the brain, and paralyzing or "muscle-relaxing" agents to prevent patient movement. The anesthesiologist must understand and manage a complicated three-way interaction: a patient and his or her comorbidities, the physiologic stress of surgical trauma, and the pharmacologic action and interaction of the selected anesthetic agents.

Given the complexity of the human nervous system and of the task of administering anesthesia, an incidence of anesthesia awareness (AA) of one to two patients per thousand is, perhaps, understandable. This philosophy, however, fails to recognize the potentially devastating and life-altering effect this experience can have on patients. In addition, this philosophy is at odds with the profession of anesthesiology's traditional concern for patient safety: decades-long efforts to improve patient outcomes have been highly successful. As the chance of actually surviving a surgical procedure has been maximized, attention has now turned to the prevention of other undesirable outcomes, such as AA. The American Society of Anesthesiologists (ASA; American Society of Anesthesiologists Task Force on Intraoperative Awareness, 2006), and other professional anesthesiology societies have recently issued statements or guidelines for the prevention and treatment of AA. Essential to prevention and treatment, however, is some understanding of how AA can occur.

Causes of Anesthesia Awareness

Anesthesia awareness occurs when there is inadequate delivery of an unconsciousness-causing agent during the course of surgery. Several reasons for inadequate delivery can be considered: patient comorbidities, unrecognized increased patient requirement, and human or equipment error. Most puzzling, however, is that some episodes of AA fall into none of these categories and the etiology must be considered unexplained.

There are clinical situations where an anesthesiologist chooses to provide what may be an inadequate amount of unconsciousness-producing agent. These situations are considered to be at high risk for AA, with an incidence as great as 1–2 percent. As mentioned above, these agents cause depression of heart function and the anesthesiologist sometimes must balance the risk of administering more agent, and potentially causing a poor cardiovascular outcome, with the risk of delivering less agent and potentially causing AA. The exsanguinating trauma patient is a good example, as is the patient with limited cardiac "pump" function undergoing open-heart or other major surgery. Women undergoing Cesarean sections with GA are often given limited amounts of these agents due to concern for transmission to, and subsequent depression of, the newborn.

AA also occurs when a patient has an unexpectedly increased requirement for anesthetic agents. This usually occurs with patients who are consuming either prescribed or illicit substances such as opioids or marijuana, or who regularly consume alcohol. If these habits are detected during the preoperative interview, the anesthesiologist may be able to adjust the delivered anesthetic appropriately. If not, the patient may experience AA before the anesthesiologist adjusts the amount of delivered agent.

As anesthesiologists are human beings and work in an environment with systems and machines, there is also the possibility of human or equipment error. For example, the vaporizer that delivers the inhalation agent to the breathing circuit may run dry or the intravenous line may become disconnected. Despite monitors and alarms, preoperative equipment checklists, and a culture of vigilance, events such as these occur.

There are patients who experience AA and who fit none of these categories. In these patients, traditional monitoring and assessment during surgery somehow "fails." Analysis of a retrospective database maintained by the American Society of Anesthesiologists revealed 61 cases of AA (Domino, Posner, Caplan, & Cheney, 1999). In 16 percent of cases, no associated causative factor could be discerned. In a prospective study of 11,785 Scandinavian patients, no causative factor could be elucidated in 10 of 18 patients who experienced AA (Sandin et al., 2000). In an Australian dataset, patients appeared to receive adequate doses of anesthetic drugs in 13 of the 81 incidents of AA (Bergman, Kluger, & Short, 2002).

In trying to understand how these patients could experience AA, it is necessary to consider how unconsciousness is traditionally assessed and the effect of muscle relaxant drugs on such assessment. Anesthesiologists learn to detect or suspect lack of unconsciousness through increases in heart rate or blood pressure, somatic signs such as sweating or lacrimation, and patient movement. While highly useful, monitoring the heart rate and blood pressure has an imperfect predicative value in detecting consciousness (Russell & Wang, 2001). Somatic signs, when present, suggest an inadequate anesthetic state, but not necessarily consciousness, and their absence does not guarantee lack of consciousness. Most patient movement is probably due to spinal reflexes and does not necessarily reflect consciousness. However, information from patient anecdotes shows that, when conscious, patients attempt to signal to their caregiver through movement. When completely paralyzed, they are unable so to communicate. Indeed, a repeated, and tragic episode reported from patient experience is the attempt to signal consciousness by moving, only to be given additional muscle relaxants.

The use of muscle relaxants increases the incidence of AA: in the ASA database, the relative risk of AA is increased 2.28-fold with muscle relaxants (Domino, Posner, Caplan, & Cheney, 1999). However, AA can occur without muscle relaxants. In the study by Sandin et al. (2000), the overall incidence of awareness was 0.15 percent, 0.18 percent when muscle relaxants were utilized and 0.10% when they were not. In another study, three patients did not move a nonparalyzed arm at the time of skin incision despite later recall of the skin incision, because they were comfortable, not in pain and not distressed (Russell & Wang, 1997). Why nonparalyzed patients do not move when conscious is not always clear, but may reflect the complexity of the nervous system-anesthetic-surgery interaction (Kerssens, Klein, & Bonke, 2003).

Experience of Anesthesia Awareness

Firsthand accounts of awareness are available in the anesthesia literature ("On Being Aware," 1979; Cobcroft & Forsdick, 1993) or from Internet sites such as anesthesiaawareness.com. Scientific information about patient experience with AA comes from both retrospective (Schwender et al., 1998; Moerman, Bonke, & Oosting, 1993) and prospective studies (Sebel et al., 2004). Retrospective studies suffer from reporting bias: those who volunteer to come forward and be interviewed may be different from other patients who experience awareness, particularly in terms of psychological outcome. Prospective studies are extremely labor intensive and difficult to perform. In addition, as AA is relatively rare, large numbers of patients must be studied to obtain useful data.

These studies reveal that most episodes of AA consist of an auditory experience; patients remember sounds from the operating room environment. They often remember a derogatory or inflammatory remark. They report anxiety with 36–92 percent of the episodes, and a feeling of helplessness in 46–62 percent. Pain is reported less often, in 18–39 percent of the episodes. It is difficult to determine how long the intraoperative consciousness lasted in some patients. Some episodes were relatively brief; others lasted for a prolonged period of time. The longer episodes were probably associated with muscle relaxant use.

Another important point that has emerged from this work is that it is insufficient to screen for AA only on the day of surgery. For some reason, the process of memory formation and recall of intraoperative events is often not immediate. In the study by Sandin et al. (2000), patients underwent structured interviews three times: in the postanesthesia care unit, postoperative day 1–3, and again postoperative day 7–14. Of the 18 patients with awareness, only 6 had recall on the day of the procedure. By the second interview, 12 patients recalled events from the operating room; it required three interviews to account for all of the awareness patients. Phobic avoidance and denial played a part in these findings: two patients admitted at the second interview to dissimulation during the first to avoid discussion of traumatic material. It is likely that many episodes of awareness go undetected because awareness patients avoid reporting their experiences for the same reasons. The anesthesiologist responsible for the episode is the last person in whom the patient may wish to confide!

In the past, some patients have hesitated to report awareness out of fear of not being believed. Their fears were not unfounded: in a retrospective series (Schwender et al., 1998), 10 of 45 awareness patients recounted that their report of awareness was met by caregivers with disbelief. Anecdotal reports suggest that caregivers sometimes downplay these episodes by explaining them as being dreams. As knowledge about the phenomenon of awareness has spread in recent years in both the anesthesia and surgical communities, initial patient reports of awareness will, hopefully, be met with a more supportive response. Indeed, the ASA's "Practice Advisory for Intraoperative Awareness and Brain Function Monitoring" (American Society of Anesthesiologists Task Force on Intraoperative Awareness, 2006) states that anesthesiologists should "speak with patients who report recall of intra-operative events to obtain details of the event and discuss possible reasons for its occurrence." The advisory also recommends that counseling or psychological sup-port be offered.

Psychological Effects of Awareness

There appears to be a spectrum of psychological aftereffects following AA. The consequences of awareness for patients are varied and are probably related to the duration of awareness, the experience of pain during awareness, and the degree of anxiety experienced while aware. Some patients do not seem overtly affected. Others, however, clearly are: retrospective studies report aftereffects such as anxiety during the day, nightmares, and sleep disturbances in 51–69 per-cent of patients. It is not clear what percentage of these patients received psycho-logical treatment or the time course of their symptomatology.

What is clear, however, is that a subset of patients develops a persistent, life-altering posttraumatic stress disorder (PTSD) and should be immediately referred for psychological counseling (Macleod & Maycock, 1992). To try to quantify the incidence of PTSD following AA, an attempt was made to perform follow-up inter-views with the 18 patients who experienced awareness in the Scandinavian dataset (Lennmarken, Bildfors, Enlund, Samuelsson, & Sandin, 2002). Of 18 patients, 2 were lost to follow-up and 6 refused to be interviewed. Of the remaining 9, 3 reported persistent but mild psychological sequelae, and 4 reported ongoing PTSD requiring psychological therapy. The authors were concerned that the patients who refused to be interviewed might also suffer from PTSD because attempted avoidance of the trauma is a symptom of the syndrome. The incidence of PTSD in this group of 11,785 patients, then, was at least 0.034 percent and perhaps as high as 0.08 percent. In another study, the Clinician Administered PTSD Scale was administered to 16 patients who reported AA and it was found that 9 of 16 patients, at a mean time of 17.9 years after the surgery, met PTSD criteria (Osterman, Hopper, Heran, Keane, & van der Kolk, 2001). They found that these patients had significant postoperative distress related to "feeling unable to communicate, unsafe, terrified, abandoned and betrayed."

Anecdotal patient reports suggest that the incidence of PTSD is correlated with the duration of intraoperative consciousness. Patients with prolonged awareness were most likely completely paralyzed with muscle relaxants, hence the repeated reports equating the sensation to being entombed, resulting in feelings of extreme terror and complete helplessness. Some awareness PTSD patients are unable to sleep in a supine position and must sleep sitting in a chair. This may be a result of experiencing intraoperative consciousness in the supine position.

Early referral for psychological support may ameliorate some of the current patient suffering, and treatment strategies are discussed below. Ideally the patient will be referred to a caregiver with both expertise in the treatment of PTSD and also an understanding of AA. The anesthesiologist may need to educate the psychologist about the issues at hand. With an incidence of AA in the United States of about 100 patients per workday, there is clearly a large group of patients who may require psychological care.

PATIENT CASE STUDIES

Patient 1

Eight years ago, at the age of 46, the patient underwent a procedure to remove an eye, the result of a chronic and painful corneal condition. At some point following the induction of general anesthesia, she returned to consciousness. She estimates that her duration of consciousness lasted 40 minutes. The first thing she remembers was hearing disco music, then her surgeon saying, "Cut deeper here. No, deeper." She experienced extreme panic when she realized that she was conscious during the surgery. She attempted to move her head to signal her consciousness, but was unable to do so.

After repeated attempts at moving, she heard the surgeon say, "She's moving." No one attempted to reassure her or communicate with her. Instead of being reanesthetized, she felt a burning sensation across her back, which was probably an additional dose of muscle relaxant being administered. As the surgery continued, she wished that she would die instead of continuing her conscious state. She continued to attempt to move and the surgeon said, "She's moving again." The anesthesiologist commented that something was wrong with his equipment, which was the apparent cause of her consciousness. Her awareness persisted for several more minutes as the surgeons tugged on her eye. She remembers the moment her optic nerve was severed.

She emerged from the anesthetic thrashing about and came out of the operating room (OR) screaming that she had been awake while her eye was removed. In the recovery room, no one would address the fact that she had been conscious during surgery. That evening she recounted her experience to her pastor, who did believe her. When the surgeon came to see her the next morning, she informed him of her experience and quoted operating room dialogue verbatim. No psychological counseling was offered.

The anesthesiologist did not visit her until the third postoperative day. He patted her hand and told her that everything she said had happened was true, but that she had also had local anesthesia, that she could not have felt pain, and therefore no harm could possibly have been done. He then left. No psychological counseling was offered.

Postoperatively, she developed PTSD; however, without proper referral, she did not begin receiving counseling until eight months following her operation. Her treatment involved "talk therapy" and she was prescribed fluoxetine and clonazepam. Her PTSD symptoms persist to this day: she is easily startled, has flashbacks, triggers, temper flare-ups, mood swings, and fatigue, and does not do well in situations over which she has no control. She has not slept for more than an hour and 15 minutes at a time, nor has she lain on her back since her operation.

Patient 2

The patient elected to have a general anesthetic for a Cesarean section. At some point following the induction of anesthesia, she awoke and felt a burning, searing pain, as if "someone were pushing something burning through me." She felt that she was "being hurled into mayhem." She thought that it was more than she could bear and that her "brain was exploding." She began to imagine herself as a speck in the room and that no one knew she was there. She tried to scream, but realized her scream was only in her mind. She tried to move multiple times, but was unable to do so. She realized that she could not communicate with her caregivers and thought she would never see her baby. She thought that she was dying and that at least then, the pain would end.

The experience "robbed her of the happiness of becoming a new mother."

She found herself dreaming about the experience over and over, the events being replayed again and again.

Several years later she needed to undergo further surgery, an appendectomy, with a different anesthesia provider. This provider tried to reassure her that she would be closely monitored and that the provider would watch over her. Although apprehensive, she agreed to be anesthetized and experienced no intraoperative consciousness.

Shortly thereafter she required a third procedure and the anesthesiologist was the same as for her Cesarean section. Again apprehensive, she thought that since the second procedure had gone without awareness, this would go well also. Again, however, she found herself conscious during the operation and was "more terrified than I have ever been before." She again felt burning pain and "could not believe that it was happening again." She had experienced anesthesia awareness twice in four years.

This patient was provided with little in the way of professional psychological intervention during the first two years following these events. Subsequently some general counseling support and cognitive behavioral therapy has been provided, but rather late in the day. She continues to experience flashback phenomena, behavioral avoidance, and depression more than 10 years later. Her marriage has also been a casualty of the awareness episodes.

Patient 3

The patient underwent a general anesthetic to drain an abscess in her jaw. She realized that she was awake and that the surgical team did not know this. She struggled to move, but was unable to do so. She experienced intense pain. She felt completely helpless and knew "her life was in someone else's hands." She remembers the sensation of the scalpel and then no more: she thinks that she actually "passed out" rather than was reanesthetized.

She experiences nightmares and dreams about lying awake on the operating room table and about "dying any minute." She has panic attacks and flashbacks, particularly from bright lights similar to those in the operating room. She has felt suicidal and realizes that her personality has changed. Before the surgery she was outgoing and vivacious, but now she is withdrawn and avoids contact with people she does not know.

Treatment began with addressing the depressive component, which was the most marked feature of her initial presentation, with both cognitive behavior therapy and selective serotonin reuptake inhibitor (SSRI) antidepressant medication. The flashbacks, which were severe, were managed using a combination of distraction techniques when they occurred and cognitive exposure to the flashback content in the clinic. This included cue exposure: stimuli that provoked flashbacks were identified and a program of graded exposure to these was implemented. The patient was taught cognitive and breathing techniques for managing the panic attacks. After six months there was a marked improvement in her condition, but she continued to experience the occasional flashback or nightmare (perhaps once every two weeks).

Treatment of Anesthesia Awareness

Management in the Immediate Postoperative Period

A suspected episode of anesthetic awareness may come to light in a number of ways: the anesthesiologist may be aware of some equipment fault or clinical error intraoperatively and realize that this may have given rise to unintended consciousness; the patient may have been unusually agitated as she/he emerged from the anesthetic; or the anesthesiologist may have heard from nursing or other staff that following or during postoperative recovery, the patient has made comments indicative of intraoperative memory or distress. It is crucial under any of these circumstances for the anesthesiologist responsible for the general anesthetic to go and speak to the patient as soon as possible, accompanied by a witness, such as a nurse.

The anesthesiologist should listen carefully, intently, and empathically to the patient's account of the experience. It is imperative that the anesthesiologist should take the account seriously and not attempt to invalidate or undermine the patient's version of events. The anesthesiologist should offer an apology where it is clear that the patient has experienced a distressing event, irrespective of the cause. Usually the patient is desperately trying to understand what has transpired, and is looking to the anesthesiologist to provide an explanation. It is understandable that anesthesiologists, finding themselves in this situation, would be concerned about the legal implications and potential for litigation: however, an apology does not constitute an admission of guilt or liability (Aitkenhead, 1990). In many cases, patients will not proceed to litigation if they receive a genuine apology from the responsible clinician along with a credible explanation as to how the episode of awareness arose.

After hearing the patient's account of the experience, in most cases, the anesthesiologist will need to be make further inquiries in order to better understand what led up to the incident, and will need to be circumscribed in her/his attempt to provide an explanation in the first instance. However, a fuller account of how the incident arose should be forthcoming within a matter of days. When listening to the patient's account, the anesthesiologist should be attentive and empathic, in other words, should show clear nonverbal and verbal indications that he/she really does understand the emotional and psychological implications of what the patient is describing.

As mentioned previously, many patients in the past have been told that their accounts of anesthetic awareness cannot possibly be true or that they have experienced a rather vivid intraoperative dream. Commonly this has led to disbelief among spouses, relatives, and friends and invariably has led to profound exacerbation of the posttraumatic stress disorder (Wang, 2001). Entirely fabricated claims of anesthetic awareness are extremely rare, and clinically the recommended policy is always to assume that the patient has genuinely had a traumatic experience (Aitkenhead, 1990). On occasion, a patient may have misattributed an awareness event that took place in the time period immediately before or after the surgery rather than during the operation, and this can be clarified through gentle and diplomatic questioning combined with verification of events with other OR staff. Providing patients with the time and attention needed for them to give a full and detailed account of their experience to the responsible anesthesiologist is likely to provide a good deal of therapeutic mitigation of the trauma they suffered, although it will rarely give rise to complete remission.

Nursing staff in the recovery area should monitor the patient during the early postoperative period and pay particular attention to the occurrence of flashbacks, nightmares, panic attacks, generalized anxiety, and depression. An early appointment with a clinical psychologist or psychiatrist experienced in the management of posttraumatic stress disorders should be arranged. Whether or not the patient manifests any of the above-mentioned phenomena during the immediate postoperative period in the hospital, the anesthesiologist should arrange a follow-up meeting with the patient within a period of two weeks of discharge (Wang, 2001).

The Role of Muscle Relaxants and Paralysis in the Genesis of Psychological Trauma

In a careful and rigorous, prospective awareness study (Sandin et al., 2000), it was found that of the sample of 11,785 patients (including both paralyzed and nonparalyzed anesthetic techniques), 11 paralyzed patients and 4 nonparalyzed patients had significant memory of intraoperative events. However, of the four nonparalyzed patients with awareness, none had found the intraoperative experience traumatic or distressing, nor did they have immediate or delayed PTSD reactions. In contrast, 11 of the 14 paralyzed patients reported intraoperative trauma and anxiety, but only 6 of the 11 experienced intraoperative pain. Persistent postoperative psychological symptoms were associated with patients who, during the operation, did not understand why they were wakeful and why they were paralyzed.

In the follow-up study two years later (Lennmarken et al., 2002), 9 out of the 18 awareness patients were interviewed. Of the 9 interviewed (7 paralyzed, 2 nonparalyzed), 4 were found to have severe psychiatric symptoms (PTSD). All 4 had received muscle relaxants during their operation, and not one had experienced intraoperative pain.

In summary, although awareness in the absence of muscle relaxants does occur (but at a lower rate than for the paralyzed patients), it rarely gives rise to serious psychological consequences. For those who do have long-term psychological sequelae, not understanding what was happening during the wakeful intraoperative experience seems to be a key component of the etiology (but not necessarily intraoperative pain).

In the second author's (MW's) clinical practice, it is commonly a catastrophic misunderstanding or misinterpretation of the cause of the paralysis that gives rise to severe intraoperative psychological traumatization. So, for example, the patient may fear that the surgeon has accidentally cut the spinal cord, or that some unusual drug interaction has occurred, rendering the patient paralyzed for the rest of her life. It is frequently the intraoperative misconception that the state of paralysis is irreversible that causes acute psychological trauma. This clinical impression appears to be supported by the Sandin and Lennmarken data, in that those patients who had unresolved PTSD were those who were described as having being "confused" and distressed by their predicament intraoperatively.

What lessons can be leaned from these data and clinical anecdotes? First, there is a strong argument for better preoperative information being provided, including the nature and actions of muscle relaxants. This is controversial, since many anesthesiologists do not wish to frighten their patients with anxiety-provoking information in relation to a risk that they consider infinitesimal. However an incidence of one in five hundred is not infinitesimal. Moreover, if such information might reliably reduce the incidence of intraoperative traumatization and postoperative PTSD for those who do experience awareness, then the small risk of increasing the preoperative anxiety of some patients may be justified, given the devastating and often chronic effects of postawareness PTSD (Wang, 2001).

Second, it is crucial that, in obtaining an account of the patient's awareness experience during the early postoperative period, the patient's understanding of the nature of his or her experience is verified. Nothing should be assumed, and assumptions of the patient's point of view based on the anesthesiologist's sophisticated knowledge of muscle relaxants and anesthesiology should be avoided. If and when detected, misunderstandings should be carefully and empathically addressed, without undermining the validity of the patient's account of the experience.

Early Psychological Intervention

In recent years, there has been much made of the importance of psychological debriefing during the first 48 hours following a traumatic experience (Dyregrov, 1997); however, there is now much empirical evidence that such intervention at best has no effect and in some patients may actually worsen the posttraumatic stress disorder, effectively retraumatizing the patient (Rose, Bisson, Churchill, & Wessely, 2002). It is imperative however, that awareness patients are followed up and monitored closely, preferably by mental health professionals with experience of posttraumatic stress disorder. There is a natural process by which an individual comes to terms with a traumatic incident, and it is important that the patient is given the time, space, and expectation to allow this process to take its course. Patients should be provided opportunities for psychological and counseling support during the first three months postoperatively, but they should not be compelled to retell their traumatic experience. The natural and common cycle of emotional and psychological avoidance of thoughts and recollections of the experience alternating with sudden, distressing, uncontrollable intrusive memories and images should be explained, and presented to the patient as a normal adaptive process. The patient should be given to expect that this cycle will occur frequently during the early days and weeks, but in most cases of general PTSD, noticeable improvement in frequency, intensity, and duration will have taken place by the end of the third month.

Psychological Intervention in the Medium Term

Nevertheless, because of the severity of trauma often associated with anesthetic awareness, many patients will continue to experience severe, disabling, and intrusive flashback phenomena and manifest pathological phobic avoidance of a variety of situations and cues associated with operations, hospitals, and medical staff. If these phenomena remain severe and show no sign of remission after three months, a period of intensive cognitive behavioral treatment is indicated (Harvey, Bryant, & Tarrier, 2003). Ideally, this should be provided by an experienced clinical psychologist with qualifications and expertise in cognitive behavior therapy for posttraumatic stress disorders. A detailed and comprehensive assessment of the patient and her/his difficulties should be undertaken by the psychologist, giving rise to an individualized clinical formulation. This formulation will then drive intervention and will take account of not only cognitive behavioral components but also the emotional, social, occupational, and community context of the patient's difficulties. The psychologist should attempt to mobilize support from family and friends in the implementation of the intervention, in order to encourage maintenance and generalization of improvement. The nature of any flashback phenomena and associated cognitive avoidance will need to be carefully assessed with particular attention to *silent assumptions* and implied but unspoken consequences and fears. Erroneous conceptions should be tested. Specific cognitive behavioral interventions will include behavioral cue exposure and habituation to the most distressing thoughts and images that constitute the disabling intrusions. Phobic avoidance phenomena should be addressed using a carefully planned and implemented program of graded exposure, which might include visits to the hospital and the operating room in which the incident took place (Harvey et al., 2003). Patients who experience depression in the postoperative period should be treated with the standard cognitive behavioral therapy (CBT) for depression protocol alongside SSRI antidepressant medication (Beck, 1976).

It is important to create appropriate expectations with regard to rate of improvement and the likelihood of residual difficulties in the longer term. Even among patients who have been carefully and competently managed, and who have responded to psychological intervention for PTSD, most, because of the severity of the trauma, will have ongoing PTSD difficulties for many years following the awareness event. In the main, these will be perhaps the occasional nightmare or flashback, perhaps once a month or less. Following successful treatment, these will no longer be functionally disabling, but they will continue to cause short-lived distress. It will also take many years for the patient to reestablish trust in medical staff and to feel comfortable in hospital environments.

Further Surgery

The need for further surgery is a common and understandably difficult scenario in which previously resolved PTSD phenomenology reemerges. Many awareness patients attempt to delay or avoid the surgery altogether. This needs to be managed with care and skill. The anesthesiologist needs to provide special reassurance that the awareness episode will not be repeated, perhaps by ensuring the use of additional monitoring equipment or procedures such as the isolated forearm technique or a brain function monitor (described below). A shared understanding of how and why the awareness occurred in the first place, and what will be different this time, becomes even more important. The patient may need additional psychological support and intervention during the period prior to the operation and on the day of admission. The anesthesiologist should set aside time to meet with the patient and his or her supporter (partner, relative, or friend) during the two weeks before the scheduled operation date, to provide reassurance, explanations, and opportunities for questions.

Prevention of Anesthesia Awareness

Preventing or limiting the incidence of AA is a multifaceted issue. As mentioned above, international professional anesthesiology societies have issued advisories and guidelines and, in the United States, the Joint Commission for

Hospital Accreditation (JCAHO) has issued a sentinel event alert about the topic (Joint Commission for Hospital Accreditation, 2004). These documents address preoperative, intraoperative, and postoperative strategies to limit the incidence or severity of AA.

Preoperatively, attention should be paid to appropriate equipment checklists and the identification of patient risk factors that may heighten the chance of AA. Patients who are identified as being at high risk should be so informed. Preoperative administration of a benzodiazepine or scopolamine may limit memory formation should intraoperative consciousness occur.

Intraoperatively, monitoring alarms should be enabled and persistent vigilance maintained. Should consciousness be detected or suspected, some feel that administration of benzodiazepine may offer retrograde amnesia; however, there is no good evidence that this is likely to be effective. Muscle relaxants should be used judiciously, and patient movement should be never treated with muscle relaxants alone; anesthetic agents should be increased.

It is currently controversial as to whether traditional operating room monitors and techniques are adequate or whether a new generation of electroenchalographic (EEG) monitors should be employed. Although several different algorithms are utilized, these "brain function" monitors display a metric to the anesthesiologists that reflects the ongoing activity of the patient's cerebral cortex. By increasing the delivery of the unconsciousness-producing agent when the metric rises over a specific amount, the anesthesiologist may be able to decrease the incidence of AA. In a prospective study of patients undergoing procedures who are known to be at high risk for AA, an 82 percent reduction in AA in patients monitored with the Bispectral index (BIS) monitor (Aspect Medical Systems, Newton, MA), compared to those cared for with only traditional monitoring, was demonstrated (Myles, Leslie, McNeil, Forbes, & Chan, 2004). Ekman, Lindholm, Lennmarken, and Sandin (2004) compared the incidence of AA in patients at average risk for awareness who were cared for with BIS monitors to the incidence in historical controls. They found a similar reduction in incidence. There is currently no clear consensus among anesthesiologists about the merits of these monitors: some use EEG-based monitoring on all patients, some on those given muscle relaxants, some only on those considered high risk, and some on no patients. Further prospective studies about brain function monitoring and AA could be very useful in fully defining these monitors' utility. Wang and Russell have argued that the isolated forearm technique (in which a tourniquet is applied to an arm prior to the administration of muscle relaxant, allowing a sufficiently conscious patient to signal to the anesthesiologist) should be used more routinely (Russell & Wang, 1995), and an authoritative review described the technique as the "gold standard" in awareness detection (Jessop & Jones, 1991). However, it remains controversial as a routine anesthesiology monitoring procedure.

Anesthesia awareness is a rare but predictable event. Despite major advances in understanding the phenomenon, it continues to occur. It is unlikely that the incidence will ever be zero, but with improved understanding and monitoring, hopefully, the incidence will decrease. As the current incidence in the routine surgery is one to two per thousand patients, and 10 times greater in the high-risk patient, every location that administers general anesthesia can be expected to have patients with this experience. It makes sense to be prepared, including having appropriate psychological counseling services prepared and caregivers with an understanding of the phenomena of AA interest and expertise in the prevention and treatment of PTSD pre-identified and perhaps even on call to attempt to lessen subsequent patient suffering.

References

Aitkenhead, A. R. (1990). Editorial: Awareness during anaesthesia—What should the patient be told? *Anaesthesia, 45*, 351–352.

American Society of Anesthesiologists Task Force on Intraoperative Awareness. (2006). Practice advisory for intraoperative awareness and brain function monitoring: A report by the American Society of Anesthesiologists Task Force on Intraoperative Awareness. *Anesthesiology, 104*, 847–864.

Beck, A. T. (1976). *Cognitive therapy and the emotional disorders.* New York: Meridian.

Bergman, I. J., Kluger, M. T., & Short, T. G. (2002). Awareness during general anaesthesia: A review of 81 cases from the Anaesthetic Incident Monitoring Study. *Anaesthesia, 57*, 549–556.

Cobcroft, M. D., & Forsdick, C. (1993). Awareness under anaesthesia: The patients' point of view. *Anaesthesia and Intensive Care, 21*, 837–843.

Domino, K. B., Posner, K. L., Caplan, R. A., & Cheney, F. W. (1999). Awareness during anesthesia: A closed claims analysis. *Anesthesiology, 90*, 1053–1061.

Dyregrov, A. (1997). The process in psychological debriefings. *Journal of Traumatic Stress, 10*, 589–605.

Ekman, A., Lindholm, M. L., Lennmarken, C., & Sandin, R. (2004). Reduction in the incidence of awareness using BIS monitoring. *Acta Anaesthesiologica Scandinavica, 48*, 20–26.

Harvey, A. G., Bryant, A. B., & Tarrier, N. (2003). Cognitive behaviour therapy for posttraumatic stress disorder. *Clinical Psychology Review, 23*, 501–522.

Jessop, J., & Jones, J. G. (1991). Conscious awareness during general anaesthesia—What are we attempting to monitor? *British Journal of Anaesthesia, 66*, 635–637.

Joint Commission for Hospital Accreditation. (2004). *Sentinel Alert No. 32: Anesthesia Awareness.* Retrieved November 25, 2006, from www.jointcommission.org/SentinelEvents/SentinelEventAlert/sea_32.htm

Kerssens, C., Klein, J., & Bonke, B. (2003). Awareness: Monitoring versus remembering what happened. *Anesthesiology, 99*, 570–575.

Lennmarken, C., Bildfors, K., Enlund, G., Samuelsson, P., & Sandin, R. (2002). Victims of awareness. *Acta Anaesthesiologica Scandinavica, 46*, 229–231.

Macleod, A. D., Maycock, E. (1992). Awareness during anaesthesia and post traumatic stress disorder. *Anaesthesia and Intensive Care, 20*, 378–382.

Moerman, N., Bonke, B., & Oosting, J. (1993). Awareness and recall during general anesthesia. Facts and feelings. *Anesthesiology, 79*, 454–464.

Myles, P. S., Leslie, K., McNeil, J., Forbes, A., & Chan, M. T. (2004). Bispectral index monitoring to prevent awareness during anaesthesia: The B-Aware randomised controlled trial. *Lancet, 363,* 1757–1763.

On being aware. (1979). *British Journal of Anaesthesia, 51,* 711–712.

Osterman, J. E., Hopper, J., Heran, W. J., Keane, T. M., & van der Kolk, B. A. (2001). Awareness under anesthesia and the development of posttraumatic stress disorder. *General Hospital Psychiatry, 23,* 198–204.

Rose, S., Bisson, J., Churchill, R., & Wessely, S. (2002). Psychological debriefing for preventing post traumatic stress disorder (PTSD) (Cochrane Review). *The Cochrane Database of Systematic Reviews,* issue 2, Art. no. CD000560. Retrieved December 12, 2006, from www.mrw.interscience.wiley.com/cochrane/clsysrev/articles/CD000560

Russell, I. F., & Wang, M. (1995). Isolated forearm technique. *British Journal of Anaesthesia, 75,* 819–821.

Russell, I. F., & Wang, M. (1997). Absence of memory for intraoperative information during surgery under adequate general anaesthesia. *British Journal of Anaesthesia, 78,* 3–9.

Russell, I. F., & Wang, M. (2001). Absence of memory for intra-operative information during surgery with total intravenous anaesthesia. *British Journal of Anaesthesia, 86,* 196–202.

Sandin, R. H., Enlund, G., Samuelsson, P., & Lennmarken, C. (2000). Awareness during anaesthesia: A prospective case study. *Lancet, 355,* 707–711.

Schwender, D., Kunze-Kronawitter, H., Dietrich, P., Klasing, S., Forst, H., & Madler, C. (1998). Conscious awareness during general anaesthesia: Patients' perceptions, emotions, cognition and reactions. *British Journal of Anaesthesia, 80,* 133–139.

Sebel, P. S., Bowdle, T. A., Ghoneim, M. M., Rampil, I. J., Padilla, R. E., Gan, T. J., et al. (2004). The incidence of awareness during anesthesia: A multicenter United States study. *Anesthesia and Analgesia, 99,* 833–839.

Wang, M. (2001). The psychological consequences of explicit and implicit memories of events during surgery. In M. Ghoneim (Ed.), *Awareness during anesthesia.* Woburn, MA: Butterworth-Heinemann.

CHAPTER 5

AIDS AND TRAUMA IN THE TWENTY-FIRST CENTURY: IMPLICATIONS FOR PREVENTION, TREATMENT, AND POLICY

Cheryl Gore-Felton and Michael DiMarco

Globally, at the end of 2005, there were an estimated 33–46 million people living with HIV (PLH) or AIDS. Worldwide surveillance data indicate that AIDS has been diagnosed in virtually every country, and while rising AIDS mortality rates have caused global HIV prevalence to stabilize, the incidence has continued to rise (UNAIDS/WHO, 2005). South Africa continues to be at the epicenter of the AIDS crisis, with approximately 25 million adults and children living with the virus at the end of 2005 (UNAIDS/WHO, 2005). In North America, approximately 1.3 million individuals are living with HIV/AIDS and an estimated 25 percent are unaware of their serostatus (Centers for Disease Control [CDC], 2003a).

In the United States, the estimated number of deaths among persons with HIV decreased by 25 percent during 1995–1996 (CDC, 2003b), by 46.4 percent in 1997 (Holmes, 1998), by 21 percent during 1997–1998 (Martin, Smith, Mathews, & Ventura, 1999), and by 8 percent during 2000–2004 (CDC, 2005). The dramatic decrease observed in 1997 is credited to the advent of antiretroviral therapy, which changed HIV from an acute, life-threatening disease to a chronic, manageable disease for many living in the United States (Beaudin & Chambre, 1996).

The number of new HIV infections in the United States is estimated at 40,000 per year (CDC, 2003b). Ethnic minority groups are disproportionately represented among HIV/AIDS cases, such that African-Americans, who represent about 13 percent of the total U.S. population, constituted 50 percent of persons living with HIV/AIDS at the end of 2004 (CDC, 2005). Similarly, people who are Hispanic/Latino comprise 13 percent of the total U.S. population (including Puerto Rico) (CDC, 2005), but accounted for 19 percent of the cumulative number of new U.S. AIDS cases during the period from 2000 to 2004 (CDC, 2005). From 2000 through 2004, approximately 72 percent of the persons diagnosed with AIDS were 25–44 years old, 40 percent were black, 40 percent white, and 19 percent Hispanic (CDC, 2005). By gender, African American and Hispanic males accounted for 57 percent of the new HIV infections and a striking 78 percent of new HIV infections among women cumulative through 2004 (CDC, 2005). It is important to note that sexual contact accounts for most of the HIV transmission for men and women. There is no imminent cure for HIV/AIDS, and until there is one, the best weapon against AIDS is prevention. In order to develop effective prevention programs, it is critical to understand the factors associated with risk behavior, particularly among populations that are vulnerable to infection and in which the incidence rates continue to increase. To date, men who have sex with men (MSM) and minority women represent most of the HIV/AIDS cases in the United States, and understanding the factors that put each group at risk, as well as those factors that serve as bridges between the groups, facilitating HIV transmission, has received a great deal of attention over the past two decades and will be the focus of the remainder of this chapter.

Sexual Risk Behavior among HIV-Positive Persons

In 1996, medication known as highly active antiretroviral therapy (HAART) transformed the trajectory of HIV/AIDS disease progression such that it extended life expectancy and improved physical health as well as quality of life (Emini, Schleif, Deutsch, & Condra, 1996; Rabkin & Ferrando, 1997; Vittinghoff et al., 1999). Although HAART enables individuals to live longer, healthier lives, there are increased challenges in reducing transmission risk behavior. For instance, research among HIV-positive men and women found that the likelihood of contracting a post-HIV sexually transmitted infection (STI) increased as the length of time living with HIV and AIDS increased (Gore-Felton et al., 2003). Additionally, an epidemiological study among over 16,000 MSM found that as HAART use increased over time, so did the reports of multiple sexual partners and unprotected anal intercourse (Katz et al., 2002). It may be that the advent of effective pharmacological interventions increases physical and psychological well-being in such a way that over time individuals begin to feel better. For many, normal activities, including new relationships and sexual activity, resume. Moreover, some individuals who have responded favorably to medication management may believe that unprotected sex poses little risk because of their decreased viral load and their perception that this lowers the probability of transmitting the virus (Vanable, Ostrow, McKirnan, Taywaditep, & Hope, 2000).

CASE EXAMPLE: MR. S

Mr. S is a 38-year-old gay-identified Caucasian male diagnosed with HIV in 1992. His viral load has been undetectable for the past six years. Overall,

Mr. S is in good health. He has a history of being victimized because of his sexual orientation, and on one occasion he was beaten so badly that he suffered three fractured ribs. He admits that he has a tendency to get involved with partners who have "tempers." For the past five years, he has been in a relationship with a male partner who has been violent toward him. He has a college degree in marketing and works on a consulting basis.

Mr. S participated in a clinical research project for men living with HIV. The project recruited men receiving treatment from an infectious disease clinic in the Midwest. The inclusion criterion for the research study was HIV risk behavior in the past three months. Participants received 15 sessions of cognitive behavioral skills training in stress management, risk reduction behavior, and strategies to improve adherence to medical treatment.

When Mr. S was originally diagnosed with HIV, he refrained from any form of sexual activity for a year and a half. He recalled going into a "deep depression," thinking his life was over. He received psychotherapy and antidepressant therapy for approximately two years after he was initially diagnosed. The psychotherapy focused on the cognitive and behavioral components of his depression with particular emphasis on the meaning of HIV in his life. Mr. S. came to understand that he took unnecessary risks such as going to bars and getting drunk to the point of suffering blackouts. He would wake up in motel rooms, sometimes beaten and robbed.

By focusing on his HIV status in therapy, Mr. S was forced to confront his own internalized homophobia, which was the result of sociocultural norms as well as the physical and emotional abuse he suffered during his elementary and junior high school years. He suffered insults, derogatory epithets, and physical bullying (e.g., being pushed, spat on, and hit) on an almost daily basis. He did not talk with anyone about the abuse and by the time he graduated high school he was a fixture at the gay bars. During high school he began to date older men, and around that time he was involved in his first abusive relationship with another man. The physical and emotional abuse that Mr. S experienced as a child created a great deal of shame, guilt, and anger toward self. Therapy focused on working through the negative affect associated with his abuse experiences. Focusing his attention on his negative feelings about his sexual orientation in a safe, nonjudgmental environment enabled him to realize that he had been reacting to others' hatred, which was separate from how he felt about himself. Through this process he was able to articulate his desire to meet a man and establish a long-term relationship. Prior to therapy, Mr. S could not articulate this desire and engaged in behaviors, such as one-night stands, excessive alcohol use, and abusive partners that ensured he would not establish a long-term, loving relationship with another man. These behaviors allowed him to suppress his "taboo" desire for a meaningful relationship with another man. After he was diagnosed with HIV, he did not think it would be possible to meet a man that would want to be in a relationship with him. His therapy focused on challenging his beliefs and attitudes about his sexual orientation and provided education related to his trauma experiences, trauma reactions, and subsequent risk behavior.

After two years of psychotherapy, Mr. S met his partner; this was approximately two years after protease inhibitors were introduced. Mr. S's partner is HIV negative and was very accepting of Mr. S's diagnosis, which is not uncommon in the gay community. Mr. S reported that he was quite nervous about sexual activity at the beginning of the relationship because he did not want to infect his partner. He reported using condoms for sexual intercourse including anal and oral sex. Over time, condom use gradually tapered off for oral sex, as both he and his partner deemed oral sex to be a low-risk behavior, particularly if ejaculation into the mouth was eliminated. Mr. S explained that he and his partner became less nervous about transmission as they increased their education on the technical transmission probabilities. Gradually, the couple began to engage in reciprocal anal sex without condom use. Ms. S, still concerned about transmission risk to his partner, refrained from ejaculation. He and his partner agreed that anal sex could occur if his viral load remained undetectable, thus lowering the probability chance for transmission.

Over the course of time, Mr. S concluded that condom use lowered the feeling of intimacy the longer the relationship progressed. Both he and his partner yearned for a closeness that they believed could only be achieved through unprotected sex. Intellectually, both Mr. S and his partner knew the risk for HIV transmission existed; however, they used mathematical probability to determine when Mr. S's viral load was significantly low and thus the probability of infection would be close to nonexistent. They did not consult a physician on this matter.

This case illustrates important key concepts in how risk behavior is influenced over time. First, risk behavior often develops in response to traumatic experiences. When physical and emotional abuse occurs during childhood, the sense of oneself is challenged and the emotional response can be overwhelming. Individuals will seek homeostasis by engaging in behaviors to numb the negative feelings. In this case, Mr. S used alcohol and sex to numb his emotional pain. He thought he was to blame for the abuse he suffered and as his punishment he continued to expose himself to risky situations that included abusive relationships. As noted earlier, he was also able to hide from his desire to have a meaningful relationship with another man.

Second, HIV-related risk behavior occurs within the context of one's relationships. Often alcohol and or drugs facilitate sexual risk behavior. Part of the reason for this is that substances impair judgment and make it difficult to have a conversation with a partner about protection. In the case of Mr. S, engaging in self-injurious behavior that was a result of years of abuse and substance use was a way to numb the emotional response to his destructive behavior. Once he got into therapy, he was able to discontinue his self-injurious behavior. Indeed, he practiced safe sex for years before meeting his current partner.

Third, HIV-related risk behavior is often linked to intimacy and closeness within couples. Mr. S's partner supported limited risk behavior, which encouraged Mr. S to engage in unprotected sexual activity. The couple attempted to minimize the risk of transmission by using statistical probability for transmission. The couple intellectualized and rationalized risk behavior as permissible under the circumstances that they believed posed the least amount of risk for transmission. Over time, there tends to be a natural evolution for sexual relationships to deepen sexual intimacy through skin to skin contact, which is part of the human experience for most individuals. Assisting couples to understand this normal desire and not pathologize it is an important aspect of interventions to reduce risk behavior. Effective therapists need to have genuine empathy for couples who are struggling with these basic human needs, so that viable alternatives are explored, as are factors that motivate safer behavior and minimize transmission risk within couples where one person is HIV positive.

Notably, once individuals learn their HIV-positive serostatus, most people change their behavior to avoid transmitting HIV to others (Crepaz & Marks, 2002; Kalichman, Rompa, & Cage, 2000); however, depending upon the sex act, 10–60 percent of HIV-positive persons report sexual behaviors that place themselves and others at risk for sexually transmitted diseases (STIs) (Crepaz & Marks, 2002). A review of the research on risk behavior among HIV-positive adults suggests that high-risk behaviors are more likely with other infected persons, but significant rates of risk behaviors are observed with HIV-negative partners and partners of unknown serostatus (Kalichman, 2000). As a result, it is critical to develop interventions that can assist HIV-positive persons in reducing high-risk sexual risk behavior and provide assistance in maintaining good physical and psychological health.

Traumatic Life Events

Interpersonal Violence

In comparison to the general population, people living with HIV tend to report experiencing more traumatic life events, particularly those that are violent and abusive. Indeed, in a nationally representative probability sample of 2,864 HIV-positive adults, 21 percent of the women and 12 percent of the MSM reported interpersonal violence. Similarly, a study among HIV-positive African American women living in the inner city found higher prevalence of physical assault, rape, and robbery compared to their HIV-negative counterparts (Kimerling et al., 1999).

Among female sex partners of male drug users, a substantial proportion reported histories of rape, assault, and threat of assault. These traumatic events were associated with HIV risk, such that women who had been raped or threatened with assault were more likely to have multiple sex partners and engage in unprotected anal sex (He, McCoy, Stevens, & Stark, 1998). Indeed, some researchers now assert that violence assessment, particularly with regard to domestic violence, is an important adjunct to effective HIV prevention (Klein & Birkhead, 2000). Men are also vulnerable to violence, and in same-sex relationships where there is abuse, HIV-positive MSM have reported difficulty leaving the relationship and for some individuals they report higher risk for HIV transmission because of difficulty engaging in safer behavior with abusive partners (Letellier, 1996).

CASE EXAMPLE: MS. B

A 32-year-old Caucasian woman with a history of childhood sexual abuse, domestic violence, rape, and injection drug use was diagnosed with human papillomavirus (HPV) and HIV six years ago. She had four children, all of whom were taken from her custody by child protective services over the past 10 years because of neglect. Ms. B has not injected drugs for six years; she stopped using heroin when she was diagnosed with HIV/HPV, but she continues to struggle with alcohol addiction and on occasion she uses crack cocaine with her current boyfriend.

Ms. B admits that she has sex for drugs and food on occasion. Ms. B's caseworker suggested she participate in a women's psychotherapy group for HIV-positive women who also were experiencing trauma-related symptoms. Ms. B was easily startled, often suffered panic attacks, and rarely got a good night's sleep because of night terrors. She was sexually abused by two of her mother's boyfriends from the age of 5 until she was 10 years old. She is sexually provocative and admits that she can get a man to do anything she wants him to by using sex. She often laughs when talking about painful memories and says sexually provocative things to other group members when they discuss interpersonal relationships. Ms. B told the group during the first session, "I don't know why I'm here with all you bitches, I was hoping at least one real man would be here!" The group facilitators picked up on the anger and fear behind that statement and assisted Ms. B in focusing on her emotions. To do this, she was directed to concentrate on her body and identify what she felt and where she felt it. Through this exercise, Ms. B was able to say that she was afraid the women wouldn't like her so she wanted to say something that would distance herself from them before they had a chance to hurt her. The women acknowledged her pain and validated her anger by discussing their own fears about being in the group and their history of being hurt by others.

The facilitators assisted Ms. B in exploring her anger, particularly toward women. Other women in the group were struggling with the same issue, which enabled Ms. B to connect to the anger she felt toward her mother for not protecting her when she was a child from sexual abuse. This feeling was validated by two other women who shared a similar history of abuse. Ms. B was also able to disclose the circumstances in which she was likely to engage in unprotected sex. Typically, it was while she was under the influence of alcohol or drugs. She stated there were times she didn't care if someone else got the virus and there were other times she was scared she was going to give it someone else.

Ms. B used sex, alcohol, and drugs to cope with the pain of her abuse memories. The group was able to provide her with skills to cope with the negative affect associated with her abuse memories and reframe her subsequent behaviors as ways she developed to survive the horrific feelings of abandonment, fear, shame, and anger. Ms. B continues to struggle with using condoms all the time. She can use them with people she is just "kickin' it with," but she finds it difficult to assert herself with her boyfriend. The gender-power differential in couples has been associated with HIV risk, particularly in cases like Ms. B's, where poverty influences behavior because certain needs like food or a place to stay have to be met. After the group, Ms. B sought treatment in an outpatient substance use program for her alcohol addiction.

The case of Ms. B is not unusual. A clinic-based sample of HIV-positive adults found that individuals who reported greater severity of sexual coercion (based on the number of times the coercion occurred) were more likely to report more unprotected sex during the past three months. This is important because it's not simply the experience of sexual coercion that is related to sexual risk behavior; it appears that the severity of abuse is an important correlate of sexual risk behavior. This is consistent with research indicating that more severe trauma-related symptoms were associated with risk behavior, such that individuals who experienced more severe intrusion symptoms (e.g., nightmares) were more likely to report unprotected sex during the past three months (Gore-Felton & Koopman, 2002). Avoidant symptoms were associated with sexual risk behavior, in that individuals reporting more severe symptoms of avoidance were less likely to report unprotected sexual intercourse in the past three months. A possible explanation for this may be that individuals who suffer from avoidant symptoms may also experience more severe disruptions in their ability to establish or maintain intimate relationships, resulting in decreased opportunities to engage in risky sexual behavior (Gore-Felton & Koopman, 2002).

Childhood Sexual Abuse and HIV/AIDS

There is a growing body of evidence that adults and adolescents who were sexually abused as children are more likely to engage in high-risk activities that could increase their risk of exposure to HIV (Allers & Benjack, 1991; Bartholow et al., 1994; Carballo-Diéguez & Dolezal, 1995; Lemp et al., 1994; Zierler et al., 1991). The sequelae of childhood sexual abuse (CSA) can have long-lasting deleterious effects on an individual's psychological, physical, and social functioning. For instance, sexual compulsivity has been linked to a history of abuse (Allers, Benjack, White, & Rousey, 1993; Carmen & Rieker, 1989) and is associated with behaviors that confer high risk for HIV transmission, such as having multiple partners or engaging in impulsive, unprotected sexual intercourse. Moreover, mood disorders that result from abuse, such as chronic depression, and behaviors that include self-destructive tendencies, revictimization, and drug/alcohol abuse can increase one's vulnerability to HIV infection (Allers et al., 1993).

In a study of HIV transmission risk, Zierler et al. (1991) reported that female and male survivors of CSA were more likely to have engaged in sex work, to change partners frequently, and to have casual sex with acquaintances than people who were never abused. Furthermore, survivors of both sexes reported more frequent use of alcohol and tranquilizers and were more likely to report a history of a sexually transmitted infection or to have serologic evidence of HIV infection. Surprisingly, abused men in this sample had a two-fold increase in prevalence of HIV infection (Zierler et al., 1991). Similar findings were found among 52 HIV-positive adults, such that almost two-thirds (65%) reported histories of childhood sexual/physical abuse (Allers & Benjack, 1991).

For women, a history of CSA is a major risk factor for becoming HIV positive (Allers et al., 1993; Lodico & DiClemente, 1994: Zierler et al., 1991). Moreover, female victims of CSA are at much higher risk than nonvictims of becoming prostitutes or drug abusers (Russell, 1986), and few women make a conscious connection between their childhood victimization and later high-risk behaviors (Russell, 1986). Sexual coercion has also been linked to CSA, such that women with a history of CSA were significantly more likely to experience unwanted sexual intercourse as adults (Messman & Long, 1996) and were at greater risk for HIV infection (Whitmire, Harlow, Quina, & Morokoff, 1999).

For men, there is also evidence indicating a strong relationship between CSA and HIV risk behavior. In a study of 1,001 adult homosexual and bisexual men attending STD clinics in three American cities, one-third of the sample had experienced sexual abuse during childhood or adolescence, and this variable was associated with HIV-risk behavior, such as unprotected anal intercourse during adulthood (Bartholow et al., 1994). Lemp et al. (1994) reported that in a sample of 425 young MSM, a lifetime history of forced sex was significantly associated with the likelihood of having unsafe anal sex in the six months prior to the interview. Similarly, a study examining high-risk sexual behavior among 182 men of Puerto Rican ancestry living in New York City who had sex with men found that men who reported a history of childhood sexual abuse were significantly more likely to engage in receptive anal sex and to do so without protection (Carballo-Diéguez & Dolezal, 1995). A study examining a conceptual model of sexual risk among gay and bisexual men found that psychopathology, drug use, and trading sex for money, drugs, or a place to stay mediated the relationship between CSA and subsequent adult HIV risk behavior (Gore-Felton et al., 2006). Victimization that confers risk of HIV infection is also more common among men with a CSA history, who are more likely to report sexually coercive events involving unprotected anal intercourse (Kalichman, Gore-Felton, Benotsch, Cage, & Rompa, 2004), which is the highest sexual risk behavior for HIV transmission.

CASE EXAMPLE: MR. M

Mr. M is a 42-year-old African American male who participated in a group stress management intervention that recruited men who reported HIV risk behavior (sexual or injection drugs) and psychological trauma symptoms. Mr. M stated that he is currently in a relationship with a woman and considers himself to be heterosexual. She does not know that he is HIV positive. He admitted that he has had sex with men, typically when using drugs and alcohol.

Mr. M has been diagnosed with AIDS for the past five years. He is also infected with Hepatitis C. He has a previous history of injection drug use. He stopped using injection drugs, including heroin and cocaine, around the time he was diagnosed with AIDS. The group members challenged Mr. M to consider whether his AIDS diagnosis had any impact on changing his drug use. Mr. M accepted that there was a connection and added that his drug use was an excuse to escape from the harsh realities of life. Mr. M occasionally uses marijuana and alcohol to help him relax.

The group helped Mr. M identify the benefits and consequences of escaping though the use of drugs. Instead of criticizing his current marijuana and alcohol use, the facilitators helped Mr. M reframe a seemingly negative behavior into a drive to survive by shielding awareness of his emotional pain. Avoidance behavior, common among individuals coping with traumatic stress, was normalized as an adaptive human survival drive rather than a character flaw. The peer support of the group helped Mr. M reduce his shame and enabled him to talk about other sensitive personal information. Mr. M disclosed that an older male cousin had sex with him when he was about 10 years old. Mr. M struggles with anger toward his cousin but has never shared his experience with his family because he fears that his manhood would be questioned.

The stress of keeping this secret is very stressful and Mr. M becomes enraged when he thinks about it. He has spent most of his life trying to forget about it. Although he had insight that the situation was stressful, he lacked awareness of how his stress manifested itself through physical feelings of tension and aggression. The group facilitators were able to provide important psychoeducational information related to the effect of trauma on the brain and subsequent emotional and physical responses. This information was key to validating the experiences of hyperarousal, avoidance, and reexperiencing that Mr. M had related to his childhood sexual abuse. The therapeutic utility of group process was evident for Mr. M when the other group members confirmed these experiences as universal, which further validated these responses as normal given exposure to trauma.

Mr. M was able to discuss his anger toward men and women, which he often acted out sexually by not using condoms. Mr. M was able to identify his anger and subsequent shame associated with his sexual abuse. After he was able to connect emotionally to the feelings he had spent years trying to bury, he was able to understand his behavior toward others and his inability to maintain intimate relationships. For Mr. M, it was important to discuss how safer sex was protection for him so that he could maintain his health. The threat of being infected with an additional HIV strain that might be resistant to his current medication regimen along with the threat of acquiring a different sexually transmitted infection that might complicate his current medical course was helpful in motivating him to use condoms with his sexual partners.

Trauma-Related Stress Symptoms and HIV/AIDS

Studies examining trauma among populations already infected with HIV underscore the strong relationship between previous trauma and subsequent

HIV infection. A chart review of 238 female patients at an HIV outpatient clinic found that almost one-third (32%) had a history of sexual abuse (Bedimo, Kissinger, & Bessinger, 1997). Gore-Felton and Koopman (2002) conducted a study among a diverse sample of 64 HIV-positive men and women living in California and found that almost a quarter of the sample reported moderate to severe trauma symptoms, suggesting a clinical diagnosis of posttraumatic stress disorder (PTSD). The types of trauma reported were heterogeneous and included interpersonal violence, childhood and adulthood sexual victimization, robbery, burglary, and witnessing violence. Moreover, the severity of the abuse (adult and childhood) and the trauma-related symptoms (avoidance and intrusion) were associated with sexual risk behavior.

In addition to the traumatic experiences of interpersonal violence and abuse, being diagnosed with a chronic, life-threatening illness has been categorized as a traumatic stressor in the fourth edition of the *Diagnostic and Statistical Manual* (American Psychiatric Association, 1994). Moreover, a growing body of research suggests that traumatic stress responses, and even full-blown PTSD syndromes, can ensue from the traumatic experience of being diagnosed with a life-threatening illness. For instance, a number of studies have documented clinically significant cancer-related posttraumatic stress symptoms: intrusion, avoidance, and anxiety (Alter et al., 1996; Butler, Koopman, Classen, & Spiegel, 1999; Cella, Mahon, & Donovan, 1990; Cordova & Andrykowski, 2003; Koopman et al., 2002). Very little empirical research has been conducted among HIV-positive persons examining this phenomenon. However, among the few studies that have examined trauma symptoms among HIV-positive adults, the results have been consistent with the cancer studies. For example, in a study among MSM examining PTSD symptoms in response to HIV infection, 30 percent met the criteria for PTSD. In this same study, PTSD associated with HIV was significantly and positively associated with a history of PTSD from other traumatic events that occurred prior to being diagnosed with HIV (Kelly et al., 1998). Additionally, HIV-positive women who reported less social support had a higher incidence of PTSD and exhibited higher rates of avoidance symptoms compared to women who reported more social support (Jones, 1999).

Posttraumatic stress symptoms complicate not only responses to traumatic stressors themselves but also the severity and course of comorbid medical and psychiatric problems, including HIV infection. The prevalence of PTSD in the general population is about 9 percent (Breslau, Davis, Andreski, & Peterson, 1991); the prevalence of partial PTSD is estimated to be close to 30 percent (Weiss et al., 1992). The rates are likely to be higher among those with HIV infection, due in part to the lifestyle associated with elevated disease risk. For instance, among HIV-positive African American women, 62 percent reported experiencing at least one traumatic life event, and 35 percent of the sample met the full criteria for PTSD diagnosis (Kimerling et al., 1999). Moreover, 87.9 percent reported symptoms of reexperiencing the traumatic event, 73.5 percent reported avoidance, and 70.4 percent reported symptoms of hyperarousal.

CASE EXAMPLE: MR. A

Mr. A is a 35-year-old Hispanic male who lives in a known gang area. He has been HIV positive since age 20. He learned that he was HIV positive as a result of going to an emergency room after being beaten with the handle of a gun. He can remember feeling completely powerless when the gun was held to his head. He disclosed this information in a group for men living with HIV disease. Mr. A is currently in a relationship with an abusive man who is 20 years older than he is. Mr. A knows that he needs to leave the relationship, but he has nowhere to go. His partner sometimes locks him out of the apartment when he is angry. As a result, Mr. A has had to sleep on the street. Mr. A often feels on edge, particularly when he is locked out of his apartment and needs to sleep on the street in a dangerous area where he may be assaulted.

In addition to coping with his partner's aggressive outbursts, he also stated that his partner makes him use methamphetamine and then lets his friends have sex with him. Mr. A stated that he wants to please his partner so he complies with the request. At times he is so intoxicated that he does not even know what is happening to him. He admits to being "passed around" for receptive anal sex at sex parties that his partner hosts. Mr. A knows that when he uses methamphetamine he does not take his antiretroviral medication as prescribed. The ongoing traumatic stress has led to inconsistent attendance at routine medical appointments, reduced access to medication, low medication adherence, and the lack of a safe place to live. Mr. A's low self-esteem and inability to leave the abusive relationship place him at high risk for reinfection with another HIV strain as well as other sexually transmitted diseases.

An all male psychotherapy group was very beneficial for Mr. A. He had a group of men affirming his manhood while at the same time empathizing with his pain. This atmosphere of acceptance and trust enabled Mr. A to reveal a childhood that was exposed to repeated physical violence and emotional abuse by his stepfather, who constantly called him "faggot." Mr. A was able to identify his low self-esteem and self-worth as motivating factors that kept him in his current abusive situation. Paradoxically, the more acceptance and affirmation Mr. A felt from the group the greater his ambivalence grew about attending the group: this was demonstrated by sporadic group attendance. The group confronted Mr. A's sporadic attendance in a caring manner that enabled him to connect to his feelings about the group. Mr. A revealed that he felt safe in the group, which was a feeling he had not experienced before, particularly among men. He knew the group was time limited and thought being too involved with the group would only hurt too much when the group ended. This disclosure allowed the group to offer support outside of the group meetings and to discuss community programs and services that were available, once the group ended, to provide ongoing social support.

To assist Mr. A cope with the transition of the discontinuation of the group, he was encouraged to access the community services while still in the group. Mr. A met other caring men and women at the community service

programs and was able to access services that enabled him to leave his abusive relationship and move into transitional housing. Mr. A agreed to attend
individual psychotherapy sessions, which began while the group was still ongoing. This provided a bridge once the group ended for Mr. A to continue to
work on bolstering his self-esteem, developing social support, and reducing
his risk behavior.

It is important to note that empirical evidence suggests that PTSD occurs only
in a minority of individuals exposed to a trauma, indicating that the stressor cannot be the sole etiologic agent of PTSD. Indeed, idiosyncratic factors such as type
of trauma, trauma severity, and biology (i.e., genetics) influence the trajectory of
trauma symptoms and functioning over time (Shalev & Yahuda, 1998). However,
for those who do develop PTSD symptomology, the symptoms follow a similar,
defined pattern of distress regardless of the particular traumatic stressor.

Mechanisms Linking Traumatic Stress to HIV Risk Behavior

An important question to ask is, "Why does trauma lead to risk behavior?"
While no studies have definitively established the mechanisms that link trauma
with HIV risk behaviors, several models have been proposed. One hypothesis is
that the psychological symptoms (e.g., intrusion, hyperarousal, and avoidance)
associated with a traumatic experience may interfere with the individual's ability
to integrate safer patterns of interpersonal and personal functioning. Clinical
observation, along with empirical research, indicates that trauma symptoms are
often accompanied by psychological distress such as frustration and anger.

Notably, cognitive behavioral interventions that have been successful in reducing PTSD symptoms have also been successful at reducing comorbid psychological distress (Zoellner, Fitzgibbons, & Foa, 2001). When specifically considering
HIV-related risk behavior, various psychological mechanisms have been identified that mediate change in HIV risk behavior, including the following: health
beliefs (Becker & Joseph, 1988), self-efficacy (Bandura, 1994), peer influence
(Fisher, 1988), and coping (Mayne, Acree, Chesney, & Folkman, 1998). The relationship of each of these mechanisms to sexual/drug use risk behaviors has
received some support.

For example, levels of self-reported self-efficacy are associated with sexual
refusal, consistency of condom use, and reduced total number of sexual partners
and anonymous partners (Aspinwall, Kemeny, Taylor, Schneider, & Dudley, 1991;
Kasen, Vaughan, & Walter, 1992; Rosenthal, Moore, & Flynn, 1991; Walter et al.,
1993). However, no single model seems to be comprehensive in explaining the
major factors influencing risk behavior. This is particularly true for populations
that have experienced a traumatic stressor. Therefore, it is important to consider
additional models and allow further theoretical understanding to emerge as new
evidence is obtained.

An alternative perspective, the distress model, states that emotional distress
is related to HIV risk acts (Richardson, Schott, McGuigan, & Levine, 1987;

Rotheram-Borus, Rosario, Reid, & Koopman, 1995). Reducing mood disturbance may be a key factor leading to reduced sexual and drug use risk behavior. Brendstrup and Schmidt (1990) observed that distress due to undertreated stressors might create a barrier against adopting safe sexual practices among homosexual/bisexual men. In longitudinal HIV risk reduction research focusing on gay/bisexual male adolescents (Rotheram-Borus et al., 1995), components of the health belief model, self-efficacy theory, peer influence, coping, and distress models were examined. Only the distress model was supported, such that the pattern of protected anal or oral acts varied with emotional distress, substance use, and conduct problems.

Previous cross-sectional studies have shown that sexual abuse is the event that most often leads to PTSD among women (Breslau et al., 1991; Resnick et al., 1993). This, coupled with evidence that there is a risk of increased drug disorders associated with an increased risk for HIV among individuals with PTSD, has led some researchers to hypothesize that PTSD psychopathology may mediate the relationship between abuse and sexual risk behavior (Miller, 1999).

A study among gay and bisexual men examined this assertion and found preliminary support for the hypothesis that psychopathology does mediate the relationship between CSA and sexual risk behavior (Gore-Felton et al., 2006). Specifically, borderline functioning, dissociative symptoms, and intrusive trauma symptoms mediated the relationship between CSA and adult sexual risk behavior (Gore-Felton et al., 2006).

The Effect of Trauma on Physiology

Physiological Indicators of Stress

The autonomic nervous system and the cardiovascular, metabolic, and immune systems protect the body by responding to internal and external stress. However, cumulative stress can disrupt this complex interactive system. McEwen's model of stress and health (McEwen, 1998) incorporates a considerable body of research suggesting that chronic elevation of cortisol caused by stress, as well as other factors, can lead to immunity problems as a function of allostatic load, which is the cumulative effect of stress on the body. In healthy individuals, cortisol levels are usually highest prior to awakening and decrease over the course of the day (Posener et al., 1996).

Experiencing chronic stress or enduring major traumatic life events may result in raising cortisol above its usual levels. Evidence suggests that chronic elevation of cortisol may increase HIV viral replication (Corley, 1995; Swanson, Zeller, & Spear, 1998). Recent research further indicates an association between depressive symptoms, cortisol, and disease progression among HIV-positive men (Leserman et al., 2000).

Traumatic and other stressful life events are highly prevalent among persons who become HIV positive. Childhood sexual abuse and other traumatic life events appear to be risk factors for sexual risk behavior and injecting and other drug use associated with HIV infection (Gore-Felton & Koopman, 2002). Clinical evidence suggests that stressful life events predict more rapid HIV disease progression. Indeed, research found that for every severely stressful life event per six-month interval, the risk of early HIV disease progression doubled (Evans et al., 1997). In research on persons recently notified of HIV-positive serostatus, PTSD symptoms of avoidance and intrusion were associated with greater distress, and avoidance was predictive of lower CD4+ percentages (Lutgendorf et al., 1997).

Research suggests that the development of PTSD is likely facilitated by an atypical biological response in the immediate aftermath of a traumatic event, which in turns leads to psychiatric symptoms (Yehuda, McFarlane, & Shalev, 1998). Thus, interventions that target both the psychological and physiological manifestations of PTSD are likely to be effective in reducing trauma-related stress symptoms.

CASE EXAMPLE: MR. M

Referring back to the case of Mr. M, the 42-year-old African American male with a history of injection drug use and childhood sexual trauma, an important function of the group was to provide Mr. M feedback on the triggers that lead to his use of drugs and alcohol to mentally escape from stress. The group helped Mr. M understand that he was using drugs and alcohol to help his body relax. The group facilitators focused the group's attention on the basic human need to feel calm and safe, which increases the desire to reduce feelings of stress such as tightness in one's stomach and chest in response to hyperarousal symptoms of trauma. This type of education helped increase awareness of how hyperarousal symptoms are associated with the avoidance and experiencing symptoms of posttraumatic stress disorder.

The group practiced diaphragmatic breathing, which helped Mr. M and others learn how to master the desired internal calmness that was sought through the use of drugs and alcohol. Paradoxically, Mr. M's use of drugs and alcohol increased the feeling of being out of control which was the cost of blocking out intrusive memories. The diaphragmatic breathing and guided imagery helped Mr. M lower his feelings of anxiety and created the calm physiological response he wanted while maintaining a sense of control. It was emphasized that Mr. M could use the diaphragmatic breathing techniques as an additional coping tool and as an alternative to drugs and alcohol.

Relationship between Adult PTSD and Substance Abuse

It is important to understand the link between trauma and substance use, because substance use and sexual risk behaviors are the principal routes for the transmission of HIV infection (DesJarlais & Friedman, 1988; Hearst & Hully, 1988) and they tend to co-occur. It is argued that alcohol and other drugs have direct causal effects on sexual behavior and condom use by impairing one's judgment about possible risks, disinhibiting one physically and psychologically, and making one less sensitive to the concerns of a partner (Strunin & Hingson, 1992). High-risk sexual behavior is strongly related to substance use (Ostrow et al., 1990). Thus, use of drugs and alcohol can increase the risk of becoming HIV infected when the sexual partner has HIV infection (Ostrow et al., 1990; Penkower et al., 1991), suggesting that an intervention aimed at decreasing risk behavior in the context of substance use, particularly among PLH, is likely to reduce HIV transmission. Indeed, the majority of persons with AIDS have been infected either through sexual risk behavior, injection drug risk behavior, or both (CDC, 2002), and risk behaviors continue among some persons already HIV infected. Even among well-educated employed women who are not intravenous drug users (IDUs), 60 percent engaged in unprotected sexual activity after learning that they were HIV positive (Brown & Rundell, 1990).

Importantly, many MSM and IDUs have changed their risk behaviors in response to the threat of AIDS (Catania et al., 1992; DesJarlais & Friedman, 1988). However, even after people have reduced their high-risk sex and drug use behaviors, relapse often occurs (DesJarlais, Friedman, & Casriel, 1990; Stall et al., 1990). One explanation may be that trauma-related stress was not assessed and, therefore, symptoms of stress were not addressed in the intervention. It should be noted that the comorbidity of PTSD and substance abuse is high (Keane & Wolfe, 1990; Kulka et al., 1990). For example, 59 percent of women with trauma histories attending a drug rehabilitation clinic experienced symptoms that met the criteria for PTSD (Fullilove et al., 1993). In the cases of undiagnosed PTSD, it may be that individuals turn to substances in an effort to self-medicate their anxiety symptoms (e.g., hyperarousal, avoidance, reexperiencing). Clinicians have long noted the association between alcohol use and anxiety disorders. Indeed, alcohol belongs to the same class of drugs, known as sedative-hypnotics, that include benzodiazepines. Benzodiazepines have been prescribed for the treatment of anxiety for years. However, today they are not the drug of choice to treat anxiety because of their tolerance and addictive properties. However, they are efficient in reducing feelings of anxiety and explain why so many individuals with anxiety disorders use alcohol to get relief from disturbing symptoms.

Implications for Disease Management and Clinical Practice

Group Interventions

As previously noted, a great deal of progress in understanding the life cycle of HIV has resulted in the development of HAART; however, at present, there is no cure for AIDS and no vaccine against HIV infection, and none seem imminent. Although HAART is responsible for prolonging life and slowing disease progression among many persons with HIV/AIDS, not everyone has been helped by the HAART regimen (Deeks et al., 1997).

Support groups and other psychosocial interventions have a role to play in enhancing the quality of life for HIV-positive persons. Research has found that psychosocial interventions may enhance survival among persons with cancer (Goodwin et al., 2001; Spiegel, 2002) and may have similar effects on individuals living with HIV/AIDS. For example, a study examining changes in immuno-logic status among 25 HIV-infected men, randomly assigned to a 10-week stress management intervention or to a wait-list control, found that men receiving stress management had higher CD4(+), CD45RA(+), and CD29(+) cell counts over a 12-month period after completion of the intervention (Antoni et al., 2002). It is important to note that this difference was found independent of the individ-ual's number of naïve T cells and HIV virus load. Thus, there is evidence that stress management is an efficacious method of immunologic reconstitution among HIV-infected men.

These findings are consistent with results among participants in a 10-week bereavement support group for HIV-positive individuals, which demonstrated health benefits such as higher CD4+ cell count, lower plasma cortisol levels, and fewer numbers of physician visits, compared to those of control group partici-pants (Goodkin et al., 1998). The clinical implications of such immune function benefits are continuing to be investigated. Given the importance of immune function in HIV/AIDS, further research on the psychoimmunology of psycho-social interventions is likely to lead to clinically useful results.

Although individual psychosocial interventions for HIV-positive persons can be effective (Markowitz, Klerman, & Perry, 1992; Perry et al., 1991), group interven-tions have the clear advantage of providing social support and validation. Research-ers have demonstrated positive effects of group intervention for HIV/AIDS patients on psychological variables, including mood, sexual and drug use risk behaviors, and beliefs and knowledge about HIV/AIDS. Moreover, psychosocial interventions using groups have proven efficacious in helping to reduce emotional distress among HIV-positive patients (Kelly et al., 1993a). For instance, frequency of unprotected anal intercourse among depressed HIV-infected men was significantly reduced by a supportive-expressive group intervention, and a cognitive behavioral group inter-vention resulted in significantly less illicit drug use (Kelly et al., 1993b). Addition-ally, a skills-training group resulted in safer sex practices among gay men and safer sexual practices among single, pregnant, inner-city women (Hobfall et al., 1994).

In addition to reducing risk behavior, cognitive behavioral group interven-tions have been successful in reducing stress symptoms. Indeed, cognitive restructuring and coping skills have produced marked improvement in "reexpe-riencing" and "avoidance" symptoms. This is an extremely important clinical finding in light of the fact that the most frequently experienced symptoms in PTSD are reexperiencing and autonomic arousal symptoms (Resnick et al., 1993; Rothbaum et al., 1992). A body of evidence amassed over the past decade indi-cates that when different treatment modalities are compared, cognitive behav-ioral interventions are the most effective in alleviating trauma symptoms (Gore-Felton, 2000; Gore-Felton, Gill, Koopman, & Spiegel, 1999).

As previously noted, improvements in antiviral treatment are prolonging the lives of people living with HIV disease. Because HIV transmission is preventable by changing and maintaining behavior, the use of behavioral skills that prevent HIV transmission is the primary available means to curtail the HIV epidemic.

The lives of HIV-positive persons are often complex, and their social as well as psychological needs often go unmet. There is substantial need for social support in the face of life-threatening illness. Fortunately, group interventions that provide social support and the opportunity to learn adaptive coping skills have been successful in helping patients manage their anxiety and depression (Markowitz et al., 1992). It is clear from the literature that distress, posttraumatic stress symptoms, social network exposure, and drug abuse can complicate the course of HIV disease and may predispose vulnerable individuals to engage in risk behavior. It is also clear that over a decade of research in the field of HIV has consistently demonstrated that group interventions can effectively reduce risk behavior, alleviate psychological distress, and improve health outcomes.

Social Support

There is substantial need for social support in the face of life-threatening illness. Under normal circumstances, social support helps individuals mobilize their psychological resources and manage emotional responses to stress as well as provide financial support, materials, skills, and cognitive guidance to handle situations optimally. Studies have shown that the mere perception that adequate support is available can serve to buffer situational stress as much as the actual level of social support.

HIV-infected patients are confronted with high levels of stress related to their health status, and their social support systems are often burdened and impaired. An AIDS diagnosis is frequently linked to a decrease in the number of supportive contacts or a change in the pattern of those contacts. For example, AIDS patients report lower levels of practical and emotional support from family members. In fact, many AIDS patients report greater availability of emotional support from friends than from family members (Kelly, Raphael, & Statham, 1996).

Problems with inadequate social support may have physiological as well as psychological consequences. In general, greater social support has been associated with better immune system function. Among HIV-positive persons, those with less deterioration in CD4+ cell count were significantly more likely to report greater social support availability (Theorell et al., 1995). Consistent with the research suggesting that more social support is associated with better immune function, bereavement, a loss of an important source of social support, has been associated with decreased immune system functioning (Goodkin et al., 1996).

Social support may be an important factor in minimizing the intensity of the stress experienced by HIV-positive individuals. An explanation as to how this may occur can be found within the theoretical framework of the stress-buffering hypothesis of social support. The stress-buffering hypothesis of social support (Cohen & Wills, 1985) refers to the protection that social support provides against the effects of stressful events and situations. This protective effect of social support is thought to operate both by contributing to the resources available to individuals to cope with the stressor and by reducing the stress response to the stressor (Cohen & Wills, 1985).

Incorporating psychosocial approaches to the standard treatment and care of HIV/AIDS patients may promote better health outcomes. Transforming how medicine views psychosocial factors within the context of chronic illness undoubtedly means treating HIV from an interdisciplinary approach, which focuses appropriate attention on the psychosocial influences that affect disease course. As individuals live longer with HIV, becoming middle- or older-aged, it will be necessary to consider developmental influences on psychosocial functioning within the context of a chronic, life-threatening disease that continues to be socially stigmatized.

Individual Interventions

Maintaining behavior change for many years requires well-developed coping skills and the use of strategies to manage mental health distress symptoms to sustain reductions in transmission acts (Gore-Felton et al., 2005).

Preventive interventions for HIV-positive individuals offer benefits for both the individual and society, including reducing psychopathology, decreasing the likelihood of transmission to uninfected persons, and reducing the probability of reinfection with drug-resistant HIV strains that may accelerate disease progression.

There are several benefits to using an individualized intervention approach. Some individuals may fear the stigmatization associated with a small-group intervention; attending the group discloses one's serostatus to other group members, which poses a risk of loss of privacy should a group member decide not to maintain confidentiality. In some settings, arriving at the site discloses one as being HIV positive. Moreover, scheduling group sessions at times that are convenient for participants and staff can be very challenging. Our current structure and organization of health services are amenable to individual sessions. For instance, medical and community-based clinics are typically organized around delivery of individual sessions; this is certainly the norm in clinics for those with sexually transmitted diseases, both in this country and internationally. When the interventions are delivered in individual sessions, the coordination and stigmatization issues are not present, which enhances the feasibility and acceptability of disseminating the intervention.

Medical Adherence and Health Outcomes

Minimizing the symptoms associated with HIV disease is imperative to restoring quality of life, which includes reducing stress responses to health-related stressors among individuals living with HIV/AIDS. As for individuals living with other chronic illnesses, HIV/AIDS presents challenges to maintaining health behaviors over an extended period of time. Adherence to treatment regimens, defined as the match between the patient's behavior and health care advice (Haynes, Sackett, & Taylor, 1980), is important because less than very high medication compliance can facilitate the development of drug-resistant HIV strains (Bangsberg, Moss, & Deeks, 2004). Moreover, there is evidence suggesting that less than very high adherence to HAART can lead to treatment failure, as evidenced by an increase of HIV-1 RNA (viral load) in the body (Bialer, Wallack, &, McDaniel, 2000). Individuals may also develop viral resistance across different classes of medications, limiting their ability to benefit from other drug therapies. Multiple factors have been associated with adherence (Johnson et al., 2003). Consequently, improving long-term utilization of and adherence to HAART is integrally related to health maintenance among PLH and requires interventions that can be tailored to meet the multiple demands of individuals.

Policy Implications

As medical interventions continue to improve health and increase the overall life expectancies of people living with HIV/AIDS, there will be more people living with HIV, suggesting that HIV prevention efforts need a broader focus that includes HIV-positive populations. Incorporating the assessment of trauma and the treatment of trauma-related symptoms among HIV-positive men and women may be a particularly effective method of reducing sexual risk behavior. Thus, intervention and prevention efforts may be able to thwart new infections by developing strategies that not only build skills needed to prevent HIV but effectively target psychological symptoms and behaviors that occur within the context of traumatic life experiences.

Policies that encourage individuals to know whether they are HIV positive or not may encourage early entry into care, which may assist in identifying individuals early in their disease and educate them about safer behavior. For instance, some infectious disease physicians advocate changing the current medical standard-of-care to include HIV testing when other sexually transmitted diseases are being tested for, without the need for special consent by patients. Similarly, there are those that consider preventive medicine to include HIV testing for high-risk age groups so that it becomes standard practice much like a colonoscopy at age 50 and mammograms for women 40 years and older. However, there are others who believe it is time to implement routine, not risk-based HIV testing (Beckwith et al., 2005).

Normalizing HIV Testing

Early in the HIV epidemic, health providers in the United States targeted high-risk groups for HIV testing and counseling, chiefly homosexual men and injection drug users. As the epidemic progressed in the 1980s and 1990s it became clear that HIV/AIDS affects men and women of all sexual orientations. Testing and prevention campaigns shifted from targeting a demographic label (gay or bisexual) to targeting actual risk behavior (unprotected sex, multiple partners, needle sharing, or sexually transmitted infections (STIs) as a way of identifying those at highest risk for HIV. Typically, health providers offer testing to patients who endorse risk factors for HIV, relying heavily upon the self-report of the patient.

Aside from objective findings of an opportunistic infection or presence of other STIs, a test is typically offered when a patient reports a history of risky behavior, such as unprotected sex, drug use, or intercourse with a partner of the same sex. This is problematic because self-report may not reliably identify risk behavior and may limit access to necessary HIV testing and prevention counseling. Integrating non-risk-based HIV testing and counseling into all aspects of health care, such as primary care, family planning clinics, and the emergency department, will normalize the role of routine testing as care standard, identify cases among those who do not know they have HIV, and create a powerful cultural shift in how testing is perceived in the eye of the public (Beckwith et al., 2005).

Imagine being given an HIV test in an annual physical exam, regardless of any stated risk, evidence of opportunistic infection, or STI, that would, under current policies and practices, prompt testing. To offer HIV testing for "no apparent reason" would require a policy change in how medicine is practiced and how Medicare, Medicaid, and other third-party payers reimburse health organizations for preventative testing. Continued reliance on risk-based testing for patients who may be reluctant to self-identify risk would limit the ability of the health care community to diagnose HIV infection. These missed opportunities to diagnose delay treatment, increase health care costs, and keep patients from receiving the necessary educational and behavioral counseling that would lower the risk of transmission to others.

In 2001, the CDC revised their guidelines for HIV testing, counseling, and referral for the screening of pregnant women (CDC, 2001). The revised guidelines call for health care providers to provide routine testing and counseling in areas where the prevalence of HIV infection is equal to or greater than 1 percent and for persons with increasing behavioral risk for infection regardless of the prevalence of HIV infection. This was the first step in recognizing the need for routine HIV testing by broadening the inclusion criteria for testing. In 2003, the prevention effort called for expanding its strategies to increase the early identification of HIV with appropriate linkage to care by making HIV testing a routine part of medical care, particularly in communities where the prevalence is greater than 1 percent, by the inclusion of rapid HIV testing in outreach outside the medical care setting, and by a focus on decreasing perinatal HIV transmission (CDC, 2003a)

In 2006, the CDC again revised their recommendations for HIV testing. These newly revised CDC recommendations advocate routine voluntary HIV screening as a normal part of medical practice, similar to screening for other treatable conditions, among populations where the prevalence of HIV is greater than 0.1 percent (CDC, 2006).

The recommendation to routinely offer testing when the local prevalence is greater than 0.1 percent is impractical. Health care providers would have to know specific population estimates, which are not easily assessable. HIV risk is based on social networks and specific risks behaviors for individuals as well as the prevalence for HIV infection in a particular social network. It would be strategic to test everyone, taking the burden away from "prevalence rates" and physician/provider perception in initiating voluntary testing.

Furthermore, the practice of relying on an accurate risk assessment is faulty because it is limited by self-reported data, which are vulnerable to social desirability, recall bias, and normal forgetting. As mentioned earlier, individuals may not feel comfortable sharing risk behavior or simply asking for testing. Not only are some patients reluctant to self-identify risk, but health providers may not seek information regarding risk because of their own discomfort in asking patients about testing or fear of being seen as offensive. If patients are inaccurate in their risk assessment and providers are reluctant to ask about testing, HIV testing that is based on risk assessment will undoubtedly fail.

Routine testing, regardless of risk, would considerably increase the early identification of HIV disease, which would assist in getting individuals into treatment early and exposing high-risk individuals to prevention messages. It is important to note that regardless of the test results, the exposure to HIV testing, in and of itself, is an intervention, because it highlights the risk of HIV infection. This process can affect decisions by increasing the cognitive dissonance related to maintaining risk behavior. Moreover, pairing testing with access to counseling can facilitate behavioral changes necessary to decrease risk behavior. Thus, a policy that encourages HIV testing as routine, standard medical care and affords individuals access to counseling and prevention messages is likely to reduce HIV incidence rates.

Early Education and Prevention

Most of the HIV that is transmitted worldwide occurs within the context of an intimate relationship, usually a sexual relationship. Policies that encourage dissemination of best prevention practices to youth before they become sexually active are necessary to build "sexual esteem." With "sexual esteem," girls will not feel the need to have sex before they are ready or because they fear losing the affection of someone they care about. Similarly, boys will not feel pressured to prove their worthiness through sexual conquests or their manhood by becoming teen fathers, or feel pressured to engage in sex before they are emotionally ready.

It is true that part of sexual education is learning how to use a condom correctly; however, when HIV prevention curricula are carefully scrutinized, it is evident that much more is being taught. This includes self-efficacy, assertive communication, social support, self-esteem, and self-worth, and for those who have experienced sexual trauma it is about reclaiming one's sexuality, learning to be sensual without sex, and restructuring the meaning of what a sexual being is. Abstinence-based programs appear to work best for early adolescents who have not yet become sexually active (Jemmott, Jemmott, & Fong, 1998). However, for adolescents who are already sexually active, education and prevention programs are necessary to decrease risk behavior and in some cases return adolescents to abstinence (Jemmott, Jemmott, & Fong, 1998).

In light of this evidence, the debate about whether or not abstinence-only programs should exist in schools seems moot. Like most human dilemmas, the problem is complex and therefore requires a multifaceted approach—one size will not fit all. Thus, incorporating abstinence-only programs into education and prevention seems like the best approach to providing our youth with information that will delay sexual activity and keep those who are sexually active safe from unwanted pregnancies, STIs, and HIV infection. The savings to society and public health of such an approach would be substantial.

References

Allers, C. T., & Benjack, K. J. (1991). Connections between childhood abuse and HIV infection. *Journal of Counseling and Development, 70,* 309–313.

Allers, C. T., Benjack, K. J., White, J., & Rousey, J. T. (1993). HIV vulnerability and the adult survivor of childhood sexual abuse. *Child Abuse and Neglect, 17*(2), 291–298.

Alter, C. L., Pelcovitz, D., Axelrod, A., Goldenberg, B., Harris, H., Meyers, B., et al. (1996). Identification of PTSD in cancer survivors. *Psychosomatics, 37*(2), 137–143.

American Psychiatric Association. (1994). *Diagnostic and statistical manual of mental disorders* (4th ed.). Washington, DC: Author.

Antoni, M. H., Cruess, D. G., Klimas, N., et al. (2002). Stress management and immune system reconstitution in symptomatic HIV-infected gay men over time: Effects on transitional naïve T cells (CD4(+)CD45RA(+)CD29(+)). *American Journal of Psychiatry, 159,* 143–145.

Aspinwall, L. G., Kemeny, M. E., Taylor, S. E., Schneider, S. G., & Dudley, J. P. (1991). Psychosocial predictors of gay men's AIDS risk-reduction behavior. *Health Psychology, 10*(6), 432–444.

Bandura, A. (1994). Social cognitive theory and exercise of control over HIV infection. In R. J. DiClemente & J. L. Peterson (Eds.), *Preventing AIDS: Theories and methods of behavioral interventions* (pp. 25–59). New York: Plenum Press.

Bangsberg, D. R., Moss, A. R., & Deeks, S. G. (2004). Paradoxes of adherence and drug resistance to antiretroviral therapy. *Journal of Antimicrobial Chemotherapy, 10.*

Bartholow, B. N., Doll, L. S., Joy, D., Douglas, J. M., Bolan, G., Harrison, J. S., et al. (1994). Emotional, behavioral, and HIV risks associated with sexual abuse among adult homosexual and bisexual men. *Child Abuse & Neglect, 18*(9), 747–761.

Beaudin, C. L., & Chambre, S. M. (1996). HIV/AIDS as a chronic disease: Emergence from the plague model. *American Behavioral Scientist, 39*(6), 684–706

Becker, M., & Joseph, J. G. (1988). AIDS and behavioral change to reduce risk: A review. *American Journal of Public Health, 78,* 394–410.

Beckwith, C. G., Flanigan, T. P., del Rio, C., Simmons, E., Wing, E. J., Carpenter, C.C.J., et al. (2005). It is time to implement routine, not risk-based HIV testing. *Clinical Infectious Diseases, 40,* 1037–1040.

Bedimo, A. L., Kissinger, P., & Bessinger, R. (1997). History of sexual abuse among HIV-infected women. *International Journal of STD & AIDS, 8*(5), 332–335.

Bialer, P. A., Wallack, J. J., & McDaniel, J. S. (2000). Human immunodeficiency virus and AIDS. In A. Stoudemire, B. Fogel, & D. B. Greenberg (Eds.), *Psychiatric care of the medical patient* (2nd ed.) (pp. 871–887). New York: Oxford University Press.

Biglino, A., Limone, P., Forno, B., Pollono, A., Cariti, G., Molinatti, G. M., et al. (1995). Altered adrenocorticotropin and cortisol response to corticotropin-releasing hormone in HIV-1 infection. *European Journal of Endocrinology, 133*, 173–179.

Brendstrup, E., & Schmidt, K. (1990). Homosexual and bisexual men's coping with the aids epidemic: Qualitative interviews with 10 non-HIV-tested homosexual and bisexual men. *Social Science Medicine, 30*(6), 713–720.

Breslau, N., Davis, G. C., Andreski, P., & Peterson, E. (1991). Traumatic events and post-traumatic stress disorder in an urban population of young adults. *Archives of General Psychiatry, 48*(3), 216–222.

Brown, G. R., & Rundell, J. R. (1990). Prospective study of psychiatric morbidity in HIV-seropositive women without AIDS. *General Hospital Psychiatry, 12*, 30–35.

Butler, L. D., Koopman, C., Classen, C., & Spiegel, D. (1999). Traumatic stress, life events, and emotional support in women with metastatic breast cancer: Cancer-related traumatic stress symptoms associated with past and current stressors. *Health Psychology, 18*(6), 555–560.

Butler, R. W., Braff D. L., Rausch, J. L., Jenkins, M. A., Sprock, J., & Geyer, M. A. (1990). Physiological evidence of exaggerated startle response in a subgroup of Vietnam veterans with combat-related PTSD. *American Journal of Psychiatry, 147*, 1308–1312.

Carballo-Diéguez, A. & Dolezal, C. (1995). Association between history of childhood sexual abuse and adult HIV-risk sexual behavior in Puerto Rican men who have sex with men. *Child Abuse & Neglect, 19*(5), 595–605.

Carmen, E., & Rieker, P. (1989). A psychosocial model of the victim-to-patient process: Implications for treatment. *Psychiatric Clinics of North America, 12*(2), 431–443.

Catania, J., Coates, T., Kegeles, S., Fullilove, M. T., Peterson, J., Marin, B., et al. Condom use in multi-ethnic neighborhoods of San Francisco: The population-based AMEN (AIDS in multiethnic neighborhoods) study. *American Journal of Public Health, 82*, 284–287.

Cella, D. F., Mahon, S. M., & Donovan, M. I. (1990). Cancer recurrence as a traumatic event. *Behavioral Medicine, 16*(1), 15–22.

Centers for Disease Control and Prevention (CDC). (2001). Revised recommendations for HIV screening of pregnant women. *Morbidity & Mortality Weekly Report, 50*(No. RR-19), 63–85.

Centers for Disease Control and Prevention. (2002). Drug-associated HIV transmission continues in the United States. Retrieved December 18, 2004, from http://www.cdc.gov/hiv/pubs/facts/idu.htm

Centers for Disease Control & Prevention. (2003a). Advancing HIV prevention: New strategies for a changing epidemic—United States, 2003. *Morbidity & Mortality Weekly Report, 52*(15), 329–332.

Centers for Disease Control and Prevention. (2003b). HIV/AIDS Surveillance Report. Cases of HIV infection and AIDS in the United States, 2002. Retrieved December 23, 2003, from http://www.cdc.gov/hiv/stats/hasr1402.htm

Centers for Disease Control and Prevention. (2005). HIV/AIDS Surveillance Report. Cases of HIV infection and AIDS in the United States, 2004, 16. Retrieved November 5, 2006, from http://www.cdc.gov/hiv/topics/surveillance/resources/reports/2004report/pdf/2004SurveillanceReport.pdf

Centers for Disease Control and Prevention (2006). Revised Recommendations for HIV Testing of Adults, Adolescents, and Pregnant Women in Health-Care Settings.

MMWR *55*(RR14), 1–17. Retrieved March 29, 2007, from http://www.cdc.gov/mmwr/preview/mmwrhtml/rr5514a1.htm

Chesney, Margaret A. (1993). Health psychology in the 21st century: Acquired immunodeficiency syndrome as a harbinger of things to come. *Health Psychology* (American Psychological Association), *12* (4), 259–268.

Cohen, S., & Wills, T. A. (1985). Stress, social support, and the buffering hypothesis. *Psychological Bulletin*, *98*, 310–357.

Cole, S. W., & Kemeny, M. E. (1997). Psychobiology of HIV infection. *Critical Reviews in Neurobiology*, *11*, 289–321.

Cordova, M. J., & Andrykowski, M. A. (2003). Responses to cancer diagnosis and treatment: posttraumatic stress and posttraumatic growth. *Seminars in Clinical Neuropsychiatry*, *8*(4), 286–296.

Corley, P. A. (1995). HIV and the cortisol connection: A feasible concept of the process of AIDS. *Medical Hypotheses*, *44*, 483–489.

Crepaz, N., & Marks, G. (2002). Towards an understanding of sexual risk behavior in people living with HIV: A review of social, psychological, and medical findings. *AIDS*, *16*(2),135–149.

Deeks, S. G., Smith, M., Holodniy M., et al. (1997). HIV-1 protease inhibitors: A review for clinicians. *Journal of the American Medical Association,*, 277, 145–153.

Delahanty, D. L., Royer, D. K., Raimonde, A. J., & Spoonster, E. (2003). Peritraumatic dissociation is inversely related to catecholamine levels in initial urine samples of motor vehicle accident victims. *Journal of Trauma and Dissociation*, *4*(1), 65–80.

DesJarlais, D. C., & Friedman, S. R. (1988). The psychology of preventing AIDS among intravenous drug users. *American Psychologist*, *43*(11), 865–870.

DesJarlais, D. C., Friedman, S. R., & Casriel, C. (1990). Target groups for preventing AIDS among intravenous drug users: The "hard" data studies. *Journal of Consulting and Clinical Psychology*, *58*(1), 50–56.

Emini, E. A., Schleif, W. A., Deutsch, P., & Condra J. H. (1996). In vivo selection of HIV-1 variants with reduced susceptibility to the protease inhibitor L-735,524 and related compounds. *Advances in Experimental Medicine and Biology*, *394*, 327–31.

Evans, D. L., Leserman, J., Perkins, D. O., Murphy, C., Zheng, B., Gettes, D., et al. (1997). Severe life stress as a predictor of early disease progression in HIV infection. *American Journal of Psychiatry*, *154*, 630–634.

Fisher, J. D. (1988). Possible effects of reference group-based social influence on AIDS-risk behavior and AIDS-prevention. *American Psychologist*, *43*(11), 914–920.

Fullilove, M. T., Fullilove, R. E., Smith, M., Michael, C., Panzer, P. G., & Wallace, R. (1993). Violence, trauma, and post-traumatic stress disorder among women drug users. *Journal of Traumatic Stress*, *6*, 533–543.

Goodkin, K., Feaster, D. J., Asthana, D., Blaney, N. T., Kumar, M., Baldewicz, T., et al. (1998). A bereavement support group intervention is longitudinally associated with salutary effects on the CD4 cell count and number of physician visits. *Clinical & Diagnostic Laboratory Immunology*, *5*, 382–391.

Goodkin, K., Feaster, D. J., Tuttle, R., et al. (1996). Bereavement is associated with time-dependent decrements in cellular immune function in asymptomatic human immunodeficiency virus type 1-seropositive homosexual men. *Clinical & Diagnostic Laboratory Immunology*, *3*, 109–118.

Goodwin, P. J., Leszcz, M., Ennis, M., et al. (2001). The effect of group psychosocial support on survival in metastatic breast cancer. *New England Journal of Medicine*, *345*, 1719–1726.

Gore-Felton, C. (2000). Acute stress reactions among victims of violence: Assessment and treatment. *Directions in Psychiatry, 10*(1), 1–13.

Gore-Felton, C., Gill, M., Koopman, C., & Spiegel, D. (1999). Acute stress reactions among victims of violence: Implications for early intervention. *Aggression and Violent Behavior: A Review Journal, 4*, 293–306.

Gore-Felton, C., Kalichman, S. C., Brondino, M., Benotsch, E., Cage, M., & DiFonzo, K. (2006). Childhood sexual abuse and HIV risk among men who have sex with men: Initial test of a conceptual model. *Journal of Family Violence, 21*, 263–270.

Gore-Felton, C., & Koopman, C. (2002). Traumatic experiences: Harbinger of risk behavior among HIV-positive adults. *Journal of Trauma and Dissociation, 3*(4), 121–135.

Gore-Felton, C., Koopman, C., Turner-Cobb, J. M., Durán, R., Israelski, D., & Spiegel, D. (2002). The influence of social support, coping, and mood on sexual risk behavior among HIV-positive men and women. *Journal of Health Psychology, 7*(6), 713–722.

Gore-Felton, C., Rotheram-Borus, M. J., Kelly, J A., Weinhardt, L. S., Catz, S. L., Chesney, M A., et al. (2005). The Healthy Living Project: Individually-tailored multidimensional intervention for HIV-infected persons. *AIDS Education and Prevention, 17* (1, Suppl, A) 21–39.

Gore-Felton, C., Vosvick, M., Bendel, T., Koopman, C., Das, B., Israelski, D., et al. (2003). Correlates of sexually transmitted disease infection among adults living with HIV. *International Journal of STD & AIDS, 14*, 539–546.

Haynes, R. B., Sackett, D. L., & Taylor, D. W. (1980). How to detect and manage low patient compliance in chronic illness. *Geriatrics, 35* (91–3), 96–97.

He, H., McCoy, H. V., Stevens, S. J., & Stark, M. J. (1998). Violence and HIV sexual risk among female sex partners of male drug users. *Women & Health, 27*(1–2), 161–175.

Hearst, N., & Hulley, S. B. (1988). Preventing the heterosexual spread of AIDS: Are we giving our patients the best advice? *Journal of the American Medical Association, 259*(16), 2428–2432.

Hobfoll, S. E., Jackson, A. P., Lavin, J., Britton P. J., & Shepherd, J. B. (1994). Reducing inner-city women's AIDS risk activities: A study of single, pregnant women. *Health Psychology, 13*(5), 397–403.

Holmes, S. A. (1998, October 8). AIDS deaths in U.S. drop by nearly half as infections go on. *New York Times*, p. A1.

Jemmott, J. B., Jemmott, L., & Fong, G. T. (1998). Abstinence and safer sex HIV risk-reduction interventions for African-American adolescents: A randomised controlled trial. *Journal of the American Medical Association, 279*, 1529–1536.

Johnson, M. O., Catz, S. L., Remien, R. H., Rotheram-Borus, M. J., Morin, S. F., Charlebois, E., et al. (2003). Theory guided, empirically supported avenues for intervention on HIV medication nonadherence: Findings from the Healthy Living Project. *AIDS Patient Care and STDS, 17*(2), 645–656.

Jones, D. L. (1999). Conceptual structure of HIV+ women with PTSD: Trauma construct elaboration. *Dissertation Abstracts International, 59*(7-B).

Kalichman, S. C. (2000). HIV transmission risk behaviors of men and women living with HIV-AIDS: Prevalence, predictors and emerging clinical interventions. *Clinical Psychology: Science & Practice, 7*(1), 32–47.

Kalichman, S. C., Gore-Felton, C., Benotsch, E., Cage, M., & Rompa, D. (2004). Trauma symptoms, sexual behaviors, and substance abuse: correlates of childhood sexual abuse and HIV risks among men who have sex with men. *Journal of Child Sexual Abuse, 13*(1), 1–15.

Kalichman, S. C., Rompa, D., & Cage, M. (2000). Sexually transmitted infections among HIV seropositive men and women. *Sexually Transmitted Infections, 76*(5), 350–354.

Kasen, S., Vaughan, R. D., & Walter, H J. (1992). Self-efficacy for AIDS preventive behaviors among tenth grade students. *Health Education Quarterly, 19*(2), 187–202.

Katz, M. H., Schwarcz, S. K., Kellogg, T. A., Klausner, J. D., Dilley, J. W., Gibson, S., et al. (2002). Impact of highly active antiretroviral treatment on HIV seroincidence among men who have sex with men. *American Journal of Public Health, 92*(3), 388–389.

Keane, T. M., & Wolfe, J. (1990). Comorbidity in post-traumatic stress disorder: An analysis of community and clinical studies. *Journal of Applied Social Psychology, 50,* 138–140.

Kelly, J. A., Murphy, D. A., Bahr, G. R., Kalichman, S. C., Morgan, M. G., Stevenson, L. Y., et al. (1993a). Outcome of cognitive-behavioral and support group brief therapies for depressed, HIV-infected persons. *American Journal of Psychiatry, 150*(11), 1679–1686.

Kelly, J. A., Murphy, D. A., Bahr, G. R., Koob, J. J., Morgan, M. G., Kalichman, S. C., et al. (1993b). Factors associated with severity of depression and high-risk sexual behavior among persons diagnosed with HIV infection. *Health Psychology, 12,* 215–219.

Kelly, B., Raphael, B., Judd, F., Kernutt, G., Burnett, P., & Burrows, G. (1998). Posttraumatic stress disorder in response to HIV infection. *General Hospital Psychiatry, 20*(6), 345–352.

Kelly, B., Raphael, B., & Statham, D. (1996). A comparison of the psychosocial aspects of AIDS and cancer-related bereavement. *International Journal of Psychiatry in Medicine, 26,* 35–49.

Kimerling, R., Calhoun, K. S., Forehand, R., Armistead, L., Morse, E., Morse, P., et al. (1999). Traumatic stress in HIV-infected women. *AIDS Education and Prevention, 11*(4), 321–330.

Klein, S. J., & Birkhead, G. S. (2000). Domestic violence and HIV/AIDS, Letter to the Editor. *American Journal of Public Health, 90*(10), 1648.

Koopman, C., Butler, L. D., Classen, C., Giese-Davis, J., Morrow, G. R., Westendorf, J., et al. (2002). Traumatic stress symptoms among women with recently diagnosed primary breast cancer. *Journal of Traumatic Stress, 15*(4), 277–287.

Kulka, R. A., Schlenger, W. E., Fairbank, J. A., Hough, R. L., Jordan, B. K., & Marmar, C. R. (1990). *Trauma and the Vietnam War generation: Report of findings from the national Vietnam veterans' readjustment study.* New York: Brunner/Mazel.

Lemp, G. F., Hirozawa, A. M., Givertz, D., Nieri, G. N., Anderson, L., Lindegren, M. L., et al. (1994). Seroprevalence of HIV and risk behaviors among young homosexual and bisexual men: The San Francisco/Berkeley young men's survey. *Journal of the American Medical Association, 272*(6), 449–454.

Leserman, J., Petitto, J. M., Golden, R. N., Gaynes, B.N., Gu, H., Perkins, D.O., et al. (2000). Impact of stressful life events, depression, social support, coping, and cortisol on progression to AIDS. *American Journal of Psychiatry, 157,* 1221–1228.

Letellier, P. (1996). Twin epidemics: Domestic violence and HIV infection among gay and bisexual men. In C. M. Renzetti & C. H. Miley (Eds.), *Violence in gay and lesbian domestic partnerships* (pp. 69–81). New York: Haworth Press.

Lodico, M., & DiClemente, R. (1994). The association between childhood sexual abuse and HIV related risk behaviors. *Clinical Pediatrics, 33,* 498–502.

Lutgendorf, S. K., Antoni, M. H., Ironson, G., Klimas, N., Fletcher, M.A., & Schneiderman, N. (1997). Cognitive processing style, mood, and immune function following HIV seropositivity notification. *Cognitive Therapy & Research, 21,* 157–184.

Malik, M., & Camm, A. J. (1993). Components of heart rate variability: What they really mean and what we really measure. *American Journal of Cardiology, 72*, 821–822.

Markowitz, J. C., Klerman, G. L., & Perry, S. W. (1992). Interpersonal psychotherapy of depressed HIV-positive outpatients. *Hospital & Community Psychiatry, 43*(9), 885–890.

Martin, J. A., Smith B. L., Mathews, T. J., & Ventura, S. J. (1999). Births and deaths: preliminary data for 1998. *National Vital Statistics Reports, 47*(25), 1–8.

Mayne, T. J., Acree, M., Chesney, M. A., & Folkman, S. (1998). HIV sexual risk behavior following bereavement in gay men. *Health Psychology, 17*(5), 403–411.

McEwen, B. S. (1998). Protective and damaging effects of stress mediators. *New England Journal of Medicine, 338*, 171–179.

Messman, T. L., & Long, P. (1996). Child sexual abuse and its relationship to revictimization in adult women. A review. *Clinical Psychology Review, 16*(5), 397–420.

Metzger, L. J., Orr, S. P., Berry, N. J., Ahern, C. E., Lasko, N. B., & Pitman, R. K. (1999). Physiological reactivity to startling tones in women with PTSD. *Journal of Abnormal Psychology, 108*(2), 347–352.

Miller, M. (1999). A model to explain the relationship between sexual abuse and HIV risk among women. *AIDS Care, 11*(1), 3–20.

Nyamathi, A., Flaskerud, J., Leake, B., & Chen, S. (1996). Impoverished women at risk for AIDS: Social support variables. *Journal of Psychosocial Nursing, 34*, 31–39.

Orr, S. P., Lasko, N. B., Shalev, A. Y., & Pitman, R. K. (1995). Physiologic responses to loud tones in Vietnam veterans with posttraumatic stress disorder. *Journal of Abnormal Psychology, 104*(1), 75–82.

Ostrow, D. G., VanRaden, M. J., Fox, R. Kingsley, L. A., Dudley, J., & Kaslow, R. A. (1990). Recreational drug use and sexual behavior change in a cohort of homosexual men. *AIDS, 4*(8), 759–765.

Penkower K., Dew M. A., Kingsley, L., et al. (1991). Behavioral, health and psychosocial factors and risk for HIV infection among sexually active homosexual men: The multicenter AIDS cohort study. *American Journal of Public Health, 81*(2), 194–196.

Perry, S., Fishman, B., Jacobsberg, L., Young, J., et al. (1991). Effectiveness of psychoeducational interventions in reducing emotional distress after human immunodeficiency virus antibody testing. *Archives of General Psychiatry, 48*(2), 143–147.

Porges, S. W. (1995). Cardiac vagal tone: A physiological index of stress. *Neuroscience and Biobehavioral Reviews, 19*, 225–233.

Posener, J. A., Schildkraut, J. J., Samson, J. A., & Schatzberg, A. F. (1996). Diurnal variation of plasma cortisol and homovanillic acid in healthy subjects. *Psychoneuroendocrinology, 21*, 33–38.

Rabkin, J. G., & Ferrando, S. (1997). A "second life" agenda. Psychiatric research issues raised by protease inhibitor treatments for people with the human immunodeficiency virus or the acquired immunodeficiency syndrome. *Archives of General Psychiatry, 54*(11), 1049–1053.

Resnick, H. S., Kilpatrick, D. G., Dansky, B. S., Saunders, B. E., & Best, C. L. (1993). Prevalence of civilian trauma and posttraumatic stress disorder in a representative national sample of women. *Journal of Consulting & Clinical Psychology, 61*(6), 984–991.

Richardson, J., Schott, J., McGuigan, K., & Levine, A. (1987). Behavior change among homosexual college students to decrease risk for acquired immune deficiency syndrome. *Preventive Medicine, 16*, 285–286.

Rosenthal, D., Moore, S., & Flynn, I. (1991). Adolescent self-efficacy, self-esteem and sexual risk-taking. *Journal of Community & Applied Social Psychology, 1*(2), 77–88.

Rothbaum, B. O., Foa, E. B., Riggs, D. S., Murdock, T., & Walsh, W. (1992). A prospective examination of post-traumatic stress disorder in rape victims. *Journal of Traumatic Stress, 5*(3), 455–475.

Rotheram-Borus, M. J., Murphy, D. A., Miller, S., & Draimin, B. H. (1997). An intervention for adolescents whose parents are living with AIDS. *Clinical Child Psychology and Psychiatry, 2*, 201–219.

Rotheram-Borus, M. J., Rosario, M., Reid, H., & Koopman, C. (1995). Predicting patterns of sexual acts among homosexual and bisexual youths. *American Journal of Psychiatry, 152*(4), 588–595.

Russell, D.E.H. (1986). *The secret trauma: Incest in the lives of girls and women.* New York: Basic Books.

Sarna, L., Van Servellen, G. L., & Padilla, G. (1996). Comparison of emotional distress in men with acquired immunodeficiency syndrome and in men with cancer. *Applied Nursing Research, 9*, 209–212.

Saul, J. P., Berger, R. D., Albrecht, P., Stein, S. P., Chen, M. H., & Cohen, R. J. (1991). Transfer function analysis of the circulation: unique insights into cardiovascular regulation. *American Journal of Physiology, 261*, 1231–1245.

Shalev, A. Y., Orr, S. P., Peri, T., Schreiber, S., & Pitman, R. K. (1992). Physiologic responses to loud tones in Israeli patients with posttraumatic stress disorder. *Archives of General Psychiatry, 49*, 870–875.

Shalev, A. Y., & Yahuda, R. (1998). Longitudinal development of traumatic stress disorders. In R. Yahuda (Ed.), *Psychological trauma* (pp. 31–66). Washington, DC: American Psychiatric Press.

Spiegel, D. (2002). Effects of psychotherapy on cancer survival. *Nature Reviews Cancer, 2*, 383–389.

Stall, R., Ekstrand, M., Pollack, McKusick, L., & Coates, T. J. (1990). Relapse from safer sex: The next challenge for AIDS prevention efforts. *Journal of Acquired Immune Deficiency Syndromes, 3*(12), 1181–1187.

Strunin, L., & Hingson, R. (1992). Alcohol, drugs, and adolescent sexual behavior. *International Journal of the Addictions, 27*(2), 129–146.

Swanson, B., Zeller, J. M., & Spear, G. T. (1998). Cortisol upregulates HIV p24 antigen production in cultured human monocyte-derived macrophages. *Journal of the Association of Nurses in AIDS Care, 9*, 78–83.

Theorell, T., Blomkvist, V., Jonsson, H., Schulman, S., Berntorp, E., & Stegendal, L. (1995). Social support and the development of immune function in human immunodeficiency virus infection. *Psychosomatic Medicine, 57*, 32–36.

UNAIDS/WHO Joint United Nations Programme on HIV/AIDS. (2005, December). *Global Summary of the HIV/AIDS Epidemic, December 2005.* Geneva, Switzerland: UNAIDS/WHO.

Vanable, P. A., Ostrow, D. G., McKirnan, D. J., Taywaditep, K. J., & Hope, B. A. (2000). Impact of combination therapies on HIV risk perceptions and sexual risk among HIV-positive and HIV-negative gay and bisexual men. *Health Psychology, 19*(2), 134–145.

Vittinghoff, E., Scheer, S., O'Malley, P., Colfax, G., Holmberg, S. D., & Buchbinder, S. P. (1999). Combination antiretroviral therapy and recent declines in AIDS incidence and mortality. *Journal of Infectious Diseases 179*(3), 717–20.

Walter, H. J., Vaughan, R. D., Gladis, M. M., Ragin, D. F., Kasen, S., & Cohall, A. T. (1993). Factors associated with AIDS-related behavioral intentions among high school students in an AIDS epicenter. *Health Education Quarterly, 20*(3), 409–420.

Weiss, D. S., Marmar, C. R., Schlenger, W. E., Fairbank, J. A., Jordan, B. K., Hough, R. L. et al. (1992). The prevalence of lifetime and partial post-traumatic stress disorder in Vietnam theater veterans. *Journal of Traumatic Stress, 5*(3), 365–376.

Whitmire, L. E., Harlow, L. L., Quina, K., & Morokoff, P. J. (1999). *Childhood trauma and HIV: Women at risk.* Philadelphia: Brunner/Mazel.

Williams, C. L., Haines, J., & Sale, I. M. (2003). Psychophysiological and psychological correlates of dissociation in a case of dissociative identity disorder. *Journal of Trauma and Dissociation, 4*(1), 101–118.

Yasuma, F. & Hayano, J. (2004). Respiratory sinus arrhythmia: Why does the heartbeat synchronize with respiratory rhythm? *Chest, 125,* 683–690.

Yehuda, R., McFarlane, A. C., & Shalev, A. Y. (1998). Predicting the development of post-traumatic stress disorder from the acute response to traumatic event. *Biological Psychiatry, 44,* 1305–1313.

Zierler, S., Cunningham, W. E., Anderson, R., Shapiro, M. F., Bozzette, S. A., Nakazono, T. M., et al. Violence victimization after HIV infection in a US probability sample of adult patients in primary care. *American Journal of Public Health, 90*(2), 208–215.

Zierler, S., Feingold, L., Laufer, D., Velentgas, P., Kantrowitz-Gordon, I., & Mayer, K. (1991). Adult survivors of childhood sexual abuse and subsequent risk of HIV infection. *American Journal of Public Health, 81,* 572–575.

Zoellner, L. A., Fitzgibbons, L. A., & Foa, E. B. (2001). Cognitive behavioral approaches to PTSD. In J. P. Wilson, M. J. Friedman, & J. D. Lindy (Eds.), *Treating psychological trauma and PTSD* (pp. 159–182). New York: Guilford Press.

CHAPTER 6

EMOTIONAL TRAUMA FOLLOWING BURN INJURY IN CHILDREN

Rhonda S. Robert

In 1947, one of the most significant industrial disasters in the United States occurred in the Texas City port. A ship carrying 7,700 tons of ammonium nitrate caught fire and exploded. The explosion blew nearly 6,350 tons of the ship's steel into the air at supersonic speed, causing a number of other fires and explosions, including a fire on a second ship carrying a large amount of ammonium nitrate and sulfur. The official death toll was 581. Five thousand were injured, and 1,784 were admitted to 21 area hospitals (Minutaglio, 2003). Many of the Texas City disaster burn injury survivors were cared for at the University of Texas Medical Branch (UTMB). The extensive clinical experience gained due to this disaster by medical professionals resulted in significant advances in burn care.

Given the excellent care for adults at the University of Texas Medical Branch Blocker Burn Unit and the potential for shared resources, the Shriners of North America built their first burns institute in Galveston, Texas, in 1966.[1]

Improving the survival rates of persons who sustained major burn injuries became a major medical focus. As survival rates improved, quality of life issues became more salient. The mental health clinicians were integrated into the burn care team and psychosocial research followed.

Posttraumatic stress is one of the most commonly occurring psychiatric symptoms experienced by the burn injury survivor (Thomas, Meyer, & Blakeney, 2002) and is the primary focus of this chapter. In the initial portion of the chapter, background literature on burn trauma is summarized. This is followed by clinical considerations, a case vignette, and policy recommendations.

Background Literature on Traumatic Stress in Burn Injury

Persons who survive trauma frequently report symptoms of emotional distress. Symptoms of both acute stress disorder (ASD), which are present during the first month following a traumatic event, and posttraumatic stress disorder (PTSD), which describes stress symptoms occurring after one month, will be discussed in terms of burn injury.

Traumatic stressors experienced by the burn injury survivor may be numerous and ongoing. In addition to the injury event, the burn injury survivor experiences pain throughout the period of acute physical healing, and may experience long-term changes in physical abilities and the permanent social stigmatization of scarring (Thomas et al., 2002). The life-saving medical procedures themselves are often experienced as traumatic (Stuber, Shemesh, & Saxe, 2003). Given the uniqueness of the burn injury event and long-term traumatic losses, treatment and recovery expectations derived from other populations may not generalize to this population. However, information based on other populations may be informative.

Lifetime prevalence estimates for PTSD in adults vary. Variance is largely attributed to sampling and assessment methods (Meichenbaum, 1994). Estimates of lifetime prevalence of PTSD in the adult population of the United States based on community-based studies vary from 8 percent (American Psychiatric Association, 2000) to 25 percent (Robins, Helzer, Croughan, & Ratcliff, 1981), making it one of the most common psychiatric disorders in the United States. No estimate of lifetime prevalence for ASD has been established. However, there have been studies of the prevalence of ASD after some events such as road traffic accidents.

People respond to trauma differently. Investigators have explored a dose-response relationship between trauma severity and distress response. Sustaining physical injury and the extent of that injury (Kilpatrick et al., 1989), encountering the grotesque and macabre (Green, 1991), enduring physical torture (Thygesen, Hermann, & Willanger, 1970), loss of a loved one in the trauma event, and prolonged events (Horowitz, 1986) are aspects of the dose-response relationship that have been considered.

Dose variables and the ASD response have not been reported in the literature. Regarding the PTSD response, the dose variables in burn injury that have been considered include percentage of total body surface area burn, length of hospitalization, visible disfigurement, digital amputation, age, gender, and electrical versus thermal burn injury. The findings are equivocal for these variables (Baur et al., 1998). Patterson, Carrigan, Questad, & Robinson (1992) and van Loey, Maas, Faber, & Taal (2003) found patients' total body surface area burn and length of hospital stay to be associated with PTSD. In contrast, El Hamaoui and colleagues (2002), Powers and colleagues (1994), and Perry and colleagues (1992) all reported no relationship between development of PTSD and length of hospitalization or severity of burn. Tedstone and Tarrier (1997) found that patients with small burn injuries of 1 percent or less experienced clinically significant levels of psychological difficulties post-burn. In children between the ages of 12 and 48 months, size of the burn was related to PTSD (Stoddard et al., 2006). Perhaps the burn survivor's perception is as important as the size of the burn. For the adult, perception may be primarily focused on threat to body integrity, while the toddler's perception may be more closely linked to physiological pain.

The relationship between PTSD and visible burn disfigurement has also been studied. Madianos, Papaghelis, Ioannovick, & Dafni (2001) found facial disfigurement to be the only burn characteristic significantly associated with the presence of psychiatric problems and illness. Williams and Griffiths (1991) found visibility of the burn to be a useful factor in the prediction of psychological outcome. Taal and Faber (1998) counter these findings. In their study of 174 participants, visibility of the burn scars was not a predictor of pathological feelings.

No results were found regarding major limb amputation. Fukunishi (1999) addressed digital amputation. Japanese women with digital amputation were at risk of developing PTSD. Emotional problems associated with digital amputation would lead one to suspect that a limb amputation would be a major risk factor for emotional adjustment post-burn injury.

Frequency of PTSD in those with electrical burn injury as compared to those thermally injured was not uncovered in the literature. Mancusi-Ungaro, Tarbox, and Wainwright (1986) compared emotional problems, but not PTSD specifically, in electrical and thermal injuries. Those with electrical injuries scored differently on the Minnesota Multiphasic Personality Inventory from those with thermal injuries. Graham (1987) reported that the differences may be tapping cognitive problems post-electrical injury, but do not establish PTSD. Other investigators have concluded that emotional problems are associated with electrical injury, but have not utilized a thermally injured comparison group (Hooshmand, Radfar, & Beckner, 1989). Premalatha (1994), Laforce and colleagues (2000), and van Zomeren and colleagues (1998) presented case studies in which a person with electrical shock developed PTSD.

In the literature specific to pediatric burn survivors, the relationship between age and PTSD is mixed. In a sample inclusive of children and adults, El Hamaoui et al. (2002) found that PTSD was related to being of a younger age, whereas Kravitz et al. (1993) found no relationship between age at time of burn and the incidence of nightmares. With a nonburned population of Hurricane Andrew survivors, Garrison et al. (1995) found that PTSD increased with age in an adolescent sample. Perhaps a relationship between PTSD and age exists, though not linear in nature. For example, at certain developmental stages, individuals may be more susceptible to the occurrence of PTSD than at other stages. The relationship between PTSD and age warrants further investigation in future research.

The relationship between gender and PTSD has also been examined. In burn survivors, Patterson et al. (1992) studied a U.S. sample in which female patients were more likely to have PTSD. In other cultures, the results have varied. In a

Moroccan burn survivor population, El Hamaoui et al. (2002) found no relationship between PTSD and gender. In a Japanese sample, female burn survivors
were at greater risk for PTSD (Fukunishi, 1999). In a Dutch sample, female gender was associated with PTSD (van Loey et al, 2003). In a community-based
sample of adults from the United States, Kessler (1995) found that 20 percent of
women exposed to a trauma developed PTSD, compared to 8 percent of men.

Ethnic group relationship to the occurrence of PTSD in burn survivors is not
known. Some information is known about the relationship between ethnic group
and the occurrence of PTSD in veterans and disaster survivors, though the findings are mixed. In some samples of combat veterans, occurrence of PTSD was
similar across ethnic groups (Penk et al., 1989; Zatzick, Marmar, Weis, & Metzler,
1994). In contrast, a sample of Puerto Rican Vietnam veterans had a higher risk
for PTSD and experienced more severe PTSD symptoms than white, non-
Hispanic Vietnam veterans, and these differences were not explained by exposure to stressors or acculturation (Ortega & Rosenheck, 2000). Hispanic ethnicity
was a predictor of PTSD in the neighborhoods near to the 9/11 terrorist attacks
(Galea et al., 2002). In addition to different rates of expression, PTSD might also
be expressed differently between ethnic groups. Norris, Perilla, and Murphy
(2001) found that symptom expression was different between Mexican and
American groups. The Mexican sample was higher in intrusion and avoidance
symptoms, whereas the U.S. sample was higher in arousal symptoms.

Others have suggested that event and injury characteristics will not fully
explain why some persons experience PTSD and others do not. For example, in
a diathesis-stress model, the individual's characteristics and long-standing environmental elements, rather than the event characteristics, are emphasized (Butler,
Koopman, Classen, & Spiegel, 1999). Experiencing a traumatic event is not necessarily associated with negative psychological outcomes or psychiatric disorders.

Some survivors report positive outcomes of surviving extreme stress (Frankl,
1959). Researchers have found a number of ways to describe positive outcomes,
including benefit finding (Tomich & Helgeson, 2004), posttraumatic growth
(Ickovics et al., 2006), and stress-related growth (Frazier & Kaler, 2006).

The diathesis-stress model does not discount the dose-response relationship,
but highlights the importance of taking into consideration a person's personal
characteristics and factors in the person's environment. Variables of interest
include the following:

- Social support (Bum-Hee & Dimsdale, 1999; Buckley, Blanchard & Hickling,
  1996; Gilboa, 2001; Perry et al., 1992)
- Coping style (Fauerbach, Richter, & Laurence, 2002; Lawrence & Fauerbach,
  2003)
- Attribution of responsibility (Lambert, Difede, & Contrada, 2004)
- Dimensions of personality (with special interest in introversion/extroversion;
  Taal & Faber, 1998)
- Pre-event trauma history and pre- and posttrauma mental health (with special
  interest in mood disorders; Bum-Hee & Dimsdale, 1999; Fauerbach et al., 1997)

- Anxiety disorders and enuresis (Stoddard, Norman, Murphy, & Beardslee, 1989)
- Substance abuse and attention problems (Caffo & Belaise, 2003)
- Cognitive style (e.g., locus of control; Harvey & Bryant, 1999)
- Relationship between children's symptoms and trauma-related symptoms in parents (Kratochwill, 1996)
- Fear of dying during the traumatic event and initiation of litigation (Blanchard et al., 1996)
- Level of hypnotizability (Bryant, Guthrie, Moulds, Nixon, & Felmingham, 2003; DuHamel, Difede, Foley, & Greenleaf, 2002).

In a study conducted at Shriners Burns Hospital in Galveston, Texas, a negative relationship was found between psychological history (i.e., abuse, neglect, or a mental disorder) and response to pharmacotherapy treatment for acute stress disorder. If the patient had a significant psychological history, the patient was significantly less likely to respond to treatment.

Since 1995, burn survivors at Shriners Hospital–Galveston have been assessed for acute stress disorder (ASD) throughout hospitalization. About 9 percent of that acutely injured population experienced ASD. What distinguishes the 9 percent of the group who present with ASD from the remainder of the population is not known. How the trauma is evidenced across time post-burn is also unclear. The research literature is limited regarding childhood trauma, course of ASD, effects of early treatment, and the relationship between ASD and PTSD (Bryant & Harvey, 1997; Marshall, Spitzer, & Liebowitz, 1999). In child-based studies, parents have been asked to retrospectively describe how their child fared after a traumatic event (Harvey & Bryant, 2000). Retrospective studies lack generalizability, given the influence of current symptoms on recall of acute symptoms. Knowledge gleaned from parent versus child reports also lacks generalizability given the disparity between reporters of internalized emotional experiences (Davis et al., 2000).

The development of trauma symptoms in the burn survivor after the acute hospitalization should be assessed. Delayed onset PTSD is seen in 7–30 percent of the adult populations sampled (Buckley et al., 1996; Pfefferbaum, 1997). Richard Bryant (1996) found that one-third of burn survivors develop posttraumatic stress disorder within two years of their injury. Delayed onset of PTSD is defined as a minimum of 6 months posttrauma before symptoms develop.

PTSD can be enduring and debilitating (Rothbaum, Foa, Riggs, Murdock, & Walsh, 1992). For adult burn survivors in the Netherlands who were one to two years post-burn, symptoms of PTSD were the most important predictor in the desire for burn-specific aftercare (van Loey et al., 2001). Though spontaneous remission occurs in about half the adult population, the other half have enduring concerns. Remission in children is less well understood, though war-related studies indicate that 26–31 percent of children sampled had PTSD 6–10 years post-event (Sack et al., 1993). Given this delayed expression of emotional trauma and the long-standing potential for the symptoms seen in adults and children surviving war, long-term evaluation of burn injury survivors is desired.

Clinicians treating persons posttrauma suspected that early treatment of ASD would have prevented PTSD, and initial studies of adults receiving early treatment showed remission of symptoms (Cardena et al., 1998). Early treatment was also supported by reports that early occurrence of trauma symptoms was predictive of the development of later PTSD in adults (Liebowitz et al., 1998). In subsequent studies, no relationship between the occurrence of ASD and PTSD has been detected, raising doubts about the positive effect of early treatment on subsequent expression of PTSD (Foa, Keane, & Friedman, 2000).

In adults sustaining burn injuries, Ehde, Patterson, Wiechman, & Wilson (2000) found that PTSD symptoms at one month postinjury were the only significant predictor of posttraumatic stress symptoms at one year. Difede and colleagues (2002) found that hospitalized adult burn patients who were diagnosed with ASD were at high risk for chronic PTSD.

For traumatized children, the impact of early intervention is not known (Cohen, Mannarino, & Deblinger, 2006). In a study of long-term psychosocial sequelae of pediatric burn injuries, an unusually high incidence of anxiety disorders other than posttraumatic stress disorder has been reported. Blakeney, Thomas, Berniger, Holzer, & Meyer (2001) sampled 50 adolescent burn survivors who were described by their parents as distressed. This sample was biased in that only survivors who were identified as distressed by their parents were represented. However, the information captures the nature of the symptoms experienced by adolescent burn survivors. Anxiety disorders were the most common diagnoses with 34 percent of this sample reporting one or more anxiety disorders. In this study, the Computerized Diagnostic Interview Schedule for Children (C-DISC) was the structured diagnostic tool utilized. Psychiatric disorders were recorded for the past six months. All were at least two years postburn. Forty percent did not meet the criteria for a psychiatric diagnosis, while the other 60 percent met the criteria for one to three disorders. Anxiety disorders were the most commonly described, including agoraphobia, separation anxiety, social phobia, specific phobia, obsessive compulsive disorder, general anxiety, panic disorder, and posttraumatic stress.

Additional long-term follow-up data are needed to increase understanding of the unique distress of traumatized children by providing necessary information to clarify the complex relationships between stress exposure, ASD, PTSD, and person-environment variables.

Clinical Course of Care

Assessment of Preexisting Mental Health Problems

Accidents occur. Many injuries occur irrespective of the survivor's behavior. Blame is not ascribed to victims of burn injury. For some, however, premorbid mental health problems increase the risk of likelihood of injury. For example, adult burn survivors are more likely to have substance abuse problems or mood disorders as compared to the general population (Patterson et al., 2003). Children and adolescents are more likely to have problems of inattention and poor impulse control (including attention deficit/hyperactivity disorder; Thomas, Ayoub, Rosenberg, Robert, & Meyer, 2004), substance abuse (especially use of flammable inhalants), mood disorders, developmental disorders, cognitive impairment, and behavior problems (including oppositional defiant disorder and conduct disorder; Thomas et al., 2002). In rare instances, self-immolation as a suicide attempt is seen (Stoddard, 1993; Stoddard, Pahlavan, & Cahners, 1985). Thus, screening for preexisting mental health disorders in burn-injured patients is an essential beginning to treatment.

Fire setting is a noteworthy behavior that requires thorough assessment and intervention (Kolko, 2000; Wilcox & Kolko, 2002). The problem behavior of fire setting varies in nature. Based on the teachings of David Wilcox (2000), the Texas state fire marshal, Juvenile Fire Setting Division, utilizes the following categories for fire-setting types: curious, crisis, delinquent, and pathological. The curious fire setter is typically in the preschool age range. The curious fire setter is motivated to explore the environment. Based on the consequence of the action, the likelihood of repeating the behavior will be increased or decreased to the point of habituation or extinction. School-age children typically exhibit crisis fire setting. In this case, fire setting is a behavioral manifestation of distressing emotions. The fire may serve as an outcry or an attempt to garner the assistance of others in the child's crisis. The child may also find the fire soothes feelings of distress, eliciting feelings of power, warmth, and calm. The fire can induce a trance-like state , similar to that elicited by visual imagery or hypnosis. The older school-age child typically exhibits delinquent fire setting. Delinquent fire setting may be a manifestation of habituated misbehavior, with the intent to belong and be recognized (Wilcox, 2000). Fire involvement is a misbehavior that can result in attention, power, retribution, peer acceptance, and excitement. Delinquent fire setting may also be attributed to unmanaged problems of poor impulse control, for example, attention deficit/hyperactivity disorder, and bipolar mood disorder. The older teenager typically exhibits pathological fire setting. The goals of pathological fire setting vary and include suicide or suicide attempt, homicide or homicide attempt, pyromania, and arson. The pleasure or relief when setting a fire motivates pyromania. Arson is motivated by the potential for monetary gain or improvement in living circumstances. In a sample of 796 admissions between 2000 and 2002 at Shriners Hospital–Galveston, 11 percent (n = 88) were due to fire setting. Of these 88, 67 percent (n = 59) were curious, 10 percent (n = 9) crisis, 17 percent (n = 15) delinquent, and 6 percent (n = 5) pathological (Robert, Rosenberg, Rosenberg, & Meyer, 2004).

Assessment and treatment for fire-setting behavior is not commonly taught in traditional mental health training programs and is an area in which to develop skills if working with the burn trauma population. According to the prevalence estimate noted above, more than 1 out of every 10 pediatric burn patients were injured due to fire setting. No evidence has been found that a burn injury brings an end to problem fire-setting behaviors. Thus, the problem behavior of fire

setting is a primary component of psychological assessment and treatment with
a pediatric burn survivor population.

One resource for cross training and referral can be found through fire departments. Juvenile fire setting prevention programs are available through fire
departments across the nation. The S.O.S. Fires Youth Intervention Program
has an online database at www.sosfires.com, on which prevention programs
across the nation are listed. Package programs are available for those interested
in developing assessment and intervention skills or a fire-setting prevention program for the local community. One such program has been created and determined to be effective by Irene Pinsonneault (2002c), and the related materials are
sold through Fire Solutions in Fall River, Massachusetts. The intervention is
formatted for eight weekly sessions and available for pre-school-aged children,
school-aged children, and adolescents. Franklin and colleagues (2002) as well as
Kolko (2001) have tested efficacious treatment interventions. Barry Bennett, the
burn team social worker at Loyola University Medical Center, and his colleagues,
Gamelli, Duchene, Atkocaitis, and Plunkett (2004) created and established the
efficacy of a juvenile fire setter assessment and treatment program entitled Burn
Education Awareness Recognition and Support (BEARS). Fire and burn injury
safety, product regulations and design issues, and criminal acts are also aspects
of burn trauma. Regarding fire and burn injury safety, some persons do not have
an emotional, cognitive, or behavior disorder but act without understanding the
physical laws of fire. For example, a child who is learning to mow the lawn
naively pours gas into a hot lawnmower. Education regarding fire and burn
injury safety would likely prevent such an accident. Given the preventable nature
of injuries such as these, burn care professionals including mental health professionals provide community-based fire and burn injury safety education. The second week of October is fire safety week and the first week of February is burn
awareness week. Both are perfect opportunities for community educational
involvement.

Product regulations and design issues are also highlighted in a thorough pre-
history interview and assessment. Though the attention of the mental health
professional is directed toward the psychological adjustment of the patient post-
burn injury, the information gleaned from the psychological interview is pertinent to safety standards and policies. Clothing, household appliances, and
building features and materials are commonly questioned in the occurrence of
burn injury, despite current safety standards and policies. Working with the professionals at the Consumer Product Safety Commission can be helpful in both
clinical and research-related work. Clinically, people ask the question, "Why
me?" After an accident, persons seek meaning in traumatic events. Some people
answer that question by taking a role in making the world a safer place. Many
patients report giving talks, writing articles, and teaching others about lessons
learned through their burn injury trauma. If this is an aspect of personal adjustment posttrauma, placing a report on an injury through the Consumer Product

Safety Commission can serve an emotionally therapeutic purpose. Patient or caregiver online reporting is encouraged at www.cpsc.gov.

Some burn injuries are caused by a criminal act by a third party. The trauma is twofold. Both the injurious event and the betrayal by another are traumatic. Vulnerable persons are abused by burning, including children, disabled people, and the elderly. Assault, arson, and attempted murder, though less common, are examples of crimes that result in a burn injury. The prevalence of children abused by burning is staggering. In one sample at the Shriners Hospital–Galveston, 22 percent of the children who were hospitalized for burn injuries were suspected of having been injured by maltreatment, including abuse and neglect. The reported range is as high as 30 percent (Bennett & Gamelli, 1998). For the clinician completing the history, the risk for abuse and neglect needs to be thoroughly assessed. Assessing for abuse and neglect has been described in a chapter on child maltreatment in the third edition of *Total Burn Care* (Robert, Blakeney, & Herndon, 2006). Identifying possible abuse and neglect is necessary both for the personal safety of the patient and for emotional recovery from trauma.

A thorough preinjury history is the first step in providing comprehensive psychological services. Those who have a significant premorbid mental health problem will have more challenges in trauma recovery (Fauerbach, Lawrence, Haythornthwaite, McGuire, & Munster, 1996). Given the intertwined nature of premorbid mental health problems and posttrauma recovery, both should be treated.

Assessment and Treatment of Emotional Trauma

Trauma in a child impacts the entire family. Traumatic distress in one family member is associated with traumatic distress in other family members. Family-based services are optimal and thus both caregivers and survivors are addressed in the following section.

Recommendations for the Treatment of Caregivers

Trauma symptoms are reported as common and severe in caregivers (Stuber et al., 2003). Family stress and caregiver stress are predictive of acute stress symptoms in children hospitalized with injuries (Saxe et al., 2005). Given the high risk for caregiver trauma and the impact of caregiver trauma on the child's emotional recovery, early intervention is recommended. The caregiver is usually available to be seen before the patient, as the patient receives medical evaluation and treatment upon arrival. Caregivers typically describe dissociative symptoms and hypervigilance, as well as survivor guilt. Posttraumatic stress symptoms can be disruptive to a parent's feeling of being capable of caring for a burn-injured child (Rizzone, Stoddard, Murphy, & Kruger, 1994). For example, a parent's anxiety is associated with increased parent-child conflict and conflict with the extended family (Hall et al., 2006). Interventions should be aimed at decreasing parental distress. The following are recommended:

- Normalize trauma response as a normal person's reaction to an abnormal event.
- Provide structure and reassurance without establishing false expectations.
- Educate the caregiver on common trauma reactions. Knowing what is normal allays fears about losing one's mind or identity.
- Keep interventions simple and relevant to the next 24 hours, as a person's ability to attend to and learn new information is compromised by the emotional trauma and physical exhaustion related to rescue efforts. For example, traumatic stress symptoms that might negatively impact the caregiver in the next 24 hours should be described, for example, insomnia, loss of appetite.
- Predict the likely symptoms and provide suggestions as to how to cope effectively with the symptoms likely to occur within the next 24 hours.
- Guide the caregiver in helping the patient within the bounds of the caregiver's capacity.

Many caregivers need to be desensitized to the stimuli associated with burn injury. Desensitization is the process of gradually introducing anxiety-provoking stimuli so that a person increases tolerance and is able to approach that which was previously overwhelming and distressing. Desensitization is most commonly described in phobia research and well established as effective in decreasing anxiety (Taylor, 2006). The clinician can help with the desensitization of the caregiver by understanding the caregiver's apprehension about visiting the patient. After the concerns are elicited, the clinician can make suggestions regarding gradual exposure, attention and neglect, and competent caregiving goals. Gradual exposure might involve the caregiver sitting outside the room and incrementally moving closer to the patient. The clinician might accompany the caregiver to coach the caregiver as needed. The clinician can prompt the caregiver as to what is important to acknowledge and what can be ignored for the time being. For example, making eye contact with the patient calms many caregivers. Touching the patient can also be comforting to both the patient and the caregiver. A common location spared from injury is the top of the head. The importance of caregiver presence is complemented with words of reassurance that describe the caregiver's availability and love for the patient and the patient's current safety. Many caregivers fear that the patient will ask a difficult question for which they are not prepared. The most important rule is to be truthful. Establishing a false expectation can be more damaging than speaking the truth. The patient needs to be able to trust the caregiver during this time. The caregiver is a port in the storm. Caregivers may fear that the truth will be an assault to the patient. The caregiver may not know how to state the difficult answer and may not be emotionally prepared. When a need exists to balance truth with preparedness, the patient may be provided with incomplete answers. The information that is provided establishes a foundation for the remaining information. Another option is for the caregiver to validate the importance of the question, acknowledge not having an answer, reassure the patient that someone does have the answer, and note that the caregiver will secure the answer for the patient. The caregiver is encouraged to bring the question to the clinician, who can help the caregiver develop both an answer and a method by which to deliver the answer.

The delivery of distressing answers deserves consideration (Matsakis, 1996). The traumatic loss information should be embedded in a narrative that includes a beginning. The events preceding the trauma need to be recalled, including routinized aspects of daily living and the presence of caring others. The trauma event needs a label, and the patient's injury consequent to the trauma needs to be stated. Thereafter, the rescue efforts and the personnel involved, as well as current safety status, should be emphasized. The love and reassurance embedded in rescue offset the impact of the traumatic events.

Many clinical techniques utilized with those traumatized by burn injury can be derived from non–burn specific trauma literature. Comprehensive books for clinicians include *Effective Treatments for PTSD: Practice Guidelines from the International Society for Traumatic Stress Studies* (Foa et al., 2000); *Clinician's Guide to PTSD: A Cognitive-Behavioral Approach* (Taylor, 2006); and *Treating Trauma and Traumatic Grief in Children and Adolescents* (Cohen, Mannarino, & Deblinger, 2006).

Recommendations for the Assessment and Treatment of Children

At this time, there is no profile that can reliably predict which patients will suffer which mental health problems at which time points in the future (Thomas et al., 2002). For this reason, all patients should have access to mental health services. Throughout the course of recovery, traumatic stress symptoms should be assessed for both caregivers and patients, including toddlers and pre-school-age children. Children as young as one year of age can be reliably assessed, as recently described in a series of articles by Fred Stoddard, Glenn Saxe, and colleagues (see two articles by Stoddard and colleagues published in 2006).

Intrusion symptoms (reliving the event) are the most salient trauma symptoms in the medically ill child (Shemesh et al., 2006). Nightmares and altered sleep patterns are usually the symptoms first noted by the burn-injured patient (Robert, Blakeney, Villarreal, Rosenberg, & Meyer, 1999). Utilizing a numeric rating subsequent to endorsement of an item adds to the ability to monitor changes in distress level. A number of assessment tools are available and a sampling follows. The first two tools are specific to the burn patient population.

> "About Your Burn Injury" (see Shakespeare, 1998) is a 10-item questionnaire developed at the Odsstock Burns Unit. No reliability and validity data were found. The self-completion questionnaire assesses self-perception of physical, social, and psychological functions specific to burn rehabilitation.
> The "Child Stress Disorders Checklist" (Saxe et al., 2003) is a new measure that holds promise in use with burned patients. The items are specific to burn trauma and recovery, and this checklist is the only standardized, burn-specific measure available.
> The "University of California at Los Angeles Post-Traumatic Stress Disorder Reaction Index" (Steinberg, Brymer, Decker, & Pynoos, 2004) is a widely used

structured interview for diagnosing childhood PTSD. Investigators have used the 20-item test to assess children who witnessed sexual assaults on their mothers, who were exposed to gunfire, and who were injured in a severe boating accident. Adults can also complete this scale. The children's version has simplified wording appropriate for the language capacities of school-age children, and the scale has been modified to enable diagnosis. A parallel form is available for questioning parents about symptoms exhibited by their traumatized children. Both instruments have well-established validity and reliability and are frequently utilized by investigators of childhood PTSD.

The "Children's Impact of Events Scale" (C-IES) (Yule, 1990) includes subscales for intrusion and avoidance and is used to assess posttraumatic symptoms in children. This measure was adapted from the well-established adult version and has been established as equivalent. Nelson is the vendor.

The "Trauma Symptom Checklist for Children" (TSCC; Briere, 1996) is a self-report for children aged 8 to 16 years of age who have experienced traumatic events. The 54-item TSCC includes two validity scales (Underresponse and Hyperresponse), five clinical scales (Anxiety, Depression, Anger, Posttraumatic Stress, Dissociation), and eight critical items. The TSCC scales are internally consistent (alpha coefficients for clinical scales range from .77–.89 in the standardization sample) and exhibit reasonable convergent, discriminant, and predictive validity in normative and clinical samples. This test has been translated into Spanish. PAR is the vendor.

The "Children's PTSD Inventory—A Structured Interview for Diagnosing Posttraumatic Stress Disorder in Children and Adolescents" (Saigh, 2004) is a structured interview for children aged 6 through 18 years. The items directly correspond to the *DSM-IV* diagnostic criteria for PTSD. The inventory is currently available in English and Spanish. Harcourt is the distributor.

"When Bad Things Happen" and "Parent Report of the Child's Reaction to Stress" (Fletcher, 1992) are parallel child and parent interviews used to diagnose disorders and emotional responses posttrauma. Internal consistency was uniformly high for all scales (.89–.94). Convergent and divergent validity have been established (Fletcher, 1996). Both child and parent interviews are available in Spanish.

Other Aspects of Mental Health Care during Acute Hospitalization

During the acute phase of treatment, the physical and emotional recovery processes are intertwined. For example, emotional trauma is recurrent and trauma responses are rekindled if the pain and anxiety specific to physical treatment are unmanaged (Stoddard, Saxe, Ronfeldt, Drake, Edgren, Sheridan, 2006a; Saxe et al., 2005).

Assessment and management of pain and anxiety require an interdisciplinary team, including physicians, nurses, physical therapists, mental health professionals, and pharmacists. Background pain, procedural pain, generalized hospital anxiety, preprocedural anxiety, and procedural anxiety need to be assessed and treated consistently. Assessment and treatment guidelines improve care and, consequently, pain and anxiety management protocols are recommended (Patterson, Tininenko, & Ptacek, 2006; Patterson, Hofland, Espey, & Sharaar, 2004; Ratcliff, Brown, Rosenberg, Rosenberg, Robert, & Cuervo, 2006; Sheridan, Hinson, Nackel, Blaquiere, Daley, Querzoli, et al., 1997).

Psychological techniques for acute pain and anxiety management complement pharmacotherapy. Psychological preparation can greatly reduce anticipatory anxiety. Procedural and sensory preparatory information strategies are particularly effective techniques (Everett, Patterson, & Chen, 1990). Procedural-based preparatory information is focused on the mechanics of the procedure. With sensory information, common patient feeling states are described. The cognitive behavioral techniques included in types of relaxation training (e.g., deep breathing, visual imagery, progressive muscle relaxation, hypnosis) have been shown to counteract procedural anxiety and thus minimize the cyclical interaction between anxiety and acute pain (Cromes, McDonald, & Robinson, 1980; Knudson-Cooper, 1981). The cognitive aspects of interpreting painful stimuli affect pain perception (Patterson, 1995). For example, if pain is equated with death, perceived pain increases; however, when pain is equated with cleaning and healing, perceived pain decreases. Another cognitive behavioral strategy found to be effective in reducing perceived pain involves patient participation in decision making during wound care (Kavanaugh, Lasoft, & Eide, 1991).

With procedural pain and anxiety managed, traumatic stress symptoms can be addressed (Tcheung, Robert, Rosenberg, Rosenberg, Villarreal, & Thomas, 2005; Robert, Brack, Blakeney, Villarreal, Rosenberg, & Thomas, 2003). Both pharmacotherapy and psychotherapy should be considered (Robert, Villarreal, Blakeney, & Meyer, 1999). Theoretically, symptoms of traumatic stress have a biological component, most notably symptoms in the intrusive reexperiencing and hyperarousal categories (Kirtland, Prout, & Schwarz, 1991). From a utilitarian perspective, prompt relief of symptoms is important, as persistent ASD symptoms have a negative impact on physical recovery from burn injury (Kavanagh et al., 1991). For example, a child who is agitated may move, and movement may compromise skin grafts. In addition, ASD symptoms in the pediatric burn population are associated with poor sleep and poor appetite. Children with burn injuries need both increased food intake and rest for maximal recovery. Also, patients may be too physically impaired to engage in psychotherapy, for example, unable to focus cognitively, developmentally unable to process emotions verbally, or too distraught or agitated to verbalize emotions. Thus, psychopharmacological agents may be a primary treatment option (Tcheung, 2005).

Psychological services are recommended throughout the acute hospitalization period. One component of adjustment post-burn injury involves the grieving process. The patient grieves for the loss of self, perceived invincibility, objects, pets, home, family members, physical function, and/or aspects of appearance. A bereavement model may be helpful to the clinician working with patients during this phase (Knudson-Cooper, 1982). Shock and denial may predominate during the initial hospitalization; anger and depression often follow (Thomas et al., 2002; Koon et al., 1992).

Though individual treatment is variable, some techniques have been established as efficacious in decreasing trauma symptoms with this population. Stress management tools have been shown to be effective, for example, deep breathing, visual imagery, hypnosis, and self-hypnosis. Psychologist David Patterson at Harborview Medical Center in Seattle, Washington, has established the efficacy of stress management tools in facilitating adjustment postinjury and coping with the medical procedures necessary for physical recovery and tailored burn-specific interventions including a self-hypnosis induction specific to wound care (Patterson & Jensen, 2003). Burn injury patients are particularly amenable to hypnotic suggestion due to motivation, regression, and dissociation (Hoffman, Doctor, Patterson, Carrougher, & Furness, 2000). Ewin (1983) asserts that hypnosis should be used early and has a number of applications. Hypnosis is effective in impeding the progression of the burn injury when utilized with the first few hours of injury. Altering the physiological stress response to the injury minimizes subsequent soft tissue damage. Ewin (1984) also notes the positive impact of hypnosis on pain and anxiety management during the acute phase of recovery. Dr. Patterson has also used virtual reality technology as the vector for stress management interventions with the burn-injured patient (Hoffman, Seibel, Richards, Furness, Patterson, & Sharar, 2006; Patterson, Tininenko, Schmidt, & Sharar, 2004; Patterson, Wiechman, Jensen, & Sharar, 2006). Psychologists James Fauerbach and John Lawrence have investigated the efficacy of coping strategy interventions in the emotional rehabilitation from burn trauma (Lawrence & Fauerbach, 2003; Fauerbach, Richter, & Lawrence, 2002; Fauerbach, Lawrence, Haythornthwaite, & Richter, 2002; Haythornthwaite, Lawrence, & Fauerbach, 2001). For example, reducing catastrophic thinking and increasing sensory focusing have been established as effective tools in the acute phase of recovery.

Self-help texts can be a helpful resource during the acute emotional recovery phase of the patient. The staff of the Baltimore Regional Burn Center developed a self-help book specifically aimed at the burn patient and family members, entitled *Severe Burns: A Family Guide to Medical and Emotional Recovery* (Munster, 1993). Though it is not specific to burn injury, one book that guides both the professional development of the clinician and the emotional recovery of the patient is *I Can't Get Over It: A Handbook for Trauma Survivors* (Matsakis, 1996). Cohen, Mannarino, and Staron (2006) have recently established as efficacious a 12-session cognitive behavioral therapy intervention for children with treatment components in both posttraumatic stress and grief. Though not specific for burn-injured patients, the combination of trauma- and grief-related interventions is most fitting for this population.

Beyond Acute Recovery

Psychologist Patricia Blakeney of the Shriners Hospital–Galveston, Texas, has compiled a substantive body of research that establishes an expectation that burn survivors can thrive emotionally and socially (Blakeney, Robert, & Meyer, 1998; Blakeney et al., 1998; Meyers-Paal et al., 2000). Yet burn injury increases a child's risk of developing a major mental illness. Visible distinction and physical limitations have the potential to negatively impact adjustment across the lifespan. Young adults who sustained burn injuries as children have a 45.5 percent prevalence rate of current Axis I major mental illness and a lifetime Axis I prevalence rate of 59.4 percent, with anxiety disorders, major depression, and substance abuse being the most frequently occurring disorders (Meyer et al., 2007). The current and lifetime prevalences of mood, substance abuse, behavior, sleep, and anxiety disorders in this population are higher than those of some other traumatized populations (Stoddard et al., 1989). Extreme anxiety, fear, phobias, generalized anxiety disorder, and traumatic stress are seen beyond the acute hospitalization period (Thomas et al., 2002). Given the elevated risk, young adults who suffered major burn injury as children should be screened for these illnesses in order to initiate appropriate treatment.

Compensatory and coping strategies have the potential to stave off maladjustment and facilitate adjustment across time. Self-confidence, extroversion, and relationship-based skills are a few examples of compensatory strategies beneficial to the survivor of burn injury; in contrast, social introversion predicts the development of pathological shame (Taal & Farber, 1998). An example of a group format curriculum for the development of social skills is *Reach Out! Developing the Tools for Successful Social Interaction after Burns: A 2, 3, or 4-Day Program* (Clarke, Cooper, Partridge, Kish, & Rumsey, 1999). This program is a product of the organization Changing Faces, which was founded by James Partridge, an educator and survivor of burn trauma and injury. Partridge advocates the importance of taking the initiative in social encounters and moving the agenda quickly away from issues of appearance and on to more substantive aspects of social communication. Social psychologist Nicola Rumsey has provided an empirical base for the thesis that behavior rather than appearance predicts successful social encounters. Partridge and Rumsey are engaged in a joint venture to explore the impact of the Changing Faces social communication curriculum on those with visible distinction consequent to burn injury. A list of publications from Changing Faces can be accessed from the charity's Web site, www.changingfaces.co.uk. Nicola Rumsey is a professor at the University of the West of England, located in Bristol, and has published extensively on visible distinction.

Patricia Blakeney, Walter J. Meyer, III, and Christopher Thomas have applied the Changing Faces Social Skills Program to both adolescent and young adult long-term survivors of childhood burn injury (Blakeney et al., 2005). One year subsequent to the training program, survivors' psychosocial competence had been enhanced.

CASE VIGNETTE

Joanna is a Caucasian female burned in a house fire. She sustained a 50 percent total body surface area burn (TBSA) injury, with 45 percent being 3rd degree. She was three years of age at the time of her injury. Joanna was in the house playing with her toys and found herself engulfed in flames. Her face, arms, legs, hands, and feet were burned. Skin donor sites were from her torso. Now seven years of age and four years postinjury, Joanna receives reconstructive burn care.

Joanna is enrolled in the first grade. She repeated pre-kindergarten due to months missed post-burn injury. Joanna's uncle has been tutoring Joanna, and the uncle has noticed a marked decrease in memory and attention post-burn. Intelligence testing revealed a deficit in verbal intelligence and achievement.

Joanna is physically active, has a bright affect, enjoys school, is loving to friends and family, and is pleasing to the adults in her family and community. Joanna's mother reported that Joanna is having significant attention problems. She is having difficulty concentrating and sitting still. Her mother notes problems with daydreaming, poor coordination, and poor schoolwork. Her mother first noticed the problems post-burn injury. Joanna's schoolteacher notices attention difficulties and difficulty completing work.

Joanna's mother perceives Joanna's life to have changed for the worse consequent to the burn injury. In regard to Joanna's post-burn adjustment, her mother has been concerned about the impact of Joanna's physical appearance on her self-esteem. Initially, Joanna was reportedly timid and tried to hide her burn scars. For example, she would not wear clothing that would reveal the burn scars. Joanna has progressed from that point and is now able to wear such clothes. However, some of the post-burn timidity remains. Joanna has not worn jewelry on her burned hand, though she adorns her nonburned hand with jewelry. Her mother is concerned that Joanna is uncomfortable with the appearance of her burned hand. Her mother perceives that Joanna is aware of how people talk about her burns in public situations and perceives Joanna to feel hurt. Joanna's family drawing does reflect a sense of feeling separate or different from the others in the family. Joanna has asked her mother on occasion during bath time, "When will all the burns go away?" Her mother is concerned about Joanna's feelings as she gets older, and how Joanna will deal with her scars as a young adult. Changes in Joanna's development leave her mother with unanswered, anxiety-provoking questions. Her mother also expressed concern about regression. Joanna continues to suck her thumb every night prior to bedtime and clings to adult caregivers.

Joanna experiences a significant degree of posttraumatic stress. She experiences intrusive thoughts, exhibits avoidant behavior, and has numerous anxiety symptoms. Joanna recalls the fire and burn as an upsetting and bothersome event. She sometimes experiences bad dreams that appear to be anxiety related. She has scared, upset, or sad feelings that she tries to avoid. An example of avoidant or compartmentalized thought was exhibited in the contrast between her assertion that she does not recall post-burn events and her drawing of her experience in the hospital, in which she portrays herself in her hospital bed, surrounded by medical accoutrements and family members, while imagining what happened to her pets in the house fire. Joanna refused to draw a picture of the burn event. She reported feeling nervous and jumpy since the injury. She believes that most of the time thoughts or feelings about what happened get in the way of remembering things, including new learning. She believes paying attention is much more difficult post-burn than pre-burn. And she stays away from things that make her remember what happened and what she went through.

During the parent interview, Joanna's mother was unable to recall the burn injury history. She began to cry once the burn history was broached and cried throughout her description of her impaired attention, concentration, and memory post-burn injury. She also described having a sleep disturbance, which involves difficulty initiating sleep, staying asleep, and awakening prematurely. She exhibits hypervigilance as evidenced by calling home frequently (about twice daily) to check on Joanna's well-being, as well as changing her work schedule to maximize her time at home when Joanna is at home. The mother restricts her activities to those that include Joanna, which reassures her of Joanna's safety, and she avoids activities and situations that remind her of the event. The sound of an ambulance siren triggers intrusive thoughts of Joanna's burn and recovery, as well as fear that other family members are currently in danger. She continues to reexperience the event through nightmares.

Joanna and her family have survived a traumatic house fire. During her hospitalization, Joanna endured multiple surgeries; frequent wound care, which family members likely participated in as well (e.g., staple removal, line replacement, dressing changes, wound debridement); daily stretching and strength-building exercises; and intrusive medical procedures throughout each day (e.g., x-rays, breathing treatments, wound culture samples, blood samples). Distress came from any number of sources, for example, the immobilization of a three-year-old, pain of exposed and damaged nerve endings in the skin, acute traumatic stress symptoms, itch, generalized anxiety, short-term changes in appearance such as cropping of her long hair to the nap, and long-term changes to the body's appearance and function (burn and donor site together comprise far more than 50 percent of the body surface area).

Once Joanna was discharged from the hospital, much of the hospital routine continued in the home environment. Joanna's mother was trained to complete daily wound care in the home. The daily bath and wound care routine took several hours. Joanna wore pressure garments for about one year, for the purpose of minimizing disfigurement and maximizing function. To facilitate flexibility and range of motion, Joanna completed her rehabilitation exercises thrice daily. She was encouraged to incorporate stretching and exercise into her daily life and consequently became active in sports. To maintain skin integrity, Joanna's mother frequently massaged her scars. Joanna wore pressure garments 23 hours per day on all skin that sustained deep second or third degree burns. One pair of garments was hand washed and air dried daily. Donning the garments was a struggle because of their binding capacity, which applied 12 pounds of pressure. Once the garments are on, wearing them is difficult because of the heat and itch. Thermal regulation is different for Joanna in that she has lost the sweat glands for 45 percent of her body. She may be less tolerant of high outdoor temperatures or require more hydration when exposed to high outdoor temperatures. For the first one to two years, she was hypermetabolic and maintaining a normal body weight was a struggle as she needed to increase caloric intake. She is at risk for less dense bones and consequent orthopedic problems. For her lifetime, sunscreen and/or clothing need to be applied to all burned areas before she goes outside, to prevent skin damage and hyperpigmentation.

Joanna and her family have been diligent in adhering to these numerous and enduring demands, while displaced from their home, which was being rebuilt. They have insured that Joanna attends each of the annual burn camps provided through her medical facility and engages in a physical activity program that combats skin contracture.

Joanna and her mother continue to have the emotional scars of trauma. The first several years post-burn are spent in the reorganization of the family. The daily survival demands postpone emotional healing. Emotional healing comes after the physical crisis. Cross-sectional studies have shown that three to four years are the average amount of time post-burn required for a sample population to look similar to a nonburned normative sample in some areas of emotional and behavioral functioning (Blakeney et al., 1998), which is consistent with Joanna's and her mother's experience.

Ideally, Joanna will develop compensatory skills to deal with new, unique, and distressing situations. About 30 percent of pediatric burn survivors adjust abnormally (Blakeney et al., 1998). To adapt to the emotional demands post-burn, Joanna will need a supportive, organized family that encourages her independence and can consistently adhere to a medical and rehabilitation treatment plan that lasts a lifetime. Joanna does have a dedicated mother who has provided a family with such qualities.

Joanna's verbal intelligence deficit will put her at high risk for adapting to "beyond normal" circumstances. As Joanna's academic curriculum is increasingly based more on abstract, verbal reasoning, Joanna's achievement will likely lag. Strengths for Joanna are visual-spatial reasoning and visual-motor abilities. Joanna will naturally learn best kinesthetically (by doing) and modeling from others. What caused the low average intelligence and verbal comprehension deficit for Joanna is not clear. Though neurocognitive damage is associated with burn injury (hypoxia and closed head injury) and electrical injury, Joanna did not have any measures of learning pre-burn beyond family observation and experience, for example, school performance, standardized academic achievement or estimate of intelligence, allowing for attribution of neurocognitive damage to burn injury.

Joanna has lost her body as it was, as well as a sense of safety that existed prior to the traumatic injury. Burn survivors frequently experience staring and teasing because of their visible distinction. Struggles are frequently seen regarding losses and grief consequent to the burn injury. Joanna currently has PTSD symptoms, as does her mother.

The long-term consequences for Joanna are not fully known. She will face social dilemmas beyond those of others. She will choose her career differently. She will need to be sheltered from the sun and heat. She will likely need a job that balances standing and sitting, rather than a job that is exclusively a standing job. She will not have jobs that focus on her body, for example, modeling. Joanna will need access to academic tutoring throughout her academic career. She will need access to intermittent counseling and medical care all of her life. Her mother will need access to counseling intermittently throughout Joanna's childhood and adolescence.

Summary

The science of psychosocial rehabilitation from burn injury is advancing. Standardized assessment tools and their application with the burn injured have developed substantially across the past decade. Pain management standards have improved. Posttraumatic stress, depression, pain, sleep disorders, and body image of the burn survivor are better understood due to the persistence of clinician-scientists committed to the emotional rehabilitation of this important population (Esselman, Thombs, Magyar-Russell, & Fauerbach, 2006). Intervention efficacy studies have been sparse in the literature but are slowly gaining in prevalence and need to be further pursued.

Policy Recommendations
Public Education on the Prevention of Burn Injury

Strategies for the prevention of burn injury are greatly needed. Much of the mental health professionals' general training and many of their skills can be applied to prevention-related interventions, such as knowledge in the area of learning, behavior, and the process of change. Injuries consequent to maltreatment, fire-setting, other un- or undertreated mental health disorders, and retail products need to be addressed.

Research on Causes of Self-Injury and Abuse by Burning

Better understanding of maltreatment by burning could be accomplished through large sampling of patients and survivors. When events occur infrequently, as do some of the most dangerous signs of maltreatment, large sampling is needed. A national database established under a public safety initiative would allow for larger sampling and greater disclosure of information between agencies. One initial step has been accomplished. As of 1995, the American Burn Association initiated collaboration with the American College of Surgeons and created the TRACS/ABA Burn Registry. Ninety burn centers participate and by 2002, the National Burn Repository (NBR) was well established and generated an annual report. The NBR collects data on some behavioral parameters of burn injury, including suspected self-inflicted injury, child abuse, assault or abuse of adults, and arson. The total of all behavioral parameters reported in the NBR accounts for 4.9 percent of burn injuries.

What is lacking is thorough assessment of behavioral parameters and consistent methods of reporting on them. The 4.9 percent prevalence rates of total problem behaviors in the burn injury population is likely an underestimate. Fire setting alone accounted for 11 percent of the burn injury population and suspected maltreatment accounted for another 22–30 percent in non-NBR samples cited above. In addition, data are not collected on many significant behavioral parameters, such as neglect and fire setting.

Maltreatment needs to be pursued more aggressively. However, making a determination of maltreatment can be difficult. Breadth of knowledge is needed to understand the plausibility of injury stories. When a burn injury story is provided, investigating the plausibility of the events requires the knowledge base of professionals not typically found in the burn center. Forensic experts, fire dynamics experts, and mechanical engineers, combined with the experts in burn injury pathophysiology, the burn care professionals, would allow the plausibility of the story to be tested (Hansen & Barnhill, 1982). Such collaborative relationships and studies are needed.

Reporting of Burn Injuries

Fire setting destroys and compromises human lives. The burn-injured fire setter, however, is at risk for not having the fire-setting behavior addressed. Some states have no laws addressing the reporting of burn injuries to fire service officials, while others clearly regulate burn injury reporting and clarify related limitations of patient confidentiality. Massachusetts law mandates the reporting of all burn injuries >5% TBSA. State police manage the Massachusetts Burn Injury Reporting System (M-BIRS), which delineates procedures, forms, and education on both toll-free telephone and facsimile reporting. Excerpted below is the Massachusetts General Law Chapter 112, Section 12A, amended by the Act of 1986:

> Every physician ... examining or treating a person with a burn injury affecting five percent or more of the surface area of his body, or, whenever any such case is treated in a hospital, sanitarium or other institution, the manager, superintendent or other person in charge thereof, shall report such cases ... at once to the commissioner of public safety and to the police in the community where the burn occurred.

Advocating for such legislation in all 50 states would be a meaningful mission, as has been accomplished with child abuse and neglect laws.

Improvements in Product Safety Standards and Laws

Retail products are repeatedly associated with burn injury stories. After improvements in product safety standards, laws, or codes, some products have ceased to be associated with burn injuries. Improvements in product safety are commonly left to victim advocates. Change may be more effective or expedient if products involved in burn injury are subject to mandated reporting. For example, the Consumer Product Safety Commission has collaborated with burn centers for the purpose of gathering a large data sample within a short amount of time. In one such national initiative, the role of clothing in burn injury is being studied. In less than five months, 107 patients provided data that have allowed for clothing safety to be studied. Other products, codes, and standards associated with burn injury need to be studied as well.

Resources

Books that address social challenges such as teasing can be clinically helpful:

Sticks and Stones: Seven Ways Your Child Can Deal with Teasing, Conflict, and Other Hard Times, by Scott Cooper (2000)

How to Handle Bullies, Teasers and Other Meanies: A Book That Takes the Nuisance Out of Name Calling and Other Nonsense, by Kate Cohen-Posey (1995)

Organizations

The Phoenix Society, a national burn survivor organization, sponsors an annual conference, a monthly publication entitled Burn Support News, and the Web site www.phoenix-society.org.

The Texas burn survivors support organization can be contacted at www.texasburnsurvivors.org.

The National Ability Center, at www.discovernac.org, is committed to the development of lifetime skills (e.g., self esteem, confidence, physical development), thereby enhancing active participation in all aspects of community life.

Online Support

The Burn Survivors Throughout the World Web site is www.burnsurvivorsttw.com.

Hundreds of survivors display their autobiographies at www.burnsurvivorsonline.com.

The National Center for PTSD Web site is NCPTSD.va.gov. It provides resources for trauma survivors, family members, and professionals.

Safety Tips

Steps to bath safety:
> Set the hot water heater at 120 degrees or less.
> Install and set a pressure balance tub and shower valve, for example, Delta Scald-Guard.
> Use a thermometer and hand to test the water temperature before bathing;
> ALWAYS have a bathing child within eyesight.

When drinking a hot beverage while supervising children, use a lid-
    ded travel mug.
Fit propane tanks with quick release valves.
When working outdoors, apprise yourself of the location of high-tension
    wires and STAY CLEAR—both person and tools.
Install hot water heater 18 inches above the foundation OR use a water
    heater that does not have a pilot light.
Check to see that free-standing oven-range units are installed with mount-
    ing brackets, ensuring that the units cannot tip.
Keep children out of kitchens and baths, unless:
    The activity is focused on the child
    The child is within arm's reach, and
    The child is within eyesight.
In addition to supervision, try doorknob slipcovers; use cabinet locks;
    make cleaning materials and chemicals inaccessible to children; child
    safety gates can be of assistance.
Place small appliances AND THEIR CORDS out of child's reach. Look for
    cords that have a quick release and are coiled.
Gas is a tool, so:
    Store in sealed container
    Make inaccessible to children
    Store away from source of ignition
    Put in a cool engine (e.g., before you begin mowing)
    Use only in a well-ventilated area (e.g., outdoors)
    Use with machines, not people (e.g., never use to kill lice).
Baby walkers with wheels should only be used in secured spaces,
    e.g., with no stairs, no hot materials, no electrical outlets, no ap-
    pliances/tools. Imagine the bumper car ride at the carnival—a
    flat surface that is fenced in.
Install fire and smoke detectors in the home.
Change the batteries in the fire and smoke detectors biannually, when you
    reset your clocks.
Place fire extinguishers in the home.
Create a house fire escape plan and discuss with the family, including escape
    routes, how to proceed out of the home, how to get help, and where to
    meet once outside the home.
Place lit candles and space heaters in the same room as adults, so candle
    activity is always in eyesight.
NEVER use fuel, including accelerants:
    On existing flame
    In unventilated area
    When burning trash
    On a recreational camp fire
    When barbecueing.
NEVER store fuel by ignition source.
Use sealed fuel can.
Cover unused outlets.

Use electrical cords that have an approval tag from Underwriters Labora-
tories. Do not use damaged electrical cords, for example, cords that
are frayed, worn. Use only for designated application.

Small kitchen appliances are safe when:

The base is wider than the top

The base is heavier than the top

The lid seals the liquid when cooking

The cord is not accessible to a child.

Kill lice with lice shampoo. No other options exist.

When putting out campfires, use water. If you do not have water and use
dirt, stir the dirt and embers until the embers extinguish. Do not
bury the embers with dirt, as this creates a long-lasting "oven."

When you have a concern about product safety, contact the Consumer
Product Safety Commission: phone (800) 638 2772; Web site www.
cpsc.gov.

Note

1. The Shriners of North America are a philanthropic group whose original mission was to provide free medical care to children affected by polio. After polio was eradicated from the United States, the Shriners established a mission beyond orthopedics, which was to provide free medical care for children who sustain burn injuries. A number of organizations generously funded research at the Shriners Hospital–Galveston across the past 10 years, which advanced the psychological rehabilitation services for the burn survivor. These organizations and programs include the International Association of Fire Fighters Burn Foundation Research Grant Program, the Shriners Hospitals for Children Research Grant Program, the University of Texas Medical Branch (UTMB) Small Grants Program, the National Institutes of Health, and the National Institute for Disability and Rehabilitation research program. Much of which follows is a summary of experience gleaned while a member of the burn care team in Galveston, Texas.

References

American Psychiatric Association. (1980). *Diagnostic and statistical manual of mental disorders* (3rd ed.). Washington, DC: Author.

American Psychiatric Association. (1994). *Diagnostic and statistical manual of mental disorders* (4th ed.). Washington, DC: Author.

American Psychiatric Association. (2000). *Diagnostic and statistical manual of mental disorders* (4th ed., text revision). Washington, DC: Author.

Andreasen, N. J. (2004). Acute and delayed posttraumatic stress disorders: A history and some issues. *American Journal of Psychiatry, 161*, 1321–1323.

Baur, K. M., Hardy, P. E., & Van Dorsten, B. (1998). Posttraumatic stress disorder in burn populations: A critical review of the literature. *Journal of Burn Care and Rehabilitation, 19*(3), 230–240.

Bennett, B., & Gamelli, R. (1998). Profile of an abused burned child. *Journal of Burn Care and Rehabilitation, 19*(1, Pt. 1), 88–94.

Bennett, B., Gamelli, R., Duchene, R., Atkocaitis, D., & Plunkett, J. (2004). Burn education awareness recognition and support (BEARS): A community-based juvenile firesetters assessment and treatment program. *Journal of Burn Care and Rehabilitation, 25*(3),
324–327.

Blakeney, P., Meyer, W., Robert, R., Desai, M., Wolf, S., & Herndon, D. (1998). Long-term
psychosocial adaptation of children who survive burns involving 80% or greater total
body surface area. *Journal of Trauma: Injury, Infection, and Critical Care, 44*(4), 625–634.

Blakeney, P., Robert, R., & Meyer, W. (1998). Psychological and social recovery of children
disfigured by physical trauma: Elements of treatment supported by empirical data.
International Review of Psychiatry, 10, 196–200.

Blakeney, P., Thomas, C., Berniger, F., Holzer, C., & Meyer, W. J., III. (2001). Long term
psychiatric disorders in adolescent burn survivors [Abstract 41, p. 81]. *EBA Programme and Abstract Book.* Ninth Congress of the European Burns Association 2001,
Lyon, France.

Blakeney, P., Thomas, C., Holzer, C., Rose, M., Berniger, F., & Meyer, W. (2005). Efficacy of
a short-term, intensive social skills training program for burned adolescents. *Journal of
Burn Care and Rehabilitation, 26*(6), 546–555.

Blanchard, E., Hickling, E., Taylor, A., Loos, W., Forneris, C., & Jaccard, J. (1996). Who
develops PTSD from motor vehicle accidents? *Behavioral Research and Therapeutic,
34*(1), 1–10.

Briere, J. (1996) *Trauma Symptom Checklist for Children: Professional Manual.* Florida: Psychological Assessment Resources Inc.

Bryant, R. (1996). Predictors of post-traumatic stress disorder following burns injury.
Burns, 22(2), 89–92.

Bryant, R., Guthrie, R., Moulds, M., Nixon, R., & Felmingham, K. (2003). Hypnotizability
and posttraumatic stress disorder: A prospective study. *Journal of Clinical and Experimental Hypnosis, 51*(4), 382–389.

Bryant R., & Harvey, A. (1997). Acute stress disorder: A critical review of diagnostic
issues. *Clinical Psychology Review, 17*(7), 757–773.

Buckley, T., Blanchard, E., & Hickling, E. (1996). A prospective examination of delayed
onset PTSD secondary to motor vehicle accidents. *Journal of Abnormal Psychology,
105*(4), 617–625.

Bum-Hee, Y., & Dimsdale, J. (1999). Post traumatic stress disorder in patients with burn
injuries. *Journal of Burn Care and Rehabilitation, 20*(5), 426–433.

Caffo, E., & Belaise, C. (2003). Psychological aspects of traumatic injury in children and
adolescents. *Child and Adolescent Psychiatric Clinics of North America, 12,* 493–535.

Cardena, E., Holen, A., McFarlane, A., Solomon, Z., Wilkinson, C., & Spiegel, D. (1998).
A multisite study of acute stress reactions to a disaster. In T. Widiger, A. Frances, H.
Pincus, R. Ross, M. First, W. Davis, & M. Kline (Eds.), *DSM–IV sourcebook, volume 4* (pp.
377–391). Washington, DC: American Psychiatric Association.

Cardena, E., Koopman, C., Classen, C., Waelde, L., & Spiegel, D. (2000). Psychometric
properties of the Stanford Acute Stress Reaction Questionnaire (SASRQ): A valid and
reliable measure of acute stress. *Journal of Traumatic Stress, 13*(4), 719–734.

Clarke, A., Cooper, C., Partridge, J., Kish, V., & Rumsey, N. (1999). *Reach out! Developing
the tools for successful social interaction after burns: A 2, 3, or 4-day programme.* London:
Changing Faces Publication.

Cohen, J. A., Mannarino, A., & Deblinger, E. (2006). *Treating trauma and traumatic grief in
children and adolescents.* New York: Guilford.

Cohen, J. A., Mannarino, A., & Staron, V. (2006). A pilot study of modified cognitive-behavioral therapy for childhood traumatic grief (CBT–CTG). *Journal of the American Academy of Child and Adolescent Psychiatry, 45*(12), 1465–1473.

Cohen-Posey, K. (1995). *How to handle bullies, teasers and other meanies: A book that takes the nuisance out of name calling and other nonsense.* Highland City, FL: Rainbow Books.

Cooper, S. (2000). *Sticks and stones: Seven ways your child can deal with teasing, conflict, and other hard times.* New York: Three Rivers Press.

Cromes, G., McDonald, M., & Robinson, C. (1980). The effects of relaxation training on anxiety and pain during burn wound debridement. Paper presented at the 12th Annual Meeting of the American Burn Association, San Antonio, TX.

Davis, W., Racusin, R., Fleischer, A., Mooney, D., Foord, J., & McHugo, G. (2000). Acute stress disorder symptomatology during hospitalization for pediatric injury. *Journal of the American Academy of Child and Adolescent Psychiatry, 39*(5), 569–575.

Difede, J., Ptacek, J., Roberts, J., Barocas, D., Rives, W., Appeldorf, W., et al. (2002). Acute stress disorder after burn injury: A predictor of posttraumatic stress disorder? *Psychosomatic Medicine, 64*, 826–834.

Dollinger, S. J. (1985). Lightning-strike disaster among children. *British Journal of Medical Psychology, 75*, 383–385.

DuHamel, K. N., Difede, J., Foley, F., & Greenleaf, M. (2002). Hypnotizability and trauma symptoms after burn injury. *International Journal of Clinical and Experimental Hypnosis, 50*(1), 33–50.

Ehde, D., Patterson, D., Wiechman, S., & Wilson, L. (2000). Post-traumatic stress symptoms and distress 1 year after burn injury. *Journal of Burn Care and Rehabilitation, 21*, 105–111.

El Hamaoui, Y., Yaalaoui, S., Chihabeddine, K., Boukind, E., & Moussaoui, D. (2002). Posttraumatic stress disorder in burned patients. *Burns, 28*(7), 647–650.

Esselman, P., Thombs, B., Magyar-Russell, G., & Fauerbach, J. (2006). Burn rehabilitation: State of the science. *American Journal of Physical Medicine and Rehabilitation, 85*(4), 383–413.

Everett, J., Patterson, D., & Chen, A. (1990). Cognitive and behavioral treatments for burn pain. *The Pain Clinic, 3*(3), 133–145.

Ewin, D. M. (1983). Emergency room hypnosis for the burned patient. *American Journal of Clinical Hypnosis, 26*(1), 5–8.

Ewin, D. M. (1984). Hypnosis in surgery and anesthesia. In W. C. Wester, II, & A. H. Smith, Jr. (Eds.), *Clinical hypnosis: A multidisciplinary approach.* Philadelphia: Lippincott Williams & Wilkins.

Fauerbach, J., Lawrence, J., Haythornthwaite, J., McGuire, M., & Munster, A. (1996). Pre-injury psychiatric illness and post injury adjustment in adult burn survivors. *Academy of Psychosomatic Medicine, 37*(6), 547–555.

Fauerbach, J., Lawrence, J., Haythornthwaite, J., & Richter, L. (2002). Coping with the stress of a painful medical procedure. *Behavioral Research and Therapy, 40*(9), 1003–1015.

Fauerbach, J., Lawrence, J., Haythornthwaite, J., Richter, D., McGuire, M., Schmidt, C., et al. (1997). Preburn psychiatric history affects posttrauma morbidity. *Psychosomatics, 38*, 374–385.

Fauerbach, J., Lawrence, J., Stevens, S., & Munster, A. (1998). Work status and attrition from longitudinal studies are influenced by psychiatric disorder. *Journal of Burn Care and Rehabilitation, 19*, 247–252.

Fauerbach, J., Richter, L., & Lawrence, J. (2002). Regulating acute posttrauma distress. *Journal of Burn Care and Rehabilitation, 23*(4), 249–257.

Fletcher, K. (1992). When Bad Things Happen Scale. Washington DC: National Center for PTSD Assessments.

Fletcher, K. (1996). Psychometric review of the When Bad Things Happen Scale (WBTH). In B. H. Stamm (Ed.), *Measurement of stress, trauma, and adaptation* (pp. 435–437). Lutherville, MD: Sidran Press.

Foa, E., Keane, T., & Friedman, M. (Eds.). (2000). *Effective treatments for PTSD: Practice guidelines from the international society for traumatic stress studies.* New York: Guilford.

Frankl, V. (1959). *Man's search for meaning.* Boston: Beacon Press.

Franklin, G., Pucci, P., Arbabi, S., Brandt, M., Wahl, W., & Taheri, P. (2002). Decreased juvenile arson and firesetting recidivism after implementation of a multidisciplinary prevention program. *Journal of Trauma-Injury Infection and Critical Care, 53*(2), 260–4.

Frazier, P. A., & Kaler, M. E. (2006). Assessing the validity of self-reported stress-related growth. *Journal of Consulting and Clinical Psychology, 74*(5), 859–869.

Fukunishi, I. (1999). Relationship of cosmetic disfigurement to the severity of posttraumatic stress disorder in burn injury or digital amputation. *Psychotherapy and Psychosomatics, 68*(2), 82–86.

Garrison C. Z., Bryant, E. S., Addy, C. L., Spurrier, P G., Freedy, & J. R., Kilpatrick D. G. (1995). Posttraumatic stress disorder in adolescents after Hurricane Andrew. *Journal of the American Academy of Child Adolescent Psychiatry, 34*(9), 1193–1201.

Gilboa, D. (2001). Long-term psychosocial adjustment after burn injury. *Burns, 27*, 335–341.

Graham, J. R. (1987). *The MMPI: A practical guide* (2nd ed.). New York: Oxford University Press.

Green, B. (1991). Evaluating the effects of disaster. *Journal of Consulting and Clinical Psychology, 3*, 538–546.

Hall, E., Saxe, G., Stoddard, F., Kaplow, J., Koenen, K., Chawlan, N., et al. (2006). Posttraumatic stress symptoms in parents of children with acute burns. *Burns, 31*(4), 403–412.

Hansen, J. C., & Barnhill, L. R. (1982). *Clinical approaches to family violence* (p. 157). Rockville, MD: Aspen.

Harvey, A., & Bryant, R. (1999). Predictors of acute stress following motor vehicle accidents. *Journal of Traumatic Stress, 12*(3), 519–525.

Harvey, A., & Bryant, R. (2000). Memory for acute stress disorder symptoms: A two-year prospective study. *Journal of Nervous and Mental Disorders, 188*(9), 602–607.

Haythornthwaite, J., Lawrence, J., & Fauerbach, J. (2001). Brief cognitive interventions for burn pain. *Annals of Behaviour Medicine, 23*(1), 42–49.

Hoffman, H., Doctor, J., Patterson, D., Carrougher, G., & Furness, T. (2000). Use of virtual reality for adjunctive treatment of adolescent burn pain during wound care: A case report. *Pain, 85*, 305–309.

Hoffman, H., Seibel, E., Richards, T., Furness, T., Patterson, D., & Sharar, S. (2006). Virtual reality helmet display quality influences the magnitude of virtual reality analgesia. *Journal of Pain, 7*(11), 843–850.

Hooshmand, H., Radfar, F., & Beckner, E. (1989). The neurophysiological aspects of electrical injuries. *Clinical Electroencephalography, 20*(2), 111–120.

Horowitz, M. (1986). *Stress response syndromes* (2nd 3d). Northvale, NJ: Jason Aronson.

Ickovics, J., Meade, C., Kershaw, T., Milan, S., Lewis, J., & Ethier, K. (2006). Urban teens: Trauma, posttraumatic growth, and emotional distress among female adolescents. *Journal of Consulting and Clinical Psychology*, *74*(5), 841–850.

Kavanaugh, C. K., Lasoft, E., & Eide, Y. (1991). Learned helplessness and the pediatric burn patient: Dressing change behavior and serum cortisol and beta endorphins. *Advances in Pediatrics*, *38*, 335–363.

Kazak, A., Barakat, L., Meeske, K., Christakis, D., Meadown, A., & Casey, R. (1997). Post traumatic stress, family functioning, and social support in survivors of childhood leukemia and their mothers and fathers. *Journal of Consulting and Clinical Psychology*, *65*, 120–129.

Kessler, R. (1995). Posttraumatic stress disorder in the national comorbidity survey. *Archives of General Psychiatry*, *52*(12), 1048–1060.

Kilpatrick, D., Saunders, B., Amick-McMullan, A., Best, C., Veronen, L., & Resnick, H. (1989). Victim and crime factors associated with the development of crime-related post-traumatic stress disorder. *Behavior Therapeutics*, *20*, 199–214.

Kirtland, P., Prout, M., & Schwarz, R. (1991). *Post-traumatic stress disorder: A clinician's guide.* New York: Plenum Press.

Knudson-Cooper, M. (1981). Relaxation and biofeedback training in the treatment of severely burned children. *Journal of Burn Care and Rehabilitation*, *2*(2).

Knudson-Cooper, M. (1982). Emotional care of the hospitalized burned child. *Journal of Burn Care and Rehabilitation*, *3*, 109–116.

Kolko, D. (2000). *Juvenile firesetter intervention clinical training.* Pittsburg, PA: University of Pittsburgh School of Medicine, Department of Psychiatry.

Kolko, D. (2001). Efficacy of cognitive-behavioral treatment and fire safety education for children who set fires: Initial and follow-up outcomes. *Journal of Child Psychology and Psychiatry & Allied Disciplines*, *42*(3), 371–380.

Koon, K., Blakeney, P., Broemeling, L., Moore, P., Robson, M., & Herndon, D. (1992). Self-esteem in pediatric burn patients. *Proceedings of the American Burn Association*, *24*, 112.

Kratochwill, T. (1996). Posttraumatic stress disorder in children and adolescents: Commentary and recommendations. *Journal of School Psychology*, *34*(2), 185–188.

Kravitz, M., McCoy, B. J., Tompkins, D. M., Daly, W., Mulligan, J., McCauley, R L., et al. (1993). Sleep disorders in children after burn injury. *Journal of Burn Care and Rehabilitation*, *14*(1), 58–64.

Laforce, R., Jr., Gibson, B., Morehouse, R., Bailey, P. A., & MacLaren, V. V. (2000). Neuropsychiatric profile of a case of post traumatic stress disorder following an electric shock. *Medical Journal of Malaysia*, *55*(4), 524–526.

Lambert, J., Difede, J., & Contrada, R. (2004). The relationship of attribution of responsibility to acute stress disorder among hospitalized burn patients. *Journal of Nervous and Mental Disease*, *192*(4), 304–312.

Lawrence, J., & Fauerbach, J. (2003). Personality, coping, chronic stress, social support and PTSD symptoms among adult burn survivors: A path analysis. *Journal of Burn Care and Rehabilitation*, *24*(1), 63–72.

Liebowitz, M., Barlow, D., Ballenger, J., Davidson, J., Foa, E., Fyer, A., et al. (1998). DSM-IV anxiety disorders: Final overview. In T. Widiger, A. Frances, H. Pincus, R. Ross, M. First, W. Davis, & M. Kline (Eds.), *DSM-IV sourcebook, volume 4* (pp. 1047–1076). Washington, DC: American Psychiatric Association.

Madianos, M. G., Papaghelis, M., Ioannovick, J., & Dafni, R. (2001). Psychiatric disorders
    in burn patients: A follow-up study. *Psychotherapy and Psychosomatics*, 70(1), 30–37.
Mancusi-Ungaro, H. R., Jr., Tarbox, A. R., & Wainwright, D. J. (1986). Posttraumatic
    stress disorder in electric burn patients. *Journal of Burn Care and Rehabilitation*, 7(6),
    521–525.
Marshall, R, Spitzer, R, & Liebowitz, M. (1999). Review and critique of the new
    DSM–IV diagnosis of acute stress disorder. *American Journal of Psychiatry*, 156(11),
    1677–1685.
Matsakis, A. 1996. *I can't get over it: A handbook for trauma survivors*. Oakland, CA: New
    Harbinger.
Meichenbaum, D. (1994). *A clinical handbook/practical therapist manual for assessing and
    treating adults with post traumatic stress disorder (PTSD)*. Waterloo, Ontario, Canada:
    University of Waterloo Institute Press.
Meyer, W., Blakeney, P., Thomas, C., Russell, W., Robert, R., Holzer, C. Prevalence of
    major psychiatric illness in young adults who were burned as children. *Psychosomatic
    Medicine*, 2007, in press.
Meyers-Paal, R., Blakeney, P., Murphy, L., Robert, R., Chinkes, D., Meyer, W., et al. (2000).
    Physical and psychological rehabilitation outcomes for pediatric patients who suffer >
    80% total body surface area burn and > 70% 3rd degree burns. *Journal of Burn Care and
    Rehabilitation*, 21(1, Pt. 1), 43–49.
Minutaglio, B. (2003). *City on fire*. New York: HarperCollins.
Munster, A. M. (1993). *Severe burns: A family guide to medical and emotional recovery*.
    Baltimore: Johns Hopkins Press.
Norris, F. H., Perilla, J. L., & Murphy, A. D. (2001). Postdisaster stress in the United States
    and Mexico: A cross-cultural test of the multicriterion conceptual model of posttrau-
    matic stress disorder. *Journal of Abnormal Psychology*, 110(4), 553–563.
Ortega, A. N., & Rosenheck, R. (2000). Posttraumatic stress disorder among Hispanic
    Vietnam veterans. *American Journal of Psychiatry*, 157(4), 615–619.
Patterson, D. (1995). Nonopioid based approaches to burn pain. *Journal of Burn Care and
    Rehabilitationitation*, 16(3), 372–376.
Patterson, D. R., Carrigan, L., Questad, K. A., & Robinson, R. (1992). Post-traumatic
    stress disorder in hospitalized patients with burn injuries. *Journal of Burn Care and
    Rehabilitation*, 13(1), 20.
Patterson, D., Finch, C., Wiechman, S., Bonsack, R., Gibran, N., & Heimbach, D. (2003).
    Premorbid mental health status of adult burn patients: Comparison with a normative
    sample. *Journal of Burn Care and Rehabilitation*, 24(5), 347–350.
Patterson, D., Hofland, H., Espey, K., & Sharaar, S. (2004). Nursing committee of the
    International Society for Burn Injuries: Pain management. *Burns*, 30(8), 10–15.
Patterson, D., & Jensen, M. (2003). Hypnosis and clinical pain. *Psychological Bulletin*,
    129(4), 495–521.
Patterson, D., Tininenko, J., Schmidt, A., & Sharar, S. (2004). Virtual reality hypno-
    sis: A case report. *International Journal of Clinical and Experimental Hypnosis*, 52(1),
    27–38.
Patterson, D., Tininenko, J., & Ptacek, J. (2006). Pain during burn hospitalization predicts
    long-term outcome. *Journal of Burn Care and Rehabilitation*, 27(5), 719–726.
Patterson, D., Wiechman, S., Jensen, M., & Sharar, S. (2006). Hypnosis delivered through
    immersive virtual reality for burn pain: A clinical case series. *International Journal of
    Clinical and Experimental Hypnosis*, 54(2), 130–142.

Pelcovitz, D., Libov, B., Mandel, F., Kaplan, S., Weinblatt, M., & Septimus, A. (1998). Post-traumatic stress disorder and family functioning in adolescent cancer. *Journal of Traumatic Stress, 11*(2), 205–221.

Penk, W. E., Robinowitz, R., Black, J., Dolan, M., Bell, W., Dorsett, D., et al. Ethnicity: post-traumatic stress disorder differences among black, white, and Hispanic veterans who differ in degrees of exposure to combat in Vietnam. *Journal of Clinical Psychology, 45*(5), 729–735.

Perry, S., Difede, J., Musngi, G., Frances, A., & Jacobsberg, L. (1992). Predictors of post-traumatic stress disorder after burn injury. *American Journal of Psychiatry, 149*, 931–935.

Pfefferbaum B. (1997). Posttraumatic stress disorder in children. *Journal of the American Academy of Child and Adolescent Psychiatry, 36*(11), 1503–1511.

Pinsonneault, I. L. (2002a). Developmental perspectives on children and fire. In D. Kolko (Ed.), *Handbook on firesetting in children and youth*. San Diego: Academic Press.

Pinsonneault, I. L. (2002b). Fire safety education and skills training. In D. Kolko (Ed.), *Handbook on firesetting in children and youth*. San Diego: Academic Press.

Pinsonneault, I. L. (2002c). Three models of educational interventions with child and adolescent firesetters. In D. Kolko (Ed.), *Handbook on firesetting in children and youth*. San Diego: Academic Press.

Powers, P. S., Cruse, C. W., Daniels, S., & Stevens, B. (1994). Posttraumatic stress disorder in patients with burns. *Journal of Burn Care and Rehabilitation, 5*(2), 147–153.

Premalatha, G. D. (1994). Post traumatic stress disorder following an electric shock. *Medical Journal of Malaysia, 49*(3), 292–294.

Purdue G., & Hunt J. (1990). Adult assault as a mechanism of burn injury. *Archives of Surgery, 125*, 268–269.

Ratcliff, S., Brown, A., Rosenberg, L., Rosenberg, M., Robert, R., Cuervo, L., et al. (2006). The effectiveness of a pain and anxiety protocol to treat the acute pediatric burn patient. *Burns, 32*, 554–562.

Rizzone, L., Stoddard, F., Murphy, J., & Kruger, L. (1994). Posttraumatic stress disorder in mothers of children and adolescents with burns. *Journal of Burn Care and Rehabilitation, 15*(2), 158–63.

Robert, R., Blakeney, P., & Herndon, D. (2006). Child maltreatment. In D. Herndon (Ed.), *Total burn care* (3rd ed.) (pp. 771–780). New York: W. B. Saunders..

Robert, R., Blakeney, P., Villarreal, C., Rosenberg, L., & Meyer, W. J., III. (1999). Imipramine treatment in pediatric burn patients with symptoms of acute stress disorder: A pilot study. *Journal of the American Academy of Child and Adolescent Psychiatry, 38*(7), 873–882.

Robert, R., Brack, A., Blakeney, P., Villarreal, C., Rosenberg, L., Thomas, C., et al. (2003). A double-blind study of the analgesic efficacy of oral transmucosal fentanyl citrate and oral morphine in pediatric patients undergoing burn dressing change and tubbing. *Journal of Burn Care and Rehabilitation, 24*(6), 351–355.

Robert, R., Rosenberg, L., Rosenberg, M., & Meyer, W. J., III. (2004). Firesetting behavior. Paper presented at the annual meeting of the American Burn Association, Vancouver, British Columbia, Canada.

Robert, R., Villarreal, C., Blakeney, P., & Meyer, W. (1999). An approach to timely treatment of acute stress disorder. *Journal of Burn Care and Rehabilitation, 20*(3), 250–258.

Robins, L., Helzer, J., Croughan, J., & Ratcliff, K. (1981). National Institute of Mental Health interview schedule. *Archives of General Psychiatry, 38*, 381–389.

Rothbaum, B., Foa, E., Riggs, D., Murdock, T., & Walsh, W. (1992). A prospective examination of post-traumatic stress disorder in rape victims. *Journal of Traumatic Stress, 5,* 455–475.

Sack, W., Clarke, G., Him, C., Dickason, D., Goff, B., Lanham, K., et al. (1993). A six year follow-up of Cambodian adolescents. *Journal of the American Academy of Child and Adolescent Psychiatry, 32,* 3–15.

Saigh, P. (1996). Posttraumatic stress disorder among children and adolescents: An introduction. *Journal of School Psychology, 34*(2), 103–105.

Saigh, P. A., Yasik, A. E., & Oberfield, R. A. (2000). The Children's PTSD Inventory: Development and reliability. *Journal of Traumatic Stress, 13,* 369–380.

Saigh, P. A. (2004). *Children's PTSD Inventory [Manual].* San Antonio, TX: PsychCorp.

Saxe, G., Chawla, N., Stoddard, F., Kassam-Adams, N., Courtney, D., Cunningham, K., et al. (2003). Child Stress Disorders Checklist: A measure of ASD and PTSD in children. *Journal of the American Academy of Child and Adolescent Psychiatry, 42*(8), 972–978.

Saxe, G., Miller, A., Bartholomew, D., Hall, E., Lopez, C., Kaplow, J., et al. (2005). Incidence of and risk factors for acutes stress disorder in children with injuries. *Journal of Trauma 59*(4), 946–953.

Shakespeare, V. (1998). Effect of small burn injury on physical, social and psychological health at 3–4 months after discharge, *Burns, 24,* 739–744.

Shemesh, E., Annunziato, R., Newcorn, J., Rockmore, L., Bierer, L., Cohen, J., et al. (2006). Assessment of posttraumatic stress symptoms in children who are medically ill and children presenting to a child trauma program. *Annals of New York Academy of Science, 1071,* 472–477.

Sheridan, R., Hinson, M., & Nackel, A. (1997). Development of a pediatric burn pain and anxiety management program. *Journal of Burn Care and Rehabilitation, 18,* 455–459.

Steinberg, A., Brymer, M., Decker, K., & Pynoos, R. (2004). The University of California at Los Angeles Post-Traumatic Stress Disorder Reaction Index. *Current Psychiatry Reports, 6*(2), 96–100

Stoddard, F. (1989). A diagnostic outcome study of children and adolescents with severe burns. *Journal of Trauma, 29*(4), 471–477.

Stoddard, F. (1993). A psychiatric perspective on self-inflicted burns. *Journal of Burn Care and Rehabilitation, 14*(4), 480–482.

Stoddard, F., Norman, D., Murphy, M., & Beardslee, W. (1989). Psychiatric outcome of burned children and adolescents. *Journal of the American Academy of Child and Adolescent Psychiatry, 28*(4), 589–595.

Stoddard, F., Pahlavan, K., & Cahners, S. (1985). Suicide attempted by self-immolation during adolescence. I. Literature review, case reports, and personality precursors. *Adolescent Psychiatry, 12,* 251–265.

Stoddard, F., Saxe, G., Ronfeldt, H., Drake, J., Burns, J., Edgren, C., et al. (2006a). Acute stress symptoms in young children with burns. *Journal of the American Academy of Child and Adolescent Psychiatry, 45*(1), 87–93.

Stoddard, F., Ronfeldt, H., Kagan, J., Drake, J., Snidman, N., Murphy, J., et al. (2006b). Young burned children: The course of acute stress and physiological and behavioral responses. *American Journal of Psychiatry, 163*(6), 1084–1090.

Stuber, M., Kazak, A., Meeske, K., Barakat, L., Guthrie, D., Garnier, H., et al. (1997). Predictors of posttraumatic stress symptoms in childhood cancer survivors. *Pediatrics, 100*(6), 958–964.

Stuber, M., Shemesh, E., & Saxe, G. (2003). Posttraumatic stress responses in children with life-threatening illnesses. *Child and Adolescent Psychiatric Clinics of North America*, *12*(2), 195–209.

Taal, L., & Faber, A. (1998). Posttraumatic stress and maladjustment among adult burn survivors 1 to 2 years postburn. Part II: The interview data. *Burns, 24*, 399–405.

Taylor, S. (2006). *Clinician's guide to PTSD: A cognitive-behavioral approach.* New York: Guilford.

Tcheung, W. J., Robert, R., Rosenberg, L., Rosenberg, M., Villarreal, C., Thomas, C., et al. (2005). Early treatment of acute stress disorder in children suffering from major burn injury. *Pediatric Critical Care Medicine, 6*(6), 676–681.

Tedstone, J. E., & Tarrier, N. (1997). An investigation of the prevalence of psychological morbidity in burn-injured patients. *Burns, 23*(7–8), 550–554.

Thomas, C., Ayoub, M., Rosenberg, L., Robert, R., & Meyer, W. (2004). Attention deficit hyperactivity disorder and burn injury. *Burns, 30*(3), 221–224.

Thomas, C., Meyer, W. J., III, & Blakeney, P. (2002.) Psychiatric disorders associated with burn injury. In D. Herndon (Ed.), *Total burn care* (2nd ed., pp. 766–773). New York: W. B. Saunders.

Thygesen, P., Hermann, K., & Willanger, R. (1970). Concentration camp survivors in Denmark: Persecution, disease, disability, compensation. *Danish Medical Bulletin, 17*, 65–108.

Tomich, P., & Helgeson, V. (2004). Is finding something good in the bad always good? Benefit finding among women with breast cancer. *Health Psychology, 23*, 16–23.

van Loey, N. E., Maas, C. J., Faber, A. W., & Taal, L. A. (2003). Predictors of chronic posttraumatic stress symptoms following burn injury: Results of a longitudinal study. *Journal of Traumatic Stress 16*(4), 361–369.

van Zomeren, A. H., ten Duis H. J., Minderhoud, J. M., & Sipma, M. (1998). *Journal of Neurological and Neurosurgical Psychiatry, 64*(6), 763–9.

Wicks-Nelson, R., & Israel, A. C. (1991). *Behavior disorders of childhood* (2nd ed.). Englewood Cliffs, NJ: Prentice Hall.

Wilcox, D. (2000, June 14-16). What is juvenile firesetting? The scope and complexity of the problem. Paper presented at the Juvenile Firesetting Intervention Conference sponsored by the Houston fire department, Houston, Texas.

Wilcox, D., & Kolko, D. (2002). Assessing recent firesetting behavior and taking a firesetting history. In D. Kolko (Ed.), *Handbook on firesetting in children and youth.* San Diego: Academic Press.

Williams E. E., & Griffiths, T. A. (1991). Psychological consequences of burn injury. *Burns, 17*(6), 478–480.

Yule, W., & Williams, R. (1990). Post-traumatic stress reactions in children. *Journal of Traumatic Stress, 3*, 279–295.

Zatzick, D. F., Marmar, C. R., Weis, D. S., & Metzler, T. (1994). Dose trauma-lined dissociation vary across ethnic groups? *Journal of Nervous and Mental Disorders, 182*(10), 576–582.

CHAPTER 7

The Trauma of Spinal Cord Injury

Frank J. Padrone

This chapter brings together the often devastating experience of spinal cord injury (SCI) and the phenomenon of trauma that can result in posttraumatic stress disorder (PTSD). It opens with a series of brief descriptions of the onset of the injury, and then to capture more closely a person's actual experience, information on spinal cord functioning and the consequences of injury is presented. There is an interlacing throughout of the effects of SCI and those of trauma, beginning with the emotional impact of SCI. The phenomenon of trauma is presented, followed by actual case illustrations of the impact of SCI and its long-term effects. The path through adjustment, healing, and psychological treatment is reviewed, with a closing section on policy issues.

> I was diving into the water, and then my head hit something.... There I was at the bottom, and I couldn't move. (Quadriplegia, now called tetraplegia, 21-year-old male)

> We were moving along, and then skidding ... and the tree.... The next thing I woke up in the hospital, and looked down at the catheter (I learned later) coming out of the end of the penis. I knew I couldn't feel it. (Quadriplegia, now called tetraplegia, 26-year-old male)

> The elevator fell like a rock. And then I was lying there in the dark ... and realized I couldn't move my legs, and slowly realized that I couldn't feel a thing below my waist. (Paraplegia, 21-year-old female)

> I knew it was serious by the time I got to the emergency room, but then the questions ... I couldn't feel.... the shouting ... the lights. (Paraplegia, 20-year-old female)

> And whenever I have a bowel accident, she says I go crazy. (Paraparesis, 42-year-old male)

Whenever she catheterizes me, I'm like in a different world. I'm really not there.
(Quadriplegia, now called tetraplegia, 29-year-old male)

When considering the experiences described above, we might ask not only
what is the trauma, but also where does it begin and where does it end? To com-
prehend the trauma of SCI, it is necessary to have some appreciation of the
circumstances of the initial injury, as well as the numerous losses and changes
that result. Such losses have an ongoing impact that affects not only the survivor
but also anyone who is close to him/her.

Significant physical disability usually affects more aspects of life than one can
initially realize, which can be said about most disabilities. The fact that SCI can
affect so many of the body's physical systems, however, has led victims to comment in anguish at times that there is no area of life that has gone untouched by
their injury and disability. The initial experiences of the physical, emotional, and
interpersonal consequences of SCI may represent only the starting points of the
impact, as one moves forward into daily living. These consequences reappear and
are reexperienced over time, often with dismay, frustration, and the painfully
acute awareness that only personal experience can produce.

The following is a brief outline of spinal cord function. The spinal cord extends
from the base of the brain and ends in the mid-lumbar region. It is essentially a
bundle of nerves, surrounded by a boney column of vertebrae, which carries messages to and from the brain. Messages from the brain provide movement and
strength to all muscles of the body, including the ability to breathe and control
bowel and bladder functions. Messages to the brain provide physical feelings or
sensations from all areas of the body.

To provide a better understanding of the physical effects of SCI, a brief overview of the regions of the spine and parts of the body that they innervate may be
helpful. These regions are numbered in descending order from the brain.

Cervical Region (C1–C8): Located in the neck and controls the back of the head, the
    neck, shoulders, arms, hands, and diaphragm.
Thoracic Region (T1–T12): Located in the upper back and controls the torso and
    parts of the arms.
Upper Lumbar (L1–L5): Middle of the back, below the ribs and controls hips/legs.
Sacral Segments (S1–S5): Located just below the upper lumbar region and controls
    the groin, toes, and some parts of the legs.

There are two types of spinal cord injuries: complete and partial. If a spinal cord
injury is complete, there is no voluntary function below the point of injury. This
means the person will experience no sensation or voluntary movement below that
point. A complete injury at the cervical level results in paralysis and loss of sensation to all four limbs and the trunk (quadriplegia or tetraplegia) and loss of ability
to control all functions below that level, such as bowel and bladder control and
many sexual functions. Furthermore, if the spinal cord injury is high, for example
C1 or C2, the person may need a respirator or diaphragmatic pacemaker to breathe
properly. Other complications that may result from a spinal cord injury are low

blood pressure, an inability to regulate blood pressure, reduced control of body temperature, an inability to sweat that occurs below the level of injury, and chronic pain. Patients with cervical spinal injuries also have an increased susceptibility to respiratory disease, especially due to the fact that they are often unable to cough and due to difficulties with blood pressure regulation, known as autonomic dysreflexia. Complete injury below the cervical level results in dysfunction to the lower parts of the body (paraplegia) (Cleveland Clinic, 2006).

As noted above, many victims experience incomplete losses (partial injury), where some of the neurological pathways necessary for motor activity and sensory experience continue to be able to route their messages. Some or all of the physical systems may have partial function, such as some voluntary movement of legs or even a toe, with varying degrees of strength. There also may be partial or spotty sensation, in addition to varying degrees of voluntary control over different bodily functions.

The loss of the ability to move voluntarily below the level of the injury has a myriad of implications that most people do not imagine unless trained in the area. The full awareness of losses requires firsthand knowledge of their implications for living, which is acquired over time through daily experience. The loss of bowel and bladder control, the loss of sensation, the loss of many or even most of the physical aspects of sexual functioning, and potential infertility in men round out the beginning of the losses. To list the systems that have suffered damage yields a deceptively simple description of what the effects of SCI truly are. The real life consequences of each of these areas of functioning, ranging from the obvious to the subtle, become apparent to those affected only over time.

Emotional and Psychological Impact of Spinal Cord Injury

To understand more clearly the extent of stress and trauma of SCI, an awareness of the obvious and subtle losses in function is necessary. It has been our experience both clinically and in our Internship Training Program in Clinical Psychology at Rusk Institute of Rehabilitation Medicine, New York University Medical Center, that to begin to become aware of the impact of SCI, it is necessary first to know what the physical losses involve, before one can begin to understand the psychological impact.

As an example of the need for experience, the case of a 24-year-old man can be illustrative. He had been recuperating in bed for weeks after SCI, and expressed an eagerness to start using a wheelchair. Within two days of beginning to use the wheelchair, he became irritable, glum, and depressed. Not until he was actually using the wheelchair did he begin to process the full experience of his loss of the ability to walk. In this same way, the first full awareness for many people that they cannot embrace a loved one, hold a baby in their arms, pursue a toddler, or defend a loved one can be an excruciating experience. Such a level of awareness may not be reached until the actual event is thought through in detail or actually encountered. Additionally, it seems that this emotional pain can be reexperienced with future encounters. Similarly, to hear that one very likely may not be able to have an orgasm, or at least not one similar to previous experience, may be a shock. Consider on an individual basis the repeated exposure to sexual experiences with arousal but not orgasm. At the interpersonal level, the individual experiences can become reciprocal and intensified. Overall then, it seems that before a genuine appreciation can be developed for the impact of SCI, some knowledge of the obvious and subtle losses is essential.

If one is totally or completely paralyzed below the injury, mobility is restricted, and one probably requires the use of a wheelchair to get around. Obvious! It may be ultimately true that a wheelchair is not a problem but a solution to a problem. Initially however, getting around in the chair leads to the firsthand experience that "I can't walk," or other difficult realizations, which derive from the actual living and experiencing of what is known.

Additionally, not so obvious with various levels of paralysis may be the inability to move one's body from one surface (wheelchair) to another (commode), called a transfer. Depending on the level of disability, a transfer may require considerable help, ranging from verbal guidance to total assistance with the maneuver, which involves essentially being lifted from one surface to another. The actual experience can include associated acute feelings of dependence, helplessness, and embarrassment as the process is learned through repeated daily experiences that will interact with personality factors. Similarly, depending on the level of the injury, varying degrees of assistance with dressing may be necessary. Such a need can bring on a host of feelings, which can increase when the helper shifts from hospital personnel to a home attendant or loved one.

If bladder and bowel control are lost, one may have "accidents." Obvious! Not so obvious is that catheterizations may be necessary until the end of life, performed by the person with the disability, or a stranger, or a loved one. Bowel routines that prevent unexpected bowel accidents may involve insertion of rectal suppositories to prepare for elimination or digital removal of the stool from the bowel by the victim or someone else. The stress of such an experience in our culture has led some young men, when approached for education on the process, to "curse out" a nurse repeatedly, until they were able to tolerate what they perceived as a humiliating horror.

If all sensation is lost, one does not have the sense of touch, temperature, or pain. Obvious! Not so obvious is the pressure sore that can develop on the buttocks as a result of paralysis and the lack of sensation. The sore or decubitus can result in the need to lie on a special mattress for a month, in order to heal. The new sense of vulnerability and helplessness that one now feels is a byproduct. In addition, feelings of shock and embarrassment can follow from awareness of a noxious odor, when one suddenly realizes that a bowel accident has occurred that was not perceived in any way.

Although sexual feelings of arousal and sexual activity continue after SCI, there are often distressing experiences of losses and changes in sexual functioning (Sipski & Alexander, 1992) that may be even less apparent than other losses. Such losses are contingent upon the extent of the injury (complete or incomplete) and on the level of SCI (lower or upper level). Sexual functions affected can include the following: orgasm for men and women, erection and ejaculation for men, vaginal lubrication for women, and fertility for men but not for women once menstruation resumes (Bors & Comarr, 1960; National Spinal Cord Injury Information Network, 2000). An extensive literature exists on SCI and sexual functioning, including treatment approaches to the various difficulties (Sipski, Alexander, & Gomez-Marin, 2006).

These losses can remain unnoticed, unless actually experienced or actively considered, as is expected in acute rehabilitation. The realization that there is no longer direct sexual pleasure from the sense of touch below the level of injury can be disheartening. Obvious! Less apparent are the actual experiences of the losses, for example, orgasm, and what the actual sexual experience might be for a person with SCI. For example, after five months of rehabilitation, a 40-year-old woman with complete tetraplegia, was stunned when she realized that sexual intercourse would no longer include internal vaginal sensation. The realization developed only after she had been gently led to the awareness through a series of leading questions.

Emotional reactions following SCI can be varied and significant. Depression following SCI has been examined extensively. It has been considered a secondary complication that negatively impacts the quality of life for primary and secondary victims (Elliot & Frank, 1996). Although much of the literature reports less depression with SCI than is commonly believed, most of this research focuses on major depressive disorder (MDD), which may tend to omit the less intense depressive reactions that are commonly observed. With major depression there can be the risk of suicide. DeVivo, Black, Richards, and Stover (1991) found that the suicide rate among SCI victims was almost five times greater than among the general population, with the highest rate occurring within five years after injury. The University of Washington Rehabilitation Medicine update on spinal cord injury (2001) points out that the highest rate of MDD among medical patients occurs with SCI at 23–30 percent.

It should also be noted that the data on the question of suicide rates do not include information on what has been called passive suicide, which can occur when efforts at maintaining health or treating the medical complications from SCI are not applied. A more accurate estimate of the incidence of suicide in SCI requires a consideration of other variables, such as the presence of psychiatric illness, the existence of previous suicide attempts, and whether the onset of SCI had been the result of a suicide attempt. The psychological impact of SCI is made even more vivid when considering vulnerability to suicide. The consensus in the mental health community is that MDD is a treatable condition. Combined use of antidepressant medication and psychotherapy has been found to be effective, although access to medication may be more readily available than psychotherapy.

Heinrich, Tate, and Buckelew (1994) examined the responses to the Brief Symptom Inventory of 225 people with SCI at three points over a period of more than two years. They found significantly higher scores on all of the symptom scales for

SCI victims than for the normative group. They concluded that the patterns of response were less indicative of psychopathology than of reaction to traumatic injury. Symptoms decreased after 24 months had elapsed, suggesting a greater need for mental health services during this initial period. The fact that the initial assessment was conducted at discharge from inpatient rehabilitation, which often represents a period (one to four months) of increased psychological distress, suggests the possibility of even greater distress following injury. Dryden et al. (2005) reviewed depression and SCI, with a focus on risk factors. Results of this review showed that of 201 SCI patients, 28.9 percent were treated for depression. Such a classification might suggest that the incidence of depression is in fact higher, since it does not include those with depression who were not treated. Psychological risk factors included a history of depression and/or substance abuse.

In addition to psychological sequelae of SCI, another area of investigation has been that of possible neuropsychological or cognitive effects. Clinical observations and analyses of injuries, which consider the extent of the physical forces on the body during SCI, have led to a body of work on the incidence of mild traumatic brain injury (MTBI) as a comorbidity. A review by Hess, Marwitz, and Kreutzer (2003) concludes that as many as 40 percent of SCI victims may have suffered some MTBI, not only from a blow to the head but also from the acceleration and deceleration forces involved in the incident. They report disagreement in the SCI literature; for example, Trieschmann's work (1988) asserts that the incidence is overestimated and that the findings are based more on emotional trauma. Hess, Marwitz, and Kreutzer reasonably conclude that treatment planning should screen for cognitive deficits, and appropriate modifications in treatment can be provided to assist with learning new skills as indicated. Following a neuropsychological evaluation, cognitive rehabilitation, which research has shown to be effective, also can be provided.

The literature on SCI abounds with descriptions and evidence of the broad range of emotional reactions and disruptions that flood the injured person and all those involved. Heinemann and Rawal (2005) provide an excellent review of the work in the field, including emotional and behavioral reactions, models of adjustment, life satisfaction, coping, family support, and substance abuse. They conclude, drawing somewhat on Hammell's (1992) conclusions, that adjustment may be a long-term process, which only begins in acute rehabilitation, and that recognition of individual differences by health care providers is essential when assisting people with SCI.

With this brief overview of examples of the onset of SCI and some of the initial and long-term stressful experiences, consideration of trauma phenomena in the context of SCI now can be more meaningful. The proposition can be advanced that there is more trauma today than ever before. More people survive trauma as primary and secondary victims than ever before, given widespread technological advances in recent decades. These advances have a direct bearing on both the occurrence of and survival from SCI. A total of 11,000 individuals per year survive SCI in the United States, with approximately 250,000 people currently living in the United Sates with SCI (National Spinal Cord Injury Information Network, 2006).

Etiology and demographics reported by Richards, Kewman, and Pierce (2000), regarding both complete and partial SCI, show that more than 50 percent of injuries occur between 16 and 30 years of age, with 82 percent of those injured being male. Heinemann and Rawal (2005) offer the following statistical data on SCI victims. Males continue to account for 80 percent of SCIs, but there is an increase noted in persons 60 years of age and older. The latter group now makes up 10 percent of the SCI population, probably due to falls and other injuries. Following rehabilitation, 94 percent of persons with SCI return to live in a private residence; this percentage increases to 98 percent within 10 years after injury. Within two years after injury, 13 percent are competitively employed, increasing to 38 percent within 12 years. Divorce rates are noted to be 19 percent higher with SCI than in the general population, eight years after injury. The past 20 years have seen an increase in injuries due to violence, for example, gunshot wounds. Carey and Lakso (2006) find half of SCIs result from motor vehicle accidents, with substance abuse continuing to be a major risk factor at onset.

Trauma and Posttraumatic Stress Disorder

Certainly trauma is not new, but over recent decades there has been an increase in the study of the phenomenon, resulting in a growing body of knowledge. When examining the experience of trauma, consideration of stress is essential. Stress can be viewed as the mental tension and strain (*Webster's New World Dictionary*, 1991) that accompanies adjustment or coping with change. Stress can result from positive and negative experiences. When people are coping with traumatic experiences, the resulting stress is labeled traumatic stress. When stress following a traumatic incident continues, it has been called posttraumatic stress (PTS; Rothschild, 2000).

PTSD is defined in the *Diagnostic and Statistical Manual* of the American Psychiatric Association (*DSM-IV*, 1994), as follows: "The essential feature of Posttraumatic Stress Disorder is the development of characteristic symptoms following exposure to an extreme traumatic stressor " (p. 424). The formal diagnosis of PTSD in the same manual requires the following detailed considerations: The event must involve actual or threatened death or serious injury, or a threat to the physical integrity of self or others, and the person needs to experience intense fear, helplessness, or horror.

These events overwhelm the ability to cope. They pose danger and produce feelings such as helplessness and terror. One does not need to imagine but only review the previously listed narratives of those SCI victims, to see how well their experiences fit into this PTS category. In addition to what can be viewed as the emotional scarring of an experience, there has been a growing body of literature on the physiological reactions to stress that can help to form an understanding of just how traumatic experiences lead to PTS and PTSD. Both the onset of SCI and the ongoing life experiences with this disability can be traumatic, so that PTS can be an ongoing reality for many with SCI. Such a conclusion is underscored by Bracken and Shepherd (1980), who observed that SCI is "one of the most extreme psychological insults of all forms of trauma" (p. 74).

Koren, Hemel, and Klein (2006) suggest that if a traumatic event is accompanied by a physical injury, there is an increased risk for PTSD, and that this relationship may not be related to the severity of the injury, but rather to psychophysiological reactions that involve threat.

Psychological Reactions to Trauma Are Relative

Although trauma may be one of those aspects of human experience that some can describe as "You know it when you see it," such as surviving a horrific accident, being assaulted, or suffering a SCI (often referred to as "breaking one's neck or back"), not all such events are equally traumatic to people who experience them. Krystal (1985) suggests that trauma is defined by the person's perception of it, which involves affective and cognitive processes. Although the events are objective, they are recorded in a person's subjective experience of his/her helpless situation. Personal meaning is given to these events based on past experiences and views one has of oneself.

Since trauma can be conceptualized as personally defined, which has been this author's experience in working directly and indirectly (in supervision of others) with more than 1,000 SCI victims. It cannot be assumed that all people who experience the same horrible event will experience it as equally traumatizing. Not all people in the same horrific accident, even if they suffer the same injuries, have the same experience. So too, it has been our experience that not all people with a C4–5 tetraplegia experience exactly the same emotional impact, even though the physical losses may be identical. Such differences seem to be based in part on the meaning ascribed to the event from pretrauma experiences.

Giller (1999) also emphasizes that the key element in trauma is the person's subjective experience. An event or ongoing condition can be said to be traumatic when it overwhelms the person's ability to integrate the emotional experience, and the person subjectively experiences that life, body integrity, or even sanity are threatened. "Psychologically, the bottom line of trauma is overwhelming emotion and a feeling of utter helplessness, with physiological upheaval that plays a leading role in the long range effects" (p. 14).

Consideration has been given to the possibility of a greater vulnerability in some individuals to developing PTSD. Scharff and Scharff (1994) suggest that trauma in childhood and genetic factors may contribute to this predisposition. Such trauma in the context of the absence of healthy attachment to caretakers may result in a diminished ability to regulate stress during later traumatic experiences (Rothschild, 2000). More recently, attempts to expand our understanding of trauma, as well as the treatment of PTS and PTSD, are bringing together notions from neurobiology, childhood development, and psychodynamic psychotherapy, leading to a new paradigm that posits an ongoing interaction between experience and biology (Shore, 2002). The implication is that just as trauma may modify brain function, so too may positive life experiences. Since psychotherapy can be such a positive experience, this proposition may bode well for the treatment of trauma, to be addressed later. Cappas, Andres-Hyman, and Davidson (2005) are more explicit on this subject, when listing their principles of brain-based psychotherapy, which include the principle that "Experience transforms the brain" (p. 375).

PTSD is not uncommon. Approximately 8 percent of the population (Green & Kaltman, 2003) will suffer this malady at some point. The incidence of PTSD following SCI is extensively reviewed by Nielson (2003). Rates vary from 10 percent to 45 percent. Nielson concludes that the differences in rates may be explained by methodological issues. Distinction between one-time traumas and repeated traumas has been made by Terr (1991). She notes that physical disability represents a type of repeated trauma, in that the reexperiencing of physical limitations is retraumatizing. Persistent pain and the existence of previous unrelated trauma are two risk factors that can increase the risk for PTSD following physical injury (Martz, 2005).

In addition, it reasonably can be proposed that there are many people who have suffered and survived traumas, including SCI, who do not meet the criteria for a diagnosis of PTSD but who have some or many of the symptoms, with which they and their loved ones are quite familiar. Blanchard, et al. (1995) suggest that in such situations, criteria have been met for partial PTSD. These victims likely suffer from PTS (Rothschild, 2000). The incidence of PTS and PTSD in families of children with SCI was reviewed by Boyer, Knolls, Kaflakas, Tollen, and Swartz (2000). They found evidence for PTSD in 25 percent of the patients, 41 percent of the mothers and 35 percent of the fathers, demonstrating the traumatic impact on secondary victims.

Although the subjective meaning of experience significantly contributes to trauma, that meaning is not simple or readily apparent. For example, regarding a disability there is the practical meaning, such as physical dependence and the inability to perform specific tasks. There is also the psychological meaning, experienced at onset and ascribed to losses of function that are based on psychodynamic factors, which can be disruptive. There may be specific threats to the ego and to strategies or defenses that had been used to cope in the past with inner conflict but that may no longer be useful (Padrone, 1999). Meaning then exists at multiple levels.

Recent work on the role of responsibility or causal attributions in PTSD and trauma is relevant. Massad and Hulsey (2006) propose that the development and maintenance of causal attributions contribute to the meaning of the experience. Self blame, for example, that continues on a long-term basis may contribute to the development of PTSD. It is noted, however, that causal attribution is only one of the aspects to be considered in treatment of the trauma of SCI.

Case Examples

The following case examples are presented to demonstrate some of the traumatic aspects of SCI, ranging from experiences at onset through reintegration into the community and well into full participation in life. They are drawn from the experience of many different people with SCI. Descriptions of persons involved have been modified and experiences integrated to preserve anonymity, while retaining the relevant issues. Each of the people described had the following stressful experiences in common: They endured the trauma of the injury and the emergency room experience, including threat to life and feelings of helplessness. The victims each had repeated experiences with bladder and bowel accidents due to incontinence. They each subjectively experienced the incontinence as more emotionally intolerable than had initially been apparent. Psychological symptoms developed, despite the fact that the incontinence was managed after discharge from rehabilitation through regimens and devices.

The three people had the following losses in common. None of the three any longer experienced orgasmic reactions, and the men no longer experienced psychogenic erections. The two SCI victims with tetraplegia regained some abilities, through intensive rehabilitation, that reduced the amount of help they needed, but they were both dependent in most activities of daily living. They needed significant assistance moving in and out of a wheelchair to any other surface, and help with bladder and bowel management, showering, dressing, and other activities of daily living. They were able to perform some upper body grooming and eating/drinking with adaptive devices. They both had lost all sensation below the level of the injury, which when combined with paralysis resulted in the need for scheduled turns in bed and weight shifting in their wheelchair to prevent pressure sores on the buttocks. Such sores or "skin breakdowns" can require many weeks on a special bed to heal, and can lead to life-threatening infections unless properly addressed. Both victims also had difficulty coughing, due to paralysis of the intercostals and abdominal muscles, resulting in increased vulnerability to upper respiratory infections. The PTSD symptoms of numbing, dissociation, explosiveness, vigilance, and avoidance can be found among their experiences.

CASE EXAMPLE 1

A 40-year-old man suffered a lower thoracic (T10) incomplete injury in a motor vehicle accident, while working as a salesman. He later reported being trapped in the car, unable to move or feel his legs, and in considerable pain. He reported the increasing odor of something smoldering, and feared the car would go up in flames while he was trapped. Following his rescue, his emergency room experiences included ongoing pain, while the various tests confirmed he was not able to feel. There was the need to insert a urinary catheter into the penis, which he suddenly realized he was able to see but not feel. Surgery was performed to stabilize his spine.

Two weeks later he was admitted to inpatient rehabilitation with a disability of paraparesis, which involved extreme muscle weakness of the legs and bowel and bladder incontinence due to sphincter dysfunction. There was loss of most sensation from the level of injury downward, although there were areas of spared sensation. He was physically helped from a wheelchair to all other surfaces. He was wheeled into the shower, where he required assistance. Initially he needed help with dressing and undressing. His reactions to experiences with bowel and bladder accidents were considered to have been muted. Overall, in addition to irritability and angry outbursts at staff and his wife, there was considerable difficulty in compliance with various schedules and the typical skin precautions.

By the time of discharge there was some additional return of spotty sensation. Muscle strength improved so that he was eventually able to use crutches to walk short distances, although he still required a wheelchair for long distances. He was able to manage the necessary intermittent catheterizations three times daily and his own bowel routine, requiring suppositories. He was seen only periodically by a psychologist due to his resistance to the contact throughout his inpatient stay, and participated in only two sessions with his wife for sexual counseling, as he was not able to experience psychogenic or reflex erections.

Two years after discharge he was referred by his physician for outpatient psychotherapy for treatment of a reactive depression. His increasing depression was marked by angry outbursts, followed by several days of agitation and withdrawal, following most bowel accidents. His wife's description of his reaction: "It's as if he'd been boiled in oil."

Treatment revealed that by history this man had derived considerable self-esteem from what might be considered "traditional" values of manliness. He had taken some pride in being a "take charge guy," who did not shrink from challenges and was a successful breadwinner. The experience of bowel accidents at home, away from the clinical setting of the hospital, was acutely agonizing for him. He felt like a "helpless child." Such thoughts, when allowed to flow, gave way to memories of the helplessness and fear he had experienced in his smoldering car, while awaiting rescue. These and subsequent repeated experiences of his loss of strength and virility, in the context of a significantly diminished standard of living, had shattered his view of himself.

Bowel accidents seemed to be both the trigger for and a condensed version of his combined experience of helplessness, fear, and inadequacy, which was as intolerable as the "boiling" that his wife had sensed. In addition, the extensive list of health regimens and precautions that he experienced as emasculating was an ongoing confirmation and reminder of the nightmare of his journey, which he avoided through noncompliance.

CASE EXAMPLE 2

An 18-year-old woman involved in a motor vehicle accident as the driver, soon after she had earned her license, suffered a C4–5 fracture, with a complete spinal cord injury. She awakened in the emergency room, tetraplegic and intubated (a tube had been passed through her mouth and down her windpipe to mechanically ventilate her), since she could not breathe adequately on her own. She soon underwent neurosurgery for spinal fusion to stabilize cervical vertebrae. Later, during hospitalization in acute rehabilitation she progressed to using a wheelchair with rubber "quad tips" that enabled her to propel the chair for short distances. Neurogenic bladder was managed with an indwelling catheter that required periodic cleaning and changing by another person. She used a urinary collection leg bag, which she was able to empty independently, but which also required periodic cleaning. Bowel routines required oral colonic stimulants and rectal suppositories, inserted by family or attendant, usually over a commode or in bed, depending on the condition of her skin. Bowel accidents were rare, but could occur with gastrointestinal (GI) illness or eating the "wrong foods," following which she required total assistance for cleansing.

During her six months in rehabilitation, she had considerable emotional support from family and friends. Such support continued after her discharge and return home. She was included in all family gatherings. Interactions with her were almost always upbeat and encouraging. From the onset, depressed or sad feelings were quickly neutralized and met with distractions. The family provided a 12-hour attendant at home to provide for all of her physical needs, later including an increase to 24-hour help, so that the attendant accompanied her to college. It was as if every possible effort to prevent or minimize sadness or frustration was successful. She eventually became a successful writer, and married at age 27 to a man aged 30. They had two children for whom she cared, with the help of an attendant, some family members, and her husband.

At age 39 she sought psychotherapy at her husband's urging. Increasing marital conflict over daily interactions, routines, and responsibilities was the presenting problem. It soon was revealed that her dissatisfaction with home attendants had led to her routinely firing them every three to six months. She and her husband had frequent spats over her minor needs, for example, a glass of water. She also was experiencing an increase in the "insensitivity" of her children, now nine and seven years old, and becoming quite critical of them.

Work in therapy revealed that her experience of frustrations, which resulted from her disability and which were not anticipated by others or immediately relieved by them, was certainly contrary to her experiences over the years with her family. Her surface reaction was that they did not care enough to help her with what "anyone could see" was a problem for her. She soon angrily accused others of being inconsiderate or selfish. Attendants were held to a similar standard, including taking the responsibility to remember what she might need when away from home, for example, medications. They were labeled as irresponsible and undependable. Treatment revealed that these reactions were rather surface defenses to protect herself from the painful realization and natural grieving over losses that would occur if she were to endure the reality of her dependence. Such feelings of grief eventually did appear, when for the very first time since her injury, she wept, as she related the lost pleasure and freedom she once had felt, when running on a beach.

As this layer of shielded grief was experienced and dissolved, access to other layers became possible. There were more powerful feelings of impending panic in situations that forced a fuller experience of her disability. She was being protected from the overwhelmingly traumatic feelings of helplessness, which she had experienced in the emergency room, and then throughout much of her daily rehabilitation, as the "good patient." In addition, treatment revealed that the experience of total dependence connected to a lifelong conflict over maturation and independence, which had been marked by ambivalence. The natural process of separation and independence from the security provided in her home apparently had been slowed during her early years by several major disruptions in her family, leading to emotional reactions that had been repressed. Her conflict over independence had been disowned, and now led to intolerable anxiety, with the awareness of her total dependence. During the treatment of this intense anxiety, another terror emerged. Although her children were bused to school, she had refused to allow them to ride in a vehicle with any driver other than her husband. Her vigilance and avoidance of panic took the form of carefully detailed and elaborately organized arrangements for all of the children's outings, so that they and she did not experience the anxiety of a possible accident. There were also elements of guilt for her accident, since she had been an inexperienced driver.

CASE EXAMPLE 3

While practicing for a diving competition, a 19-year-old man was injured in a dive from the 40-foot platform. As he was emerging from a backward flip, he struck his head on the platform, suffering a C5–6 fracture with a complete injury. He then fell the 40 feet into the water, and remained well below the surface of the pool completely paralyzed. Even though stunned, he was desperately trying not to breathe, as he hoped he would be rescued in time. After what "seemed like ages," his colleagues pulled him up to the air, which he had difficulty breathing in, due to his inability to expand the muscles required.

His neck was placed in a supportive collar by the emergency medical technicians (EMTs). His emergency room experiences included the tests to confirm that he was not able to feel or move anything, except his face and head. Stabilization of his neck was assured by a halo traction device, which is composed of a narrow metal circle through which four pin-type posts are placed in the scalp. The posts were screwed into the scalp to the outer table of the skull. Two posts were placed near the top of his temples, and two others to the rear of his head to secure the circle, like spokes protruding from the hub of a wheel. The metal circle (the halo) was supported by rods extending downward to a shoulder/chest jacket that supported the halo. Following surgery to stabilize his spine, he was admitted with the halo in place and with tetraplegia for seven months of rehabilitation. His physical experiences were typical, although his skin required extra care to prevent pressure sores, to which he seemed more prone to develop than is usual.

At discharge from rehabilitation, he remained bladder incontinent, used a condom catheter and urine collection leg bag. Periodic catheterizations, which he was not able to perform himself, were necessary. Bowel routines required rectal suppositories, inserted by an attendant or family member either in bed or over a commode, depending on the condition of his skin. Bowel accidents were rare, but could occur with GI illness or eating the "wrong foods." He was capable of reflex erections.

He was able to propel his wheelchair for moderate distances, with rubber-tipped protrusions from the rim, called "quad tips." He also learned that he was prone to develop pressure sores on his buttocks, one of which required three weeks to heal, while he was confined to a special bed. A more careful than usual regimen of pressure relief, while seated in his wheelchair, in addition to planned turns in bed, was necessary to protect his skin. Finally, at some point in the future he would be able to learn to drive a specially-equipped motor vehicle.

His parents, especially his mother, had an extremely difficult time adjusting to the reality of the injury. His mother frequently would utter comments of desperation to him, and on occasion wail throughout the house that she didn't deserve this life. He avoided being at home as much as possible through his college years. His mother became increasingly depressed over time, and this worsened five years after his injury, when his father suddenly died. Although there was some home attendant care and assistance from two younger brothers, more of the work was assumed by his mother after his father's death. At age 29, he married a woman, aged 40, who had two pre-school-age children younger than 5 years of age. He was able to drive a specially equipped van, and was employed by an insurance company, dealing with customer complaints. Although he had a home attendant for four hours a day to help, his wife assumed many of the personal care needs when necessary, such as bladder catheterizations, bowel care, bathing, and dressing.

He entered psychotherapy six years later in reaction to feeling increasingly stressed, and when told by a physician that his significant increase in leg pain during muscle spasms might have a stress component. The sources of his stress seemed to be related to a number of experiences with the children. For example, he agonized over the fact that he was not able to attend parent-teacher conferences at the children's school, because there were flights of stairs leading to the three entrances. His initial reaction to this realization was a level of rage that he never before had experienced. In addition to such frustrations and his stress and pain, additional elements emerged in his treatment: While he was being catheterized and during his bowel routines, he tended to "space out," in a somewhat dissociated state. It was as if he were no longer present, and the voice of the person in attendance became a distant droning. There was also some intense anxiety regarding the children's well-being, especially their safety. If a family outing involved swimming, he would position himself nearby, assuring a direct line of sight, as he vigilantly watched over them.

The treatment revealed the ongoing elements of the trauma, which began with this capable athlete near the bottom of the pool. They continued through his helplessness in rehabilitation, and persisted through the "tortured years," bearing his mother's suffering. Apparently elements of dissociation began while at home. He struggled to ignore the stress of repeated experiences of physical helplessness, dependence, and added vulnerability due to his skin problems. Such stress increased in the presence of his wife, if there were any detectable signs of effort, strain or fatigue on her part. He could not so easily dismiss her reactions as merely histrionic, as he had his mother's reactions. His new found parenthood placed him in closer proximity to scenes similar to his accident, over which he now vigilantly and helplessly stood guard, while containing an inner terror.

Case Examples Review: Trauma Summary

In the vignettes sited, all three victims experienced the fear of death and helplessness at the time of accident and/or during treatment in the emergency room. Feelings of helplessness and vulnerability continued for two of the three for many years. One showed increased arousal with bouts of explosiveness, signs of an inability to tolerate inner experience. Two showed signs of avoidance of experiences that might result in hypervigilance or panic for them. One showed signs of dissociation. All three experienced being repeatedly traumatized by various aspects of their situation, which then intertwined with long-standing personal conflicts. It should be noted that only one of the three people suffered the pressure and stress of major financial concerns. Two of the three were gainfully employed, which spared them the more common experience of financial concerns that can lead to considerable distress for SCI victims.

The outcomes of treatment for these three people were all successful, in that the symptoms of PTS and PTSD were significantly reduced or eliminated. For example, for one, explosive rages and days of withdrawal no longer followed bowel accidents. There was certainly distress and reactions of "damn the [accidents, disability, or auto accident]," which seemed appropriate to the situation. These reactions were not nearly so disruptive, however, to his life or to his experiences with others. The other two patients experienced similar changes in coping with their own stressful experiences, in that symptoms of avoidance, dissociation, panic, or vigilance were no longer so significant. Distress continued to be experienced in many of the same situations, but at more appropriate levels. The treatment included: education regarding PTSD symptoms, a detailed review of trauma experiences, with careful attention to monitoring levels of stress, and psychodynamic psychotherapy.

Adjustment Process to SCI and Trauma

Much of the research does not support a linear or sequential stage model of adjustment. Apparently there is no single predictable sequence of reactions that

all victims of SCI experience. Catherall (2004) proposes a model for primary and
secondary victims of trauma on the road to healing, which builds on previous
models (Remer, 1984). Because of individual differences among victims and
variations in the nature of the trauma, there may not be universal applicability,
but the process is very similar to clinical experience. The stages are not distinct
or linear; they overlap and recycle, with some dependence among them. There is
also an interaction between the processes of the primary and secondary victims,
which much of the research in the area does not seem to consider. Unique to
Catherall's model is an initial stage that precedes the trauma and addresses
the background of the victims, which in clinical experience is seen as critical.
The complexity of the model is seen as its strength, in that it seems to describe
the reality of the healing process more accurately than other models do.

As Catherall (2004) explains, the primary victim's process includes six
stages:

(1) The *pretrauma stage* of the person's socialization background. To this background
    might be added the preexisting psychological factors or pretrauma personality
    for each of the victims and the dynamics of the preexisting relationship.
(2) The *trauma event* (for the primary victim) *and trauma awareness* for the sec-
    ondary victim may be multidimensional, especially with SCI. Clinical experi-
    ence suggests that awareness is an experiential process, which takes place
    over time and involves more than information. It also can involve emotionally
    laden insights about the present or inferences about the future.
(3) *Crisis/disorientation* can be marked by shock, denial, and a state of disorgani-
    zation. As this process moves forward, it may be revisited repeatedly by all
    involved.
(4) *Outward adjustment* occurs when the primary and secondary victims reinsti-
    tute old coping mechanisms on a personal and interpersonal level. This tem-
    porary adjustment eventually falters in the face of the need for significant
    personal and interpersonal change.
(5) *Reorganization* needs to occur on the personal (intrapsychic) and interper-
    sonal (relationship) level, as a result of the experience of what is called the
    "secondary traumatic impact." Integration of these changes needs to occur
    in this stage, once again in the pretrauma context (Catherall, 2004). Most
    important, and supported by clinical experience, is that this stage may be
    unsuccessful or incomplete, which can lead to a recycling to previous stages.
(6) *Integration and resolution*, the final healing stage, follows, when all involved have
    managed intrapsychic and relationship changes. The difference in the process
    between the primary and secondary victim is clearly the trauma event for the
    former. One of the key elements in this system is the ongoing interaction be-
    tween the stages of each of the victims, so that stresses in one can result in
    recycling for both, and progress in one can assist the progress of the other.

Although it may be disheartening to note that there may not be a final end
point to the process, since there can continue to be need for repeated adjust-
ments, the success achieved can be demonstrated by the extent of the need in the
future to return to previous steps. With success, the crisis stage will not be revisited. Recycling only to the *reorganization* stage, rather than a return to the crisis

stage, is the hallmark of success. The new challenges are now worked through more rapidly. Such ongoing experiences may be similar to the adjustment to psychological challenges and conflicts that most people face in their lives, but without the stress of trauma.

Healing and Seeking Help Following SCI

In keeping with the core meaning of trauma as a wound, there is an emphasis in the literature on recovery that focuses on the process of healing (Herman, 1997; Schiraldi, 2000). Since helplessness and disempowerment are two of the key aspects of trauma that are often concretized by physical disability, the field of rehabilitation advocates strongly for empowerment as an essential element to healing, as does Herman (1997).

Bearing in mind that healing is not an event, Schiraldi (2000) offers some insight into and indicators of the process, which is likened to having been thrust into a dark valley, out of which one may need to climb rather than emerge. This metaphor seems quite applicable to healing from the trauma of SCI. The healing is not a passive event and does not simply develop over time, although time may allow a necessary respite, so that inner resources can be called upon. Possibly due to the demands of the physical changes incurred with SCI, living with this disability is an active process that requires effort. Returning to the community and engaging life is usually a struggle. Having climbed back out of the valley, one will be able to feel strong and whole again after the process. One will be able to think or not to think about the traumatic events, and do so without a slide into a host of disturbing thoughts, but rather with feelings that are appropriate in intensity. The successful effort also can allow one to tolerate feelings that one was not able to endure, without states of arousal or numbing of the feelings of associated anxiety or depression. During the process, the mourning of losses will have occurred, along with reestablishing a personal sense of worth and strength, based on a realistic self-evaluation. Overall the outcome will reestablish a comfort level with all feelings, and a commitment to turning one's energy to living in the future, with a realistic sense of responsibility.

The process may be quicker for some than others, with movement up and back down. Dealing with the memories may require more than simply thinking about them; rather they will need to be processed in a such a way that one is able to assimilate and come to terms with them. Although this outcome is what may be meant by the term "acceptance," the use of the term is often experienced by SCI victims as glib. Notions of acceptance can be thought by victims to be based in insensitivity, ignorance, or denial. Constructs of assimilation, integration, or adjustment seem to more accurately include the idea of a process, rather than a decision to embrace, which acceptance may connote.

Despite signs of growing psychological distress, reluctance to seek and engage qualified help may persist. It may be helpful to bear in mind, in addition to the reluctance suggested by Good et al. (2006), that the feelings of helplessness and the fact of increased dependence following SCI can contribute to the reluctance to seek help. Of equal if not greater influence may be cultural factors that influence perspectives on health, medical care, physical disability, and psychological problems and their treatment. Schiraldi (2000) offers an overview of indicators for treatment and useful considerations in the selection of a treatment path, outlining various effective approaches that can be taken.

Psychological Intervention Following SCI

Various forms of psychological treatment are offered following SCI. The type of intervention provided can be determined by the setting and by the primary purpose of the treatment, for example, treatment of depression, PTSD, or adjustment to disability. Different techniques are employed, such as cognitive behavioral psychotherapy (CBT) and psychodynamic psychotherapy, in an individual and/or group format. Pharmacological treatment is also commonly used for treatment and to assist in the adjustment process. For people who require inpatient rehabilitation, psychological services are offered almost routinely, often as part of the interdisciplinary team approach to rehabilitation. Rehabilitation services to outpatients, who by definition have less physical disability, are usually prescribed on a discipline-specific basis, so that psychological services are offered less frequently.

Coping effectiveness training (CET), which is based in CBT techniques, has been found to be an effective group approach to improving psychological adjustment. Following treatment, a significant improvement in depression and anxiety was noted, when compared to controls (Kennedy, Duff, Evans, & Beedie, 2003). It was concluded that participants found the results of SCI to be more manageable, in addition to the benefit derived from group discussion and problem solving. Mixed findings have been reported on CBT by Craig, Hancock, Dickson, and Chang (1997). Significant change was not noted between treatment and control groups following treatment, but beneficial long-term effects on high levels of depression were reported a year later. It was concluded that CBT was effective over time with more intense depression.

Elliot and Kennedy (2004) conducted a review of research in the area of SCI and the treatment of depression. They note that although there is considerable literature on depression and SCI, it often includes descriptive and anecdotal data. Studies that do employ control groups contain methodological problems, and rarely use randomized clinical trials. Elliot and Kennedy conclude that many of the assumptions regarding the efficacy of treatment remain empirically untested, and discuss some of the reasons for the current state of research in this area.

There are a number of modalities for the treatment of PTSD, as cited by the National Center for PTSD of the Department of Veterans Affairs. The most common treatment techniques are CBT, pharmacotherapy, eye movement desensitization and reprocessing (EMDR) and brief psychodynamic psychotherapy. Common to most approaches are the following elements: education regarding the development of PTSD as an anxiety disorder that develops in normal people when they are exposed to extreme stress; carefully monitored exposure to the traumatic memories, through recall and imagery in a safe setting; experience of feelings of anger or shame, which are not uncommon following trauma; and training in coping skills to deal with memories or reminders, without numbing or becoming overwhelmed. There is agreement that if a person is in crisis at the start of treatment, these issues should be addressed prior to PTSD treatment.

Currently, the University of Southern California Institute for Creative Technologies is developing an approach called the Full Spectrum PTSD treatment system (Rizzo et al., 2005) to address the increase in PTSD among returning veterans of the Iraq war. It is an approach based on virtual reality scenarios that was introduced in 1997.

In the three vignettes above, the treatment approach employed is a multidimensional one that has evolved in our work over the years. It clearly is not the only useful approach. Although various constraints have limited our ability to gather data, our approach is one in which we have developed confidence. It includes elements of a number of different models for the treatment of the emotional difficulties found with SCI and trauma. The treatment is heavily psychodynamic, with interpersonal and existential underpinnings. It is interlaced with concepts and strategies from a cognitive behavioral model of psychotherapy, in addition to the somatic (neurobiochemical) considerations of trauma. Neuropsychological principles are employed as necessary. This integrated approach is contained within the context of a rehabilitation psychology frame.

The treatment presumes that SCI results in emotional upheaval, and that trauma is an emotional and somatic experience. The intervention requires the development of a working relationship marked by empathic relatedness. Herman (1997) offers support for aspects of such a model via a survivor's comment: "Good therapists were those who really validated my experience and helped me to control my behavior rather than trying to control me" (p. 133). Validation and empathy are seen as critical to the therapeutic relationship, which McCabe and Priebe (2004) indicate is one of the essential ingredients for effective treatment. In this regard, our supervision of psychologists in training at Rusk Institute focuses on the elements implied in the victim's description of a good therapist. Empathy is considered crucial to success. Of equal importance is the goal of empowerment of the patient, which includes resisting the possible tendency of the psychologist to take control, in an attempt to rescue the patient.

As the phenomena of trauma and its treatment have become delineated over the years, an additional component of education has been added to our approach; it explains the physiological phenomenon of trauma and its naturally following symptoms. The extent and timing of the education is a judgment based on clinical considerations, such as the extent of PTSD symptoms. In this regard, the process of treatment is based on the psychologist's ability to be primarily a clinician, flexibly calling upon knowledge from the facets of the model cited above, rather than a focus on a particular model or technique. The focus is on the current moment, in the context of the past and future. Such flexibility in approach is necessitated by the variety of situations and reactions that are presented by our SCI population.

Our process of treatment begins with current difficulties, followed by an exploration of the onset and later aspects of the ongoing experiences with SCI to assure that they include an appropriate level of emotion for this person, rather than one that is muted, disorganizing, or in some other way symptomatic. The extent of the focus on historical information and experience is determined by clinical judgment. In the process, and probably more specific to the treatment of PTS and PTSD, one function of the psychologist is to modulate the amount of emotion experienced, although there may be frequent and necessary expressions of grief, depression, and rage. Reviews of these experiences may require many repetitions. In this way, the traumatic experiences and losses can be more readily placed into memory, a process that the experience of trauma possibly had prevented. In this course of treatment, the traumatic experiences lose the ability to generate symptoms of trauma.

Further highlighting the need for treatment following SCI is the possibility that the incidence of PTSD and PTS among SCI victims may be even higher than reported (Nielson, 2003). Since much of the research is quantitative and not qualitative, and since findings are also based on self-report to questionnaires, outcomes may be questionable. It has been our experience that most SCI victims, especially males, tend to minimize their personal distress and actively employ mechanisms that avoid experiences that might trigger emotional distress. Many, who show signs of more intense distress as reported by staff, diligently avoid contact with mental health providers. Some results in the literature, then, may be thrown into question, since many investigations are not based on a total sample but rather on the percentage who agree to participate. In this regard, Good et al. (2006) studied rehabilitation outcomes among men recovering from serious injuries, and found that more than half of the masculine characteristics included were negative indicators for seeking psychological help. Such a finding may explain some of the reluctance to engage in psychological treatment. Hoge et al. (2004) also reported that of combat veterans returning from duty whose evaluations showed positive indicators for mental disorder only 23–40 percent sought mental health services. As additional support for the proposition that the incidence of PTSD and PTS among SCI victims is underrepresented in the literature, our experience has noted that contact with psychological services for men with SCI has required outreach and creatively designed programs to engage them.

In order to better engage SCI patients, a program was designed at Rusk Institute, called the "Seminar in Personal Functioning," which was led by a physician and a psychologist. Each of four 90-minute group sessions addressed a specific area of physical loss, beginning with a didactic presentation on the anatomy and physiology of the loss and followed by experiential group discussion on living with such a loss. The topics presented were paralysis, bowel and bladder incontinence, physical sensation, including care and protection of skin, and sexual functioning. Additional experiential groups on sexual functioning, which included audiovisuals and discussions, then followed.

To manage the consequences of SCI involves work and daily attention to physical needs. Partners often may serve as caregivers and they may be seen as members of the rehabilitation team, with insufficient attention paid to them as secondary victims (Padrone, 1999). Daily attention to the needs of the victim can be traumatizing for a caregiver, while ironically the work can be a distraction and a haven from addressing the emotional impact of personal losses and trauma. The consequent increase in stress can be amplified by worry about the primary victim and personal exhaustion, as exemplified in the recent proliferation of caregiver stress tests, developed by specific illness/disability organizations.

Rehabilitation and Adaptation to SCI

Losses from SCI are once again both obvious and subtle, ranging from loss of functions to loss of beliefs in fairness and in oneself. Herman (1997) speaks to the necessity to mourn losses, in order to resolve trauma. She suggests that incomplete mourning can perpetuate trauma. The social rituals that usually enable mourning are not available to trauma victims, resulting in an increased probability of psychological symptoms. Experience suggests that since mourning is an inner experience, and since it is culturally influenced, the actual process may vary among people. Since SCI always involves loss, the need for mourning may be clear, but it is often resisted or avoided. It may be seen as weakness or giving in (Herman, 1997) to weakness, to growing feelings of grief, loss, and even the disability itself. Actually one might say that in the face of such experiences, it is an act of courage.

Incomplete mourning also has been seen to diminish a victim's empathy for the suffering of others, since by implied comparison their suffering is relatively meager. In the context of such a lack of empathy, cynicism may develop. Cynicism can be seen not necessarily as a feature of personality but rather as a sign of a depression or mourning that was indicated but never happened. As victims truly experience the injustice of their situation, with the validation of a trained professional, anger and indignation may rise. Experience supports the proposition that such feelings of indignation often release a person to reclaim a lost sense of power and dignity. Herman (1997) poignantly concludes: "Mourning is the only way to give due honor to loss; there is no adequate compensation" (p. 190).

Finally, disability and trauma persist throughout an ever-changing life span that moves forward through many of life's milestones, which are made numerous by the relative youth of the victims (Padrone, 1999). Such milestone experiences bring with them their own challenges, which can exacerbate feelings of loss and helplessness and retraumatize the victims. As one moves through the life cycle, relationships will begin and end, challenges will result in success, failure, or disappointment. Families will evolve, and later experiences certainly will scrape the wound. The extent to which resolution has been accomplished will limit the recycling of the adjustment process through each milestone and stressful experience.

The trauma of SCI profoundly and irrevocably changes one's life. In varying degrees and under the myriad influences suggested here, it presents a series of traumatic events that can go on indefinitely, unless there is appropriate intervention. Notions of "coping with adversity," "getting through," and "hard work" can be said to be the mantra of rehabilitation, which most often has at its core not the goal of cure but that of empowerment. Although resolution of trauma may be successful, it is not necessarily complete. Experiences of stress and trauma can often be revisited, but the litmus test of success is that they do not lead to the full recycling symptoms of PTS or PTSD. With the necessary assistance, people with spinal cord injury can and do go on to lead full and productive lives.

As mentioned earlier, discharge from rehabilitation may be only the beginning of the road back from the trauma of SCI, but the soil will have been prepared with the empowerment that rehabilitation can provide. Possibly unique to the trauma of SCI, when compared to other traumas, is the existence of a network of well-established rehabilitation facilities and services throughout the country for treatment and ongoing research.

The disability of SCI, when viewed in the context of trauma, makes a commitment to rehabilitation more relevant. Howard Rusk, who has been called the "Father of Rehabilitation Medicine," has spoken eloquently on the strength of the human spirit, which he viewed as the unique quality that fuels the courage to live actively, despite the losses and trauma of disability. When well into his late 80s, Howard Rusk delivered a brief address to a small gathering at Rusk Institute, which concluded with a personal recognition of the losses that aging can bring. It seemed to epitomize his view of suffering loss while retaining the ability to remain open to life, feelings, and being human. He concluded his message with the following comment: "I may no longer be able to run about and accomplish the things I did once, and I may not be able to [do other things]... , but I can love as good as ever." In the closing line in his autobiography, he expressed his genuine respect for our human struggle with loss and his conviction that people can climb back up from the trauma of disability, when he said: "To believe in rehabilitation is to believe in humanity" (Rusk, 1977, p. 238).

Public Policy Issues and SCI

Following SCI, the need for rehabilitation and for psychological services is clear. The selection of a treatment facility is an important decision, in which consideration should be given to the range of services provided, the availability and intensity of those services, and the quality of the rehabilitation program. Inpatient services are provided in a number of different settings, including hospital-based units and rehabilitation centers. Most desirable programs deliver treatment through an interdisciplinary team, which includes providers of psychological services. Some inpatient programs provide treatment in a designated unit or program, delivered by a specialized team. Standards of care are assured by program approval from the Commission on Accreditation of Rehabilitation Facilities

(CARF), established in 1966. Outpatient rehabilitation programs also provide an interdisciplinary program of treatment, although some patients may not require all services (Hagglund, Kewman, Wirth, & Riggert, 2005).

Rehabilitation following SCI with significant disability is generally automatic, but the availability and extent of psychological services offered, as well as other services, may not be. This development in the treatment of SCI reflects the major changes in delivery of all rehabilitation services over recent decades. As the need for services and the number of facilities to provide them has increased significantly, efforts to control costs also have been necessary. Length of stay for inpatient treatment has been significantly reduced for all hospital stays. As a result, there is a greater need for services on an outpatient basis. There has been pressure to eliminate some services, by "streamlining" the rehabilitation team, and to institute dual training for others, both of which suggestions have raised quality of care objections. Insurance coverage by managed care companies now includes 95 percent of insured workers. The management of costs has led to capitation initiatives, which place the care providers in a potentially difficult position; if more care is recommended, there is a negative financial consequence. The government Medicaid and Medicare programs provide an increasing proportion of payment for inpatient coverage. Since SCI tends to strike at a relatively early age, before careers, employment, and finances have stabilized, a significant portion of patients are in need of Medicaid coverage. Furthermore, the Medicare program provides health care coverage for an increasing number of SCI patients. There has been a rise in the number of SCI patients who are elderly, and a person is eligible for Medicare following two years of permanent disability, both of which result in Medicare assuming the responsibility for health coverage. Increasing the problem is the fact that the "limitations of these programs ... often exacerbate the health problems of persons with disabilities" (Hagglund et al., 2005, p. 805). Additionally, the psychological and behavioral difficulties with which many people with disabilities contend can result in increased medical and emotional difficulties when they go untreated, ironically increasing health care costs.

Two additional Medicare cost containment strategies currently are impacting inpatient rehabilitation services, and these strategies tend to affect all other third party payers. A Prospective Payment System (PPS) has been implemented, which provides for a single payment to hospitals based on type of disability, for example, stroke or SCI, and on level of care needed, which is similar to the Diagnostic Related Groupings (DRG) payment system in acute hospitals. In this system an average length of stay is calculated for each disability and level, and the facility receives a fixed payment, which can increase with comorbidities. This method of payment has resulted in reduced costs and reduced lengths of stay in inpatient rehabilitation (Hagglund et al., 2005). Although the achievement of rehabilitation goals seems to have become more efficient, patients are being discharged to their home or to a subacute rehabilitation facility with greater levels of dependence than in the past. Although treatment and progress can continue at home or at the subacute facility, the patient will receive less intensive treatment. Little attention has been paid to the psychological price paid by patients and family.

A second strategy is known as the 75–25 percent rule, which specifies that 75 percent of patients admitted to acute inpatient rehabilitation facilities (IRFs) must be drawn from a specific list of diagnostic groups, for the facility to continue to be classified as an IRF and continue to receive the current rate of reimbursement. Although spinal cord injury is included on the approved list, the impact of the rule may be to reduce the number of available beds in rehabilitation facilities, thereby leading to additional pressure on the facility to discharge patients sooner. Since it has been estimated that only half of patients being treated in an IRF facility meet the specified criteria, the rule is being phased in with annual increments to allow time for necessary reorganization, such as bed reductions. In addition to the estimated cost reduction, it is anticipated that many patients will be denied admission to acute rehabilitation, because they do not fall into the designated diagnostic categories (Hagglund et al., 2005), and will be sent to subacute rehabilitation facilities.

Furthermore, something of a "catch-22" situation has now developed. As access to intensive and long-term inpatient treatment is being reduced, limits are also being placed on the number of outpatient treatment sessions that a patient may receive. The search for outpatient psychological assistance may require some effort to deal with the maze of daunting funding issues. The psychological issues that need to be addressed here are complex. They often require more than the limited number of counseling sessions that may be provided by a managed care company to "get through" or stave off a crisis. Overall, the availability of professional and financial resources for treatment is limited, while the need has grown.

Should seeking help through physicians and rehabilitation personnel be unproductive, additional sources of information can be found through the Commission on Accreditation of Rehabilitation Facilities (CARF) at http://www.carf.org/consumer.aspx?Content=content/about/providerlist.htm&ID=6. Extensive listings of qualified mental health practitioners also are available through state professional organizations. Hurdles do include, however, limited availability of wheelchair accessible offices, even following the Americans with Disabilities Act, which took effect in 1992. The number of clinicians who are experienced with SCI may be limited, although competent clinicians should be able to assimilate new information rapidly and integrate it into the work. On a positive note, the pool of professionals is growing. There is an increase in the number of training sites for mental health professionals in the field of rehabilitation. At another level, board certification for psychologists is now provided (since 1995) by the American Psychological Association in the area of rehabilitation psychology as a specialization.

Community reentry is a major goal of rehabilitation. Considerable legal progress has been made toward the removal of barriers to full participation in life for people with disabilities. Legislation has been enacted that addresses accessibility issues, employment opportunities, and safety issues in the workplace. In this context, awareness of one's rights can be empowering for those with disability. An excellent review of such information is provided by Bruyere and van Looy (2005).

Overall, there are complex rehabilitation needs following SCI, which are addressed most effectively in CARF-accredited inpatient programs. If such programs are not readily available, recommendation is made for acute rehabilitation programs, with a complete interdisciplinary team that provides regular psychological services as part of the team effort.

Although cost containment in health care is needed, people with disabilities do have special health care needs that can be complex, which brings into question the blanket application of cost-cutting efforts across disabilities. Many of these policies take into account only the physical needs of patients, with little attention paid to the psychological and neuropsychological needs. Finally, government spending on research in the area of SCI is subject to budget reductions and politicizing of certain efforts, such as has been seen in the stem cell debate. People with disabilities often do not have advocates in the legislature who can speak for the needs of this vulnerable and high-risk group. There needs to be a reasonable balance between cost reduction and the quality of health care.

Acknowledgments

I would like to express my gratitude to the many people with spinal cord injury for their permission to bear witness to and share in their journey and to Jung Ahn, MD, clinical professor of rehabilitation medicine, New York University School of Medicine.

References

Adams Carey, M. G., & Lakso, M. (2006). Acute stages of spinal cord injury. *Perspectives: Recovery strategies from the OR to home, 6*(3), 1, 5–7.

Allen, J. G. (1995). *Coping with Trauma: A Guide to Self Understanding*. Washington, DC: American Psychiatric Press.

American Psychiatric Association. (1994). *Diagnostic and statistical manual of mental disorders* (4th ed.). Washington, DC: Author.

Blanchard, E. B., Hickling, E. J., Vollmer, A. J., Loos, W. R., Buckley, T. C., & Jackard, J. (1995). Short term follow-up of post-traumatic stress symptoms in motor vehicle accident victims. *Behaviour Research and Therapy, 33*(4), 369–377.

Bors, E., & Comarr, A. E. (1960). Neurological disturbances of sexual function with special reference to 529 patients with spinal cord injury. *Urology Survey, 110*, 191–221.

Boyer, B. A., Knolls, M. L., Kafkalas, C. M., Tollen, L. G., & Swartz, M. (2000). Prevalence and relationships of posttraumatic stress in families experiencing pediatric spinal cord injuries. *Rehabilitation Psychology, 45*(4), 339–355.

Bracken, M. B., & Shepherd, M. J. (1980). Coping and adaptation following acute spinal cord injury: A theoretical analysis. *Paraplegia, 18*, 74–85.

Bruyere, S. M., & van Looy, S. A. (2005). Legislation and Rehabilitation Professionals. In H. H. Zaretsky, E. F. Richter III, & M. G. Eisenberg (Eds.), *Medical aspects of disability: A handbook for the rehabilitation professional* (3rd ed., pp. 827–850). New York: Springer Publishing Company.

Cappas, N. M., Andres-Hyman, R., & Davidson, L. (2005). What psychotherapists can begin to learn from neuroscience: Seven principles of a brain-based psychotherapy. *Psychotherapy: Theory, Research, Practice, Training, 42*(3), 374–383.

Carey, M. G., & Lakso, M. (2006). Acute stages of spinal cord injuries. *Perspectives, 6*(5), 1–7. Retrieved September 30, 2006, from www.perspectivesinnursing.org

Catherall, D. R. (2004). *Handbook of stress trauma and the family.* New York: Brunner-Rutledge.

Cleveland Clinic, Department of Patient Education and Health Information (2006). The spinal cord and injury. Retrieved October 15, 2006, from http://www.clevelandclinic.org/health/health-info/docs/2000/2036.asp?index=8720

Craig, A. R., Hancock, K., Dickson, H., & Chang E. (1997). Long-term psychological outcomes in spinal cord injured persons: Results of a controlled trial using cognitive behavior therapy. *Archives of Physical Medicine and Rehabilitation, 78*(1), 3–38.

DeVivo, M. J., Black K. J., Richards J. S., & Stover S. L. (1991). Suicide following spinal cord injury. *Paraplegia, 29*(9), 620–627.

Dryden, D. M., Duncan Saunders, L., Rowe, B. H., May, L. A., Yiannakoulias, N., Svenson, L. W., et al. (2005). Depression following traumatic spinal cord injury. *Neuroepidemiology, 25*(2), 55–61.

Elliot, T., & Frank, R. G. (1996). Depression following spinal cord injury. *Archives of Physical Medicine and Rehabilitation, 47*, 131–143.

Elliott, T. R., & Kennedy, P. (2004). Treatment of depression following spinal cord injury: Evidence-based review. *Rehabilitation Psychology, 49*(2), 134–139.

Giller, E. (1999). What is psychological trauma? The Sidran Institute. Retrieved September 9, 2006, from http://www.sidran.org/whatistrauma.html

Good, G. E., Schopp, L. H., Thomson, D., Hathaway, S., Sanford-Martens, T., Mazurek, M. O., et al. (2006). Masculine roles and rehabilitation outcomes among men recovering from serious injuries. *Psychology of Men and Masculinity 7*(3), 165–176.

Green, B. L., & Kaltman, S. I. (2003). Recent research findings on the diagnosis of post-traumatic stress disorder: Prevalence, course, comorbidity and risk. In Simon, R. I., (Ed.) *Posttraumatic Stress Disorder in Litigation: Guidelines for Forensic Assessment* (2nd ed.) (pp. 19–39). Washington, DC: American Psychiatric Press, Inc.

Hagglund, K. J., Kewman, D. C., Wirth, N. E., & Riggart, S. C. (2005). Trends in medical rehabilitation delivery and payment systems. In H. H. Zaretsky, E. F. Richter, III, & M. G. Eisenberg (Eds.), *Medical aspects of disability: A handbook for the rehabilitation professional* (3rd ed., pp. 797–826). New York: Springer Publishing Company.

Hammell, K.R.W. (1992). Psychological and sociological theories concerning adjustment to traumatic spinal cord injury: The implications for rehabilitation. *Paraplegia, 30*, 317–326.

Havik, O. E., & Maeland, J. G. (1988). Verbal denial and outcome in myocardial infarction patients. *Journal of Psychosomatic Research, 32*, 145–157.

Heinemann, A. W., & Rawal, P. H. (2005). Spinal cord injury. In H. H. Zaretsky, E. F. Richter, III, & M. G. Eisenberg (Eds.), *Medical aspects of disability: A handbook for the rehabilitation professional* (3rd ed., pp. 611–647). New York: Springer Publishing Company.

Heinrich, R. K., Tate, D. G., & Buckelew, S. P. (1994). Brief symptom inventory norms for spinal cord injury. *Rehabilitation Psychology, 39*(1), 49–56.

Herman, J. (1997). *Trauma and recovery.* New York: Basic Books.

Hess, D. W., Marwitz, J. H., & Kreutzer, J. S. (2003). Neuropsychological impairments after spinal cord injury: A comparative study with mild traumatic brain injury. *Rehabilitation Psychology, 48* (3), 151–156.

Hoge, C. W., Castro, C. A., Messer, S. C., McGurk, D., Cotting, D. I., & Koffman, R. L. (2004). Combat duty in Iraq and Afghanistan, mental health problems, and barriers to care. *The New England Journal of Medicine, 351,* 13–22.

Kennedy, P., Duff, J., Evans, M., & Beedie, A. (2003). Coping effectiveness training reduces depression and anxiety following traumatic spinal cord injuries. *British Journal of Clinical Psychology, 42*(1), 41–52.

Koren, D., Hemel, D., & Kelin, E. (2006). Injury increases the risk for PTSD: An examination of potential neurobiological and psychological mediators. *CNS Spectrum, 11*(8), 616–624.

Kortte, K. B., & Wegener, S. T. (2004, August). Denial of illness in medical rehabilitation populations: Theory, research and definition. *Rehabilitation Psychology, 49*(3), 187–199.

Krystal, H. (1985). Trauma and the stimulus barrier. *Psychoanalytic Inquiry, 5*(1), 131–61.

Martz, E. (2005). Associations and predictors of posttraumatic stress levels according to person-related, disability-related, and trauma-related variables among individuals with spinal cord injuries. *Rehabilitation Psychology, 50*(2), 149–157.

Massad, P. M., & Hulsey, T. L. (2006). Causal attributions in posttraumatic stress disorder: Implications for clinical research and practice. *Psychotherapy: Theory, Research, Practice, Training, 43*(2), 201–215.

McCabe, R., & Priebe, S. (2004). The therapeutic relationship in the treatment of severe mental illness: A review of methods and findings. *International Journal of Social Psychiatry, 50,* 115–128.

National Spinal Cord Injury Information Network. (2006). Spinal cord injury, facts and figures at a glance. Retrieved October 15, 2006, from http://www.spinalcord.uab.edu/show.asp?durki=21446

Neufeldt, V., & Guralnik, D. B. (Eds.). (1991). *Webster's new world dictionary of American English* (3rd college ed.). New York: Simon and Schuster.

Nielson, M. S. (2003). Prevalence of posttraumatic stress disorder in persons with spinal cord injuries: The mediating effect of social support. *Rehabilitation Psychology 48*(4), 289–295.

Padrone, F. J. (1999). Psychotherapeutic issues in treating family members. In K. G. Langer, L. Laatsch, & L. Lewis (Eds.), *Psychotherapeutic interventions for adults with brain injury or stroke: A clinician's treatment resource.* Madison, CT: Psychosocial Press.

Remer, P. (1984). *Stages in coping with rape.* Unpublished manuscript, University of Kentucky at Lexington.

Richards, J. S., Kewman, D. G., & Pierce, C. A. (2000). Spinal cord injury. In R. G. Frank & T. R. Elliott (Eds.), *Handbook of rehabilitation psychology* (pp. 11–25). Washington, DC: American Psychological Association.

Rizzo, A., Pair, J., McNerney, P J., Eastlund, E., Manson, B., Gratch, J., et al. (2005). Development of a VR therapy application for Iraq war military personnel with PTSD. *Studies in Health Technology and Informatics 111,* 407–413.

Rothschild, B. (2000). *The body remembers. The psychophysiology of trauma and trauma treat-ment.* New York: W. W. Norton and Company.

Rusk, H. A. (1977). *A world to care for: The autobiography of Howard A. Rusk, MD.* New York: Random House.

Scharff, J. S., & Scharff, D. E. (1994). *Object relations therapy of physical and sexual trauma.* Northvale, NJ: Jason Aronson.

Schiraldi, G. R. (2000). *The posttraumatic stress disorder sourcebook.* Lincolnwood, IL: Lowell House.

Selye, H. (1982). History and present status of the stress concept. In L. Goldberger & S. Breznitz (Eds.), *Handbook of stress: Theoretical and clinical aspects* (pp. 7–17). New York: Free Press.

Sexual function for men with spinal cord injury. (2000). Spinal Cord Injury Information Network, American Spinal Cord Injury Association, Medline. Retrieved October 20, 2006, from http://www.spinalcord.uab.edu/show.asp?durki = 22405

Shore, A. N. (2002). Dysregulation of the right brain: A fundamental mechanism of trau-matic attachment and the psychopathogenesis of posttraumatic stress disorder. *Austra-lian and New Zealand Journal of Psychiatry, 36,* 9–30

Shore, A. N. (2003). *Affect regulation and the repair of the self.* New York: W. W. Norton.

Sipski, M. L. (1997). *Sexuality and spinal cord injury: where we are and where we are go-ing.* Retrieved September, 29 2006 from http://www.ed.gov/pubs/AmericanRehab/spring97/sp9707.html#sr.

Sipski, M., Alexander, C. J., & Gomez-Marin, O. (2006, June 27). Effects of level and de-gree of spinal cord injury on male orgasm. *Spinal Cord, 1.* Retrieved October 26, 2006 from http://www.nature.com/sc/

Terr, L. C. (1991). Childhood traumas: An outline and overview. *American Journal of Psychiatry, 148,* 10–20.

Trieschmann, R. B. (1988). *Spinal cord injuries: Psychological, social and vocational rehabilita-tion* (2nd ed.). New York: Demos.

United States Department of Veterans Affairs, National Center for PTSD. (n.d.). Treatment of PTSD. Retrieved December 8, 2006, from http://www.ncptsd.va.gov/facts/treatments/fs_treatment.html

University of Washington Rehabilitation Medicine. (2001). Depression and Spinal Cord Injury. *Research: Spinal Cord Injury Update, 10*(2). Retrieved October 15, 2006, from Uni-versity of Washington Rehabilitation Medicine Web site: http://depts.washington.edu/rehab/sci/updates/01sum_depression.html

Van der Kolk, B. A. (1987). *Psychological trauma.* Washington, DC: American Psychiatric Press.

CHAPTER 8

Disclosure of Trauma in the Medical Setting

Ruth Q. Leibowitz

When traumatic life experiences create problems in a person's life, disclosure to a caring other is often an important first step toward healing. However, people hesitate to disclose for many reasons. The two veterans quoted below waited many years before sharing their stories:

> I think the reason that people don't come and open up is because they're too damn proud.... you don't want to be a whiner. You can handle anything, because that's what you're taught. I was 26 years in the military so you're Mr. Macho and you don't want to open up with what's really in your heart to somebody that you don't know, because then you ... are real vulnerable for some more hurt that you don't deserve. (Male veteran, age 63. Experienced childhood physical and sexual abuse, exposure to toxic substance, combat trauma, atrocity, death of son. Disclosed a year and a half prior to being interviewed)

> Because I went all those years growing up as a young person into having children and then going into the military and I felt that if I survived it without no one knowing it that it was best to wait and just get my 20 years in. Then I would be able to seek help without feeling threatened.... I hung in there ... even if it meant being stressed out, depressed, and crying.... I cried behind closed doors, but I held it in, and it wasn't easy. (Female veteran, age 60. Experienced serious transportation or other accident, childhood sexual and physical assault, military sexual trauma. Disclosed six months prior to being interviewed)

Why did these and many other individuals wait years before seeking help for trauma-related distress? Why is trauma of importance to health providers, even those who focus primarily on biomedical issues? How can clinicians invite patients to disclose earlier in the course of their symptoms—or should they?

This chapter was conceptualized first and foremost with the primary care practitioner (PCP) in mind. In addition to providing preventive treatment, PCPs are often the first professionals sought when a health problem is suspected. In many health care systems, patients cannot make appointments for specialty care without a referral from their PCP. Thus, of all types of medical environments, primary care may well be the most important arena for recognition and referral for treatment of trauma-related distress.

It is hoped that providers in specialty areas will also benefit from this chapter. A number of specialty-care medical populations are noted for high incidences of significant trauma histories. Particularly prevalent in PTSD samples are disorders of the cardiovascular, gastrointestinal, respiratory, musculoskeletal, endocrine, neurological, gynecological, and immune systems (Schnurr & Jankowski, 1999). Finally, mental health professionals who accept referrals from, work alongside, and/or provide training for colleagues of more biomedical specialties may find additional ideas for this interdisciplinary work.

PTSD is not the only mental health diagnosis that can develop in the aftermath of trauma. Other anxiety disorders, depression, eating disorders, and somatic symptoms are also commonly associated with traumatic life experiences (e.g., Mayou, Bryant, & Ehlers, 2001; O'Donnell, Creamer, & Pattison, 2005; Rayworth, Wise, & Harlow, 2004; Zatzick, Russo, & Katon, 2003). Early, repeated trauma is associated with borderline personality disorder (Bandelow, Wedekind, Broocks, Hajak, & Ruther, 2005; Lee, Geracioti, Kasckow, & Coccaro, 2005; Sansone, Songer, & Miller, 2005). Increased rates of suicide are seen among individuals with trauma histories (Roy, 2004; Tarrier & Gregg, 2004). Thus, although I will focus on PTSD in this chapter, it is important to acknowledge other ways in which trauma-related distress can manifest itself.

The information and viewpoints contained in this chapter emerge from extensive literature reviews, my own clinical training experience, and the early results of a recent study conducted in a southwestern Veterans Health Administration (VHA) system (see acknowledgments; and Leibowitz, Jeffreys, Copeland, & Noel, 2006b) in which surveys with questions about trauma history and disclosure experiences were collected from 173 veterans in PTSD outpatient treatment and 395 patients visiting outpatient primary care clinics, and interviews were conducted with 56 veterans and eight providers. This research is referred to as the disclosure study, and the words of participants are interspersed throughout the chapter.

Screening versus Disclosure

There is presently debate among professionals about whether routine screening for trauma (in particular, intimate partner violence) should occur in primary care. The details of this controversy are beyond the scope of this chapter; however, the interested reader can read Ramsay, Richardson, Carter, Davidson, & Feder (2002), U.S. Preventive Services Task Force (2005), and Nicolaidis &

Touhouliotis (2006) for a taste of the issues. Screening and disclosure are different processes that do not necessarily overlap. Screening is a formalized written or spoken attempt by a health professional to learn the absence or presence of a patient's experience or symptoms.

Screening can and sometimes does occur impersonally and without context. For example, the Veterans Health Administration (VHA) currently requires that patients be screened for military sexual trauma and PTSD symptoms. The good news is that implementation of this requirement has led to increased identification of trauma-related distress. The bad news is that in some clinics this screening is done in an impersonal manner by a nurse, medical assistant, or physician who the patient may or may not have ever met before. Although the screening itself is required, there is no requirement to provide an explanation of why the questions might be meaningful or relevant to the patient's health or quality of life.

The act of screening may or may not lead to disclosure. Conversely, disclosure can occur in the absence of screening. As will be illustrated, disclosure is most likely to occur when the patient is in a state of readiness and in the context of a relationship with the provider. The PCP quoted below noticed the following about several women who initially denied their trauma histories but later sought help:

> Some women have dealt with it and so they will volunteer that information and it doesn't seem to bother them at all. Others will deny it, and if it has happened and they have never disclosed I have no knowledge of that. But there have been patients who have told me that it didn't happen, and then they will come back later and subsequently they will say, well, you know that really DID happen to me but I was afraid to say anything…. I think it's the trust factor more than anything else. I think that they have to get to know me…. You know, before you disclose anything to anybody you have to have some sort of confidence about what they're going to do with your information.

Trauma and Health

Many published studies connect trauma and its aftermath with various aspects of physical health. In the biopsychosocial model described by Wilson and Cleary (1995) and further elucidated by Schnurr and Green (2003), health is conceptualized as a multidimensional construct that includes but goes far beyond purely biological conditions and processes, including functional status and quality of life.

Traumatic experiences and PTSD interact with health in numerous domains including physiological changes, diagnosable biomedical illness, perceived symptoms, well-being, health behaviors, ideas, and functional abilities.

Trauma Survivors in the Medical Setting: Prevalence and Trauma-Health Associations

Many individuals with mental health issues, including trauma-related distress, do not initially seek specialty mental health care. Instead, they appear in medical clinics with multiple psychosocial problems that may remain unrecognized by busy providers. Some authors (Norquist & Regier, 1996, Regier, Narrow, Rae, Manderscheid, Locke, & Goodwin, 1993) have conceptualized the general medical setting as part of a "defacto mental health care system." The tendency to seek help from medical rather than mental health professionals for trauma-related distress has cultural as well as individual components. For example, for survivors of a volcanic eruption in Japan, more severe symptoms of PTSD and depression were associated with more frequent help-seeking from medical but not mental health professionals (Goto, Wilson, Kahana, & Slane, 2002). Goto and colleagues conceptualized this as being "related to cultural norms regarding shame and self disclosure of emotional distress" (p. 157).

Patients and providers frequently do not recognize links between physical and psychological symptoms of traumatic events (Munro, Freeman, & Law, 2004). In the disclosure study, the most frequent reasons individuals with PTSD gave for initially disclosing to a health professional were those that were external to themselves, such as pressure from a friend or family member to seek help for emotional or behavioral problems. A VHA psychologist who assessed many individuals recently returned from Iraq and Afghanistan mentioned that those young men and women with symptoms of trauma-related distress do not generally ask their medical providers about PTSD. Rather, they seek help for individual symptoms that they do not realize are part of a larger pattern, such as sleep disturbance and worsening relationships with co-workers.

Patients are not the only ones who often fail to make the connection between past trauma and present symptom patterns. A psychiatrist who has worked with trauma survivors for 20 years expressed surprise that even with all the media coverage and generally increased public knowledge of PTSD, patients with trauma histories referred to her by primary care colleagues are generally not explicitly referred for potential PTSD, but for depression or chronic pain.

Primary care providers see a substantial proportion of patients with trauma histories. Researchers who cast a wide net by including many different categories of trauma find the highest prevalences. For example, the prevalence of at least one traumatic experience has been detected at more than 85 percent in one primary care sample (Applegate, 2001). Eighty-one percent of the women in one sample reported significant trauma histories (Escalona, Achilles, Waitzkin, & Yager, 2004) More than 80 percent of the veterans surveyed in primary care waiting rooms for the disclosure study reported at least one category of trauma in their lifetime, with 65 percent reporting more than one, and approximately 25 percent reporting more than four.

When the focus is narrowed to specific types of trauma, the number of traumatized individuals presenting in primary care remains high. Beebe, Gulledge, Lee, & Replogle (1994), found a sexual assault prevalence of 30 percent among female patients, and Friedman, Samet, Roberts, Hudlin, & Hans (1992) found a prevalence of 16 percent and 19 percent for physical and sexual abuse respectively among two samples of male and female primary care patients.

Of female family practice patients currently in a relationship, 10 percent reported being physically hurt by their partner in the past year, and 39 percent reported lifetime intimate partner violence (Burge, Schneider, Ivy, & Catala, 2005).

Not everyone who experiences trauma develops PTSD; in fact, the majority do not. Schnurr and Green (2003) estimate that between 8 and 14 percent of men and 20 to 31 percent of women who have experienced Criterion A traumas develop PTSD.[1] Whether or not PTSD develops appears to be related to a wide variety of variables, including gender, type and intensity of trauma, number of traumatic events experienced, ethnicity, education, and social support (e.g., Beckham et al., 2000; Kessler, Sonnega, Bromet, Hughes, & Nelso, 1995; Stretch Knudson, & Durand, 1998). Some trauma experiences are more likely than others to lead to PTSD. For example, PTSD rates following rape are reported to be as high as 50–80 percent (Solomon & Davidson, 1997). In contrast, the lifetime prevalence of PTSD for male combat veterans is generally believed to be 20–30 percent (e.g., Blake et al., 1990). Though the majority of individuals who experience a Criterion A type of trauma do not develop full-criteria PTSD or chronic trauma-related distress, those who do constitute a sizable minority. Of primary care patients who experience trauma, approximately one-third report trauma-related distress (Seville et al., 2003).

At least as early as 1988 it was observed that the aging combat veteran population appeared to have more medical problems than other individuals in their age cohort. Lipton and Schaffer (1988) wrote: "A major problem in dealing with this group of men has been their reluctance to admit to symptoms, either physical or psychological. They have usually suffered in silence for years, unable or unwilling to ask for help despite urging by family and friends" (p. 317). Though almost 20 years have passed since this paper was written and media coverage about the psychological effects of trauma has increased, these words still describe many veterans today. Even the youngest remain hesitant to tell their stories.

A landmark 2004 study by Hoge and colleagues of soldiers deployed to Iraq and Afghanistan found a high degree of combat exposure. Of those who screened positive for a mental health disorder, only 23–40 percent had sought mental health care. Major reasons for not doing so were fears of stigmatization and potential harm to their military careers. Though this study focused on active-duty soldiers, similar barriers were mentioned by several veterans in the disclosure study, for whom fears of stigma and job loss in the civilian sector continued to be a concern.

Patients' trauma experiences remain underidentified in medical settings. Coker, Bethea, Smith, Fadden, &Brandt (2002) conducted interviews with female primary care patients and matched their findings on the prevalence of intimate partner violence (IPV) with medical record documentation, finding that IPV remained undocumented for 84 percent of those patients who experienced it. Of 18 battered women who reported having seen their "regular doctor" in the prior year; only one in three had discussed their abuse with their provider (McCauley, Yurk, Jenckes, & Ford, 1998). Magruder et al. (2005) found that slightly less than one half of the cases of PTSD that were uncovered by rigorous study procedures had been diagnosed by primary care clinicians.

Trauma-related distress can affect the health of the patient, the provider-patient relationship, and the larger health care system. Female medical patients with a history of physical/sexual abuse have lower pain thresholds and report more frequent use of maladaptive coping strategies than do those without abuse histories (Scarinci, Mcdonald-Haile, Bradley, & Richter, 1994). Zayfert, Dums, Ferguson, and Hegel (2002) found that patients with PTSD reported significantly worse physical functioning than did patients with panic disorder, generalized anxiety disorder, or major depression. Williamson, Thompson, Anda, Dietz, and Felitti (2002) found that childhood abuse was associated with adult obesity. Health behaviors such as increased substance use, risky sexual behaviors, poor exercise habits, nicotine dependence, binge drinking, and poor nutritional habits have been associated with a wide range of trauma types, and with PTSD (e.g., Beckham et al., 1997; Breslau, Davis, & Schultz, 2003; Lang et al., 2003, McNutt, Carlson, Persaud, & Postmus, 2002). A Vet Center counselor described one client's cycle of behaviors that resulted from trauma triggers:[2]

> She's a Vietnam era vet, sexual trauma, subject to depression. When she is depressed she will eat a lot of fatty foods, sweets.... She has developed diabetes and doesn't take her medication so then the depression worsens. Obesity is a problem. She doesn't exercise at all. And she'll present with ... "I'm not taking medication correctly. I'm having problems with my diabetes. My blood pressure is going up." She works in a setting where if she has a male supervisor it's very difficult for her ... and often [there are] environmental cues that relate to the trauma in the military and then she just rolls right into the poor self-care.

Both trauma experience and PTSD appear to be related to physical health outcomes. Cloitre, Cohen, Edelman, & Han (2001) studied childhood abuse survivors and found that trauma exposure but not PTSD was associated with an increased number of self-reported medical conditions. However, PTSD rather than trauma exposure was associated with decreased perceived physical health. Wolfe, Schnurr, Brown, and Furey (1994) found that war zone exposure contributed to health effects independently of whether study participants had PTSD. In contrast, the results of a study of firefighters suggest that PTSD rather than exposure to fire-related disaster accounted for an increase in reported physical symptoms (McFarlane, Atchison, Rafalowicz, & Papay, 1994).

Given these varied results, an obvious question arises: is it trauma exposure by itself or PTSD that is most associated with changes in health? A study by Seville and colleagues (2003) may shed light on this issue: In a primary care patient population, trauma by itself did not predict greater physical and psychosocial impairment, but continued distress related to the trauma did. A number of authors have found that distress patterns that do not meet the full criteria for PTSD nevertheless affect multiple life domains, including health (Gillock, 2001; Marshall et al., 2001; Schlenger, Fairbank, Jordan, & Caddell, 1999). In fact,

Gillock, Zayfert, Hegel, and Ferguson (2005) recently reported that primary care patients with partial PTSD showed greater similarities to full-PTSD patients in their levels of medical utilization, physical symptom intensity, and health functioning than they did to patients without PTSD. Thus, perhaps, trauma-related distress (regardless of whether it meets PTSD criteria) mediates or moderates health-related outcomes.

Trauma-related issues reach beyond the level of the individual. They affect health care systems in numerous ways, including provider-patient interactions, services utilization, and overall costs. In a community sample, the total number of traumas and a history of physical or sexual abuse correlated with both PTSD prevalence and increased use of medical services (Rosenberg et al., 2000). High users of VHA primary care services are much more likely than low users to have current PTSD (Deykin et al., 2001). Veterans with more severe PTSD are greater utilizers of both mental and physical health services than those without (Calhoun, Bosworth, Grambow, Dudley, & Beckham, 2002). Schnurr, Spiro, and Paris (2000) found that for male veterans with PTSD, increased use of medical services was not completely attributable to comorbid (concurrent) Axis I disorders such as depression.

Trauma can affect the provider-patient relationship and patient satisfaction with health care. In a study by Plichta, Duncan, and Plichta (1996), women who reported abuse by a spouse during the past year also reported greater dissatisfaction with their health care than those who reported no abuse. Only about one-tenth of these women had talked with a physician about their abuse. In contrast, Lang et al. (2005) found that women with more PTSD symptoms expressed more satisfaction with overall care than did those with other mental health diagnoses. In a study of physicians' reactions to working with patients with rheumatological complaints, Walker, Katon, Keegan, Gardner, and Sullivan (1997) found that a patient's having been abused or having been raped during adulthood were two of a number of factors that were significantly associated with physicians' reports of frustration with patient care.

Patients with trauma-related distress sometimes have strong reactions to both personal and physical aspects of medical visits that are not generally as problematic for nontraumatized peers. A Vet Center counselor specializing in women's sexual trauma spoke of spending a great deal of time helping patients negotiate relationships with their health providers. A mental health professional who works primarily with combat veterans stated:

> It's extremely difficult for them to ask for help and any apparent hint of rejection will cause them to withdraw, and they'll either blow up or they just walk away and don't come back…. And the reason they walk away is they're afraid they'll blow up and sometimes because the waiting room is crowded and noisy and they can't tolerate it, and neither can they tolerate the effort it takes to explain to somebody that they just can't be here right now.

A psychiatrist described how trauma survivors may present with very different emotional exteriors:

My interest dates back to the mid-80s when … it always seemed that the women who were the most chronically depressed had histories of childhood trauma. Then, the Vietnam patients began to come in—on the outside they seemed very angry and violent. But once you got to know them it became clear that they had experienced a great deal of trauma during the war. Then also in the mid-80s we started learning more about PTSD and realizing it fit many of these people. So I've gotten to see two major forms of PTSD—the more passive, depressed presentation of it and the more irritable, angry presentation.

The veteran quoted below denied the extent of his problems to both himself and others for many years, opting not to tell providers about symptoms of PTSD from combat experiences that included witnessing atrocities in Vietnam:

I only told them what they wanted to hear, which helped me somewhat, but I was breaking appointments. I wasn't stable in my mind. I wasn't able to connect with anyone at that time, that's why I blew off…. I was scared because I had never had a one-on-one with anybody that was digging into my head…. For all these years I was telling everyone I was fine and I didn't want to really find out that I was crazy.

This patient's narrative illustrates how fears related to disclosure and help-seeking can interact with health behaviors—in this case, failing to follow through with appointments.

A primary care provider related how she had first become aware of potential issues for survivors of sexual abuse during physical exams:

At a conference a midwife who was talking about … how sexual trauma would cause people to dissociate and so during a pelvic exam you need to … keep them engaged with you personally and try to minimize this retraumatization as much as you can. She worked in a public health clinic and one of the residents referred to it as a snake pit. She was perfectly horrified and asked him, "Why do you say that?" He said, "Because the women when you go to touch them … recoil from you." That was a red flag to her, and she began to wonder about the sexual trauma history of these women and did some evaluation on her own and realized that many had been victims of sexual trauma and consequently the exam was awful for them, and they would recoil. And [the resident] was referring not to the patients as snakes, but their behavior is like a snake trying to slither away…. And it opened her awareness.

One provider voiced several examples of situations in which trauma-related distress could interact with various aspects of medical treatment:

If you're a primary care provider and you are sending your patient in for an MRI and it's a closed MRI … I have had patients walk out of there with panic attacks…. So radiology needs to know about it … how to address those types of patients that tend to be very anxious in those settings…. Even technicians, even phlebotomists should know how to deal with anxious patients because they are drawing blood with a needle and if they don't know that they've got somebody in there who witnessed torture in Vietnam and you ask them to just come and draw blood and they walk out of your office in a tirade because they can't stand that, they're going to label them as psychotic or some other problem versus really understanding, this person went through this [and it] makes them more anxious in this type of setting.

A Vietnam veteran recently told me that after a surgical procedure, he lost control of his temper in the hospital when informed that he had been administered morphine. He himself did not realize the reasons for the outburst until after discharge, as he recalled memories of morphine being administered to dying men and to silence the suffering wounded so that they would not give their positions away to the enemy. Had both he and his providers been aware of these associations, the anger might have been avoided, or apologies quickly made and accepted.

Some providers come up with "tricks of the trade" for helping their patients to cope with discomforts in medical settings that are related to their trauma histories. This social worker found a strategy to help clients feel more comfortable in the dentist's chair:

> I've had people who have worked in morgues, or have been on body recovery missions, to where the smell and taste of the blood—olfactory kinds of stimulation— will trigger off their PTSD symptoms. I teach them to go lay the eucalyptus right under the nose and they're not going to smell or taste anything other than that stuff. And they say well, what will the dentist think? And I say, you tell your dentist you have PTSD and that this helps you to manage your symptoms ... and the dentist will say, "I don't have a problem with that. Thank you for letting me know." Then a few days later they come back and say, "I told the dentist that and he said, 'I don't have a problem with that.'"

Trauma Disclosure

Why Would a Patient Disclose?

Why may it benefit certain patients to disclose trauma to their medical providers? "May" is a key word here. Many individuals who experience trauma do not develop chronic forms of trauma-related distress and would not perceive any reason to bring up the topic during a medical visit. The majority of primary care patients who had experienced traumatic events reported no need for professional help (Mol et al., 2002). The minority who did want help, however, believed the primary care physician could play an important role.

For a variety of trauma populations, confiding in others in a naturally occurring context is associated with better mental and physical health. For example, Holocaust survivors who spoke in more detail about their World War II experiences had greater self-reported health controlling for preinterview health status (Pennebaker, Barger, & Tiebout, 1989). Schwarz and Kowalski (1992) followed a population of individuals exposed to school violence and found that those who did not seek help had more PTSD symptoms (especially avoidance), recall of life threat, and depression after the event than did those who had sought follow-up counseling.

A number of researchers have explored the constructs of self-disclosure and self-concealment and their relationship to physical and mental health. Cepeda-Benito and Short (1998) found that students who scored high on a measure of self-concealment evidenced greater psychological distress and avoidance of psychological treatment. Larson and Chastain (1990) found a relationship between higher scores on a validated self-concealment measure and increased physical and psychological symptoms, even after controlling for such variables as the occurrence of trauma and social support. Of the disclosure study's sample of 173 veterans in active treatment for PTSD, 42 percent reported at least one category of trauma that they were still not ready to disclose. This group of veterans reported significantly more PTSD-related and health-related distress than their peers did.

Individuals with good support systems may benefit from disclosure to nonprofessionals such as friends or family members. In their study of peacekeepers who had returned from Somalia, Bolton, Glenn, Orsillo, Roemer, and Litz (2003) found that individuals who had disclosed to significant supportive others about their experiences showed better adjustment than those who had not disclosed. Not everyone, however, has a good support system or wishes to disclose to people they know. One-half of the PTSD outpatients in the disclosure study reported that a health professional was the first person to whom they had disclosed. This 72-year-old veteran of both Korea and Vietnam expressed his reasons for preferring to talk to a professional:

A: Well I didn't think anybody would be interested.... I didn't want to unload.... It's ... a little gory and some of them a little shaky, memories of bad situations. Especially when you see somebody with their intestines all open and he's still living. These are stories that you don't want to tell kids or family or friends or anybody, the general public.
Q: What about telling a health professional? Like a nurse or a doctor?
A: That would be fine. That's what they're trained for.

For individuals with trauma-related symptoms that affect their lives to a moderate or extreme degree, friends and family—no matter how well-meaning—may not be able to provide what is needed to reduce these symptoms. Chronic trauma-related distress is not so different from a chronic physical disease. For example, effective treatment of diabetes requires behavioral and/or medical interventions that a lay person is not trained to handle. In fact, few people would expect family and friends to alleviate or treat their diabetes. Likewise, individuals with chronic PTSD can benefit from psychotherapy and/or medications that are available from trained professionals.

Finally, as stated previously, many people suffer from trauma-related distress without realizing the source of their suffering. If a patient is unaware of the connections between trauma experience and present problems, why would he or she elect to bring up painful experiences?

Why (Not) Ask? Providers' Worries

A number of researchers have explored the attitudes, beliefs, and practices of providers related to screening for trauma in primary care and other medical environments. The majority have focused on intimate partner violence/domestic violence (IPV/DV), particularly with female patients. Most physicians appear to believe that IPV screening is an appropriate clinical practice for physicians and that assistance of victims is part of the physicians' role (Chamberlain & Perham-Hester, 2002; Garimella, Plichta, Houseman, & Garzon, 2000), yet screening is seldom accomplished consistently. For example, Elliott, Nerney, Jones, and Friedmann (2002) showed that only 6 percent of physicians screened all female patients for DV and 10 percent reported that they never screened. Another study found that even though more than 70 percent of physicians believed they could be of help with problems associated with physical and sexual abuse and more than 85 percent of their patients agreed, most physicians nevertheless did not routinely inquire about these forms of abuse at either initial or annual visits (Friedman et al., 1992).

In a landmark study, Sugg and Inui (1992) asked primary care physicians about their responses to IPV. One overarching response theme was discomfort regarding the possibility of opening up a "Pandora's box" or a "can of worms" by inquiring about domestic violence. Although that study was conducted approximately 15 years ago, its results still ring true. Below, several of the barriers most commonly mentioned by the physicians interviewed by Sugg and Inui will be listed and discussed.

First, in the study, physicians expressed concerns about offending the patient. Physicians feared that posing questions about domestic violence might be insulting to patients, or constitute a betrayal of trust that could compromise the patient-physician relationship. A similar concern on the part of nurses was echoed by Gallop, McKeever, Toner, Lancee, and Lueck (1995), who found that although a majority of nurses were supportive of inquiry about patients' past sexual abuse, many were nevertheless concerned about being perceived as intrusive by the patient.

Physicians also felt powerless to be of help to a patient who is a victim of domestic violence. Many physicians wanted to "fix" the problem and lacked confidence in their ability to do this, largely due to lack of training. A barrier reported by physicians in a more recent study (Garimella et al., 2000) was lack of knowledge about resources. In fact, 70 percent of physicians queried believed they did not have resources available to assist victims of violence. An internist who participated in the disclosure study admitted that, although she was interested in her patients as individuals, psychiatric care was not her area of expertise:

> I would like to take care of the whole person. If I could have a feeling for what's going on and provide some degree of counseling or reassurance to the patient and send them to a psychiatrist or some facility that knows how to better manage it, I would be very happy with that ... but not actually manage [psychiatric issues], because that is hard for me to do.

Physicians also expressed frustration about not having control over the outcome. Just over 40 percent of the physicians in Sugg and Inui's study (1992) expressed frustration that even if they intervened—for example, making a referral—the patient was ultimately in control. As one physician said, "I try to refer to resources. But that is part of my sense of impotence. I can't give this woman a job. I can't hold her hand. I can't do it for her" (p. 3159). This source of provider frustration has been found in other studies as well, and appears to be accompanied by negative judgment about the patient at least in some circumstances (e.g., Nicolaidis, Curry, & Gerrity (2004a).

Several of the concerns mentioned above are quite realistic and merit consideration and caution. Disclosure of trauma *can* "open a can of worms" for both provider and patient. The "tyranny of time" was mentioned by most physicians in the Sugg and Inui study (1992), and time continues to pose practical limitations. Other provider concerns, such as offending the patient by asking and/or not having control over the outcome of the disclosure, can be set aside with more confidence.

Revisiting Providers' Concerns

Q: Are there any conditions you can imagine where you think a health provider should not inquire about a patient's trauma history?

A: No. I don't think so. I think [the provider] should at least ask that "yes" or "no" question and leave it up to the patient to either say, "I'm ready to share this. Yes I've had that experience" or "no." And the next question should be, "Are you willing to talk about it?" And then it's back on [the patient], "yes" or "no." (male combat veteran, age 55)

The act of disclosure involves not only behavior but also relationship. The person telling his or her story to another does not do so in a void. The person who hears the story plays a role that can inspire anything from the trust and openness that may lead to obtaining real help to the silence or negative response that may mean no help at all, or even retraumatization.

As we saw, one concern raised by providers regarded offending patients by asking about trauma. Two separate, interrelated bodies of literature tell us that patients look for more than a strict biomedical focus from their primary care providers. The first focuses on the preferences, expectations, and beliefs of patients related to speaking with medical providers about general nonmedical issues, such as emotional distress and personal problems. This literature tells us that the majority of medical patients welcome providers' interest in nonmedical or psychosocial issues (Yaffe & Stewart, 1986; Brody, Khaliq, & Thompson, 1997; Burge, Schneider, Ivy, & Catala, 2005).

A number of factors appear to predict whether patients bring up psychosocial issues with medical providers. In a study by Del Piccolo et al. (1998), the level of emotional distress and positive attitudes about confiding predicted disclosure of nonmedical problems. Patients of community-based primary care practices were most likely to disclose psychosocial problems with prior physician inquiry, greater physician-patient familiarity, and more intense self-perceived distress (Robinson & Roter, 1999).

Even patients who desire help from medical providers often do not disclose their psychosocial needs. Barriers include patients' beliefs that they can handle distress on their own, embarrassment or hesitation to bother their physician, perceived lack of time, belief that the doctor is not interested, and negative experiences with physicians' behavior (Cape & McCulloch, 1999).

Gender is a predictor of disclosure and help-seeking in general, and studies indicate that women are more likely both to seek help and confide in providers than are men (Bland, Newman, & Orn, 1997; Steinert & Rosenberg, 1987). Suggested theoretical reasons for gender differences in help-seeking include gender-role socialization and degree of acceptance of the social construction of masculinity (e.g., Addis & Mahalik, 2003).

A growing body of literature specific to disclosure and identification of trauma in the medical setting has, to date, focused primarily on the intimate partner violence/domestic violence (IPV/DV) and childhood sexual abuse (CSA) experiences of female patients. The responses of the mostly male veteran population associated with the disclosure study suggest that barriers and supports for trauma disclosure are similar for both men and women, and across trauma type.

As was the case for the general psychosocial issues mentioned above, a majority of medical patients welcome inquiry about interpersonal violence from their physicians. For example, in a large sample of female primary care patients, 85 percent agreed that physicians should routinely screen for abuse (Caralis & Musialowski, 1997). Likewise, 85 percent of predominantly male primary care patients surveyed for the disclosure study agreed or strongly agreed that providers should ask questions about their patients' trauma histories, In fact, a major deterrent to disclosure cited by a number of researchers is simply the provider's failure to ask (Walker et al., 1993; Friedman et al., 1992). Other barriers to disclosure of IPV and/or family violence in medical settings include perceived lack of privacy, lack of confidence in the provider's ability to handle the issues, uncertainty about whether abuse/trauma was a valid topic to bring up during a medical appointment, and feelings of shame, guilt, and/or embarrassment (Bacchus, Mezey, & Bewley, 2003; Chang et al., 2003; Fogarty, Burge, & McCord, 2002; McCauley et al., 1998).

None of the veterans in the disclosure study reported feeling offended by trauma questions or screening per se. In contrast, they were offended by other aspects of the disclosure experience and the medical encounter, such as perceived provider failure to listen to them, lack of privacy, and feeling rushed. Thus, instead of being overly concerned about offending patients by asking about trauma at all, providers would better serve patients by learning to ask these questions most effectively, appropriately, and compassionately.

The issue of competency was also raised by providers in the Sugg and Inui (1992) study. Physicians in that study mentioned lack of training. Today it is more common for physicians to have received training in recognition and treatment of trauma (IPV specifically) than it was 15 years ago. In addition, U.S. medical schools now typically require courses in provider-patient communication. The good news is that the medical establishment has begun to realize the importance of communication in the health arena and to make this a part of medical education. However, the required communications course may only be a few hours long. This allows for teaching only the basics and conveys the implicit message that provider-patient communication is not truly an important aspect of professional identity.

Given that the time for communications training in many curricula is limited and that trauma is only one of many psychosocial issues of importance in the medical environment, perhaps training geared toward better communication with patients about difficult issues in general may be most valuable. After all, trauma does not stand alone as a potentially "difficult" issue.

An internist in the disclosure study made the point that building a relationship in which the patient feels comfortable bringing up difficult or potentially embarrassing issues opens the door not only to disclosure of trauma but to discussion of more "biomedical" issues as well, such as concerns about pinworms or a hernia in the scrotal sac: "Things like that, that matter to them but they might not really want to tell you about—it's easier to say, 'I'm fine.' So I could do those little things that if they trust you enough they want to tell you."

Several resources for communications training are listed at the end of this chapter. For helpful publications specific to the identification and management of IPV, see Fogarty et al. (2002); McCauley et al. (2003); Nicolaidis (2002, 2004); Nicolaidis and Touhouliotis (2006); and Thompson et al. (1998).

As a nurse-practitioner in the disclosure study voiced her perceptions of how and why providers fear patient disclosure during the medical encounter, she wove together a number of common provider concerns:

> For a lot of the providers [trauma's] just one more thing they have to screen for, and they're really not interested in taking the time to hear how that's going to affect that patient's interaction with them.... Doctors do not like to be in situations where they raise an issue and then they can't take care of it and patients can what I call "crater." You raise the subject and they can fall apart on you and end up retraumatizing themselves. You have to put limits on that and not allow them to go through the trauma history in detail. They need to do that with a person who is qualified. I think people avoid it because they're like, "I don't want to deal with this. When she starts to cry, I don't know what to do." We've offered in-services on it but the staff around here changes quite a bit and so it's very hard to keep people up to date on that.

The nurse-practitioner echoes the theme of competency and several other themes raised by participants in Sugg and Inui's (1992) study, also touching upon the themes of feeling powerless to help, and not having control over the outcome. Her narrative pertains not only to individual providers but also to the system in which they work. Two issues on an organizational level are mentioned. The opening statement about screening pertains to institutional and professional guidelines. Presently, within the VHA system, providers are required to screen for both military sexual trauma and PTSD. As in all health care systems, they are also expected to follow numerous other clinical guidelines. The requirements of multiple guidelines in the context of the short time typically allowed for a medical visit create a context of competing demands that are difficult for providers to balance.

The other organizational issue mentioned in the above quotation is the challenge of training medical staff in an environment of high turnover. This is particularly pertinent in training institutions such as VHA medical centers and university hospitals, where a high number of patients are seen by resident physicians who then move on to their next rotation.

Another "ingredient" of the medical environment that has not yet been explicitly mentioned is that of the community outside a particular practice or institution. The importance of a community level of support is implicit when providers express their discomfort related to lack of resources for patients. Community resources are important even in systems that have built-in educational, referral, and treatment sources. For example, within the VHA system, patients are considered entitled to treatment for PTSD if it stems from trauma experienced during military duty. There are a number of challenges inherent in this policy. First, if a veteran suffers from PTSD that is not related to military trauma, treatment for PTSD within the system is not guaranteed. Second, trauma-related distress is not always synonymous with PTSD. A veteran whose symptoms do not meet the full criteria for PTSD is also not guaranteed treatment.

Therefore, even in a system as comprehensive as the VHA, it is incumbent on providers to know of mental health resources available elsewhere in their communities. This was not the case in the system in which the disclosure study was completed, where 77 percent of primary care providers surveyed knew where to refer patients within the VHA for PTSD evaluation or treatment; however, only 15 percent knew where to refer in the outside community.

Primary care organizations need to find ways to maintain information about in-house, community, and national resources. Gathering and updating such information doesn't take long to do, but requires ongoing maintenance. Some large practices with collaborative, interdisciplinary staff may have employees such as nurse educators or social workers who are designated to collect, maintain, and check resources such as psycho-educational materials and nearby sources of referral. Practices without this built-in resource may have to come up with creative methods such as assigning an interested member of the office staff or collaborating with other small practices in the area to collect, maintain, and share information.

The PCP cannot be a specialist in all areas, and does not need to solve all problems on his or her own. Allies and colleagues within the treatment environment (including nonmedical office staff) and in the community can collaborate with PCPs to provide support to both patient and PCP. Some health care systems are interdisciplinary and integrative to the degree that a PCP is a short walk down the hall from a mental health colleague. Those without such resources challenge PCPs to collaborate with trauma specialists outside their own practice or organization.

Competency is not just an individual issue but a team and organizational issue. A number of disclosure study providers spoke about the importance of a team approach in meeting patients' needs. Below, a nurse-practitioner describes coordinated efforts to treat a "difficult" patient:

> Pelvic pain is one of those things.... I'm thinking of two particular patients who insisted they wanted severe radical surgeries. They were absolutely convinced that they needed their colon resected or they needed their ovaries out or these kinds of things, and it was all healthy tissue.... We were able to get [one patient] some good counseling. We were able to all stay on the same page and my job was to coordinate all the providers, because she would bounce from provider to provider and try to split and manipulate. We kept her all on the same page and she was able to get [to] a place [where] that was not her focus ... and her level of functioning was much higher than when she first came to see us.

This provider benefited from the mentorship of a psychiatrist in her organization:

> I watched her in action and probably the most instructive thing that I could do was to watch her set limits with patients, and just be very matter-of-fact about it. "No, we're not going to do that and here's why, but here's what we can do." We try to give people options. You never just want to shut somebody down. On the other hand, you don't want to be manipulated. So you stand on the same page with everybody else who has seen them, and you use them for support.

The chronic care model (e.g., Wagner et al., 2001, 2005) was developed as a way to conceptualize treatment of chronic physical and mental illnesses. It presents treatment in terms of multiple interactions and partnerships among patients, the practice team, the health system, and the community. If the identification and treatment of trauma-related distress is conceptualized in this manner, competency does not rest on the shoulders of the PCP alone but is shared by the members of the medical team and organization, the greater community, and the patient. The comprehensive website at http://www.improvingchroniccare.org/change/index.html provides additional information about this model. Also see Nicolaidis and Touhouliotis (2006) for an exploration of the relevance of the chronic care model to health care for IPV survivors.

Another concern of providers mentioned in Sugg and Inui (1992) was control over the outcome. This concern may stem in part from providers' unrealistic (i.e., inflated) sense of their responsibilities. For example, Nicolaidis, Curry, and Gerrity (2004a) found that a majority of primary care health care workers agreed with the statement that "A provider's responsibility includes making sure a patient gets to a shelter right away if he or she discloses abuse." In fact, this is not a responsibility of the provider, and is not the only or the best solution for everyone who experiences domestic violence; people who experience domestic violence often go through different stages of readiness to change and are not necessarily ready to take dramatic steps immediately upon disclosure (Nicolaidis, 2002).

A number of women interviewed by Chang et al. (2003) said they benefited simply from speaking about their abuse with someone whom they respected and whom they perceived cared about them. They did not necessarily expect a major change to occur at that moment, but often described the experience as one in which a door was opened or a seed planted. Mol et al. (2002), who surveyed both male and female primary care patients with trauma histories, found that they primarily wanted "sympathy, 'a number of good talks,' and care for physical complaints" (p. 390).

Another way for providers to reframe the issue of control is to consider that it is positive that the patient, not the provider, controls the outcome. Individuals who have suffered trauma—especially interpersonal violence—have been controlled at the hands of others, whether the "other" is a parent, a spouse, or a military interrogator. Thus, in the medical setting it is important for them not to be or feel controlled by others. Veterans and providers interviewed for the disclosure study emphasized that although it is good to ask about trauma, it is equally important not to push the patient to disclose or seek help or to label him or her as "crazy." Choices must be left in the hands of the patient.

Familiarity with the transtheoretical or stages of change model (e.g., Prochaska et al., 1994; Prochaska & Diclemente, 1986) can help clinicians to understand, accept, and work with patients' readiness to disclose and/or seek treatment. This model features five stages. In the precontemplation stage, the individual is unwilling to change and/or unaware of the need for change. In the contemplation stage, the individual is considering action, but has not taken practical steps toward it. In the preparation stage, the individual intends to take steps soon. In the action stage, the individual takes practical, observable steps toward change. Finally, in the maintenance stage, an individual maintains positive changes that have already been made, and takes steps to avoid relapse.

Although this model has traditionally been used in the context of overcoming addiction, it has more recently been applied to more general aspects of health-related behavior and the first two stages in particular could be conceptualized in terms of trauma disclosure for a patient suffering from trauma-related distress. For example, if a patient is in the precontemplation stage with regard to disclosure and help-seeking, it is doubtful that queries about traumatic distress or suggestions to seek help for symptoms will elicit much if any response. Two male combat veterans expressed this in their own ways:

I wasn't ready to sober up until I got to the point to where I was ready, and then I wasn't willing to deal with my trauma. I wasn't ready to deal with the war until I got sober enough to have my brain to where I could think. So there was just a sequence of preconditions practically before it got me in the habit of giving the facts.

You get ticked off for no reason and you don't want to accept that. You feel like nobody understands you. You don't want to accept the responsibility for your actions. You want to blame somebody else. You want to rationalize….You did this. No I didn't. Ah! You're full of shit! Then you walk out or you punch him out…. So when you come to see the PTSD person for the first time, you've got to admit to yourself and to your spouse … that you've got some problems. And if you're not willing to admit that, you're not going to get any help.

In the contemplation stage the individual begins to consider embarking on a journey of change. This stage is often marked by ambivalence, as expressed by this veteran:

> Okay, well, I'll accept the help. That's the next step. You got to be willing to say, "Yeah, maybe I do need help." But there is always that doubt there that everybody else is full of shit and you're right!

These two stages are most likely the most frustrating for the provider, to whom it may be obvious that the patient is suffering and perhaps causing suffering to those around him or her as well. These are the stages in which providers tend to make negative judgments and assumptions about patients, such as, "It's obvious that she ought to take her children and go to a shelter—she must want to be abused," or "This man is an idiot not to see how his anger is affecting his family—no wonder his children aren't talking to him." These are the stages in which the provider may also have unkind feelings toward him- or herself or the helping professions, such as, "Why do I even bother? Nothing I do with this patient makes a difference," or "Perhaps I should have been a car mechanic instead of a doctor—at least then my relationship with my 'patients' would be more straightforward."

These stages of change are normative, and regardless of the provider's wishes, the patient will go at his or her own speed. This does not mean clinicians cannot make a difference. For example, screening or a concerned inquiry at the pre-contemplation stage might plant a seed that will help move the patient along to contemplation. Providing information, a specific referral, or a list of community resources can help the patient plan or take action, or in terms of the model move on to the preparation or action stages. As stated previously, many of the veterans in our disclosure study waited years before they disclosed or sought help. Some received multiple messages from family members, providers, friends, and work supervisors that they could benefit from making changes. Ultimately, most listened, but their "listening timetable" did not conform to that of the well-wishers around them.

Finally, providers in the Sugg and Inui study (1992) mentioned time as a barrier. This is an important and real limitation mentioned frequently by patients as well. In fact, many trauma survivors are hypervigilant for any sign that their PCP is in a rush or otherwise unavailable to them. Any hint that a provider is concerned about time is sometimes interpreted as a sign of not caring or being untrustworthy. One veteran in the disclosure study likened the primary care clinic to a fast food restaurant where "You come in. Order. Then you go out.... And that's why I didn't go into detail with them." Another stated:

> ..... I was pushed in and I was pushed out very quickly.... I felt lonely. I felt betrayed. Then I said, well, I've lived with this problem for so long that I don't need them and they didn't understand how I felt. Most of them were interns and probably never experienced a trauma situation in their life so they didn't know how I felt.

Patients mentioned body language (such as fidgeting), manner of asking questions, and actions such as looking repeatedly at the clock as cues that providers were overly concerned about moving on.

If patients are not revealing important aspects of their physical and emotional health due to time issues, their best interests are not being served. On the other hand, providers in modern health care systems have very real time pressures that cannot be ignored. Conceptualizing the identification of trauma-related distress as a team rather than an individual responsibility, as described above, can help. Comfort and skill in setting limits with patients can also help.

Finally, some providers make the decision that spending more time with a patient under certain circumstances is worthwhile. Physicians in a study by Glowa, Frazier, Wang, Eaker, & Osterling (2003) acknowledged that IPV disclosure meant more work for the physician, yet also expressed a belief that it improved the doctor-patient relationship.

Is Disclosure Always "Good?" And How Can Providers Be Sensitive to Potential Pitfalls?

Providers' caution about the potential of opening Pandora's box is sometimes well founded. Disclosure can be difficult and the responses of those who hear the disclosure can have a powerful effect on the speaker. Previously, I cited Bolton et al.'s study (2003) showing that returning peacekeepers appeared to benefit from disclosing to supportive others. The word "supportive" is key, because those who did not feel their listeners were supportive experienced adjustment problems similar to those who had not disclosed at all. Campbell, Ahrens, Sefl, Wasco, and Barnes (2001) reported that women who had received supportive social reactions to their experience of rape had fewer health and emotional problems than those who reported responses they perceived as hurtful.

Although a number of veterans in the disclosure study expressed ambivalence about disclosure, the majority (more than 70%) were glad that they had disclosed that first time. Some of the most positive things veterans had to say about disclosure are as follows:

> I've been given like a reprieve, I mean like an awakening [laughs], slowly but surely. I'm understanding a lot of things that I didn't understand then.... I'm learning so much just from that little class [PSTD 101] that we're having.... I've learned that I have to learn by opening up my ears and opening up my eyes and shutting my mouth. (58-year-old male veteran)

> It was a big relief, like I had been locked in a cage for so many years and then all of a sudden someone just opened the door. It was a relief of ... finally I admitted it to somebody, and not be afraid. Because you were always being threatened, being threatened, being threatened.... I'm glad. I'm grateful and thankful to God that I came, even if it meant saying that to somebody about incest. I don't care now. I just wanted to feel better about myself. (60-year-old female veteran)

Not all veterans interviewed, however, were as positive about their disclosure experiences. Several experienced increased symptoms for some time afterward, including more frequent nightmares, flashbacks, and/or urges to use substances. A psychologist who works with combat veterans said this about the experiences of some of her patients following Compensation and Pension (C&P) interviews:[3]

> They don't know if they are ever going to see us again, and that's one of the things that they have a really hard time with when they go to see C&Ps.... They are being asked to disclose traumatic events.... I have had people hospitalized from having to go through that process.

Disclosure of past trauma can bring up issues that pertain not only to the original trauma but to later, connected events. One disclosure study veteran who expressed negative feelings about her disclosure had experienced military rape. Her adolescent son, who had not yet been told about his origins, was conceived as a result. Once she disclosed the trauma to health care providers, she began to consider whether she should also disclose to her son, a decision that was fraught with very real concerns and fears related to their relationship and his emotional well-being. As she expressed it, "I said to myself I opened a whole freaking can of worms, and I said to myself, my wall is tumbling down and it's cracking. My steel wall is cracking."

Because disclosure can be painful, it's important to imagine and empathize with the potential emotional state and beliefs of the trauma survivor, who may dread disclosure yet simultaneously wish for it. In the following disclosure study quotation, a 53-year-old veteran who had not yet disclosed past trauma from early adulthood shared his fears and wishes:

> I'm in control now. To relive the things that happened to me ... I'm afraid would rekindle the anger again, and I'm not sure that I really have a handle on it, I'm gonna be honest with you, because I still get very mad. The good thing about it is that further disclosure might help me understand on how to not let that happen. You know, to me it's a gamble. Do I further educate myself about my problem and seek the medical help from professionals who could help me? ... I got to have confidence in your end of the field.... That's like a marriage. Are you going to be truthful to me? And faithful to me?

Many trauma survivors spend years fending off traumatic memories through dissociation, distraction, overwork, or substance abuse. This combat veteran, who had not yet disclosed to a health provider, described what happened once when he allowed himself to be sober for a short time:

> I was going through the 28-day program ... and when I got sober I had a nightmare, and it was like I had two broken legs and I'm on the ground and here comes a guy with a big bayonet and he's going to pig-stick me, and I couldn't get away. And the next thing I knew I was standing on my feet in a dark room with my fists clenched, ready to swing, cold sweat and all that, and I said wait a minute. There is something wrong here.

He, like many survivors, would not easily surrender his defenses against the difficult memories and feelings that could emerge when the traumas are admitted into consciousness.

The Disclosure Experience: Keeping It Safe

> I think it should be a routine question…. Do you have any traumas that you have suffered that we need to know about? It's like saying, yeah I'm allergic to penicillin. Yeah, I had an incident in Vietnam where I saw a guy that got killed. Repetition is the mother of all skills, and the more that it's brought up the more that the health providers treat it as, it's normal for you to have these problems…. Like a guy comes in, have you had any problems in traumas this week? Have you seen anybody get killed on the freeway? (53-year-old male Vietnam veteran)

This veteran's emphasis on the importance of routine trauma queries may be conceptualized on more than one level. There is the explicit level related to gathering information. Above and beyond that, routine inquiries about trauma deliver important meta-messages, such as, "Trauma is a valid topic to bring up in this environment," "We are concerned about you as a whole person, not just a biological entity," and "Many people experience trauma and it is normal to have reactions to it."

As stated previously, providers sometimes (rightly) fear that first disclosure can bring up strong emotions they have neither the skills nor the time to handle. Veterans and health professionals interviewed for the disclosure study offered excellent words of advice on this issue. Both groups converged in the viewpoint that it can be injurious to the patient to disclose in too great a detail during a time-limited medical appointment. As one Vet Center counselor put it:

> Don't bring a veteran with sexual or war trauma, and … then you start asking about their trauma and shut them down…. There is no perfect solution. But I think you can [educate] the veteran. Be up front. Just say, listen I only got ten minutes … and this is what we're going to do. I'm going to ask you this. If I think you have posttraumatic stress I'm going to refer you to [someone who can help], so before we start do you have any questions? … The second thing is if you don't have the training and the background to deal with trauma issues you shouldn't put yourself in that kind of position where you can't deal with how to teach people how to process their emotions. And then along with that, be aware of your own emotions. Be aware of your transference. Because you're going to have some angry people at times, and what you do and say can escalate that situation. And the last thing you want is a client jumping on your desk and trying to choke you.

The psychiatrist quoted below agreed with the benefit of educating and setting limits with the patient prior to inquiring about trauma-related experiences or symptoms.

> Providers get into this pattern when they are overwhelmed themselves. The situation creates a lot of stress because the provider realizes he or she is not helping the patient or not providing as much as the patient needs. It's OK to be explicit that the problem is an important one but not appropriate to discuss right now…. It is probably better to handle the situation explicitly, rather than communicating implicitly that it's not OK to bring the topic up.

Another example of helpful advice is demonstrated in a nurse-practitioner's words for medical providers who do not have the training or time to explore trauma details with patients, but need to or want to screen:

> The standard response is supposed to be, "Do you feel you need to see someone today?" If they start first of all to go into details, you need to stop them and say, "I'm not the right person to tell this to and I want you to get the right care, so I'll be glad to take you to see someone and get you down there to urgent care." If they don't, you know, they want to be seen but they're not in a state of acute distress, then we recommend that they [PCPs] refer them [elsewhere] depending upon the problem.

Thus, detailed disclosure of actual incidents can lead to retraumatization and is best done with the support of a provider who has experience in trauma treatment. There are ways, however, to effectively inquire about trauma without causing new trauma.

Guidelines for Effectively Inquiring about Previous Trauma

Based on the advice of both provider and patient participants in the disclosure study, the following guidelines are offered.

First, if the patient begins to disclose details of past trauma in a manner that indicates strong affect, the professional can provide explicit information about the limits of the present session, and help to "contain" the event in a healthy, compassionate manner. For example, the provider can communicate that seeking to limit disclosure details at this moment comes from a position of caring, because opening up only to be cut off can cause the patient additional pain, which the provider does not want the patient to suffer. These limits are practical, not personal.

The provider can offer that for further aspects of disclosure, and/or potential help for distress, a future appointment can be made with the same provider (if handling trauma is within the provider's range of competence) or a referral can be made to someone with expertise in this area. Some providers may feel comfortable openly and directly stating that trauma is not their area of expertise, so they are afraid that they will not be able to help the patient properly if the patient goes too deeply into the trauma. This lack of expertise is the provider's "problem," not the patient's.

The provider can also "normalize" the distress by conveying that trauma is part of the human condition, and it is possible to feel better. By "normalize," I do not mean to imply that trauma is not of concern—simply that it affects many people.

Finally, as previously stated, it is the patient who must decide what next step to take, if any. The provider is well within the realms of appropriateness to offer help if desired (e.g., a follow-up appointment or referral), to provide psycho-education (e.g., a pamphlet about PTSD, a list of community resources), or even an opinion or observation (e.g., "I have seen a number of people that have been through a similar experience feel a lot better after x, y, or z, and I think you could benefit from it too"). As stated above, it is important to remember how vulnerable and/or angry trauma survivors can feel if they suspect that they are being pushed or controlled. Of course, if the disclosure relates to current, ongoing trauma such as IPV, the scenario is different, and must include an active exploration of the patient's present level of physical safety to determine if imminent action is warranted.

These approaches will not work for all patients. An experienced provider who has a strong, long-term relationship with a patient can generally "push" more than one who barely knows the patient and/or is not yet trusted or respected by the patient. Although many patients are comforted by knowing that they are not alone in what they have experienced, others might interpret negatively the reassurance that others have gone through similar experiences ("So, you're saying that lots of people go through this? So what's wrong with me that I can't live with it?"). No matter how helpfully a provider offers a potential referral, there will always be patients who interpret this as an assertion that they are "crazy." As stated above, patients with trauma-related distress can be hypervigilant for any sign that the provider cannot be trusted, and there is no sure way to know what word or glance will send the patient into either anger or disconnection. Generally, however, patients realize that the PCP is primarily trained as a biomedical and not a mental health expert. Although they want their PCP to be interested in them as a whole person, they are, at the same time, often all too cognizant of the time limitations inherent in today's health care system. Thus, by setting compassionate limits, the provider is generally not communicating anything that the patient does not already know. Not every patient will be happy with such limits, but many will appreciate the containment.

How questions are asked was viewed as important by veterans in the disclosure study. They preferred a direct, matter-of-fact style that invites the patient to identify whether or not trauma or trauma-related distress is an issue without eliciting detailed explanation of the event or feelings about it. Veterans expressed this opinion in a number of ways:

A: I think if you ask the questions that basically say "yes" or "no" versus explaining to somebody, you'd get a better result. Because it's like you're sitting there with this person who wants to interview you and she doesn't know jack shit about what you've been through. So how can she ask you questions about what you've done, see? So if you would ask the questions as it would require a "yes" or "no" answer, a series of those, I think you would get a lot more out of an individual....

Q: ... It sounds like you're saying that you found it helpful to have very specific questions rather than putting it in your lap and saying, "Tell me what's wrong?"

A: Exactly, "Did you take mortar fire? ... Did you kill anybody? Did you see anybody get killed?" You know, instead of "What was your traumatic experience?" ... You'll find a lot of people don't want to talk about what happened because all it does is bring back the flashbacks and then you go into a depression and you don't care if you would kill yourself. And that's why I say if you could answer "yes" or "no."

Providers must be aware that sometimes individuals who may not have disclosed a trauma for many years will come forward to disclose it because they are in extreme distress. For a patient prompted to disclose due to intense levels of distress, it is both appropriate and important to assess for suicidality. Quick instrumental assistance may be needed, whether it be inpatient hospitalization, referral to specialty mental health care, and/or medication.

There was no consensus among disclosure study participants regarding the preferred format of questions. Some veterans believed the questions should be presented on paper in the form of a questionnaire. That way, the patient might feel more comfortable responding to the question honestly rather than under the perceived pressure of an interpersonal process (i.e., the provider asking the questions verbally). Others preferred an interpersonal mode of asking and responding to questions.

Unfortunately, the research does not yet exist that tells us definitively what forms of inquiry are best for patients or under exactly what circumstances inquiries about trauma-related distress lead to the best outcomes. This is where providers' common sense, intuition, knowledge of their patients, wisdom gained from similar situations, and support and training from others can make important differences in the health and lives of patients, as well as the meaningfulness of the work.

The PLISSIT Model: Borrowing from Sexual Rehabilitation

Primary care clinicians may consider borrowing a model of psycho-education and intervention from another discipline—sexual rehabilitation. The PLISSIT model was introduced in the 1970s (see Annon, 1976), and remains in use in the fields of sexual counseling and rehabilitation. Unlike the stages of change model, which capitalizes on the patient's stage of readiness to act or change, the PLISSIT model focuses on the state of readiness and comfort of the provider. Briefly, the levels of professional comfort represented in this hierarchical model are permission (P), limited information (LI), specific suggestions (SS), and intensive therapy (IT). At the most basic level or rung of the hierarchy, the health profes-sional can acknowledge that sexuality is an important, natural part of life, and convey to the patient that discussion about sexuality is permissible (P). Limited information (LI) can be provided concerning specific concerns the patient might have. Specific suggestions (SS) of behavior change are used to help the patient explore viable sexual potentials and techniques. Finally, the health professional at the highest rung of the model can provide intensive therapy (IT), which might deal with complex personal and social issues related to sexuality.

This model can be easily and practically applied to the recognition and treat-ment of trauma-related distress. It is reasonable to expect PCPs to be minimally at the permission level—this would correspond to being able to comfortably inquire about trauma experiences and communicate to the patient that discus-sion of this topic is appropriate and permissible within the health care setting. At the limited information level, a provider might ascertain if the patient is experiencing trauma-related distress and provide psycho-education related to these symptoms. The clinician might also provide information related to educational and/or treatment options available within the health care system or larger community. This is where a discussion of a potential medication trial or an offer for a specific type of referral would fit. With practice and compassionate limit-setting, both of these levels could conceivably be navigated without going into depth at that moment about the patient's trauma experiences.

The specific suggestions and intensive therapy levels of intervention would be outside of most PCPs' capacity to handle during the course of a primary care encounter, and would most likely involve collaboration and/or referral. This level might correspond to something like a "PTSD 101" group, where the patient learns both information and skills to better cope with PTSD-related issues. The intensive therapy level would correspond to formal group or individual therapy.

Conclusion

Several important themes and research studies related to disclosure of trauma in the medical setting have been outlined. Clearly, different situations call for different responses. An individual who is currently being victimized by an intimate partner has different needs from a combat veteran whose major trauma took place 40 years ago. Someone who experienced repeated childhood abuse over a period of many years may present very differently to the health professional than the recent victim of violent assault whose world up to that event has felt secure. Regardless of the cause or presentation of trauma-related distress, the first step is often the same—for the trauma to be disclosed. Once this occurs, a wide variety of steps can be taken, from none if this is the patient's preference, to immediate instrumental help (such as linking up a battered woman with a shelter and/or law enforcement or the legal system), or referrals for medication, psychotherapy, or other types of support.

Trauma is not only an individual experience; it is a public health issue affecting the mental and physical health of millions. Because of its prevalence in the medical environment, and because of the central place of primary care in a wide variety of healthcare systems, PCPs are in a position to be of tremendous support to patients suffering from trauma-related distress.

Acknowledgments

The disclosure study cited numerous times in this text was supported by the Department of Veterans Affairs, Veterans Health Administration, Health Services Research and Development Service and the Office of Academic Affiliations (TPP 98-002) while Dr. Leibowitz was a post doctoral fellow at the VERDICT Health Services Research Center at the South Texas Veterans Health Care System. The views expressed in this article are the author's and do not necessarily reflect the position or policy of the Department of Veteran Affairs. Gratitude is extended to study collaborators Matt Jeffreys, MD, Polly Noel, PhD, and Laurel Copeland, PhD, Dianne, Dunn, Ph.D., John Casada, MD and Yvette Huerta, MSW lent their combined expertise to the interview process, and Nedal Arar, PhD is providing mentorship with ongoing interpretation and coding. F. David Schneider, MD, contributed conceptually to this chapter. The author extends a particularly hearty thank-you to the veterans and clinicians who gave of their time and wisdom to teach us about the phenomenon of disclosure.

Notes

1. A *Criterion A* trauma is defined in the fourth edition of the American Psychiatric Association's *Diagnostic and Statistical Manual of Mental Disorders (DSM–IV,* 1994) as experiencing or witnessing an event "that involved actual or threatened death or serious injury, or a threat to the physical integrity of self or others" in which "the person's response involved intense fear, helplessness, or horror."

2. Vet Centers provide numerous services, including counseling to veterans who have served in a combat zone.

3. Clinical interviews used to help determine whether veterans will receive ongoing support for service-connected injury or disability.

References

Addis, M. E., & Mahalik, J. R. (2003). Men, masculinity, and the contexts of help seeking. *American Psychologist, 58,* 5–14.

American Psychiatric Association. (1994). *Diagnostic and statistical manual of mental disorders* (4th ed.). Washington, DC: Author.

Annon, J. (1976.) The PLISSIT model: a proposed conceptual scheme for the behavioural treatment of sexual problems. *Journal of Sex Education Therapy.* 2, 1–15.

Applegate, B. W. (2001). Traumatic life events, posttraumatic stress disorder, and health outcomes in a low-income, primary care population. *Dissertation Abstracts International: Section B: the Sciences and Engineering, 61*(8-B), 4387.

Bacchus, L., Mezey, G., & Bewley, S. (2003). Experiences of seeking help from health professionals in a sample of women who experienced domestic violence. *Health and Social Care in the Community, 11,* 10–18.

Bandelow, B. K., Wedekind, D., Broocks, A., Hajak, G., & Ruther, E. (2005). Early traumatic life events, parental attitudes, family history, and birth risk factors in patients with borderline personality disorder and healthy controls. *Psychiatry Research, 134,* 169–179.

Beckham, J. C., Kirby, A. C., Feldman M. E., Hertzberg, M. A, Moore, S. D., Crawford, A. L., et al.. (1997). Prevalence and correlates of heavy smoking in Vietnam veterans with chronic posttraumatic stress disorder. *Addictive Behavior, 22,* 637–647.

Beebe, D. K., Gulledge, K. M., Lee, C. M., & Replogle, W. (1994). Prevalence of sexual assault among women patients seen in family practice clinics. *Family Practice Research Journal, 14,* 223–228.

Blake, D. D., Keane, T. M., Wine, P. R., Mora, C., Taylor, K. L, & Lyons, J. A. (1990). Prevalence of PTSD symptoms in combat veterans seeking medical treatment. *Journal of Traumatic Stress, 3,* 15–27.

Bland, R. C., Newman, S. C., & Orn, H. (1997). Help-seeking for psychiatric disorders. *Canadian Journal of Psychiatry—Revue Canadienne de Psychiatrie, 42,* 935–942.

Bolton, E. E., Glenn, D. M., Orsillo, S., Roemer, L., and Litz, B. T. (2003). The relationship between self-disclosure and symptoms of posttraumatic stress disorder in peacekeepers deployed to Somalia. *Journal of Traumatic Stress, 16*, 203–210.

Breslau, N., Davis, G. C., & Schultz, L. R. (2003). Posttraumatic stress disorder and the incidence of nicotine, alcohol, and other drug disorders in persons who have experienced trauma. *Archives of General Psychiatry, 60*, 289–294.

Brody, D. S., Khaliq, A. A., & Thompson, T. L. (1997). Patients' perspectives on the management of emotional distress in primary care settings. *Journal of General Internal Medicine, 12*, 453–454.

Burge, S. K., Schneider, F. D., Ivy, L., & Catala, S. (2005). Patients' advice to physicians about intervening in family conflict. *Annals of Family Medicine, 3*, 248–254.

Calhoun, P. S., Bosworth, H. B., Grambow, S. C., Dudley, T. K., and Beckham, J. C. (2002). Medical service utilization by veterans seeking help for posttraumatic stress disorder. *American Journal of Psychiatry, 159*, 2081–2086.

Campbell, R., Ahrens, C. E., Sefl, T., Wasco, S. M., & Barnes, H. E. (2001). Social reactions to rape victims: Healing and hurtful effects on psychological and physical health outcomes. *Violence and Victimization, 16*, 287–302.

Cape, J., and McCulloch, Y. (1999). Patients' reasons for not presenting emotional problems in general practice consultations. *British Journal of General Practice, 49*, 875–879.

Caralis, P. V., & Musialowski, R. (1997). Women's experiences with domestic violence and their attitudes and expectations regarding medical care of abuse victims. *Southern Medical Journal, 90*, 1075–1080.

Cepeda-Benito, A, & Short, P. (1998). Self-concealment, avoidance of psychological services, and perceived likelihood of seeking professional help. *Journal of Counseling Psychology, 45*, 58–64.

Chamberlain, L., and Perham-Hester, K. A. (2002). The impact of perceived barriers on primary care physicians' screening practices for female partner abuse. *Women and Health, 35*, 55–69.

Chang, J. C., Decker, M., Moracco, K. E., Martin, S. L., Petersen, R., & Frasier, P. Y. (2003). What happens when health care providers ask about intimate partner violence? A description of consequences from the perspectives of female survivors. *Journal of the American Medical Womens Association, 58*, 76–81.

Christensen, A. J., Edwards, D. L., Wiebe, J. S., Benotsch, E. G., McKelvey, L., Andrews, M., et al. (1996). Effect of verbal self-disclosure on natural killer cell activity: Moderating influence of cynical hostility. *Psychosomatic Medicine, 58*, 150–155.

Christensen, A. J., & Smith, T. W. (1993). Cynical hostility and cardiovascular reactivity during self-disclosure. *Psychosomatic Medicine, 55*, 193–202.

Cloitre, M., Cohen, L. R., Edelman, R. E., & Han, H. (2001). Posttraumatic stress disorder and extent of trauma exposure as correlates of medical problems and perceived health among women with childhood abuse. *Women and Health, 34*, 1–17.

Coker, A. L., Bethea, L., Smith, P. H., Fadden, M. K., & Brandt, H. M. (2002). Missed opportunities: Intimate partner violence in family practice settings. *Preventive Medicine, 34*, 445–454.

Del Piccolo, L., Saltini, A., & Zimmermann, C. (1998). Which patients talk about stressful life events and social problems to the general practitioner? *Psychological Medicine, 28*, 1289–99.

Deykin, E. Y., Keane, T. M., Kaloupek, D., Fincke, G., Rothendler, J., Siegfried, M., et al. (2001). Posttraumatic stress disorder and the use of health services. *Psychosomatic Medicine, 63*, 835–841.

Elliott, L., Nerney, M., Jones, T., & Friedmann, P. D. (2002). Barriers to screening for domestic violence. *Journal of General Internal Medicine, 17,* 112–116.

Escalona, R., Achilles, G., Waitzkin, H., & Yager, J. (2004). PTSD and somatization in women treated at a VA primary care clinic. *Psychosomatics. 45,* 291–296.

Ferris, L. E. (1994). Canadian family physicians' and general practitioners' perceptions of their effectiveness in identifying and treating wife abuse. *Medical Care, 32,* 1163–1172.

Fogarty, C. T., Burge, S., & McCord, E. C. (2002). Communicating with patients about intimate partner violence: Screening and interviewing approaches. *Family Medicine, 34,* 369–375.

Friedman, L. S., Samet, J. H., Roberts, M. S., Hudlin, M., & Hans, P. (1992). Inquiry about victimization experiences. A survey of patient preferences and physician practices. *Archives of Internal Medicine, 152,* 1186–1190.

Gallop, R., McKeever, P., Toner, B., Lancee, W., & Lueck, M. (1995). Inquiring about childhood sexual abuse as part of the nursing history: Opinions of abused and nonabused nurses. *Archives of Psychiatric Nursing, 9,* 146–151.

Garimella, R., Plichta, S. B., Houseman, C., & Garzon, L. (2000). Physician beliefs about victims of spouse abuse and about the physician role. *Journal of Women's Health & Gender-Based Medicine, 9,* 405–411.

Gillock, K. L., Zayfert, C. Z., Hegel, M. T., & Ferguson, R. J. (2005). Posttraumatic stress disorder in primary care: Prevalence and relationships with physical symptoms and medical utilization. *General Hospital Psychiatry, 27,* 392–399.

Gillock, K., Zayfert, C., Hegel, M., Ferguson, R. , Hayes, S., & Hill, J. (2001, July). Relationships between PTSD, physical health, and medical utilization in a civilian primary care sample. Paper presented at the World Congress of Behavioral and Cognitive Therapies, Vancouver, BC, Canada.

Glowa, P. T., Frazier, P. Y., Wang, L., Eaker, K., & Osterling, W. L. (2003). What happens after we identify intimate partner violence? The family physician's perspective. *Family Medicine, 35,* 730–736.

Goto, T., Wilson, J. P., Kahana, B., & Slane, S. (2002). PTSD, depression and help-seeking patterns following the Miyake Island volcanic eruption. *International Journal of Emergency Mental Health, 4,* 157–171.

Hoge, C. W., Castro, C. A., Messer, S. C., McGurk, D., Cotting, D. I., & Koffman, R. L. (2004). Combat duty in Iraq and Afghanistan, mental health problems, and barriers to care. *New England Journal of Medicine, 351,* 13–22.

Howe, A. (1996). "I know what to do, but it's not possible to do it"—General practitioners' perceptions of their ability to detect psychological distress. *Family Practice, 13,* 127–232.

Kessler, R. C., Sonnega, A., Bromet, E., Hughes, M., & Nelso, C. B. (1995). Posttraumatic stress disorder in the National Comorbidity Survey. *Archives of General Psychiatry, 52,* 1048–1060.

Kubany, E. S., Hill, E. E., Owens, J. A., Iannce-Spencer, C., McCaig, M. A., & Tremayne, K. J. (2004). Cognitive trauma therapy for battered women with PTSD (CTT-BW). *Journal of Counseling and Clinical Psychology, 72,* 3–17.

Lang, A. J., Rodgers, C. S., Laffaye, C., Satz, L. E., Dresselhaus, T., & Stein, M. B. (2003). Sexual trauma, posttraumatic stress disorder, and health behavior. *Behavioral Medicine, 28,* 150–158.

Lang, A. J., Rodgers, C. S., Moyer, R., Laffaye, C., Satz, L., Dresselhaus, T. R., et al. (2005). Mental health and satisfaction with primary health care in female patients. *Women's Health Issues, 15,* 73–79.

Larson, D. G., & Chastain, R. L. (1990). Self-concealment: Conceptualization, measurement, and health implications. *Journal of Social and Clinical Psychology, 9*, 439–455.

Lee, R., Geracioti, T. D., Kasckow, J. W., & Coccaro, E. F. (2005). Childhood trauma and personality disorder: Positive correlation with adult CSF corticotropin-releasing factor concentrations. *American Journal of Psychiatry, 162*, 995–997.

Leibowitz, R. Q., Copeland, L. A., Jeffreys, M. D., & Noel, P. H. (2006a). Trauma disclosure and health status of primary care patients in a VHA setting. Unpublished manuscript.

Leibowitz, R. Q., Jeffreys, M. D., Copeland, L. A., & Noel, P. H. (2006b). *Trauma disclosure to healthcare providers of veterans in outpatient treatment for PTSD.* Manuscript submitted for publication.

Lipton, M. I., & Schaffer, W. R. (1988). Physical symptoms related to post-traumatic stress disorder (PTSD) in an aging population. *Military Medicine, 153*, 316–318.

Magruder, K., Frueh, B., Knapp, R., Davis, L., Hamner, M., Martin, R., et al. (2005). Prevalence of posttraumatic stress disorder in Veterans Affairs primary care clinics. *General Hospital Psychiatry, 27*, 169–179.

Marshall, R. D., Olfson, M., Hellman, F., Blanco, C., Guardino, M., & Struening, E. L. (2001). Comorbidity, impairment, and suicidality in subthreshold PTSD. *American Journal of Psychiatry, 158*, 1467–1473.

Mayou, R., Bryant, B., & Ehlers, A. (2001). Prediction of psychological outcomes one year after a motor vehicle accident. *American Journal of Psychiatry, 158*, 1231–1238.

McCauley, J., Jenckes, M. W., & McNutt, L. (2003). ASSERT: The effectiveness of a continuing medical education video on knowledge and attitudes about interpersonal violence. *Academic Medicine, 78*, 518–524.

McCauley, J., Yurk, R. A., Jenckes, M. W., & Ford, D. E. (1998). Inside "Pandora's box": Abused women's experiences with clinicians and health services. *Journal of General Internal Medicine, 13*, 549–555.

McFarlane, A. C., Atchison, M., Rafalowicz, E., & Papay, P. (1994). Physical symptoms in post-traumatic stress disorder. *Journal of Psychosomatic Research, 38*, 715–726.

McNutt, L. A., Carlson, B. E., Persaud, M., and Postmus, J. (2002). Cumulative abuse experiences, physical health and health behaviors. *Annals of Epidemiology, 12*, 123–130.

Mol, S. S., Dinant, G. J., Vilters-van Montfort, P. A., Metsemakers, J. F., van den Akker, M., Arntz, A., et al. (2002). Traumatic events in a general practice population: The patient's perspective. *Family Practice, 19*, 390–396.

Munro, C. G., Freeman, C. P., & Law, R. (2004). General practitioners' knowledge of post-traumatic stress disorder: A controlled study. *British Journal of General Practice, 54*, 843–847.

Nicolaidis, C. (2002). The voices of survivors documentary: Using patient narrative to educate physicians about domestic violence. *Journal of General Internal Medicine, 17*, 117–124.

Nicolaidis, C. (2004). Intimate partner violence: A practical guide for primary care clinicians. *Women's Health in Primary Care, 7*, 349–362.

Nicolaidis, C., Curry, M., & Gerrity, M. (2004a). Healthcare workers' expectations and empathy toward patients in abusive relationships. *Journal of the American Board of Family Practitioners, 18*, 159–165.

Nicolaidis, C., Curry, M., McFarland, B., & Gerrity, M. (2004b). Violence, mental health, and physical symptoms in an academic internal medicine practice. *Journal of General Internal Medicine, 19*, 819–827.

Nicolaidis, C., & Touhouliotis, V. (2006). Addressing intimate partner violence in primary care: Lessons from chronic illness management. *Violence and Victims, 21,* 101–115.

Norquist, G. H., & Regier, D. A. (1996). The epidemiology of psychiatric disorders and the defacto mental health care system. *Annual Review of Medicine, 47,* 473–479.

O'Donnell, M. L., Creamer, M., & Pattison, P. (2004). Posttraumatic stress disorder and depression following trauma: Understanding comorbidity. *American Journal of Psychiatry, 161,* 1390–1396.

Pennebaker, J. W., Barger, S. D., & Tiebout, J. (1989). Disclosure of traumas and health among Holocaust survivors. *Psychosomatic Medicine, 51,* 577–589.

Petrie, K. P., Booth, R. J., & Pennebaker, J. W. (1998). The immunological effects of thought suppression. *Journal of Personality and Social Psychology, 75,* 1264–1272.

Plichta, S. B., Duncan, M. M., & Plichta, L. (1996). Spouse abuse, patient-physician communication, and patient satisfaction. *American Journal of Preventive Medicine, 12,* 297–303.

Prochaska, J. O., & DiClemente, C. C. (1986). Toward a comprehensive model of change. In W. R. Miller and N. Heather (Eds.), *Addictive behaviors: Processes of change* (pp. 3–27). New York: Plenum Press.

Prochaska, J. O., Velicer, W. F., Rossi, J. S., Goldstein, M. G., Marcus, B. H., Rakowski, W., et al. (1994). Stages of change and decisional balance for twelve problem behaviors. *Health Psychology, 13,* 39–46.

Ramsay, J., Richardson, J., Carter, Y. H., Davidson, L. L., & Feder, G. (2002). Should health professionals screen women for domestic violence? Systematic review. *British Medical Journal, 325,* 314–327. [Also see response letters beginning p. 1417 of same volume].

Rayworth, B. B., Wise, L. A., & Harlow, B. L. (2004). Childhood abuse and risk of eating disorders in women. *Epidemiology, 15,* 271–278.

Regier, D. A., Narrow, W. E., Rae, D. S., Manderscheid, R. W., Locke, B. Z., & Goodwin, F. K. (1993). The de facto US mental and addictive disorders service system. Epidemiologic catchment area prospective 1-year prevalence rates of disorders and services. *Archives of General Psychiatry, 50* , 85–94.

Robinson, J. W., and Roter, D. L. (1999). Psychosocial problem disclosure by primary care patients. *Social Science and Medicine, 48,* 1353–1362.

Rodriguez, M. A., Bauer, H. M., McLoughlin, E., & Grumbach, K. (1999). Screening and intervention for intimate partner abuse: Practices and attitudes of primary care physicians. *Journal of the American Medical Association, 282,* 468–474.

Rodriguez M. A., Sheldon, W. R., Bauer, H. M., & Perez-Stable, E. J. (2001). The factors associated with disclosure of intimate partner abuse to clinicians. *Journal of Family Practice, 50,* 338–344.

Rosenberg, H. J., Rosenberg, S. D., Wolford, G. L., Manganiello, P. D., Brunette, M. F., & Boynton, R. A. (2000). The relationship between trauma, PTSD, and medical utilization in three high risk medical populations. *International Journal of Psychiatry in Medicine, 30,* 247–259.

Roy, A. (2004). Relationship of childhood trauma to age of first suicide attempt and number of attempts in substance dependent patients. *Acta Psychiatrica Scandinavica, 109,* 121–125.

Roy-Byrne, P., Smith, W. R., Goldberg, J., Afari, N., & Buchwald, D. (2004). Posttraumatic stress disorder among patients with chronic pain and chronic fatigue. *Psychological Medicine, 34,* 363–368.

Sansone, R. A., Songer, D. A., & Miller, K. A. (2005). Childhood abuse, mental healthcare utilization, self-harm behavior, and multiple psychiatric diagnoses among inpatients with and without a borderline diagnosis. *Comprehensive Psychiatry, 46,* 117–120.

Scarinci, I. C., Mcdonald-Haile, J., Bradley, L. A. & Richter, J. E. (1994). Altered pain perception and psychosocial features among women with gastrointestinal disorders and history of abuse: A preliminary model. *American Journal of Medicine, 97,* 108–118.

Schlenger, W. E., Fairbank, J. A., Jordan, B. K., & Caddell, J. M. (1999). Combat-related posttraumatic stress disorder: Prevalence, risk factors, and comorbidity. In P. A. Saig and B. J. Douglas (Eds.), *Posttraumatic stress disorder: A comprehensive text* (pp. 69–91). Needham Heights, MA: Allyn & Bacon.

Schnurr, P. P., & Green, B. L. (2003). A context for understanding the physical health consequences of exposure to extreme stress. In P. P. Schnurr & B. L. Green (Eds.), *Trauma and health: Physical health consequences of extreme stress* (pp. 3–10). Washington DC: American Psychological Association.

Schnurr, P. P., & Jankowski, M. K. (1999). Physical health and post-traumatic stress disorder: Review and synthesis. *Seminars in Clinical Neuropsychiatry, 4*(4), 295–304.

Schnurr, P. P., Spiro, A., & Paris, A. H. (2000). Physician-diagnosed medical disorders in relation to PTSD symptoms in older male military veterans. *Health Psychology, 19,* 91–97.

Schwarz E. D., & Kowalski, J. M. (1992). Malignant memories. Reluctance to utilize mental health services after a disaster. *Journal of Nervous and Mental Disease, 180,* 767–772.

Seville, J. L. Ahles, T. A., Wasson, J. H.,. Johnson, D., Callahan, E., & Stukel, T. (2003). On-going distress from emotional trauma is related to pain, mood, and physical function in a primary care population. *Journal of Pain and Symptom Management, 25,* 256–63.

Solomon, S. D., & Davidson, J. R. (1997). Trauma: prevalence, impairment, service use, and cost. *Journal of Clinical Psychiatry, 58*(Suppl. 9), 5–11.

Steinert, Y., & Rosenberg, E. (1987). Psychosocial problems: What do patients want? What do physicians want to provide? *Family Medicine, 19,* 346–350.

Stretch, R. H., Knudson, K. H., & Durand, D. (1998). Effects of premilitary and military trauma on the development of post-traumatic stress disorder symptoms in female and male active duty soldiers. *Military Medicine, 163,* 466–470.

Sugg, N. K., & Inui, T. (1992). Primary care physicians' response to domestic violence: Opening Pandora's box. *Journal of the American Medical Association, 267,* 3157–3160.

Tarrier, N., & Gregg, L. (2004). Suicide risk in civilian PTSD patients: Predictors of suicidal ideation, planning and attempts. *Social Psychiatry and Psychiatric Epidemiology, 39,* 655–661.

Thompson, E. H., Jr., Pleck, J. H., & Ferrera, D. L. (1992). Men and masculinities: Scales for masculinity ideology and masculinity-related constructs. *Sex Roles, 27,* 573–607.

Thompson, R. S., Meyer, B. A., Smith-DiJulio, K., Caplow, M. P., Maiuro, R. D., Thompson, D. C., et al. (1998). A training program to improve domestic violence identification and management in primary care: Preliminary results. *Violence and Victims, 13,* 395–410.

U.S. Preventive Services Task Force (2004). Screening for family and intimate partner violence: Recommendation statement. *Annals of Internal Medicine, 140,* 283–386. [And see comments in volume 141, pp. 81–83].

Wagner, E. H., Austin, B. T., Davis, C., Hindmarsh, M., Schaefer, J., & Bonomi, A. (2001). Improving chronic illness care: Translating evidence into action. *Health Affairs, 20,* 64–78.

Wagner, E. H. Bennett, S. M. Austin, B. T. Greene, S. M., Schaefer, J. K. & Vonkorff, M. (2005). Finding common ground: Patient-centeredness and evidence-based chronic illness care. *Journal of Alternative and Complementary Medicine, 11*(Suppl.), S7–15.

Walker, E. A., Katon, W. J., Keegan, D., Gardner, G., & Sullivan, M. (1997). Predictors of physician frustration in the care of patients with rheumatological complaints. *General Hospital Psychiatry, 19,* 315–323.

Williamson, D. F., Thompson, T. J., Anda, R. F., Dietz, W. H., & Felitti, V. (2002). Body weight and obesity in adults and self-reported abuse in childhood. *International Journal of Obesity and Related Metabolic Disorders: Journal of the International Association for the Study of Obesity, 26,* 1075–1082.

Wilson, I. B. & Cleary, P. D. (1995). Linking clinical variables with health-related quality of life. *Journal of the American Medical Association, 273,* 59–65.

Wolfe, J., Schnurr, P. P., Brown, P. J., & Furey, J. (1994). Posttraumatic stress disorder and war-zone exposure as correlates of perceived health in female Vietnam war veterans. *Journal of Consulting and Clinical Psychology, 62,*1235–1240.

Yaffe, M. J., & Stewart, M. A. (1986). Patients' attitudes to the relevance of nonmedical problems in family medicine care. *Journal of Family Practice, 23,* 241–244.

Zatzick, D. F., Russo, J. E., & Katon, W. (2003). Somatic, posttraumatic stress, and depressive symptoms among injured patients treated in trauma surgery. *Psychosomatics, 44,* 479–484.

Zayfert, C., Dums, A. R., Ferguson, R. J., & Hegel, M. T. (2002). Health functioning impairments associated with posttraumatic stress disorder, anxiety disorders, and depression. *Journal of Nervous and Mental Disease, 190,* 233–240.

Resources

Please note that the Web sites and organizations listed below are only a few of many helpful ones available. Many have links to other related resources.

Resources Specific to Trauma and Trauma-Related Distress

American Psychological Association Online: Resources on Coping with Traumatic Events

http://www.apa.org/practice/ptresources.html

Lists a number of trauma resources that are helpful for both providers and patients.

The Center on Women, Violence, and Trauma

http://www.mentalhealth.samhsa.gov/womenandtrauma/

Part of Substance Abuse and Mental Health Services Administration (SAMHSA). Two goals of the center are to "develop leadership networks" and to "stimulate local change."

Childhelp U.S.A.

http://www.childhelpusa.org

This organization provides a National Child Abuse Hotline at 1-800-4-A-CHILD for abused children, caregivers, professionals, and adults survivors of child abuse. The organization has information on a wide network of local resources.

Family Violence Prevention Fund

383 Rhode Island St., Suite #304

San Beverlyco, CA 94103-5133

Phone: 415-252-8900

http://endabuse.org/

This organization "works to prevent violence within the home, and in the community, to help those whose lives are devastated by violence because everyone has the right to live free of violence." It does legislative work, promotes community education about family violence, and has excellent resources for providers.

From Within: An International Nonprofit Organization for Survivors of Trauma and Victimization

http://www.giftfromwithin.org/

Features Internet links, publication links, support group information, and more.

Healing Resources.info: Preventing and Healing Stress-Related Problems

http://www.traumaresources.org/

This nonprofit site includes a wide range of resources for people with stress-related disorders, including PTSD.

The International Society for Traumatic Stress Studies

This international organization includes researchers, providers, laypeople, educators, and more, and focuses on all aspects and types of trauma.

Trauma resources and links: http://www.istss.org/resources/index.htm

National Center for PTSD

http://www.ncptsd.va.gov/index.html

Contains information on PTSD assessment (including screening instruments), treatment, literature, links to other organizations, and more.

The PTSD Alliance

http://www.ptsdalliance.org/home2.html

877-507-PTSD

"A group of professional and advocacy organizations that have joined forces to provide educational resources to individuals diagnosed with PTSD and their loved ones; those at risk for developing PTSD; and medical, healthcare and other frontline professionals."

Rape Abuse and Incest National Network (RAINN)

"RAINN operates the National Sexual Assault Hotline and carries out

programs to prevent sexual assault, help victims and ensure that rapists are brought to justice."
http://www.rainn.org/
This group's national sexual assault hotline is free and confidential. Hotline: 1-800-656-HOPE
It provides information on local rape crisis centers.

The Sidran Institute: Traumatic Stress Education and Advocacy
http://www.sidran.org/
200 E. Joppa Road, Suite 207
Towson, MD 21286
Phone: 410-825-8888
"We help people understand, manage, and treat trauma and dissociation."

Miscellaneous Resources

Information on the Transtheoretical Model
http://www.uri.edu/research/cprc/transtheoretical.htm
Introduces and describes the stages of change model, and lists publications in this area.

Information on the Chronic Care Model
http://www.improvingchroniccare.org/change/model/components.html
Introduces, summarizes, and illustrates the model, and provides clinical tools and resources.

American Academy on Communication in Healthcare
http://www.aachonline.org/
This organization describes its goal as "to change the practice of medicine by helping clinicians and patients, and learners and teachers relate more effectively."

The Institute for Healthcare Communication
555 Long Wharf Drive
13th Floor
New Haven, CT 06511-5901
"Dedicated to enhancing the dialogue between clinicians and patients through education, research, and advocacy." This organization conducts training and does research on provider-patient communication.
http://www.healthcarecomm.com/index.php
Phone: 800-800-5907 or 203-772-8280
Fax: 203-772-1066
e-mail info@healthcarecomm.org

CHAPTER 9

YOUTH HOMELESSNESS AND TRAUMA

Sanna J. Thompson

Homeless adolescents are some of this nation's most vulnerable and underserved youth and comprise approximately one-quarter of all people who are homeless (Cauce et al., 2000). Although it is difficult to determine the exact number of youth who are homeless in the United States, estimates indicate that between 500,000 and two million youth run away and spend some period of time in emergency shelters or on the streets every year (Farrow, Deisher, Brown, Kulig, & Kipke, 1992). Since it is difficult to determine the actual number of youth identified as runaway or homeless, it is clear they are a group of youth living in precarious, unstable, and often abusive situations.

Homelessness among youth populations has serious consequences for public health. As these unaccompanied youth live in shelters and on the streets, they are at higher risk for a variety of public health concerns, such as physical/sexual abuse, high-risk sexual behavior, HIV/AIDS, suicide, and a variety of mental health problems. Engaging in high-risk behaviors often exposes these young people to high levels of violence and involvement in a variety of dangerous and illegal behaviors. These activities often prevent them from finding gainful employment and transitioning off the streets, and this leads to requiring public resources to meet basic needs, such as housing, food, and medical care. For example, health care systems are affected by homeless youth who do not receive preventative care, become seriously ill, and require expensive treatment. As they often cannot be discharged due their lack of a medically appropriate placement, hospital stays are longer and more costly. Some have suggested that an average homeless individual utilizes over $40,000 annually in publicly funded shelters, hospitals, emergency rooms, jails, and so forth (Chronic Homelessness, 2006). Thus, the costs to society of continued homelessness among young people into their adulthood are staggering.

Attempts to define and categorize homeless youth have suggested that a developmental trajectory beginning with the initial runaway episode and leading to immersion in street culture and homelessness can assist in understanding the wide range of characteristics evidenced by these youth (Patel & Greydanus, 2002; Smoller, 1999). Researchers identify "runaway" youth as adolescents under 19 years of age who have spent at least one night away from home without parental permission (Ringwalt, Greene, Robertson, & McPheeters, 1998). Runaway youth typically stay away for a day or two, mainly as a result of conflict or intolerable situations with parents/caregivers at home. For these young people, running away may be a rational decision because of the high likelihood of exposure to harm and danger. On the other hand, others run away believing that a more exciting life with few rules and limits awaits them (Lindsey, Kurtz, Jarvis, Williams, & Nackerud, 2000; Zide & Cherry, 1992). Most research, however, confirms that running away is often a last resort for adolescents dealing with unbearable situations, not simply a search for freedom and adventure (Hyde, 2005; Schaffner, 1998). Regardless of their reason for running away, these adolescents typically return to their families within a short time, do not experience the strains of living independently on the streets, and are not considered homeless.

Homeless youth, the focus of this chapter, are defined as those who have run away from their homes, remain away for extended periods of time, and have little or no connection to their families or caretakers (Smoller, 1999). These youth lack a fixed, regular, or adequate night-time residence, often seeking shelter in public places (e.g. parks, highway underpasses), in abandoned buildings, or with a stranger (Patel & Greydanus et al., 2002). In order to survive, homeless young people tend to be immersed in the "street economy," where they are associated with other street-involved youth who get most, if not all, of their needs met through eating at soup kitchens, sleeping outdoors, and "spare-changing" (begging) for money (Roy et al., 2004). The longer these youth are exposed to life on the streets, the more likely they are to become acculturated to the streets and the street economy (Auerswald & Eyre, 2002; Gaetz, 2004; Kidd, 2003).

Not all youth leave home by choice; many are pushed out or forced to leave. These youth are often referred to as "throwaway, push-outs, or forsaken youth" (Powers, Eckenrode, & Jaklitsch, 1990). Some of these youth are abandoned or deserted by parents, others are not allowed to return home even if they desire to do so, and others are coerced into leaving due to continual neglect and/or maltreatment. The members of this subgroup of homeless youth reportedly comprise approximately 50 percent of homeless adolescents and as a group are more likely to attempt suicide, abuse drugs and/or alcohol, and engage in criminal activity (Ringwalt, Greene, & Robertson, 1998).

A final category of homeless youth, termed "doubly homeless," is composed of adolescents who have been removed from their homes by state authorities, placed in unsuitable settings, and run away from those placements. Many of these youth report being abused by foster families and feel anger and resentment at placements where they do not feel a sense of belonging, comfort, or safety (Williams, Lindsey, Kurtz, & Jarvis, 2001). Although the foster care system was designed to provide temporary care, youth may remain in state custody for years. Among adolescents admitted to foster care, many "age out" or transition from foster care to legal emancipation. These youth enter society with few resources and numerous challenges, often becoming homeless due to lack of stable housing, insufficient financial support, and poor independent living skills (Zlotnick & Robertson, 1999). "Doubly homeless" adolescents are believed to represent approximately 18 percent of the homeless youth population and come from the most problematic family backgrounds of all homeless youth (MacLean, Embry, & Cauce, 1999).

Why Youth Become Homeless

Several factors have been identified as reasons why youth leave home prematurely; however, family conflict is often the primary reason adolescents give for running away (Hyde, 2005; Tyler, Hoyt, Whitbeck, & Cauce, 2001a; Whitbeck, 1999). Almost without exception, families of homeless youth experience high levels of discord and poor communication. Verbal aggression between family members is common and creates a catalyst for conflict (Slesnick & Prestopnik, 2004). Conflict is also compounded by the lack of emotional cohesion or warmth that aids in holding a family together (Thompson, Kost, & Pollio, 2003; Whitbeck, 1999). Homeless youth are more likely to come from families that lack parental responsiveness, social support, and supervision; rejection by parents/caregivers is common (Whitbeck, Hoyt, & Bao, 2000). These young people report several issues that cause conflict with their parents or guardians, including parental and/or youth substance use, religious beliefs, sexual orientation, school performance, and personal style such as dress, hair color, or body piercing (Cochran, Stewart, Ginzler, & Cauce, 2002).

For youth who run away and become homeless, family dysfunction has often escalated from interfamily conflict to maltreatment (Thompson, Zittel-Palamra, & Maccio, 2004). These severely disturbed families exhibit high levels of child abuse, neglect, and family violence that significantly contribute to runaway behavior. Several research studies confirm that 60–75 percent of youth who run away have been maltreated by their families and conclude that the amount of family violence in these young people's background is remarkable (Kufeldt, Durieux, & Nimmo, 1992; Whitbeck & Simons, 1990). Homeless youth frequently report physical abuse that involves long and severe beatings, being kicked, slapped, and generally beaten up (Powers et al., 1990). Sexual abuse, generally measured by verbal requests for sexual favors, being touched sexually against one's will, and being forced to engage in sexual activities against one's will, is more commonly reported by girls (Simons & Whitbeck, 1991). Neglect, however, is common and evidenced by parents' inadequate guardianship, abandonment, lack of supervision, and failure to provide adequate food, clothing, and medical care (Whitbeck & Simons, 1990). These situations of chronic intrafamilial violence can erode the sense of safety, security, and cohesiveness on which family life is built. Thus, physically and sexually abused youth run away more often, stay away longer, and suffer serious psychological consequences, such as depression, suicide, and posttraumatic stress disorder (Ryan, Kilmer, Cauce, Watanabe, & Hoyt, 2000).

Homeless Youth Victimization

The research literature consistently suggests that although many youth leave their homes prematurely to escape a violent environment or abusive family, life on their own is not easier or safer then the life they left behind (Safyer, Thompson, Maccio, Zittel, & Forehand, 2000; Whitbeck, Hoyt, & Ackley, 1997). The risk of victimization while on the streets becomes a constant concern and an increased problem for youth who have been abused while in the home, as abused adolescents are significantly more vulnerable to assault on the streets than are adolescents with no history of abuse (Ryan et al., 2000). Increased time spent living on the streets increases the risk for victimization as they spend large amounts of time in public places, especially at night. They also become engaged in deviant survival strategies, such as panhandling, selling sexual favors, and dealing drugs, which increase their risk for criminal assault and other forms of victimization. Other known factors contributing to increased victimization include economic deprivation, involvement with delinquent peers, being younger, staying for longer periods of time on the streets, and engaging in survival sex (Yoder, Whitbeck, & Hoyt, 2003). Reports by homeless youth indicate that 37 percent have been sexually victimized, 23 percent have been robbed, 45 percent have been beaten up, 50 percent have been threatened with a weapon, 35 percent have been assaulted with a weapon, 37 percent have been propositioned for sexual favors, and 21 percent have been sexually assaulted while on the streets (Tyler, Hoyt, Whitbeck, & Cauce, 2001b). Females are more likely to be victims of sexual assault and exploitation, while males are more likely to become victims of physial violence (Whitbeck & Simons, 1990). These high rates of exposure to various forms of violence and victimization increase the likelihood that homeless youth will develop serious psychological difficulties.

Trauma and Homeless Youth

A growing body of research suggests that traumatic experiences have numerous debilitating consequences and can impede a young person's normal development (Foa, Johnson, Feeny, & Treadwell, 2001). Exposure to trauma during critical developmental stages can derail emotional growth and adversely affect young people's self-esteem, emerging sense of self, developing conceptualization of the world, ability to relate to and trust others, manage stress, plan for the future, and avoid future victimization (Thompson, McManus, & Voss, 2006). Adolescents who lack fundamental cognitive, emotional, familial, societal, and cultural supports are more vulnerable to serious adverse effects when exposed to traumatic experiences or situations (Becker et al., 2004a). It is clear that youth who are homeless are exposed to high rates of trauma, both on the streets and prior to becoming homeless. It has also been argued that the experience of being homeless is in itself a form of psychological trauma, as life on the street is characterized by extremely impoverished conditions, constant threats to survival in terms of daily struggles to meet basic needs, repeated victimization, and frequent witness to violent crime (Ayerst, 1999; Fest, 2003). Consequently, homeless adolescents are particularly vulnerable to the detrimental effects of trauma exposure and ongoing victimization, resulting in the development of posttraumatic stress disorder symptoms (Stewart et al., 2004; Thompson, 2005).

Characteristic symptoms of posttraumatic stress disorder (PTSD) are classified in the American Psychiatric Association's *Diagnostic and Statistical Manual of Mental Disorders* (fourth edition, text revision, 2000; *DSM–IV–TR*) into three clusters: (1) intrusive thoughts and reexperiencing the trauma; (2) avoidance and numbing; and (3) increased sense of arousal or hypervigilance. The likelihood of developing these symptoms and their severity are typically associated with the frequency and duration of trauma exposure (Carrion, Weems, Ray, & Reiss, 2002; Foa, & Meadows, 1997). One of the few studies identifying PTSD among homeless youth (Stewart et al., 2004) reported rates of symptom categories among a sample of 301 homeless youth: 24.6 percent experienced intrusive thoughts, 27.2 percent avoided thinking about the traumatic event, 22.9 percent noted a decrease in their range of emotions (numbing), and 45.8 percent reported increased arousal and hypervigilance.

One of the hallmarks of trauma symptomatology is intrusive thoughts related to the traumatic event, as well as persistent reexperiencing of the event via nightmares, flashbacks, and strong physical and emotional reactions (Carlson & Dalenberg, 2000; Kaysen, Resick, & Wise, 2003). Homeless youth may continue to have upsetting images of a traumatic event or situation and reexperience the harm they suffered. If they are forced to suffer trauma-inducing situations on a continual basis, as in constant threats of sexual assault or violence while on the street, these young people may develop strong physical and emotional reactions to experiences that remind them of the trauma experienced. They may respond by overreacting to certain "triggers" associated with the trauma, such as being in certain places and similar circumstances (Stewart et al., 2004).

Avoidant behaviors, such as efforts to avert thoughts, feelings, conversations, or activities associated with the trauma, are symptoms often experienced by an individual with PTSD. These symptoms are described by homeless youth who have left home to circumvent continued abuse from a family member, only to confront constant threats to survival and ongoing, chronic exposure to traumatic experiences while living on the street (Stewart et al., 2004). Attempting to forget the painful memories of abuse or victimization often leads to drug and/or alcohol abuse (Thompson, Zittel-Palamra, & Forehand, 2005). Therefore, addiction to drugs and/or alcohol becomes increasingly likely as the youth struggle to cope with past trauma by blunting their emotions. Although society would view these young people's drug and alcohol use as a hindrance to improving their lives and successfully transitioning off the street, numbing the daily experiences of life on the street is viewed by these young people as a common and useful strategy (Fest, 2003). The experience of finding oneself alone at the age of most homeless young people can exacerbate trauma-related symptoms. Thus, using drugs and/or alcohol is a means to forget the stress and danger of street life, avoid thoughts of past traumatic experiences, and obscure distress.

Specific manifestations of other symptoms of PTSD, such as hyperarousal, difficulty concentrating, irritability, and trouble sleeping are often described by homeless youth (Thompson, 2005). They report that falling and staying asleep are extremely difficult and they intentionally remain awake for days to guard their own safety and protect their belongings. Other forms of hyperarousal can be seen in youth's marked distrust of others, especially adults (Kidd, 2003; Whitbeck & Hoyt, 1999). As many have been exploited and victimized by adults, including members of their own families, they become extremely distrustful and guarded in order to protect themselves against further victimization. This mistrust is evident in their underutilization of formal services and their suspicion of those in authority (Ayerst, 1999).

When the violence, molestation, and other trauma experiences occur repeatedly and come from several sources, the young person has little time to recover from one set of posttraumatic stress reactions before new ones are added. For example, a homeless young person may have been the victim of parental sexual abuse, then physically assaulted, raped, and/or witnessed a friend being shot while living on the street. This sequence of experiences does not "toughen up" the person; instead, each successive experience leads to more severe and chronic posttraumatic stress reactions and other developmental consequences. In fact, youth who have suffered from prior traumatic experiences may be more likely to react more intensely to successive traumatic situations (National Child Traumatic Stress Network, 2006). Thus, multiple traumatic experiences have adverse consequences on emotional processing and may impede the normal course of social and emotional development of these adolescents.

Given what we know about trauma among adolescents in general, the context of homeless youth's daily existence points to greater possibility for trauma-related experiences and symptoms. Trauma symptoms often co-occur with other disorders commonly found among homeless youth, such as mood, anxiety, substance abuse, and conduct disorders (Gadpaille, 2004). These comorbid factors, highly prevalent among homeless youth, may also exacerbate and/or mask trauma symptoms. Thus, homelessness and the experience of living on the street influence how trauma-related symptoms are manifested among these young people.

Homeless youth are more likely to experience complex responses to trauma that require special consideration from service providers (Foa, Keane, &

Friedman, 2000). Complex trauma refers to exposure to multiple, chronic, and/ or prolonged, developmentally adverse traumatic events. Most often these experiences are of an interpersonal nature (e.g., sexual or physical abuse, community violence) with onset in early life. In violent environments, each trauma exposure may cause immediate traumatic reactions from which there is only incomplete recovery. When threats are ever present, coping mechanisms such as hypervigilance, emotional regulation, and avoidance may serve to provide a sense of control (Foa et al., 2000). With exposures to traumatic situations beginning in childhood and followed by further victimization after a young person has run away and turned to life on the streets, posttraumatic stress reactions may continue to develop over prolonged periods of time. Given the continuing traumatic situations to which these young people are exposed, service providers must be extremely sensitive to their desires for interaction and assistance (Stewart et al., 2004).

Homeless Youth Case Vignettes

As an example of the types of difficulties youth experience before and after becoming homeless, two case vignettes are described. These two cases, one male and one female, were chosen as they are typical of the hundreds of thousands of homeless youth who travel across this nation each year.

CASE EXAMPLE: CHRIS

Chris grew up in a family with an alcoholic father who would often come home from a night at the bar in an aggressive mood. He would become physically and verbally abusive to Chris's mother. It wasn't long before the drunken rages also targeted Chris. When Chris was 14, the beatings became markedly more frequent and severe. Not only was he being beaten when his father came home from a night of drinking, but he was also being beaten at other times when he was unsure of the cause that initiated his father's aggressive and violent outbursts. One day after a particularly horrendous beating, Chris decided he could not tolerate it any longer. He left home with a few belongings and sought refuge at a friend's house. His friend's mother was somewhat sympathetic to Chris's predicament and allowed him to sleep in a tent in their backyard. After a couple weeks with no attempt by Chris's parents to compel him to move back home, however, she became concerned and called Child Protective Services (CPS).

With involvement from CPS, Chris's Aunt Jane was contacted and agreed to temporarily take Chris into her home. Aunt Jane was a single mother of five young children and was overwhelmed by the responsibilities required to care for them. Although she initially felt obligated to care for Chris, she was resentful of the time, energy, and resources required to care for another child. She favored the needs of her own children over those of Chris; Chris's needs were simply ignored. He was treated as an enormous burden on the family and constantly berated for being unable to provide for or financially support himself.

Chris ran away from his aunt's house, certain that living anywhere other than where he was not wanted would be an improvement. After he spent a few nights sleeping in the woods near his house and missing school, CPS was again contacted and case workers picked him up. He was temporarily placed in a county detention facility while it was decided what to do with him. His parents were not allowed to take him back into their home and Aunt Jane felt Chris was just too much to handle. Thus, Chris was finally placed in a foster home with strangers. Chris again felt he didn't belong and was uncared for. In response, he became verbally belligerent, defiant, and abusive; he instigated several physical fights with his foster father when the foster father tried to enforce rules and boundaries with regard to Chris's behavior.

Chris responded by running away again. With nowhere to go and no one to turn to, he began sleeping in the park where he met some older homeless youth. Although these new "friends" picked on Chris and made fun of his inexperience concerning life on the street, they allowed him to hitchhike to San Francisco with them. On reaching their destination, however, the older homeless youth abandoned Chris, leaving him with no food, money, or place to stay. Chris didn't know where to go and ultimately camped with a group of homeless adults he happened across. He spent nights on the street but he couldn't sleep due to nightmares and always being worried that someone was going to assault him and take what few belongings he possessed. He had little appetite for the food he found when "dumpster diving" but had no resources to buy food or other necessities.

One of the homeless men Chris had been camping with recognized his vulnerability and inexperience on the street. He spent time teaching Chris how to "fly signs" (panhandle) for cash and showed him where he could get free food and clothing. The man also introduced Chris to heroin. Heroin made Chris feel good, as if everything was OK. It made him forget being hungry, feeling lonely and hopeless about his life. But Chris couldn't afford the drug, so he began selling it to others to get money to buy his own. Eventually, Chris was picked up by the police for drug distribution. He was convicted and ultimately sent by the juvenile courts to live with an uncle. His uncle required Chris to work in the uncle's construction business after school and on weekends, but Chris felt he was barely making enough money to pay for his basic necessities. He was bored and didn't like his uncle's imposed rules after his months of freedom. He knew there was violence, danger, and cruelty on the streets, but he was dissatisfied with his living conditions and uncomfortable with his uncle's constant supervision and monitoring of his behavior.

Once again, Chris ran away, this time from his uncle's home, and returned to the streets. During the next few years, he developed what other homeless kids called "street smarts." Living among other homeless youth, Chris became known as a "crusty" (an experienced, respected, and tough street youth). He learned how to protect himself physically by being aggressive and "hard core"; he protected himself emotionally by heavily using a variety of substances. One night, Chris found another homeless young man going through his things. Chris beat up the young man so severely that the police were called and Chris was arrested again. Chris was convicted and sent to a juvenile detention center for youth convicted of violent, criminal behaviors. Although protected from the stress and violence of the streets, Chris resided with youth far more violent and dangerous than he had known in the past. Chris was eventually released from detention, but with a criminal record and no home or family to which to return, the juvenile justice system was unsure where he should be placed. Now at age 21, he had exhausted all options for staying with family. He was ultimately released and returned to life on the street.

CASE EXAMPLE: MICHELLE

Michelle was 13 when her stepfather started coming into her bedroom at night. Due to threats of harm to herself and her little sister, Michelle was afraid to tell her mother about the sexual abuse she was experiencing. Her mother was also emotionally unstable and she often reacted with little emotional support for either of her daughters. Michelle responded to the abuse and her mother's indifference by changing her typical way of behaving. She stopped showering, her grades started slipping in school, and she avoided being at home as much as possible.

By the time Michelle was 15, one of her friends had acquired a car and Michelle accepted an invitation to go to Las Vegas on an unannounced weekend "road trip." She saw this as a way to escape the sexual assaults at home and did not tell her mother and stepfather where she was going. Arriving in Las Vegas was exciting at first. Michelle's friend knew some people who lived there and they let Michelle and her friend stay for the weekend. The weekend, however, extended to days, then weeks. Michelle found that the longer she stayed in Las Vegas, the more difficult it was to consider returning home and facing her abusive family life.

Eventually, Michelle and her friend were asked to leave their friends' home due to their heavy alcohol and drug use and the fact that they were not contributing financially to household expenses. Michelle and her friend had nowhere to turn and were forced to sleep in the car. During an evening of heavy drinking, Michelle and her friend got into an argument about a boy they both liked. The friend, once trusted, got in her car and drove away, abandoning Michelle on the street.

Michelle didn't know where to go. She didn't want to return home because of her stepfather's abuse and the lack of support she felt from her mother. She had learned where to find food at the local food pantry, but was unsure where she could sleep. Michelle knew she would get arrested if she slept on the main strip where cops frequently picked up runaway youth, so Michelle chose a darker alley away from the strip. A group of homeless men chose the same place to sleep and get high. Stumbling upon Michelle, the men sexually assaulted her. Although she was hurt and scared, Michelle couldn't call the police because she would be found to be a runaway and possibly returned to her abusive family.

After experiencing multiple victimizations, Michelle felt numb, lonely, and desperate. In order to survive, she began to engage in prostitution. Even though she felt this way of life was humiliating and degrading, she saw her options as extremely limited. In response to this way of life, Michelle began to engage in self-mutilation as a way to deal with the emotional pain she experienced. She used a razor blade to cut slashes into her wrists and abdomen; seeing the blood and feeling the physical pain calmed her inner turmoil. About this same time, Michelle's drug and alcohol use noticeably increased. She found that using substances was the only way to calm the nightmares, forget the abuse experiences, and allow her to feel safe enough to sleep. However, many mornings she woke up not knowing where she was or with whom she was sleeping.

Michelle continues to live on the street, most frequently in abandoned buildings. She misses school and dislikes using her body for money, but with no address and no identification she is unable to secure a legal job or to re-enroll in the local school system. She has joined a group of homeless youth, both boys and girls, whom she views as her surrogate family. Michelle relies on this street family for protection, emotional support, and drugs, as her life continues to be filled with danger, violence, and victimization.

Intervention Options and Recommendations

Homeless youth present a unique challenge to the service providers whose responsibility it is to assist them. Not only are these youth exposed to continuous trauma-inducing situations that create complex trauma responses, but few evidence-based treatment studies have been conducted that can guide practitioners to the most appropriate and effective treatment methods. While research has begun to describe and characterize PTSD among homeless youth and has identified trauma as a major challenge for them (Stewart et al., 2004; Thompson, McManus, & Voss, 2006), no studies have been published that evaluate and provide recommendations for best practices in treating PTSD among this population. Thus, treatment methods must be drawn from the growing body of literature on adolescent trauma and extrapolated from the guidelines developed for work with adolescents in general. These methods of determining how best to assist homeless youth are obviously problematic; however, until further research can be completed, alternative options are limited.

Services to homeless youth are "low threshold" mechanisms that aim to stimulate opportunities for longer-term interventions. Drop-in centers, shelters, and street outreach services were created to address the needs of homeless young people and often act as a gateway for youth to access specialty services, such as medical, dental, mental health, and substance abuse services. Providers delivering these services have found that when they can engage these often difficult-to-reach youth, developing a trusting relationship with them and offering them a variety of service options improve the outcomes (Fest, 2003). While efforts are further complicated by the mobility and transience of the youth, service providers who cultivate collaborative relationships with these adolescents are in a key position to initiate the process of assessing and treating trauma-related issues.

One perspective that service providers and homeless youth report as being effective in opening dialogue concerning trauma and its effects is a strengths-based approach delivered in the young people's environment (Baer, Peterson, & Wells, 2004; Cauce et al., 2000). Although this framework does not identify specific treatment protocols and is not an evidence-based treatment method, it is described by practitioners as an useful conceptual framework for working with homeless youth (Rew & Horner, 2003; Slesnick, 2001; Thompson, McManus, Lantry, Windsor, & Flynn, 2006). Strengths-based approaches focus on the assets possessed by the client, as well as those found within the environment, to increase optimism for the future (Kidd, 2003; Rew, 2002). Practitioners working from this perspective assist youth in exploring solutions, mobilizing resources, and attaining desired goals, which diminish the sense of futurelessness common among traumatized persons. As the young people begin to experience identifiable accomplishments, their sense of self-efficacy increases and feelings of shame and powerlessness are reduced. Utilizing a strengths-based approach incorporating services that are flexible and nonjudgmental encourages homeless youth to believe that they have the power to effect positive change in their lives, transition out of homelessness, and overcome the symptoms associated with their traumatic experiences (Dejong & Miller, 1995).

Treatment Phases

In most cases, when homeless adolescents receive psychological counseling it occurs during a shelter stay. Typically, homeless adolescents reside in shelters for periods from a few hours to several weeks; many never seek shelter services or do so only sporadically. Their distrust of adults and formal services results in the majority of them receiving no formal counseling services (Meade & Slesnick, 2002). Perhaps the main reason homeless youth do not receive treatment is their view that services are not tailored to their unique needs or circumstances. One study evaluating the service needs of homeless youth found that they respond best to client-centered services that are flexible and realistic concerning expectations (Thompson, McManus, Lantry, et al., 2006).

Regardless of the specific intervention method, the basic needs of homeless youth must be provided before other therapeutic interventions can be introduced (Karabanow, 2003; Kidd, 2003). The ideal situation for providing care to these young people would be to immediately transition them into stable housing where a physically safe environment could be established and direct trauma work could begin. The initial goal of treatment must be the restoration of some degree of safety and control (Wilson, Friedman, & Lindy, 2001). However, the reality is that transitioning off the streets is a gradual process and one that must be initiated and endorsed by the youth. They are also extremely unlikely to seek conventional mental health services as many find it difficult to trust adults to the extent of accepting services (Kufeldt et al., 1992). Therefore, providers must find methods to encounter these young people, build rapport, and develop their trust before attempting formal treatment strategies aimed at ameliorating trauma symptoms.

Engaging Homeless Youth

The first step in working with homeless youth concerning trauma-related issues is beginning to establish communication and trust between young person and provider. Newman (2000) suggests that the goals of therapy with chronically traumatized persons are to assist them to (1) develop trust appropriately; (2) exercise control over their own lives and internal experience; (3) decrease shame; and (4) increase self-esteem and self-care. To prevent further harm to homeless youth, targeting trauma symptomatology requires an indirect approach. Engagement must focus on providers conveying respect, empathy, and a genuine desire to be of assistance while not forcing the young people to discuss traumatic experiences or issues until they voice their readiness to do so (Fall & Berg, 1996; Levy, 1998).

In the initial contact with youth, workers must cautiously approach individuals because of their distrust, anger, and perception that adults are uncaring and unwilling to help (Fall & Berg, 1996). Providers typically begin to establish rapport by providing youth with needed supplies and inquiring about their further needs. This is accomplished by asking individuals questions that demonstrate the provider's knowledge of the homeless lifestyle, such as whether they might need medicated foot powder to attend to "boot rot" (feet that have become blistered or fungal due to damp socks), clean socks, camping gear, or food. Outreach workers also attempt to causally and briefly describe drop-in and shelter services, hours of operation, and services provided. By taking this approach, the worker is trying to convey to the young person that she understands elements of street culture and that she is there to provide client-centered assistance. By not introducing potentially charged topics during the early stages of the encounter, the worker confers control of the situation, relationship, and further discussions on the young person. As youth are more likely to describe symptoms when they have engaged with a caseworker and have more than passing relationships with that caseworker, treatment can begin only after the establishment of a truly collaborative relationship between the service provider and the young person (Barry, Ensign, & Lippek, 2002).

Consonant with the need to demonstrate that the workers will respect the wishes of the homeless young people, providers must appreciate the boundaries set by the young people and cease further engagement attempts when and if requested. The expression of symptomatic avoidance of trauma material could result in youth failing to seek help; they may decline help because disclosure of disturbing memories is difficult or they lack trust that what they reveal will be believed (Pynoos, 1994). However, once communication has been initiated, the workers can gradually move toward assisting the young people with more complex and difficult to overcome problems. Through giving information on available services, the workers present young people with options, from which they can choose those that meet their specific needs and comfort level. Each time outreach workers encounter the same individual, and as the individual gains familiarity with the workers, workers gradually attempt to engage him or her in longer conversations about street experiences, needs, and ideas about what type of assistance is desired (Fest, 2003).

Once the service provider has developed a relationship and engaged a young person, the worker collaborates with him or her to identify strengths, goals, and solutions. Rapport must be established and maintained with homeless youth by allowing them to choose the subject and direction of conversation, focusing on their strengths, and not pushing them to change immediately or make any long-term plans (Fall & Berg, 1996). The focus of interactions centers on understanding the clients' perspectives and drawing upon their strengths (Levy, 1998). Emphasis should be placed on fostering a sense of control, autonomy, and self-efficacy and encouraging youth to establish how they want to interact with providers and what changes they believe are necessary and desirable.

Engaging homeless youth requires developing a working therapeutic relationship. The young people's autonomy, power, and control over themselves and their environments, independent of the traumas they may have experienced, are key (Kidd, 2003). Homeless youth want to feel optimistic and to have the opportunity for accomplishments that give them a sense of worth (Fall & Berg, 1996). Providers are more likely to successfully engage these youth when they acknowledge the strengths, courage, skills, and determination required to survive the homeless lifestyle (Fest, 2003). Being able to listen to young people's subjective experience generates a sense of authentic mutuality. Understanding that these youth must devote a great deal of their emotional resources to securing basic needs and have little energy available to deal with their reactions to ongoing victimization requires that providers proceed cautiously and gently.

Helping professionals must find a balance between respecting the young people's self-determination and providing needed assistance. Providers must acknowledge the role of choice in street involvement and not push youth to conform to "normal" societal structures and expectations. Helping youth understand that accessing services is a positive experience, rather than a surrender of their autonomy and control, is needed before trauma work can begin. As some have noted, individuals who have been traumatized are often ambivalent concerning the need to address increased dependency following victimization and the heightened need for autonomy (Marmar, Foy, Kagan, & Pynoos, 1994). Well-meaning providers must be careful in offering help, so as not to undermine the young people's need to feel in control over their responses to continuing traumatic situations. When circumstances are viewed as uncontrollable, adolescents may respond by shifting interpersonal attachments. This may be evidenced by heightened attachment to other street youth and increased identification with peer groups that act as a protective shield but tend toward aberrant rather than emotionally supportive and helpful relationships (Pynoos, 1994).

Assessment of Trauma Symptoms

A proper assessment of PTSD is required, and inquiry concerning trauma history should be part of any routine assessment of psychological functioning (Perrin, Smith, & Yule, 2000). However, special care must be taken when seeking this information so that homeless youth do not see this as probing for information they are not yet ready to divulge. The alliance building between provider and youth is often tenuous at best; therefore, deeply sensitive or trauma-provoking questions must be asked with caution. Questions must be useful to understanding the young person's needs, without appearing to be voyeuristic, probing, or intruding. One approach to address this difficulty in assessment is to list various experiences that would be traumatic and ask whether the adolescent has experienced any of these. Categories can be developed that allow the individual to answer simply yes or no for each experience (Becker et al., 2004b). For those categories responded to in the affirmative, the clinician could further explore the meaning of the traumatic exposure for the individual and his or her symptomatic responses.

Clinicians increasingly utilize clinical interviews along with several measurement tools when assessing for the presence of PTSD in adolescents. These tools require individuals to recall frightening, traumatic events, as well as ways in which such experiences have affected them. As such, the assessment process can be threatening and may induce anxiety responses. Thus, measurement instruments must not be too lengthy, insensitive, or overly stress inducing (Perrin et al., 2000). Instruments that can be completed in written form may be more acceptable, as they allow the individuals to feel a sense of control over divulging potentially upsetting material in a less intrusive manner than having to describe the experiences verbally.

It is also important to determine the number of events that individuals have experienced, the severity of their symptoms and impairment, and the meaning of the traumatic exposure to them. Encouraging individuals to describe their history of abuse, maltreatment, and victimization can assist the clinician in further understanding the cumulative effects of the traumatic experiences and the resulting damage (Becker et al., 2004b). Although there is no "gold standard" for assessing trauma-related psychopathology, structured interviews or questionnaires cannot substitute for a comprehensive interview with a trusted provider. A sensitive provider can avoid inflicting potential harm and adverse effects during the assessment of trauma-related experiences (Cauce et al., 2000).

Evidence-Based Treatment Strategies

Once a modicum of equilibrium has been attained and the young person is engaged with the clinician, specific treatment approaches can be employed more effectively, easily, and ethically to mediate trauma symptomatology among homeless youth. Research concerning effective treatments of PTSD for adolescents is relatively limited when compared to research on adults, and virtually no clinical outcome studies have been completed that evaluate evidence-based treatment methodologies for PTSD among homeless youth. The few evidence-based interventions for homeless youth are oriented toward HIV and high-risk sexual practices (Koopman, Rosario, & Rotheram-Borus, 1994) and case-management services (Cauce et al., 1994). Thus, no evidence-based treatment options are available for direct application to this youth population, and extrapolations from findings of studies with other populations must be employed to provide guidance for treating homeless youth.

Two well-researched treatment options are described here. These treatment strategies, though not empirically validated for homeless youth, have consistently indicated the most convincing evidence for effective treatment of PTSD among adolescents. Drawing from the evidence presented in research on adolescents with PTSD symptoms, these interventions are presented as possible strategies that may be appropriate to homeless adolescents if their unique lifestyles and needs are recognized. As no studies have been completed that evaluate specific treatment methods for homeless youth, these evidence-based treatment strategies are included as they are the treatments most likely to be effective, appropriate, and feasible for application to homeless youth.

Cognitive Behavioral Therapy

Cognitive behavioral therapy (CBT) is the most studied psychosocial treatment and has been subjected to the largest number of rigorously controlled investigations for PTSD in adults (Foa & Meadows, 1997; Perrin et al., 2000). Although fewer studies have been conducted with adolescents, outcome studies conducted with community and school-based samples of adolescents consistently report that cognitive behavioral treatment approaches have robust effects on improving symptoms of PTSD (Foa et al., 2000; Pine & Cohen, 2002). CBT has shown effectiveness in addressing trauma symptoms associated with diverse stressors, such as grief or loss of a loved one, interpersonal conflicts with peers, separation from parents, and social victimization (Cohen, Mannarino, Zhitova, & Capone, 2003; Green, 2004; Pine & Cohen, 2002). These findings suggest the potential utility of CBT in youth exposed to various types of trauma, such as those experienced by homeless youth.

Cognitive behavioral treatment for PTSD focuses on the reduction of symptoms and the development of positive coping skills, and it aims to increase young people's sense of control and well-being (Perrin et al., 2000). CBT generally blends both cognitive and behavioral interventions, including exposure techniques, exploration and correction of inaccurate attributions regarding the trauma, and stress management/relaxation techniques (Cohen, 2003). The principal goal of cognitive behavioral approaches in the treatment of PTSD in adolescents is to enhance coping by developing new or modified cognitive structures through which the traumatic event may be viewed and placed in perspective. CBT focuses on restructuring thinking through the identification, examination, and alteration of thoughts and beliefs that are maladaptive (Aisenberg & Mennen, 2000). Individuals are guided to develop new or modified perceptions and regain control over the apprehension and anxiety associated with traumatic experiences (Cohen et al., 2003; Green, 2004). While completely eliminating the fear, apprehension, and anxiety associated with the trauma is unrealistic, the development of coping strategies aims to increase the individual's ability to manage, even eliminate, PTSD symptoms (Perrin et al., 2000).

Traumatized youth who are homeless may expend emotional resources anticipating victimization and have few resources to deal with their trauma symptoms. They are likely to reexperience the traumatic events, both past and present, through intrusive images and preoccupation with sounds or circumstances that remind them of the trauma. Some may actively seek out opportunities to engage in reenactments ranging from high-risk, thrill-seeking behaviors to more aggressively dangerous or violent actions as a means of demonstrating their ability to overcome the feelings of victimization (Pynoos, 1994). In violent environments, each exposure may cause immediate reactions that are used to cope and create some sense of control. Avoidance and emotional regulation are typical responses in these circumstances.

EXPOSURE STRATEGIES

Exposure strategies utilized in cognitive behavioral interventions include systematic desensitization, flooding, and implosive therapy (Foa & Meadows, 1997). These methods are used to treat symptoms characterized by their intrusiveness and recurrence, such as nightmares, flashbacks, and exaggerated startle responses. Images of the traumatic events are used to assist the individual to open up memories that have not been dealt with but are connected to many reminders of the experience. These reminders trigger painful memories that the individual has learned to avoid or escape. This method of treatment "forces" a confrontation with situations and stimuli associated with the trauma. It has been found to assist individuals in managing, on a conscious level, emotions accompanying memories or reminders of traumatic situations (Green, 2004). Exposure therapy must be conducted in a safe place where it is permissible for the feared emotional responses to occur. The benefit is viewed as making it possible to reduce reactivity to painful memories and gain control over responses to those memories and associated emotions (Marmar et al., 1994).

Many homeless young people have fled from their parental homes due to abuse and maltreatment; their behaviors of running away and living on the streets may be seen as truly avoidant responses to traumatic events. They are, however, not living in stable housing or safe conditions and are continuously exposed to victimization from a variety of sources. Thus, it may not be feasible to address or treat symptoms such as avoidance and hyperarousal until the youth is in a less dangerous living situation (Stewart et al., 2004). In light of the constant threat to safety encountered by youth living on the streets, this concern seems particularly salient, as ongoing dangers of recurrence may not only exacerbate distress but lead to aggressive, even violent, reactions. In addition, the use of exposure techniques that repeatedly require youth to reexperience traumatic stimuli may increase fragility in them. Fearfulness and mistrust of adults and others may be warranted, even appropriate, given the circumstances of the lives of these young people.

COGNITIVE RESTRUCTURING

Cognitive restructuring is often used to deal with specific issues related to the individual's appraisal of the traumatic experiences. These methods focus on restructuring thinking through the identification, examination, and alteration of thoughts and beliefs that are maladaptive (Aisenberg and Mennen, 2000). The therapist's role is to assist the individual to "correct" misattributions with regard to overresponsibility and culpability for the victimization. This is accomplished by step-by-step, logical analysis of cognitive distortions and working to replace them with more accurate views. Assumptions and perceptions of the world, both before and after the traumatic experiences occurred, are exposed by the therapist's careful facilitation. The aim is for the individual to discover her or his implicit assumptions, thereby making them explicit and modifiable. In actual practice, cognitive restructuring is often conducted in conjunction with exposure therapy so that restructuring of a specific trauma is treated with concurrent flooding techniques (Marmar et al., 1994).

Coping skill development is a primary component of CBT that trains adolescents to recognize "triggers" for anxiety that diminish their ability to feel a sense of control and mastery over their situation (Perrin et al., 2000). Stress inoculation techniques, including relaxation, positive imagery, thought stopping, and positive self-talk, are strategies that can help individuals tolerate the various symptoms of PTSD (Pine & Cohen, 2002). Through training individuals to be aware of situations that stimulate anxiety concerning the trauma and detecting the cues before they become anxiety-provoking, these stress reduction strategies have been shown to facilitate reduction in PTSD symptoms (Sherman, 1998).

For homeless youth who remain in traumatizing circumstances, these CBT strategies may be helpful in diminishing the self-blame prominent in trauma survivors. Therapists facilitate and direct young people's attempts to understand how they came to their various assumptions of how the world works. Therapists who recognize these individuals' victimization and maltreatment by adults and parents who were supposed to protect them will likely not make the mistake of underestimating their trauma-related symptoms and responses. On the other hand, young people may view these strategies as attempts to minimize their fearfulness and mistrust. Addressing cognitive schemas that organize the individual's protection should be addressed with caution, as the predictions about dangerousness of the world may be well-founded and critical to survival (Wilson et al., 2001).

Group Treatment

Another treatment method that may provide helpful assistance to trauma-tized homeless youth is the use of group support structures. Although few well-controlled studies have been conducted concerning group treatment for PTSD, this intervention method is described here due to the greater feasibility of service agencies being able to provide these services to homeless youth. The rationale for using group therapy methods with adolescents is that it provides a safe, shared, therapeutic environment where trauma survivors can normalize their reactions and provide support for each other while processing their own experiences (Foy, Eriksson, & Trice, 2001). Well-functioning mutual help groups, community support groups, and formal group therapy can provide practical support for the individual temporarily overwhelmed by traumatic experiences. They can reinforce the normative nature of stress reactions, encourage sharing of mutual concerns, address fears and traumatic memories, increase the capacity to tolerate disturbing emotions, and provide opportunities to share strategies for coping (Pynoos, 1994). Group treatment can also provide opportunities to discuss and deal with secondary challenges, such as depression, substance abuse, and other psychological dysfunction.

A recent review of group therapy studies on child and adolescent trauma (Reeker, Ensing, & Elliott, 1997) revealed that two theoretically different models dominated in the 15 studies reviewed. The two models were integrated groups andcognitive behavioral groups. Integrated group therapy typically involved a collection of techniques, such as exploration of feelings, art therapy, and prevention of future sexual abuse. On the other hand, cognitive behavioral groups usually included cognitive processing, assertive training, stress inoc-ulation, and coping-skills training. Other reviews have found that behaviorally oriented group mechanisms are more likely to be effective than nonbehavioral groups (Weisz, Weiss, Han, Granger, & Morton, 1995). The treatment effect sizes for the group intervention studies reviewed by Reeker and colleagues (1997) compared favorably to the effect sizes for individual and group psycho-therapy reviewed by Weisz and others (1995).

From these reviews, it appears that the use of a group format is useful for gaining social support and validation by similarly situated others, especially those who have experienced a traumatizing event or events. In addition, groups assist in normalizing the experiences of youth and can relieve some of the self-blame and other negative affects they often suffer (Najavits, Weiss, & Liese, 1996). Groups place a strong emphasis on making the treatment accessible and engaging to maximize involvement, a major difficulty often reported by clinicians working with homeless youth (De Rosa et al., 1999).

Group treatment may require a great deal of ongoing commitment from clients. As the daily life of homeless youth comprises attempts to secure the most basic needs and fend off further victimization, setting and keeping sched-uled appointments is not a high priority (Baer et al., 2004; Karabanow, 2003). In addition, these young people are also highly mobile, often staying in the same location for only a few days at a time (Baer et al., 2004). Thus, providers must take these limitations into account and recognize that long-term and lengthy interactions are not feasible or probable. By using an open-group format, however, youth can enter and exit the groups according to their needs, without having to commit to attending groups on a regular basis or for a specified period of time. This modality is a "low-threshold" service that accommodates the transient nature of street youth culture and recognizes the priority of homeless youth, which is to meet their basic needs before addressing other issues.

Insofar as basic environmental safety and stability are prerequisites to discussing interpersonal issues or trauma material (Newman, 2000), modification of current evidence-based treatments, such as CBT, is needed to address the challenges faced by homeless youth. CBT with adolescents often involves, and in some instances requires, collaboration with parents or guardians. It also typically consists of regular therapeutic sessions over relatively long periods of time (Perrin et al., 2000; Pine & Cohen, 2001). These requirements are not practicable for youth who are homeless and lack affiliation with parents or family members. Thus, practitioners who recognize this limitation will not push to have parental involvement.

In addition, individuals who have been and continue to be assaulted or victimized require more than emotional processing and cognitive restructuring; attention must also focus on their physical safety. Safety planning involves developing ways to reduce physical and psychological danger and assess for suicidality, substance use, and involvement in high-risk behaviors, such as survival sex. The current evidence-based treatments for general adolescent populations with PTSD may not wholly lend themselves to the unique circumstances and needs of homeless youth. To avoid the potential for further harm being done to these young people, treatment approaches must be modified to the specific needs and unique concerns of homeless youth by incorporating issues of self-care, safety, and high mobility (Briere & Jordan, 2004).

Practice Recommendations

Given the issues associated with homelessness and trauma, treatment in service settings utilized by homeless youth requires brief, strengths-based approaches aimed at helping them cope with trauma-related symptoms while recognizing their continued exposure to various sources of victimization. Service providers have few empirical research findings that provide guidance for treatment of homeless youth who experience chronic and continuous trauma experiences. Brief encounters are the norm, rather than ongoing and consistent treatment sessions; thus, effectively intervening with these young people is extraordinarily challenging. However, some specific recommendations can be summarized, utilizing the previous discussion. These recommendations include the following:

   a. provide basic (food, clothing, safe shelter) needs before attempting other service options

   b. engage young people through frequent and casual encounters to develop trusting relationships

   c. encourage them to lead the interaction and discussion of their needs

   d. provide a safe place to share concerns, challenges, and needs with a strengths-based focus

   e. provide referrals to medical care or sexual assault clinics for physical and sexual victimization

   f. assess for trauma-related symptoms through gentle, client-centered inquiry

   g. provide the most appropriate treatment given agency resources, the individual's engagement, and her or his level of symptom severity (CBT, groups, or both)

      I. Individual CBT techniques:

         1. cognitive restructuring, with sensitivity to the client's current assumptions and experiences of danger and distrust

         2. exposure techniques, only after the client is stably housed and in a safe treatment environment

         3. stress-inoculation techniques, as a way to help the client manage PTSD symptoms

      II. Open support groups to discuss issues of trauma:

         1. provide education concerning trauma, its influence on their lives, and coping mechanisms (such as substance abuse) that may be maladaptive

         2. validate feelings associated with trauma

         3. normalize responses of youth to trauma experiences

Social Policy Implications

The McKinney-Vento Homeless Assistance Act (PL100–77) remains the only major federal legislative response to homelessness to date. This act originally consisted of 15 programs providing a range of services to homeless people, including emergency shelter, transitional housing, job training, primary health care, and education (National Coalition for the Homeless,2006). Amended four times from 1988 to 2002, the changes improved the shelter and housing provisions and educational opportunities for homeless youth and adults. The McKinney-Vento Act focused largely on increasing the development of low-cost housing and addressing issues of poverty. It also extended the Education of Child and Youth programs of the No Child Left Behind Act, which ensured that all homeless children and youth have equal access to the same free, appropriate education as other youth. The policy required a designated homeless education liaison to be available to assist youth with school enrollment issues, transportation, school supplies, and referrals to support services. While school is viewed as one of the few stable and secure places in the lives of homeless youth, the transient nature of their lives allows limited exposure and engagement to educational support services. In addition, the federal regulation does not recognize or provide for services aimed at mental health issues, especially issues concerning victimization and its impact. "Support services" have limited capacity to provide the intensive treatment often required by homeless youth with complex posttraumatic stress due to their ongoing, prolonged exposure to victimization.

Federal and state policies have developed and funded services for homeless youth, but often with little understanding of the culture and lifestyle of homelessness and the specific needs of these young people. This is especially true concerning mental health issues. Services typically focus on basic safety through providing night-time shelters, to prevent injuries and illness due to inclement weather, and distributing basic necessities. Services are seldom coordinated and are often found in a variety of locations; for example, shelters are located in one part of a city, breakfast and dinner are served in various locations each day, and medical services are in other locations and sections of the city. With limited means of transportation to travel between service agencies, young people become lost in the complexities and gaps in services and never receive the services they desperately need.

Policies developed for high-risk youth services have been built on moral or philosophical frameworks that reflect distinct ideological assumptions implicit in various community-based services. For example, some services have been developed based on the belief that homelessness originates in individual psychopathology rather than societal indifference. Others view homelessness as caused by a lack of employment or skills, affordable housing, and other societal structures. Adoption of these various, even competing, perceptions by workers, agencies, and service systems may greatly influence what services are delivered, how homeless youth are engaged, and what barriers they must overcome when seeking formal assistance (Karabanow & Clement, 2004). Homeless youth urgently require basic services (i.e. food, clothing, and safe shelter) and ongoing mental health support if they are to set their lives toward productive, self-enhancing goals and find a useful place in society. Solutions must consider the often deep-rooted conditions and patterns that lead to their homelessness and must involve the community and various levels of government in creative and coordinated responses (Fitzgerald, 1995). Consultation with members of this population is critical to the development of appropriate and useful services that would more likely be utilized. Service development requires making valuable connections with homeless adolescents in an effort to engage them in various services aimed at transitioning them into more stable living situations.

Providing services that appropriately address the needs of homeless youth is often difficult, as these young people exhibit low rates of service utilization. Lack of insurance or affordable care, lack of transportation, and lack of knowledge of the systems of care are primary barriers to their seeking assistance (Yates, Pennbridge, MacKenzie, & Pearlman, 1990). Homeless youth are distrustful of formal services and authority figures, due to their past exploitation and victimization. Many fear they will be reported to the police or child protective services due to status offenses or other outstanding warrants. Other barriers include poor service coordination, inadequate staff availability, limited transportation, location of services far from "hang out" areas, strict eligibility requirements, and endless referrals with limited worker/agency support (Meade and Slesnick, 2002). Policies that provide for services that are more flexible and truly safe for these traumatized young people are needed, as it has been shown that homeless youth are more likely to utilize services they perceive are tailored to their needs. They will access services that are flexible, have less restrictive rules, and require limited disclosure of personal information (De Rosa et al., 1999; Thompson, McManus, Lantry, et al., 2006).

Another major issue in policy decisions concerning the provision of treatment and appropriate mental health services to homeless youth revolves around funding. Basic service programs, as well as extensive and effective programs that target mental health needs specifically, deserve full public and government support. However, budget constraints in these agencies have resulted in providers with less training than is needed. Due to the perilous environment in which these young people live, as well as their high rates of substance abuse and trauma-related issues, service providers must be armed with a wide range of methods appropriate to the treatment of multiple problems. Advanced training is needed for workers to gain the knowledge and experience necessary to successfully engage and assist these adolescents. Ideally, services to homeless youth should employ trained counselors that can deal with pressing mental health concerns from an extensive array of therapeutic approaches (Cauce et al., 2000). Policymakers must provide greater resources so that agencies can provide advanced training for providers working with homeless youth.

Summary

High priority must be given to enabling homeless youth to escape their oppressive problems and to giving them a chance to become competent and effective adults (Kiesler, 1991). Homelessness in youth produces chronic mental health and health problems, as well as deficiencies in educational abilities, and seriously undercuts their opportunities to receive the education necessary to function as adults. Homelessness also places young people at higher risk of encounters with drugs, alcohol, HIV/AIDS, and a variety of sources of violence and victimization. As has been argued (Rafferty, & Shinn, 1991), "In the long run, the monetary costs of neglecting children's needs are likely to substantially exceed the costs of combating poverty and homelessness" (p. 1177). Even though children and youth are often regarded as highly resilient in the face of major distress, they are less resilient in the face of multiple and ongoing stressors. Only through understanding how best to engage homeless youth and "enter their world: can we hope to have an impact on their lives.

References

Aisenberg, E., & Mennen, F. E. (2000). Children exposed to community violence: Issues for assessment and treatment. *Child and Adolescent Social Work Journal, 17*(5), 341–359.

American Psychiatric Association. (2000). *Diagnostic and statistical manual of mental disorders* (4th ed., text revision). Washington, DC: Author.

Auerswald, C. L., & Eyre, S. L. (2002). Youth homelessness in San Francisco: A life cycle approach. *Social Science and Medicine, 54*(10), 1497–1512.

Ayerst, S. L. (1999). Depression and stress in street youth. *Adolescence, 34*(135), 567–575.

Baer, J. S., Peterson, P. L., & Wells, E. A. (2004). Rationale and design of a brief substance use intervention for homeless adolescents. *Addiction Research and Theory, 12*(4), 317–334.

Barry, P. J., Ensign, J., & Lippek, S. H. (2002). Embracing street culture: Fitting health care into the lives of street youth. *Journal of Transcultural Nursing, 13*(2), 145–152.

Becker, D. F., Daley, M., Gadpaille, W. J., Green, M. R., Flahery, L. T., Harper, G., et al. (2004a). Trauma and adolescence 1: The nature and scope of trauma. *Adolescent Psychiatry, 27*(special issue), 143–163.

Becker, D. F., Daley, M., Gadpaille, W. J., Green, M. R., Flahery, L. T., Harper, G., et al. (2004b). Trauma and adolescence 3: Issues of identification, intervention, and social policy. *Adolescent Psychiatry, 27*(special issue), 201–223.

Briere, J., & Jordan, C. E. (2004). Violence against women: Outcome complexity and implications for assessment and treatment. *Journal of Interpersonal Violence, 19*(11), 1252–1276.

Carlson, E. B., & Dalenberg, C. J. (2000). A conceptual framework for the impact of traumatic experiences. *Trauma Violence Abuse, 1*(1), 4–28.

Carrion, V. G., Weems, C. F., Ray, R., & Reiss, A. L. (2002). Toward an empirical definition of pediatric PTSD: The phenomenology of PTSD symptoms in youth. *Journal of the American Academy of Child and Adolescent Psychiatry, 41*(2), 166–173.

Cauce, A. M., Morgan, C. J., Wagner, J., Moore, E., Sy, J., Wurzbacher, K., et al. (1994). Effectiveness of intensive case management for homeless adolescents: Results of a 3-month follow-up. *Journal of Emotional and Behavioral Disorders, 2*(4), 219–227.

Cauce, A. M., Paradise, M., Ginzler, J. A., Embry, L., Morgan, C. J., Lohr, Y., et al. (2000). The characteristics and mental health of homeless adolescents: Age and gender differences. *Journal of Emotional and Behavioral Disorders, 8*(4), 230–239.

Chronic Homelessness (2006). *National Alliance to End Homelessness.* Chronic Homelessness Brief. Retrieved January 9, 2007, from http//: www.endhomelessness.org

Cochran, B. N., Stewart, A. J., Ginzler, J. A., & Cauce, A. M. (2002). Challenges faced by homeless sexual minorities: Comparison of gay, lesbian, bisexual, and transgender homeless adolescents with their heterosexual counterparts. *American Journal of Public Health, 92*(5), 773–777.

Cohen, D. A. (2003). Treating acute posttraumatic reactions in children and adolescents. *Society of Biological Psychiatry, 53*, 827–833.

Cohen, J. A., Mannarino, A. P., Zhitova, A. C., & Capone, M. E. (2003). Treating child abuse-related posttraumatic stress and comorbid substance abuse in adolescents. *Child Abuse and Neglect, 27*(12), 1345–1365.

Dejong, P., & Miller, S. D. (1995). How to interview for client strengths. *Social Work, 40*(6), 729–736.

De Rosa, C. J., Montgomery, S. B., Kipke, M. D., Iverson, E., Ma, J. L., & Unger, J. B. (1999). Service utilization among homeless and runaway youth in Los Angeles, California: Rates and reasons. *Journal of Adolescent Health, 24*(6), 449–458.

Fall, K. A., & Berg, R. C. (1996). Behavioral characteristics and treatment strategies with homeless adolescents. *Individual Psychology: The Journal of Adlerian Theory, Research and Practice, 52*(4), 431–450.

Farrow, J. A., Deisher, R. W., Brown, R., Kulig, J. W., & Kipke, M. D. (1992). Health and health needs of homeless and runaway youth. A position paper of the Society for Adolescent Medicine. *Journal of Adolescent Health, 13*(8), 717–726.

Fest, J. (2003). Understanding street culture: A prevention perspective. *School Nurse News, 20*(2), 16–18.

Fitzgerald, M. D. (1995). Homeless youths and the child welfare system: Implications for policy and service. *Child Welfare, 74*(3), 717–730.

Foa, E., Johnson, K. M., Feeny, N. C., & Treadwell, K.R.H. (2001). The Child PTSD Symptom Scale: A preliminary examination of its psychometric properties. *Journal of Clinical and Child Psychology, 30*(3), 376–384.

Foa, E. B., Keane, T. M., & Friedman, M. J. (2000). *Effective treatments for PTSD: Practice guidelines from the International Society for Traumatic Stress Studies.* New York: Guilford Press.

Foa, E., & Meadows, E. A. (1997). The psychosocial treatment for posttraumatic stress disorder: A critical review. *Annual Review of Psychology, 48,* 449–480.

Foy, D. W., Eriksson, C. B., & Trice, G. A. (2001). Introduction to group interventions for trauma survivors. *Group Dynamics: Theory, Research, and Practice, 5*(4), 246–251.

Gadpaille, W. J. (2004). Cross-cultural and gender considerations of trauma. *Adolescent Psychiatry, 27*(special issue), 225–258.

Gaetz, S. (2004). Safe streets for whom? Homeless youth, social exclusion, and criminal victimization. *Canadian Journal of Criminology and Criminal Justice, 46*(4), 423–455.

Green, M. R. (2004). Interventions with traumatized adolescents. *Adolescent Psychiatry, 27*(special issue), 283–305.

Hyde, J. (2005). From home to street: Understanding young people's transitions into homelessness. *Journal of Adolescence, 28*(2), 171–183.

Karabanow, J. (2003). Creating a culture of hope: Lessons from street children agencies in Canada and Guatemala. *International Social Work, 46*(3), 369–386.

Karabanow, J., & Clement, P. (2004). Interventions with street youth: A commentary on the practice-based research literature. *Brief Treatment & Crisis Intervention, 4*(1), 93–108.

Kaysen, D., Resick, P. A., & Wise, D. (2003). Living in danger: The impact of chronic traumatization and the traumatic context on posttraumatic stress disorder. *Trauma Violence and Abuse, 4*(3), 247–264.

Kidd, S. A. (2003). Street youth: Coping and interventions. *Child and Adolescent Social Work Journal, 20*(4), 235–261.

Kiesler, C. A. (1991). Homelessness and public policy priorities. *American Psychologist, 46*(11), 1245–1252.

Koopman, C., Rosario, M., & Rotheram-Borus, M. J. (1994). Alcohol and drug use and sexual behaviors placing runaways at risk for HIV infection. *Addictive Behaviors, 19*(1), 95–103.

Kufeldt, K., Durieux, M., & Nimmo, M. (1992). Providing shelter for street youth: Are we reaching those in need? *Child Abuse and Neglect, 16*(2), 187–199.

Levy, J. S. (1998). Homeless outreach: A developmental model. *Psychiatric Rehabilitation Journal, 22*(2).

Lindsey, E. W., Kurtz, D., Jarvis, S., Williams, B., & Nackerud, L. (2000). How runaway and homeless youth navigate troubled waters: Personal strengths and resources. *Child and Adolescent Social Work Journal, 17*(2), 115–140.

MacLean, M. G., Embry, L. E., & Cauce, A. M. (1999). Homeless adolescents' paths to separation from family: Comparison of family characteristics, psychological adjustment, and victimization. *Journal of Community Psychology, 27*(2), 179–187.

Marmar, C. R., Foy, D., Kagan, B., & Pynoos, R. S. (1994). An integrated approach for treating posttraumatic stress. In R. S. Pynoos, *Posttraumatic stress disorder: A clinical review* (pp. 99–130). Baltimore, MD: Sidran Institute Press.

Meade, M. A., & Slesnick, N. (2002). Ethical considerations for research and treatment with runaway and homeless adolescents. *Journal of Psychology, 136*(4), 449–463.

Najavits, L. M., Weiss, R. D., & Liese, B. S. (1996). Group cognitive-behavioral therapy for women with PTSD and substance use disorder. *Journal of Substance Abuse Treatment, 13*(1), 13–22.

National Child Traumatic Stress Network (2006). Understanding child traumatic stress. Retrieved October 21, 2006, from http://www.nctsnet.org/nccts/nav.do?pid=faq_ under

National Coalition for the Homeless (2006). Mental illness and Homelessness: National coalition for the homeless fact sheet #5. Retrieved January 9, 2007, from http://www.nationalhomeless.org

Newman, E. (2000). Treating chronically traumatized people: Known approaches and new approaches. In A. N. Savo, & L. Haven (Eds.), *The real world guide to psychotherapy practice* (pp. 267–291). Cambridge: Harvard University Press.

Patel, D. R., & Greydanus, D. E. (2002). Homeless adolescents in the United States: An overview for pediatricians. *International Pediatrics, 17*(2), 71–75.

Perrin, S., Smith, P., & Yule, W. (2000). Practitioner review: The assessment and treatment of post-traumatic stress disorder in children and adolescents. *Journal of Child Psychology and Psychiatry and Allied Disciplines, 41*(3), 277–289.

Pine, D. S., & Cohen, J. A. (2002). Trauma in children and adolescents: Risk and treatment of psychiatric sequelae. *Biological Psychiatry, 51*, 519–531.

Powers, J. L., Eckenrode, J., & Jaklitsch, B. (1990). Maltreatment among runaway and homeless youth. *Child Abuse and Neglect, 14*(1), 87–98.

Pynoos, R. S. (Ed.). (1994). *Posttraumatic stress disorder: A clinical review.* Baltimore, MD: Sidran Institute Press.

Rafferty, Y., & Shinn, M. (1991). The impact of homelessness on children. *American Psychologist, 46*(11), 1170–1179.

Reeker, J., Ensing, E., & Elliott, D. M. (1997). A meta-analytic investigation of group treatment outcomes for sexually abused children. *Child Abuse and Neglect, 21*(7), 669–680.

Rew, L. (2002). Characteristics and health care needs of homeless adolescents. *Nursing Clinics of North America, 37*(3), 423–431.

Rew, L., & Horner, S. D. (2003). Personal strengths of homeless adolescents living in a high-risk environment. *Advances in Nursing Science, 26*(2), 90–101.

Ringwalt, C. L., Greene, J. M., & Robertson, M. J. (1998). Familial backgrounds and risk behaviors of youth with throwaway experiences. *Journal of Adolescence, 21*(3), 241–252.

Ringwalt, C. L., Greene, J. M., Robertson, M., & McPheeters, M. (1998). The prevalence of homelessness among adolescents in the United States. *American Journal of Public Health, 88*(9), 1325–1329.

Roy, E., Haley, N., Leclerc, P., Sochanski, B., Bourdreau, J. F., & Boivin, J. F. (2004). Mortality in a cohort of street youth in Montreal. *Journal of American Medical Association, 292*(5), 569–574.

Ryan, K. D., Kilmer, R. P., Cauce, A. M., Watanabe, H., & Hoyt, D. R. (2000). Psychological consequences of child maltreatment in homeless adolescents: Untangling the unique effects of maltreatment and family environment. *Child Abuse and Neglect, 24*(3), 333–352.

Safyer, A. E., Thompson, S. J., Maccio, E., Zittel, K., & Forehand, G. (2000). *Working with homeless and runaway youth: A developmental perspective.* Paper presented to the Council on Social Work Education, New York.

Schaffner, L. (1998). Searching for connection: A new look at teenaged runaways. *Adolescence, 33*(131), 619–627.

Sherman, J. O. (1998). Effects of Psychotherapeutic Treatments for PTSD: A meta-analysis of controlled clinical trials. *Journal of Traumatic Stress, 11*(3), 413–435.

Simons, R. L., & Whitbeck, L. B. (1991). Running away during adolescence as a precursor to adult homelessness. *Social Service Review, 65,* 224–247.

Slesnick, N. (2001). Variables associated with therapy attendance in runaway substance abusing youth: Preliminary findings. *American Journal of Family Therapy, 29*(5), 411–420.

Slesnick, N., & Prestopnik, J. L. (2004). Perceptions of the family environment and youth behaviors: Alcohol-abusing runaway adolescents and their primary caregivers. *The Family Journal: Counseling and therapy of couples and families, 12*(3), 243–253.

Smoller, J. (1999). Homeless Youth in the United States: Description and Developmental Issues. *New Directions for Child and Adolescent Development, 85,* 47–58.

Stewart, A. J., Steiman, M., Cauce, A. M., Cochran, B. N., Whitbeck, L. B., & Hoyt, D. R. (2004). Victimization and posttraumatic stress disorder among homeless adolescents. *Journal of the American Academy of Child and Adolescent Psychiatry, 43*(3), 325–331.

Thompson, S. J. (2005). Factors associated with trauma symptoms among runaway/homeless adolescents. *Stress, Trauma, and Crisis: An International Journal, 8*(2), 143–156.

Thompson, S. J., Kost, K. A., & Pollio, D. E. (2003). Examining risk factors to predict family reunification for runaway youth: Does ethnicity matter? *Family Relations, 52*(3), 296–305.

Thompson, S J., McManus, H., Lantry, J., Windsor, L. C., & Flynn, P. (2006). Insights from the street: Perceptions of services and providers by homeless young adults. *Evaluation and Program Planning, 29*(1), 1–10.

Thompson, S. J., McManus, H. H., & Voss, T. (2006). PTSD and substance abuse among youth who are homeless: Treatment issues and implications. *Brief Treatment and Crisis Intervention, 6*(4), 1–12.

Thompson, S. J., Zittel-Palamra, K., & Forehand, G. (2005). Difference in risk factors for cigarette, alcohol, and marijuana use among runaway youth utilizing two services sectors. *Journal of Child and Adolescent Substance Abuse, 15*(1), 17–36.

Thompson, S. J., Zittel-Palamra, K. M., & Maccio, E. (2004). Runaway youth utilizing crisis shelter services: Predictors of presenting problems. *Child and Youth Care Forum, 33*(6), 387–404.

Tyler, K. A., Hoyt, D. R., Whitbeck, L. B., & Cauce, A. M. (2001a). The effects of a high-risk environment on the sexual victimization of homeless and runaway youth. *Violence and Victims, 16*(4), 441–455.

Tyler, K. A., Hoyt, D. R., Whitbeck, L. B., & Cauce, A. M. (2001b). The impact of childhood sexual abuse on later sexual victimization among runaway youth. *Journal of Research on Adolescence, 11*(2), 151–176.

Weisz, J. R., Weiss, B., Han, S. S., Granger, D. A., & Morton, T. (1995). Effects of psychotherapy with children and adolescents revisited: A meta-analysis of treatment outcome studies. *Psychological Bulletin, 117*(3), 450–468.

Whitbeck, L. B. (1999). Primary socialization theory: It all begins with the family. *Substance Use and Misuse, 34*(7), 1025–1032.

Whitbeck, L. B., & Hoyt, D. R. (1999). *Nowhere to grow: Homeless and runaway adolescents and their families.* New York: Aldine De Gruyter.

Whitbeck, L. B., Hoyt, D. R., & Ackley, K. A. (1997). Abusive family backgrounds and later victimization among runaway and homeless adolescents. *Journal of Research on Adolescence, 7*(4), 375–392.

Whitbeck, L. B., Hoyt, D. R., & Bao, W.-N. (2000). Depressive symptoms and co-occurring depressive symptoms, substance abuse, and conduct problems among runaway and homeless adolescents. *Child Development, 71*(3), 721–732.

Whitbeck, L. B., & Simons, R. L. (1990). Life on the streets. The victimization of runaway and homeless adolescents. *Youth and Society, 22*(1), 108–125.

Williams, N. R., Lindsey, E. W., Kurtz, P., & Jarvis, S. (2001). From trauma to resiliency: Lessons from former runaway and homeless youth. *Journal of Youth Studies, 4*(2), 233–253.

Wilson, J. P., Friedman, M J., & Lindy, J. D. (Eds.). (2001). *Treating psychological trauma and PTSD.* New York: Guildford Press.

Yates, G. L., Pennbridge, J. N., MacKenzie, R. G., & Pearlman, S. (1990). A multiagency system of care for runaway/homeless youth. In M. L. Forst (Ed.), *Missing children: The law enforcement response.* Springfield, IL: Charles C. Thomas.

Yoder, K. A., Whitbeck, L. B., & Hoyt, D. R. (2003). Gang involvement and membership among homeless and runaway youth. *Youth Society, 34*(4), 441–467.

Zide, M. R., & Cherry, A. (1992). A typology of runaway youths: An empirically based definition. *Child and Adolescent Social Work Journal, 9*(2), 155–168.

Zlotnick, C., & Robertson, M. J. (1999). Getting off the streets: Economic resources and residential exits from homelessness. *Journal of Community Psychology, 27*(2), 209–224.

CHAPTER 10

Trauma in the Lives of Homeless Families

Kathleen Guarino, Lenore Rubin, and Ellen Bassuk

Homelessness is a devastating national crisis that has a significant impact on the health and well-being of adults and children across the United States. Homelessness results in multiple losses, including the loss of place, belongings, loved ones, and a sense of safety and stability. Interpersonal violence in childhood and adulthood only exacerbates the effects of poverty and increases one's risk of homelessness. Experiences of homelessness and trauma result in extremely poor emotional and physical health outcomes that make homelessness a significant public health issue with major ramifications for the broader systems of education and health care. In this chapter, as we move to examine the relationship between poverty, violence, and homelessness in the lives of female-headed homeless families, we will address the impact of homelessness on women and children's health and the systemic changes necessary to mediate the effects of poverty and strengthen society's families.

Families are among the fastest-growing segments of the homeless population (National Center on Family Homelessness [NCFH], 1999). In the United States, nearly 600,000 families and 1.35 million children experience homelessness within the course of a year (National Alliance to End Homelessness [NAEH], 2005). The majority of homeless families consist of a young single mother in her late 20s and her two young children, most often under the age of six years (NCFH, 1999). Faced with a lack of affordable housing, unemployment, and exposure to many forms of violence, poor families often struggle to access and maintain adequate housing for themselves and their children. The lack of systemic resources and opportunities, along with astoundingly high rates of violence, contribute to the loss of safety and stability in the lives of poor families.

The Roots of Family Homelessness

Structural and systemic imbalances underlie family homelessness, and changes to these systems are necessary to the solution (Bassuk, 1991; Bassuk, Weinreb, Dawson, Perloff, & Buckner, 1997; Koegel, Melamid, & Burham, 1995; National Alliance to End Homelessness, 2005; Wood, Valdez, Hayashi, & Shen, 1990). Over the last 20 years, financial assistance for poor families has decreased, rents have increased, the supply of affordable housing has declined, and the minimum wage has not kept up with increased housing costs (Bassuk, 1991; National Low Income Housing Coalition, 2004). Reductions in federally funded housing programs have decreased the availability of public and Section 8 housing options as well (Bassuk, 1991). As of 2004, "there [was] not a single jurisdiction in the country where a person working full time earning the prevailing minimum wage [could] afford a two bedroom rental home" (National Low Income Housing Coalition, 2004, p. 3). Furthermore, there were only four counties in the country where a person could work for minimum wage and afford a one-bedroom apartment (National Low Income Housing Coalition, 2004). As these discrepancies between housing and wages increase, families living in extreme poverty have few resources with which to improve their situations.

Single mothers are particularly vulnerable to homelessness, due to their limited access to higher-paying jobs, child care, and other services and supports. Bassuk et al. (1996) found that "economic resources and social supports are the most critical factors distinguishing [between homeless and low-income housed mothers]" (p. 644). Homeless mothers have an average annual income of less than $8,000, and many of these families live at 63 percent of the federal poverty level for a family of three (NCFH, 1999). Entry-level positions that pay minimum wage are insufficient to provide for a family's basic needs. In addition to being single mothers, a disproportionate number of minority women with children live in poverty in the United States (Children's Defense Fund, 2004; U.S. Census Bureau, 2005). Therefore, single mothers of minority status are at even higher risk of facing homelessness. Poor families are isolated and marginalized, both in society at large and within their local communities. In summary, poor families have little access to the financial supports necessary to survive, and they lack stable and ongoing social supports to rely on for help.

Family Homelessness and Violence

In addition to economic disparities, violence plays a significant role in the lives of families living in poverty. Traumatic events such as childhood sexual abuse, physical abuse, family separation, and domestic violence in adulthood can take a severe toll on poor families, often increasing their risk of experiencing additional traumatic life events. Homeless mothers have extensive histories of violence that impact their ability to navigate already overwhelming circumstances. The impact of this violence is deeply penetrating and far-reaching, damaging a family's emotional, physical, mental, relational, and spiritual well-being.

Focus of the Chapter

Experiences of trauma are common to most people who face homelessness, whether as single adults or within a family unit. It is important to acknowledge that single adults who are homeless are also members of a family, though they may currently be separated from their children, partners, and families of origin. Though all who are homeless suffer the ramifications of poverty and violence, the women and children who represent homeless families, and who account for 40 percent of the homeless population, have a unique set of challenges and mental health profiles that are the focus of the current chapter. In this chapter, we review the literature on the prevalence of violence in the lives of homeless families. We then explore traumatic responses to violence and discuss how exposure to trauma can lead to increased vulnerability to future traumatic experiences, specifically homelessness. We then explore promising practices to address the needs of homeless families, including strategies to understand and address the relationship between violence, trauma, and family homelessness. We conclude with a brief policy review.

Violence in the Lives of Homeless Women

CASE EXAMPLE: ALICE

Alice is a 26-year-old woman who lives in a shelter with her daughter, Sarah, and son, Matthew. Alice's exposure to violence began in childhood, when her father would hit her frequently. In adulthood, soon after she was married, Alice's husband was imprisoned for theft, and after his release, the marriage became violent. Over the course of three years, Alice left her husband 15 times. Alice's five-month-old daughter, Sarah, is frail, listless, and underweight. She cannot hold down her food, is unable to grasp a rattle, and rarely vocalizes or smiles. Her brother, Matthew, who has moved seven times in his 15 months of life, is painfully shy. After arriving at the shelter, he stopped saying the few words he knew, refused to eat, and had trouble sleeping.

Alice's experience of violence in both childhood and adulthood is a familiar story in the world of homeless families. Researchers have discovered that Alice's experiences of physical abuse within her family of origin and in her intimate adult relationships are common in the lives of homeless mothers. The impact of violence on the lives of these women is far-reaching, and can be seen in their struggles to maintain health and find safety for themselves and their children. The cycle of violence is perpetuated as women and children exposed to the trauma of violence struggle to cope with life stressors and rebuild their lives.

Experiences of family violence are common in the lives of many women, and they cross the boundaries of race, ethnicity, and socioeconomic status. Since the mid-1970s, the pervasiveness of violence against women in our society has become clear (Browne, 1993). In particular, there is heightened awareness of women's vulnerability to experiences of violent trauma, most often at the hands of those closest to them, whom they rely on for safety and support: "women in the United States are more at risk of being assaulted and injured, raped, or even killed by a current or past male partner than by all other types of assailants combined" (Browne, 1993, p. 371). Furthermore, women who report extensive experiences of physical and sexual abuse in their childhoods are more likely to be victims of violence within adult intimate relationships.

For women, the risk of experiencing violence is further exacerbated by poverty. Browne and Bassuk (1997) found that "poverty constitutes a serious risk factor for both child abuse and violence by male partners, particularly for severe and life-threatening attacks" (p. 263). Living in an environment associated with minimal employment and educational opportunities, lack of affordable housing, and increased risk of violence, poor women are at higher risk of victimization than women in the general population. The ability to change or leave a violent environment is limited, and consistent sources of protection from violence are minimal (Browne, 1993). This immobility in the face of violence often leads to repeated victimization.

Research has shown the rates of violence among housed poor mothers to be staggeringly high (Bassuk et al., 1996; Browne, 1993; Browne & Bassuk, 1997; D'Ercole & Struening, 1990; Goodman, 1991), but homeless women experience even higher rates of family violence (Bassuk et al., 1996; Browne & Bassuk, 1997; D'Ercole & Struening, 1990; Wood et al., 1990). Rates of childhood physical and sexual abuse, rape, and physical assault are particularly high among homeless women, which highlights the need to examine the relationship between childhood and adult violence and risk of homelessness.

Research has shown that the rates of childhood experiences of violence are extremely high among homeless mothers. Early comparisons of homeless and housed female-headed families indicated that homeless mothers had experienced significantly more abuse in childhood than housed mothers (Bassuk & Rosenberg, 1988). Subsequent research has continued to demonstrate a significant relationship between childhood experiences of violence and homelessness. Wood et al. (1990) studied 196 homeless and 194 housed poor families in Los Angeles, California, to compare the two groups on many characteristics, including experiences of family violence. Rates of family substance abuse and violence were higher within homeless mothers' families of origin (Wood et al., 1990).

The Worcester Family Research Project studied 220 sheltered homeless mothers and 216 low-income housed mothers, and compared homeless and low-income mothers on a variety of outcome measures, including histories of violent experiences (Bassuk et al., 1996; Browne & Bassuk, 1997). When they examined the specific experiences of childhood violence in the lives of homeless and housed poor mothers, Bassuk and her colleagues found that both homeless and low-income housed women reported significant histories of violence beginning in childhood. In each sample group, the majority of homeless and housed mothers reported experiences of severe physical assault by family members or those who lived in their homes during childhood (Bassuk et al., 1996). Based on data from the Worcester Family Research Project, Browne and Bassuk (1997) found that over 60 percent of the total sample of respondents had experienced some form of severe physical violence during their childhood, and a majority had sustained injuries. Over 40 percent of the homeless and housed women sampled reported having been sexually molested at some point in childhood or adolescence (Bassuk et al., 1996). The women sampled offered few reports of adequate interventions related to these experiences, except for removal from their families for varied periods of time (Browne & Bassuk, 1997). Overall, however, data from the Worcester Family Research Project show that homeless mothers had a higher cumulative experience of violence than poor housed mothers (Bassuk et al., 1996).

In contrast, Goodman (1991) found little difference between homeless and housed mothers in experiences of abuse. However, as in other studies, rates of family violence were found to be very high for all study participants, both homeless and housed; 60 percent of homeless women reported child physical abuse, and 42 percent had experienced child sexual abuse. Regardless of the differences in findings regarding rates of family violence among homeless and poor housed women, it is clear that overall experiences of family violence are extremely high among poor women, which increases a family's vulnerability to experiencing other adverse life events.

Violence continues to plague poor and homeless women into adulthood. Childhood experiences of violence and trauma often set women on a particular path that leads to violence in adulthood. Along with extensive childhood histories of abuse, homeless mothers have high rates of adult partner abuse and general experiences of violence (Bassuk et al., 1996; Bassuk, Dawson, Perloff, & Weinreb, 2001; Browne & Bassuk, 1997; D'Ercole & Struening, 1990; Goodman, 1991; Wood et al., 1990).

Browne and Bassuk (1997) report that "childhood violence is a strong predictor of violence by an intimate male partner" (p. 272). Bassuk, Dawson, et al. (2001) found that women with histories of childhood violence were four times more likely than other women to experience violence in adulthood. Based on data from the Worcester Family Research Project, Bassuk et al. (1996) found that approximately two-thirds of each sample of homeless and low-income housed women had been physically assaulted by a male partner in adulthood. Thirty-two percent of those women had experienced violence at the hands of their most recent partner (Browne & Bassuk, 1997). Browne and Bassuk (1997) found that over one-half of all respondents had sustained some type of physical injury by an intimate partner. Similarly, Goodman (1991) found that 64 percent of homeless women reported experiences of physical abuse by a partner. Nearly one-quarter of these women needed medical attention following these assaults by male partners (Bassuk et al., 1996). When asked about their responses to these violent experiences in relationships, approximately one-third of women who reported having been in abusive adult relationships had obtained a restraining order, and 34 percent of the women who had ended a relationship continued to be threatened and assaulted after the separation (Browne & Bassuk, 1997). Wood et al. (1990) reported that, in their comparison of homeless and housed poor mothers, homeless women reported higher instances of abuse and substance use by their adult partners. In addition to partner violence, poor women were more likely to be victims of random violence (Bassuk et al., 1996). D'Ercole and Struening (1990) interviewed homeless women and compared their experiences of trauma with those of other women in the community. Based on a sample of 141 women, they found that 21 reported having been raped, 42 reported having been both raped and physically abused, and 62 reported having been physically abused.

As documented above, poor and homeless mothers have experienced chronic, prolonged violence across childhood and into adulthood, resulting in physical, emotional, spiritual, and relational injuries that are severe and long lasting. In an examination of the lifetime prevalence of violence in the lives of homeless mothers, Bassuk et al. (1996) found that 92 percent had experienced some form of physical or sexual assault, mostly in familial or intimate relationships. Repeated assaults on physical and emotional integrity allow little time for healing or recovery, which leaves mothers in a fight for their lives and the lives of their children. This takes its toll on the entire family and results in helplessness, fear, and loss of control.

Violence in the Lives of Homeless Children

CASE EXAMPLE: SARAH

Before becoming homeless, Sarah had been running from her batterer for several years, living with relatives and more than 20 other people. To Sarah, this seemed safer than living in an apartment on her own. As a result, her six-year-old child was bounced around—he moved to another city with his father, he moved back with his mother, he moved in and out of a house with a relative—and eventually stopped attending school altogether.

Like Sarah, many homeless mothers have endured multiple experiences of violence. The prevalence of violence in the lives of homeless mothers results in high rates of violence in the lives of their children. Women deeply embedded in violent relationships are constantly on guard and focused on survival, and therefore, often unable to protect their children from witnessing or experiencing violence.

Homeless children often live in chaotic and unsafe environments, where there is frequent exposure to various forms of violence, including domestic violence, physical and sexual abuse, unpredictable adult behaviors and responses, and dramatic life changes such as moving from place to place, family separations, and placement in foster care. Within a single year in the lives of homeless children, 97 percent move up to three times, 40 percent attend two different schools, and 28 percent attend three or more different schools (NCFH, 1999). Nearly one-quarter of homeless children have witnessed acts of violence within their family, a significantly higher rate than children in the general population (NCFH, 1999). Homeless children frequently worry that they will have no place to live and no place to sleep (NCFH, 1999). They worry that something bad will happen to their family members. More than one-half are frequently concerned about guns and fire (NCFH, 1999). This level of fear and unpredictability can be extremely damaging to a developing child.

Due to often violent and chaotic family environments, more than one-third of homeless children have been the subject of a child protection investigation (NCFH, 1999). Wood et al. (1990) found that homeless mothers were more likely than housed poor mothers to have a protective case opened on the family due to possible child abuse. Twenty-two percent of homeless children are separated from their families, either by placement in foster care or by being sent to live with a relative or family friend (NCFH, 1999). About 12 percent of homeless children are placed in foster care, compared to just over 1 percent of other children (NCFH, 1999). Both homeless and low-income housed mothers report stressors related to their children, including serious physical and emotional issues and having a child placed outside of the home (Bassuk et al., 1996). Just as homeless mothers have experienced histories of violence in their childhoods, the cycle of fear and helplessness begins again with a new generation.

Trauma in the Lives of Homeless Families

Although most people experience trauma at some point in their lives, the severity, frequency, and duration of such experiences and the subsequent impact of the trauma varies considerably. In the lives of homeless families, traumatic experiences are often frequent and severe. Responses to these traumatic experiences—particularly responses to repeated exposure to trauma—can be intense and long lasting, leading to more significant mental health issues.

In a study that included 300 homeless women, North and Smith (1992) found that the majority of the sample had experienced at least one traumatic event, and of those who reported having experienced such an event, almost one-half reported having experienced multiple traumas. The trauma these women face throughout their lives leads to major alterations in their biological responses to stress, which explains their intense responses to reminders of their traumatic experiences and their struggles to cope with life events (Bassuk, Dawson, et al., 2001).

In response to trauma, posttraumatic stress disorder (PTSD) may develop, which represents a more significant and severe response to trauma that continues well beyond the actual event or events and begins to impact daily functioning as survivors try to organize their lives around their symptoms (van der Kolk, McFarlane, & Weisaeth, 1996 Given the very high rates of violence among homeless mothers, it is not surprising that the prevalence of PTSD is higher than in the general population.

High rates of PTSD among homeless and extremely poor women are well documented (Bassuk et al., 1996; Bassuk, Buckner, Perloff, & Bassuk, 1998; Bassuk, Dawson, et al., 2001; Bassuk, Melnick, & Browne, 1998; Browne, 1993;

North & Smith, 1992). Among homeless mothers, 36 percent have experienced PTSD—three times the rate for women in the general population; for homeless and low-income housed mothers with two or more lifetime disorders, the PTSD rate increases to 85 percent (Bassuk, Buckner, et al., 1998).

North and Smith (1992) found that 34 percent of the homeless women in their study met the criteria for a lifetime diagnosis of PTSD. Among homeless women who experienced trauma, over one-half developed PTSD (North & Smith, 1992). Researchers have found a strong correlation between PTSD and violent experiences in childhood. When they experience violent events in adulthood, women with childhood histories of violence are six times more likely than other women to develop PTSD (Bassuk, Dawson, et al., 2001). More specifically, childhood sexual abuse and experiences of random anger from both parents are the strongest risk factors for a diagnosis of PTSD in adulthood (Bassuk, Dawson, et al., 2001).

In addition to childhood and adult experiences of violent trauma, researchers have found that the experience of being homeless is itself traumatic (Goodman, Saxe, & Harvey, 1991). First, homelessness adds an additional layer of vulnerability and deprivation that may increase a family's risk for continued exposure to various forms of violent trauma. Second, the process of becoming homeless involves the loss of belongings, community, and sense of safety. Third, the experience of living in shelters is isolating and can lead to a loss of safety and personal control that can be devastating: "Homelessness, like other traumas, may produce a psychological sense of isolation or distrust as well as the actual disruption of social bonds" (Goodman et al., 1991, p. 1220). Homelessness can also trigger symptoms associated with past traumatic experiences that may hinder a family's ability to move back into stable housing (Goodman et al., 1991). Homeless families are not able to perform the usual routines and rituals, and are often separated from any sense of community. Along with the trauma of social isolation comes the traumatic experience of helplessness and the associated loss of control (Goodman et al., 1991). Like other traumatic experiences, homelessness often renders people helpless and at the mercy of others.

Researchers and practitioners have called into question whether a PTSD diagnosis is sufficient to describe the experience and impact of ongoing pervasive trauma, particularly within care-giving systems (Herman, 1992; van der Kolk et al., 1996). The terms "Complex PTSD" or "Disorders of Extreme Stress Not Otherwise Specified" (DESNOS) have been suggested to describe a set of symptoms associated with prolonged experiences of severe interpersonal abuse (Cook et al., 2005; Herman, 1992; van der Kolk, 2002; van der Kolk, Roth, Pelcovitz, Sunday, & Spinazzola, 2005). Given the prevalence of chronic interpersonal violence, along with the stress associated with daily survival in an often unsupportive system, the experiences of homeless mothers may well fit the definition of complex trauma.

The case of Alice at the beginning of this chapter is illustrative of the majority of homeless women who have experienced prolonged violence across their lives.

Alice has experienced multiple traumatic events, including violence during child-hood and violence in her intimate adult relationships, along with the trauma of being homeless. Trauma has played a significant role in Alice's life and the lives of her children, and the family continues to suffer the ramifications of living in an environment that breeds an ongoing sense of chaos, danger, and unpredict-ability. Alice's repeated experiences of interpersonal violence shape the ways in which she thinks and behaves, the ways in which she manages her emotions, and her ability to stay connected and attuned to her children, problem solve, form healthy relationships, and assess safety in the outside world.

The ramifications of inadequate diagnoses can be extremely devastating to trauma survivors, especially those who become increasingly involved in social service systems. To adapt to prolonged traumatic experiences, trauma survivors may develop symptoms that mimic other disorders such as bipolar disorder or borderline personality disorder (Luxenberg, Spinazzola, & van der Kolk, 2001). When trauma survivors are diagnosed purely on the basis of presenting symp-toms, providers are likely to miss the underlying traumatic experiences that may be the source of the symptoms and the necessary focus of treatment. Poor or inadequate treatment will only serve to weaken a family's resolve and its ability to find and maintain housing, employment, and external supports.

Pathways to Homelessness: The Impact of Complex Trauma

The primary and foundational causes of family homelessness are systemic and related to lack of affordable housing, employment opportunities, and fair wages (Bassuk, 1991), however, the impact of complex trauma associated with long-term histories of violence can also be devastating to women and their families. Chronic trauma impacts all levels of functioning and can result in a range of emotional, physical, and relational issues. Poor families who have experienced chronic trauma are faced with unique difficulties in the face of the already over-whelming obstacles associated with poverty. Experiences of extensive violence can compromise the normal responses to stress and the ability to cope with life events. Due to their histories of abuse, experiences of violence in the present, and subsequent difficulties in establishing and maintaining a sense of safety, trauma-tized families are far more vulnerable to negative life events, including homeless-ness. Bassuk, Perloff, and Dawson (2001) found that prolonged assaults to safety throughout the lifespan lead to physical and mental health issues, perpetuate violent relationships, and result in a continued lack of social supports, separation of the family unit, and a subsequent decrease in economic self-sufficiency that, taken together, dramatically increase a family's vulnerability to one-time or re-peated episodes of homelessness.

Emotional and Physical Health

Due to extensive chronic trauma in the early lives of homeless mothers, it is important to consider the impact on emotional and physical health in adulthood.

Homeless mothers who grow up in violent families have few opportunities to develop healthy coping skills, secure attachments, and a positive, stable sense of self, because they are too often on alert for threat or danger. Constant focus on danger takes its toll on emotional and physical health, as the body is constantly under stress. Emotional and physical issues such as depression, anxiety, and ulcers are frequently the result. Self-harm and substance abuse are among the ways in which trauma survivors attempt to cope with overwhelming thoughts and feelings and a pervasive sense of danger and unpredictability.

Both homeless and low-income housed women have poor physical health compared to the general population, including higher rates of asthma, anemia, and ulcers (Bassuk et al., 1996). These mothers also report high rates of smoking (Bassuk et al., 1996). Thirty-nine percent of homeless mothers have been hospitalized (Bassuk et al., 1996). Some physical issues may come from injuries associated with violence. Physical issues and complaints may also represent a deeper physiological response to chronic trauma that results in somatic symptoms or "body memories" (Bassuk, Melnick, & Browne, 1998). Traumatic memories may not be stored with associated language and context, but instead remain deeply visceral and experienced at the physiological level (Bassuk, Melnick, & Browne, 1998). This increases one's sense of lack of control over physical sensations and experiences, and may be interpreted as physical issues that require attention and treatment (Bassuk, Melnick, & Browne, 1998). In addition to these physically felt "memories," chronic stress and the body's chemical response to repeated violent experiences and associated triggers and memories take a cumulative toll on the health of body and mind (Bassuk, Melnick, & Browne, 1998).

Along with physical health issues, there is a strong relationship between experiences of violence and increased mental health and substance abuse issues in homeless women (Bassuk, Buckner, et al., 1997; Bassuk & Rosenburg, 1988; Bassuk et al., 1996; D'Ercole & Struening, 1990; Ingram, Corning, & Schmidt, 1996). Experiences of violence can lead to symptoms such as anxiety, feelings of loss of control, fear, guilt, shame, and depression (Browne, 1993). Homeless mothers with histories of violence have had to learn to adapt to their childhood experiences. These adaptations may lead to the development of unhealthy coping mechanisms such as drug use or self harm, along with serious mental health issues that impact the ability to manage work and relationships in adulthood.

In a review of studies of the long-term impact of childhood sexual abuse on adult women, Browne (1993) noted that all areas of functioning are impacted by ongoing childhood abuse, including emotional, physical, psychological, and relational abuse. In adulthood, these women show higher rates of depression, anxiety, substance abuse, and other general impairments in functioning as well as increased vulnerability to future victimization, including battering and sexual assault (Browne, 1993). In a study of 141 homeless women, high rates of violence were associated with increased rates of "depressive symptoms; psychotic symptoms; and hospitalizations for psychiatric, medical, alcohol, and drug problems" (D'Ercole & Struening, 1990, p. 148). Ingram et al. (1996) found that homeless women reported significantly higher rates of childhood sexual victimization and that higher levels of victimization were associated with higher levels of distress.

Bassuk and Rosenburg (1988) found that homeless mothers with extensive histories of violence experienced higher rates of substance abuse and mental health problems than housed mothers. Bassuk et al. (1996) found that "four times as many homeless as housed women reported injecting drugs on at least one occasion" (p. 643). Homeless women were also more likely than housed women to have been hospitalized for emotional or substance abuse issues, and women who had been hospitalized for mental health issues in the two years prior to being homeless were at increased risk of further episodes (Bassuk et al., 1996, Bassuk, Buckner, et al., 1997). Both homeless and low-income housed women had higher rates of PTSD, alcohol and drug abuse, major depressive disorders, and attempts at suicide than did the general population of women (Bassuk et al., 1996). Two-thirds of each sample of homeless and low-income housed women had at least one lifetime psychiatric diagnosis, and 47 percent had at least two lifetime diagnoses (Bassuk et al., 1996). North and Smith (1992) found that homeless women with histories of trauma were more likely to develop major depression, generalized anxiety disorder, and alcohol use disorder. Seventy-four percent of the homeless women in their sample with a history of PTSD had developed symptoms prior to the year in which they became homeless. Wood et al. (1990) found that 32 percent of homeless mothers and 26 percent of housed poor mothers reported frequent use of drugs such as crack and heroin.

There is research to suggest that the combination of childhood abuse and adult mental health and substance abuse can increase a family's vulnerability to multiple episodes of homelessness. In comparison to first-time homeless mothers, mothers with multiple episodes of homelessness have higher rates of major depression or substance abuse; almost two-thirds had struggled with these issues (Bassuk, Perloff, & Dawson, 2001). These women are also more likely to have three or more lifetime mental health diagnoses (Bassuk, Perloff, & Dawson, 2001). Almost one-half had a substance abuse problem, a significantly higher rate than among first-time homeless women (Bassuk, Perloff, & Dawson, 2001). In childhood, twice as many multiply homeless mothers experienced sexual abuse and random, unexplained parent anger (Bassuk, Perloff, & Dawson, 2001).

Mothers struggling with substance abuse and mental health issues such as depression, anxiety, and PTSD have fewer internal resources to manage the day-to-day issues associated with going to work, paying bills, and taking care of children. Mental health issues that result in hospitalizations can lead to family separation, job loss, and possible eviction associated with inability to pay rent. Chronic health issues can have a major impact on a mother's ability to maintain work and have the strength to cope with life stressors. Poor physical and emotional health impacts all areas of functioning and can increase a family's vulnerability to further traumatic experiences, including one-time or multiple episodes of homelessness, as mothers have few reserves to manage the daily difficulties associated with poverty and violence.

Domestic Violence

Poverty and adult violence are inextricably intertwined. Browne, Salomon, and Bassuk (1999) cited statistics showing that women with annual incomes below $10,000 are four times more likely to be victims of violent attacks, most often within intimate relationships. Rates of assaults on women are higher for families living below the poverty line (Browne et al., 1999). Experiences of violence in childhood serve to exacerbate the effects of poverty and violence in adult relationships (Bassuk, Dawson, et al., 2001; Browne & Bassuk, 1997). Survivors may enter into other abusive relationships because they have little sense of what is healthy, little ability to trust themselves or others, impaired ability to accurately detect danger cues, and minimal self-worth, power, or agency.

In their comparison of homeless and housed women, Bassuk et al. (1996) found homeless women were twice as likely to have lost their home due to a male partner who was either abusive or had lost his job. As discussed earlier, many studies have shown that homeless mothers have high rates of abuse by their adult partner (Bassuk et al., 1996; Bassuk, Dawson, et al., 2001; Browne & Bassuk, 1997; Goodman, 1991; Wood et al., 1990). Bassuk et al. (1996) found that approximately two-thirds of each sample of homeless and low-income housed women had been physically assaulted by a male partner in adulthood, and 32 percent of those women had experienced violence at the hands of their most recent partner (Browne & Bassuk, 1997). Similarly, Goodman (1991) found that 64 percent of homeless women reported experiences of physical abuse by a partner.

Browne et al. (1999) cited studies of the impact of partner violence on women's ability to work, and noted high rates of violence among women on public assistance. Issues that can interfere with work include threatening partners, stalking, physical assaults and bruising, more missed days of work, and more mental health and physical health problems that interfered with work (Browne et al., 1999). Browne and her colleagues also found that, in their sample of poor and homeless mothers, more than 40 percent had experienced physical aggression by a male partner from the time of the initial interview through a 24-month follow-up period, and rates of violence were higher among homeless than among poor housed mothers. In their examination of the relationship between partner violence and maintaining work, Browne et al. (1999) found that women who had experienced partner violence in the past 12 months were less able to maintain work over the next year, and "demonstrate significantly higher rates of emotional and medical distress, medical hospitalization, and alcohol or other drug problems" (p. 421). As discussed above, this only adds to the struggle to maintain employment. Women who are unable to maintain consistent work in low-paying jobs lack the opportunity for promotion and higher pay in the future (Browne et al., 1999). Without the ability to maintain consistent work, mothers have increased difficulty meeting the financial needs of the family, including secure housing.

Lack of Support Systems

Early experiences of violence may impact women's abilities to form relationships and solidify support networks later, thus increasing their vulnerability to homelessness in the future (Bassuk & Rosenberg, 1988; Browne, 1993). Early childhood experiences in the family of origin provide the foundation for all future relationships. This is a time when the disruption of relationships or the presence of violence within the family system can be the most damaging to later development and functioning. Anderson and Rayens (2004) found that homeless women had the highest rates of childhood family conflict, and the lowest rates of social support in childhood and adulthood. The ability to form trusting relationships and sustain supportive connections is significantly impaired for homeless mothers with extensive histories of family violence. Attachment theory maintains that childhood histories of violence disrupt the attachment bonds between parent and child, thereby impacting a child's ability to form relationships and utilize supports in adulthood. A disrupted attachment impacts a child's view of self and others long into adulthood, and when children lack the skills necessary to seek and utilize support, their impaired ability to connect can be seen in a lack of adult support networks (Anderson & Rayens, 2004). Women who have experienced chronic violence struggle to identify what is safe and what is not, which often leads to a loss of ability to access help and support, and an increased tendency to enter abusive relationships.

A lack of support networks isolates families, particularly poor families already marginalized by the larger social and economic system. Researchers have found that homeless families have fewer supports than poor housed families (Bassuk, Buckner, et al., 1997; Bassuk et al., 1996; Bassuk, Weinreb, et al., 1997; McChesney, 1992; Wood et al., 1990). Wood et al. (1990) found that two-thirds of their sample of homeless mothers could not identify more than one external support. Bassuk et al. (1996) and Bassuk and Rosenberg (1988) found that homeless mothers had fewer supports than housed mothers a year prior to becoming homeless. Members of the support networks for homeless women had less access to basic resources, which impacted their ability to care for others (Bassuk et al., 1996). Research has shown that homeless mothers tend to have smaller networks of support and more conflicted relationships than housed mothers, thereby increasing their risk for further homelessness (Bassuk, Buckner, et al., 1997). When they interviewed homeless and housed mothers with preschool children, Bassuk, Weinreb, et al. (1997) found that homeless mothers were more socially isolated. McChesney (1992) interviewed 80 sheltered homeless mothers to examine the prevalence and quality of their relationships with their families of origin. McChesney (1992) found that solid support networks for homeless mothers were limited by lack of family member availability, distance from family members, lack of resources due to overcrowding already experienced by other family members, and estrangement from families of origin. Estrangement was high among mothers who had been abused as children (McChesney, 1992). Social support among family members was seen as a buffer to potential homelessness (McChesney, 1992).

In a comparison of the prevalence and quality of social supports among homeless and housed mothers, Shinn, Knickman, and Weitzman (1991) found that, although homeless mothers more frequently reported having a close female relative and friend whom they had seen recently, significantly fewer homeless than housed mothers thought that they would be able or be invited to stay with identified family members. Homeless women reported more people in their support networks, but they often did not believe that these support networks would be helpful in providing housing if needed. Shinn et al. (1991) also found that over three-quarters of homeless mothers had stayed with a family member at some point in the past year, which led them to suggest that "social support can be used up" (p. 1184), and perhaps homeless mothers in shelters believe that they have already used their support networks to capacity.

Family Separation

Wood et al. (1990) reported that more than one-third of homeless mothers interviewed had been placed with other family members or in foster care during childhood (Wood et al., 1990). In another study, approximately one-third of respondents who had experienced violence were removed from their families for some period of time (Browne & Bassuk, 1997). Bassuk et al. (1996) found that, when they compared homeless and low-income housed mothers, more than twice as many homeless women had spent time in foster care during childhood. In a comparison of multiply homeless families to first-time homeless mothers, Bassuk, Perloff, and Dawson (2001) found that women with multiple experiences of homelessness were more likely to have had an out-of-home placement. Goodman (1991) also noted a significant difference between housed and homeless mothers in the area of time spent in foster care as a child. Having been placed in foster care as a child and having had a female caretaker who used drugs are the two most significant childhood predictors of homelessness in adulthood (Bassuk, Buckner, et al., 1997). The connection between family separation and future homelessness may be related to the disruption of parent-child attachment and the documented impact of disrupted attachments on health and well-being, skill building, and problem solving. Disrupted attachments, whether due to abuse and neglect experienced by the child or family separation due to a lack of safety in the home, have a significant impact on future relationships, emotional health, use of social supports, and availability of coping skills. Homeless mothers who enter adulthood without the skills necessary to manage stress are considerably more vulnerable to the destructive impact of violence and poverty, and subsequent experiences of homelessness.

Complex Trauma: Issues for Children

The impact of chronic trauma in childhood is particularly damaging. Children rely on their caregivers to keep them safe, and they have fewer internal coping skills than adults do to manage stress or threat. Infants and young children are in a uniquely vulnerable position because their well-being and course of development depend on their attachments with caregivers. If caregivers are compromised by trauma and by complex issues that have led to homelessness, attachment with their children is adversely impacted. Young children are also negatively impacted by direct exposure to trauma, including domestic violence, abuse, and neglect.

The ways in which a caregiver responds to a child in distress and the level of support offered to that child are vital factors in a child's recovery from trauma (NCFH, 2006). Parents who have been traumatized often have greater difficulties being responsive and sensitive to their children's needs (Osofsky, 1999). If a child's primary caregiver is a victim of violence, suffering with emotional, physical, and/or substance abuse, isolated, or in a violent relationship, it is extremely difficult to be present for and attuned to a child's needs or to foster a sense of safety and security. This leads to an increased sense of helplessness and loss of control on the part of the child, who is then forced to adapt behavior in response to perceived threats. Children's experiences of violence and instability within the caregiving system, either due to abuse and/or neglect or due to unsafe situations that lead to a child's removal, can result in disruption of the fundamental parent-child attachment system in which children learn coping skills, create relationships, and understand themselves and the world. These disruptions have a significant impact on all aspects of a child's functioning and development (James, 1994). Even when primary relationships are adequate, exposure to domestic violence can significantly impact children's functioning. Chronic traumatic experiences lead to an ongoing sense of instability, and threat has a significant impact on children's growth and development, which often results in an increase in physical problems, emotional and behavioral issues, developmental delays, and learning difficulties.

Emotional and Physical Health

Exposure to ongoing traumatic experiences, both within the family and as a result of being homeless, impacts children's physical health. Homeless children are more often in poor physical health (American Academy of Pediatrics, 1996; NCFH, 1999; Rafferty & Shinn, 1991). They are more likely to suffer from acute illnesses such as fever, ear infection, cough, stomach problems, and asthma, as well as chronic diseases such as sinusitis, anemia, asthma, bowel dysfunction, eczema, visual deficits, and neurological deficits (American Academy of Pediatrics, 1996; NCFH, 1999). These appear likely to be related to experiences of trauma (American Academy of Pediatrics, 1996). Nearly 70 percent of infants, toddlers, and preschoolers have chronic illnesses (NCFH, 1999). Weinreb, Goldberg, Bassuk, & Perloff (1998) found that homeless children had more emergency room and outpatient medical visits and were more likely to experience poor health. In a study of homeless and housed preschool children, Bassuk, Weinreb, et al. (1997) found that twice as many homeless as housed children had been medically hospitalized over a one-year period.

For homeless families living in poverty, there is a lack of ongoing routine medical care, lack of access to timely care, and poor nutrition often associated with lack of money to provide adequate meals (NCFH, 1999). Research has shown (Rafferty & Shinn, 1991) that homeless families have less access to quality health care, beginning with prenatal care and continuing as their children grow older. Unhealthy living conditions prior to homelessness can weaken a child's immune system. Subsequent time in shelters also increases the risk for disease and infection (NCFH, 1999). Ongoing issues such as lack of regular health care and lack of immunizations and screening for lead poisoning contribute to the poor health of homeless children (NCFH, 1999). The combination of stress, lack of consistent resources prior to homelessness, and the trauma of homelessness itself is a contributor to poor health (NCFH, 1999).

In addition to physical health complications associated with poverty and homelessness and associated histories of family violence, homeless children have increased emotional and behavioral issues that can impact all areas of their functioning. They have high rates of anxiety, depression, sleep problems, shyness, withdrawal, and aggression (Bassuk & Rubin, 1987; Bassuk & Rosenberg, 1988). In a study of preschool-age homeless and poor-housed children, Bassuk, Weinreb, et al. (1997) found that homeless children had significantly higher externalizing scores on the Child Behavior Check-list (CBCL) and slightly higher internalizing scores. They also found that 12 percent of homeless children had clinical problems such as anxiety, depression, and withdrawal, and 16 percent had behavior problems evidenced by severe aggression and hostility. High scores on the CBCL were most closely predicted by length of time in foster care, experiences of physical abuse, death of a childhood friend, and mother's emotional status (Bassuk, Weinreb, et al., 1997). Experiences of loss or events that lead to emotional or physical separation from a child's primary caregiver have a significant impact on a child's sense of safety and well-being, and the associated helplessness and fear is played out in a child's emotional and physical responses.

Among homeless school-age children, Buckner, Bassuk, Weinreb, and Brooks (1999) found that older children demonstrated more aggressive and acting-out behaviors than younger children did. Overall, homeless children scored well above average on parents' reports of internalizing and externalizing behaviors as well as self-reports of internalizing behaviors. Buckner et al. (1999) also found higher rates of internalizing behaviors among homeless children, and they pointed to the tendency of older children to internalize their problems. Other researchers have discussed the experience of shame, self-criticism, low self-worth, and subsequent depression that may be associated with this type of behavioral presentation (Buckner et al., 1999). Like Bassuk, Weinreb, et al. (1997), Buckner et al. (1999) found that mothers' distress was strongly related to greater behavior problems in their school-age children.

In a study of homeless youths aged 6–17, Buckner and Bassuk (1997) found that homeless children struggled with high rates of mental health problems. Nearly one-third had at least one major mental disorder that interfered with their daily lives, compared to 19 percent of other school-age children. Forty-seven percent of homeless youth had problems with anxiety, depression, or withdrawal compared to 18 percent of other school-age children; and 36 percent demonstrated delinquent or aggressive behaviors, compared to 17 percent of other school-age children (Buckner & Bassuk, 1997). High rates of internalizing symptoms, such as depression and anxiety, were associated with exposure to violence (Buckner, Beardslee, & Bassuk, 2004).

Children living in shelters with their families face a variety of challenges to their well-being and healthy development. The children sometimes display many challenging behaviors and a confusing set of symptoms. Young children may lose previously acquired skills (regression) or may have problems with sleeping (insomnia, restless sleep) and eating (digestive problems). They may be highly distractible, unable to play for more than a few minutes, or their play may be narrow and repetitive. When they receive adequate mental health assessments and services, their behaviors may lead to diagnoses of attention deficit hyperactivity disorder, separation anxiety, major depression, or conduct disorder.

Child Development

The experiences of homeless children, both prior to becoming homeless and once they have become homeless, have a significant impact on growth and development (Bassuk & Rosenberg, 1990; Bassuk & Rubin, 1987; Bassuk, Rubin, & Lauriat, 1986; Rafferty & Shinn, 1991). Studies of homeless children cited by Rafferty and Shinn (1991) have documented development delays, including difficulties with attention, speech delays, immature peer interactions, language disabilities, and cognitive delays. Bassuk and her colleagues (Bassuk and Rosenberg, 1990; Bassuk & Rubin, 1987; Bassuk et al., 1986) noted that homeless children demonstrated significant delays in language development, gross motor skills, fine motor skills, and social/personal growth, and 54 percent of homeless preschoolers showed at least one major developmental lag. Coll, Buckner, Brooks, Weinreb, and Bassuk (1998) found no developmental differences between homeless and low-income housed children, but noted that older children tended to score lower than younger children on various developmental measures, and that proper growth and development occurs too slowly for 18 percent of homeless children, which suggests that, as children experience cumulative damage associated with poverty, the impact may gradually become more apparent.

Academic Achievement

According to reports by homeless mothers, approximately 43 percent of homeless children were failing or performing below average academically, and 43 percent had repeated a grade (Bassuk & Rosenberg, 1988; Bassuk & Rubin, 1987). Additional research has shown that 14 percent of homeless children are diagnosed with learning disabilities, double the rate of other children (NCFH, 1999). According to Rubin et al. (1996), 75 percent of homeless children were performing below grade level in reading, 72 percent were below grade level in spelling, and

54 percent were below grade level in math. Homeless children are far more likely than other children to change schools, are twice as likely repeat a grade, are suspended twice as often as other children, and demonstrate behaviors that significantly interfere with their learning (NCFH, 1999).

Implications for the Field

Homeless families are likely to have experienced some form of interpersonal violence or abuse, and these traumatic experiences impact their thoughts, feelings, behaviors, and relationships. In the time between the onset of traumatic experiences and development of acute stress disorder, PTSD, or complex trauma, many mediating factors can serve either to facilitate healing and recovery or to increase distress. Factors that impact trauma recovery include the following: additional traumatic experiences, past traumatic experiences, biological traits, coping style and skills, family history, level of support, and environmental response (van der Kolk et al., 1996). Each of these factors can have a dramatic impact on a person's ability to recover from trauma without becoming overwhelmed by symptoms or developing unhealthy adaptations to manage his or her distress (van der Kolk et al., 1996). Service providers may not have control over all of these factors; however, they play a pivotal role in recovery based on their capacity to facilitate safe, predictable, compassionate, and informed responses to trauma survivors that buffer the impact of the traumatic experiences.

Ineffective responses may serve to exacerbate symptoms or retraumatize individuals and families. Those who work with homeless families should be aware of the prevalence of trauma and its associated impact on the lives of women and children. This involves understanding the research on trauma in the lives of homeless families and making changes in the ways services are provided. Changes involve the creation of trauma-informed service systems; the inclusion of thorough, trauma-informed child programming; and the provision of stable, long-term external supports for homeless families, families in transition from homelessness, and poor housed families.

The Need for Trauma-Informed Services

The effects of repeated exposure to traumatic experiences can be long-term and pervasive, and can impact all areas of people's lives, including: biological functioning, cognitive functioning, emotional functioning, social interactions/relationships, and identity formation. Simply stated, people who have experienced multiple traumas do not relate to the world in the same way as those who have not been traumatized.

As we have seen, most homeless women and children have endured multiple traumas prior to being homeless and while homeless. Their understanding and perception of themselves, their environment, and the people around them is significantly impacted by these experiences. As a result, these families require specific types of services that are sensitive to their status as trauma survivors.

Service systems must adopt a certain way of responding to the needs of the women and children that keeps in mind the trauma that they have experienced and how this impacts their current functioning in all areas. Adopting a " trauma-informed" approach to service provision means viewing the lives of homeless families through a "trauma lens" and provides a way to understand their behaviors, responses, attitudes, and emotions as a collection of survival skills developed in response to traumatic experiences. Otherwise, the impact of trauma gets lost amid other mental health, substance use, health, employment, and housing issues in the lives of homeless families.

Within shelters, all aspects of programming need to be examined to ensure that the system is sensitive to the needs of families who have been traumatized, including atmosphere and environment; policies and procedures; services; and staffing and training. Creating a trauma-informed space for consumers requires meeting basic needs and creating a safe environment in which routines and responses are consistent and predictable. Along with the need to create a safe service setting is the need to create an emotional environment that enhances the consumer's sense of safety. This includes a demonstrated tolerance for a range of emotions that may be expressed by the consumer. Tolerance for emotional expression enhances the survivor's internal sense of security and ability to regain self-control. Regardless of the response that a trauma survivor exhibits under stress, the provider must understand the individual's reactions in order to provide support. Providers working with trauma survivors should have an understanding of how traumatic experiences affect the brain and the body, and how trauma survivors exhibit different reactions in the present due to their past experiences. Providers need to be able to recognize how extreme responses of dissociation or overreaction are in fact adaptations helpful to trauma survivors while managing their traumatic experiences, but may be ineffective and unhealthy in the present. This requires ongoing training and trauma education for providers that allows them to identify what is happening with the consumer and why she may be responding in particular ways.

When providers understand trauma responses, they can help a survivor better understand her experiences, provide opportunities for her to practice regaining self-control, and help her utilize techniques to de-escalate difficult situations. Important components of support for trauma survivors involve helping them to identify specific triggers; understand what is happening in their brains and bodies; ground themselves in the reality of the present situation; and develop self-soothing techniques and coping skills to manage feelings associated with past traumatic experiences. Keeping in mind the potential triggers for trauma survivors, providers can examine their agencies and programs to identify and eliminate daily practices, policies, or ways of responding to consumers that might result in loss of control or power and feeling retraumatized. In addition to education about trauma and the body, Browne (1993) discussed the need to provide education to homeless families around the impacts of family violence, including discussions about what is considered "abusive" along with strategies to prevent abuse and keep families safe.

Child Programming

For families, the path to homelessness has included serious disruptions in interpersonal relationships, financial stress, and other losses. Some children have experienced trauma associated with loss and instability, whereas others have been exposed more directly to violence. Children's programming is of vital importance to address both the problems that arise in shelter life and the issues that families and children bring to the shelter. Shelter life entails a variety of constraints. For example, families often live in a single room. Children may have given up all their familiar possessions and now have to share playthings with all the children residing in the shelter. Because meals are generally provided by the shelter, children may also miss foods that are familiar. Sometimes parents feel constrained because their parenting practices are observable by shelter staff as well as other parents. Most shelters have rules about discipline practices and supervision of children. For example, if physical discipline of children is prohibited, parents who have relied on physical discipline must learn new parenting skills.

An effective children's program includes coordination with systems of care for children in the community and services within the shelter program. The child advocate must establish a working alliance with both the parents and their children. Even parents who are compromised by stress and trauma can provide important information about their children's well-being and should remain actively engaged in their children's care. Advocates should have a basic understanding of normal child development, so they can screen for problems that might need referral and be aware of the local systems of care available to families, including pediatric, family medicine, early intervention services, mental health, child care, state human services, and school systems. Advocates also need to understand the cultural issues presented by the population served by the shelter. The advocate's proper role is that of screening, needs assessment, and linkage with appropriate resources in the community. Further, the advocate can serve as a resource on "homelessness" for the community concerning the special needs of families residing in shelters.

CASE EXAMPLE: KATHY

Kathy came to the Horizon Shelter following the arrest of her partner for selling drugs. Her partner had been heavily involved in gang activities, and sometimes exposed Kathy and her children to violence. Kathy was a stay-at-home mother for both 18-month-old Keaunna and three-year-old Samuel. They all fled from their home after gunshots were fired into the house, and then temporarily lived with family members. When the shelter advocate first met with Kathy and her children, she noticed that Kathy appeared extremely stressed. Kathy told the advocate that her children were often up through the night and Samuel had gone back to needing diapers after having been fully toilet trained. She said that spanking hadn't helped, and he still wasn't using the toilet. Kathy thought that her children seemed irritable and unhappy, and she had so many things to take care of she didn't know what to do first.

The advocate helped Kathy to develop a list of priorities and began to help her to accomplish her goals. She let Kathy know that children sometimes did regress following family disruption and that Samuel's regression to diapers was likely a sign of his stress. She recommended that Kathy support Samuel with encouraging words rather than spankings. They worked out a plan to support the children, including part-time childcare so that Kathy would have some time to take care of the work necessary to establish a new home. The childcare providers required immunization records, but both children had gaps in their medical care, and Kathy had been using urgent care clinics for their health care. The advocate helped set up a permanent medical relationship for the family, and both children received well-child checkups. When childcare providers voiced concerns about Samuel's aggressive behavior and his sister's withdrawn behavior, the advocate linked Kathy and the children to a community mental health service. Because the mental health agency had not served shelter residents before, the advocate met with the staff to educate them about shelter life and the needs of shelter residents.

A second important component of shelter programming is on-site children/family programming. As previously discussed, children may come into a shelter with a range of difficulties that can manifest in a variety of challenging behaviors, such as aggression toward peers, extreme anxiety, and withdrawal. Parents coping with homelessness may be ill-equipped to help their children navigate shelter life. A comprehensive children's program provides respite from the stress of shelter life, and helps children feel secure and safe. Structured programs can help children gain new skills to cope with the challenges of homelessness. Programming for parents can educate them about the effects of homelessness on children's well-being and provide opportunities to improve parenting skills.

External Support Networks

Homeless mothers who have histories of violence and subsequent issues of mental, emotional, and physical health and substance abuse require specialized support services for themselves and their children in order to achieve long-term success. According to Bassuk, Buckner et al. (1997), "factors that increase social or community supports or resources are protective against family homelessness" (p. 246). Unfortunately, families that are homeless are often living in a constant state of stress and fear that interferes with their ability to access help. Given the isolation experienced by homeless women and children, enhancing connections and creating support networks become extremely important. As service systems begin to address the needs of homeless families, it is imperative that social supports are incorporated into any service planning. Social networks should also be incorporated within shelter settings in the context of mental health and substance abuse treatment planning and when helping families make the transition to stable and permanent housing.

For families who are staying in shelters, the creation and strengthening of support networks can be facilitated by providers who encourage a sense of community both within the shelter and with the outside community (Goodman et al., 1991). Within the shelter community, this involves providing families with opportunities to share their cultural rituals, join together in group activities, and participate in community meetings and support and therapeutic groups. Shelter systems can keep families connected with the outside community by making referrals and connections to trauma clinics, mental health clinics, substance abuse clinics, and other service providers.

Due to the significant mental health and substance abuse issues in the lives of homeless families, shelter systems and mental health and substance abuse providers need to actively collaborate to create integrated treatment plans that involve open communication, joint service planning, and the ability to understand and utilize trauma theory and education in all interactions with homeless families. Unification of these services can help create a treatment community that understands homeless families and serves the full range of their needs, as opposed to treating just a few issues in isolation from others. Such a "service network" helps to provide a sense of safety and predictability for homeless families, who might otherwise be asked to tell their stories repeatedly, only to receive fragmented support.

Transitions are often extremely difficult for traumatized families, as they may trigger feelings of fear, anxiety, and concern about what the future holds. It is essential that external support networks remain in place as families transition from shelter living into more permanent housing. These supports include both out-of-home and in-home services such as individual therapy, family therapy, parent aids, child care services, and stabilization teams. In addition, homeless mothers may continue to require advocates who can guide, educate, and help them navigate the system, maintain housing, and find employment.

Policy Implications

The relationships between violence, trauma, and homelessness are both intimate and destructive. Research has shown that the impact of violence on homeless families is profound, all-encompassing, and life-altering. The foundational systemic imbalances and deficits in the areas of affordable housing, employment opportunities, and sufficient wages set the stage for family homelessness, and experiences of violence and isolation further increase a family's vulnerability to homelessness. Though research has shown that homeless families have significant histories of trauma, service systems continue to demonstrate a lack of understanding of the impact of trauma in the lives of these families. Service providers often work with homeless families without an adequate understanding of trauma and without an awareness of the ways in which they can do their work in a more trauma-informed manner. Women who become homeless are not provided with adequate services and supports to stabilize and rebuild their lives, and children who suffer the ramifications of family violence are largely ignored. In order to effect change, not only do trauma-informed services, child programming, and support services need to be in place as described above, but service systems need to alter their fundamental structure and mode of operation in order to create policies, procedures, and short- and long-term programming for homeless families. Defining and creating trauma-informed policies and procedures and providing adequate adult and child supports are necessary steps toward buffering the impact of trauma on families and decreasing the potential for future homelessness.

Creation of Trauma-Informed Policies and Procedures

Service systems working with homeless families often demonstrate a lack of understanding of the experiences of trauma in the lives of homeless families and the impact of trauma on daily functioning. As discussed previously, the creation of trauma-informed systems is a necessary step in providing effective services for homeless families. This requires systemic changes in the way that services are delivered to homeless families.

There is a call for the creation of standards across settings for the implementation of trauma-informed services. This involves dedication to the training and education of staff, the creation of trauma-informed environments, the establishment of trauma-informed policies and procedures, and thorough assessments of mothers and children with specific questions related to experiences of violence and the provision of trauma-specific services for children and adults. These practices must become a routine and integral part of any service system working with homeless families. Providers at all levels of various systems, whether in shelters or community-based service centers, should demonstrate an understanding of trauma and an awareness of the reasons behind providing services differently for those who have experienced trauma. Service providers should have written policies that involve a commitment to being trauma informed and acknowledge the presence of trauma in the lives of the families served. Daily procedures as well as emergency procedures should be outlined clearly and in a manner that avoids the retraumatizing of families. These policies and procedures should be reviewed on a regular basis, and an ongoing trauma work group should continually monitor and improve services in consultation with outside agencies that have expertise in trauma and trauma-specific services for adults and children.

Access to Supports

Poor women are not given access to supports necessary to remain employed and housed. The root causes of homelessness include a lack of affordable housing, low wages, lack of employment opportunities, and decrease in assistance for poor families. Homeless mothers are often immobilized by lack of opportunity, lack of resources, and lack of support. With assistance, these women can begin to take the steps necessary to obtain employment and secure housing, and begin to create a sense of safety and stability. This involves commitment and coordination on the part of many service providers and advocates to help to change the way that services are provided to homeless families.

A mother's ability to work is intimately connected to the supports that she receives. Homeless mothers need housing supports, access to day treatment and mental health services, access to primary care doctors, access to day care, employment supports when appropriate, domestic violence services, and trauma-specific interventions within individual, group, and family settings. These services must be consistent and long term. Browne et al. (1999) found that recently victimized women had more difficulties maintaining work over the next year, and they pointed to the need for longer-term public assistance and other supports as women attempt to maintain employment in the wake of violent experiences. Browne et al. (1999) explained that their findings regarding the relationship between violence and women's ability to maintain long-term work indicate that "practical supports—such as the availability of child care, a government child care subsidy, job training, and job placement services—increase the likelihood that women will maintain work over time" (p. 421).

Child-Specific Services

Homeless mothers who have experienced violence have children who have also experienced violence. The cycle of poverty, violence, mental health issues, and substance abuse continues with the next generation of homeless children who reach adulthood without the necessary skills to manage and cope with life events. Research has shown the toll that homelessness takes on children's mental and physical health and well-being, as well as on their cognitive development. However, within the homeless world, children's services are often minimally funded or completely disregarded. The need for child-specific services in shelter and transitional settings is great, and yet current funding sources do not support these services. Shelters often depend on volunteers, who are frequently young, untrained, and unreliable. Service providers often do not coordinate with each other.

Homeless children have specific emotional, physical, and educational needs that demand attention in order to prevent continued damage and future difficulties. Therefore, it is imperative that they have access to the same quantity and quality of resources as housed children. Within shelter systems there is a need for sustainable child programming, child assessments, trauma-specific services for children with greater mental health needs, access to physical health care, and opportunities for activities to support age-appropriate growth and development. As homeless families predominantly include mothers and children of various ages, these services must be family oriented, have a developmentally appropriate trauma component for children designed for children all ages, and have a parenting component. Because a subgroup of children will require more intensive services, all programs must establish referral networks in the community that are willing and able to work with homeless children and their parents. Within the community, homeless children need access to additional supports including access to early childhood services such as Head Start. There is a need for increased mental health access, such as witness to violence services, professionals who come to shelters and are supported by shelter administrators, and family reunification and stabilization teams. As outlined in the McKinney-Vento Act, homeless children have a right to the same educational access as housed children. Therefore, there is a need to maintain continuity in school placement and to support homeless mothers in maintaining their children's school attendance.

Concluding Remarks

Homeless families face multiple challenges as they attempt to stay together, obtain permanent housing, and access necessary supports and resources. Poverty and its ramifications severely limit the capacity for healthy growth and development. Lack of affordable housing, low minimum wages, and lack of employment and educational opportunities dramatically impact a family's ability to remain self-sufficient. Poverty breeds isolation and a sense of hopelessness and powerlessness that is often paralyzing to family systems.

In addition to the systemic causes of poverty and homelessness, most homeless mothers have experienced violent trauma in both childhood and adulthood. These experiences of trauma often result in severe emotional and physical health issues and compromised relationships that impact homeless mothers' ability to access and utilize systems of care. Given the prevalence of trauma in the lives of homeless families, it is imperative that service providers understand the impact of trauma on the lives of homeless women and children. Those who best understand trauma dynamics are best able to foster recovery and healing in the lives of these families.

In recent years, some states have created 10-year plans to reduce or eliminate homelessness. This increase in awareness and motivation offers renewed hope; however, there is a need for additional resources, services, and political will to effect change on a broader scale. As a society, it is imperative that we support those with the fewest resources and the greatest need, in an effort to break the cycle of poverty, violence, and homelessness for those who are currently most vulnerable and for the generations of families to come.

References

American Academy of Pediatrics. (1996). Health needs of homeless children and families. *Pediatrics, 98*(4), 351–353.

Anderson, D. G., & Rayens, M. K. (2004). Factors influencing homelessness in women. *Public Health Nursing, 21*(1), 12–23.

Bassuk, E. L. (1991). Homeless families. *Scientific American, 265*(6), 66–74.

Bassuk, E. L., Buckner, J. C., Perloff, J. N., & Bassuk, S. S. (1998). Prevalence of mental health and substance abuse disorders among homeless and low-income housed mothers. *American Journal of Psychiatry, 155*(1), 1561–1564.

Bassuk, E. L., Buckner, J. C. Weinreb, L. F., Browne, A., Bassuk, S. S., Dawson, R., et al. (1997) .Homelessness in female-headed families: Childhood and adult risk and protective factors. *American Journal of Public Health, 87*(2), 241–248.

Bassuk, E. L., Dawson, R., Perloff, J., & Weinreb, L. (2001). Post-traumatic stress disorder in extremely poor women: Implications for health care clinicians. *Journal of the American Medical Women's Association, 56*(2), 79–85.

Bassuk, E. L., Melnick, S., & Browne, A. (1998). Responding to the needs of low-income and homeless women who are survivors of family violence. *Journal of the American Medical Women's Association, 53*(2), 57–64.

Bassuk, E. L., Perloff, J. N., & Dawson, R. (2001). Multiply homeless families: The insidious impact of violence. *Housing Policy Debate, 12*(2), 299–320.

Bassuk, E. L., & Rosenberg, L. (1988). Why does family homelessness occur? A case-control study. *American Journal of Public Health, 78*(7), 783–788.

Bassuk, E. L., & Rosenberg, L. (1990). Psychosocial characteristics of homeless children and children with homes. *Pediatrics, 85*(3), 257–261.

Bassuk, E. L., & Rubin, L. (1987). Homeless children: A neglected population. *American Journal of Orthopsychiatry, 57*(2), 279–286.

Bassuk, E. L., Rubin, L., & Lauriat, A. S. (1986). Characteristics of sheltered homeless families. *American Journal of Public Health, 76*(9), 1097–1101.

Bassuk, E. L., Weinreb, L. F., Buckner, J. C., Browne, A., Salomon, A., & Bassuk, S. S. (1996). The characteristics and needs of sheltered homeless and low-income housed mothers. *Journal of the American Medical Association, 276*(8), 640–646.

Bassuk, E. L., Weinreb, L. F., Dawson, R., Perloff, J. N., & Buckner, J. C. (1997) Determinants of behavior in homeless and low-income housed preschool children. *Pediatrics, 100*(1), 92–100.

Browne, A. (1993). Family violence and homelessness: The relevance of trauma histories in the lives of homeless women. *American Journal of Orthopsychiatry, 63*(3), 370–383.

Browne, A., & Bassuk, S. S. (1997). Intimate violence in the lives of homeless and poor housed women: Prevalence and patterns in an ethnically diverse sample. *American Journal of Orthopsychiatry, 72*(2), 261–277.

Browne, A., Salomon, A., & Bassuk, S. S. (1999). The impact of recent partner violence on poor women's capacity to maintain work. *Violence against Women, 5*(4), 393–423.

Buckner, J. C., & Bassuk, E. (1997). Mental disorders and service utilization among youths from homeless and low-income housed families. *Journal of the American Academy of Child and Adolescent Psychiatry, 36*(7), 890–900.

Buckner, J. C., Bassuk, E. L., Weinreb, L. F., & Brooks, M. G. (1999). Homelessness and its relation to the mental health and behavior of low-income school-age children. *Developmental Psychology, 35*(1), 246–257.

Buckner, J. C., Beardslee, W. R., & Bassuk, E. L. (2004). Exposure to violence and low-income children's mental health: Direct, moderated, and medicated relations. *American Journal of Orthopsychiatry, 74*(4), 413–423.

Children's Defense Fund (2006). *Cradle To Prison Pipeline Initiative: Poverty.* Retrieved December 14, 2006, from http://www.childrensdefense.org/site/PageNavigator/c2pp_poverty

Coll, C. G., Buckner, J. C., Brooks, M. G., Weinreb, L. F., & Bassuk, E. L. (1998). The developmental status and adaptive behavior of homeless and low-income housed infants and toddlers. *American Journal of Public Health, 88*(9), 1371–1373.

Cook, A., Spinazzola, J., Ford, J., Lanktree, C., Blaustein, M., Cloitre, M., et al. (2005). Complex trauma in children and adolescents. *Psychiatric Annals, 35*(5), 390–398.

D'Ercole, A. & Struening, E. (1990). Victimization among homeless women: implications for service delivery. *Journal of Community Psychology, 18,* 141–151.

Goodman, L. (1991). The prevalence of abuse among homeless and housed poor mothers: A comparison study. *American Orthopsychiatric Association, 61*(4), 489–500.

Goodman, L., Saxe, L., & Harvey, M. (1991). Homelessness as psychological trauma. *American Psychologist, 46*(11), 1219–1225.

Herman, J. (1992). *Trauma and recovery.* New York: Basic Books.

Ingram, K. M., Corning, A. F., & Schmidt, L. D. (1996). The relationship of victimization experiences to psychological well-being among homeless women and low-income housed women. *Journal of Counseling Psychology, 43*(2), 218–227.

James, B. (1994). *Handbook for treatment of attachment: Trauma problems in childrene.* New York: Free Press.

Koegel, P., Melamid, E., & Burnam, A. (1995). Childhood risk factors for homelessness among homeless adults. *American Journal of Public Health, 82*(12) 1642–1649.

Luxenberg, T., Spinazzola, J., & van der Kolk, B. (2001). Complex trauma and disorders of extreme stress (DESNOS) diagnosis, part one: Assessment. *Directions in Psychiatry, 21*(25) 373–392.

McChesney, K. Y. (1992). Absence of a family safety net for homeless families. *Journal of Sociology and Social Welfare, 19*(4), 55–72.

National Alliance to End Homelessness. (April 2005). *Family homelessness in our nation and community: A problem with a solution.* Retrieved November 2006, from http:// www. naeh.org

National Center on Family Homelessness. (1999). *Homeless children: America's new outcasts.* Newton, MA: Better Homes Fund.

National Low Income Housing Coalition. (2004). *Out of reach 2004.* Retrieved November 2006, from http://www.nlihc.org/oor2004/introduction.htm

North, C. S., & Smith, E. M. (1992). Posttraumatic stress disorder among homeless men and women. *Hospital and Community Psychiatry, 43*(10), 1010–1016.

Osofsky, J. D. (1999). The impact of violence on children. *The Future of Children, 9*(3), 33–49.

Rafferty, Y., & Shinn, M. (1991). The impact of homelessness on children. *American Psychologist, 46*(11), 1170–1179.

Rubin, D. H., Erickson, C. J., San Augustin, M., Cleary, S.D., Allen, J. K., & Cohen, P. (1996). Cognitive and academic functioning of homeless children compared with housed children. *Pediatrics 97*(3), 289.

Shinn, M., Knickman, J. R., & Weitzman, B. C. (1991). Social relationships and vulnerability to becoming homeless among poor families. *American Psychologist, 46*(11), 1180–1187.

U.S. Census Bureau. (2005). *Historical Poverty Tables.* Retrieved December 14, 2006, from http://www.census.gov/hhes/www/poverty/histpov/hstpov2.html

van der Kolk, B. A. (2002). Assessment and treatment of Complex PTSD. In R. Yehuda (Editor), *Treating trauma survivors with PTSD.* Washington, DC: American Psychiatric Press, Inc.

van der Kolk, B., McFarlane, A. C. & Weisaeth, L. (Eds.). (1996). *Traumatic stress.* New York: Guilford Press.

van der Kolk, B. A., Roth, S., Pelcovitz, D., Sunday, S., & Spinazzola, J. (2005). Disorders of extreme stress: The empirical foundation of a complex adaptation to trauma. *Journal of Traumatic Stress, 18*(5), 389–399.

Weinreb, L., Goldberg, R., Bassuk, E., & Perloff, J. N. (1998). Determinants of health and service use patterns in homeless and low-income housed children. *Pediatrics*, *102*(3), 554–562.

Wood, D., Valdez, R. B., Hayashi, T., & Shen, A. (1990). Homeless and housed families in Los Angeles: A study comparing demographic, economic, and family function characteristics. *American Journal of Public Health*, *80*(9), 1049–1052.

CHAPTER 11

TRAUMATIC IMPACT OF VIOLENCE AGAINST WOMEN

Anne M. Dietrich

The World Health Organization has estimated that in the year 2000, 1.6 million people worldwide died from self-inflicted, interpersonal, or collective violence (Krug, Dahlberg, Mercy, Zwi, & Lozano, 2002). Society's awareness of violence against women in particular has greatly increased over the past several decades, as violence against women is recognized as a significant public health issue in both industrialized and developing countries. From 10 to 69 percent of women worldwide report *intimate partner violence*, and studies from various countries, including Australia, Canada, Israel, South Africa, and the United States, show that 40–70 percent of murdered women are killed by their partners, usually in the context of an ongoing abusive relationship. Women who are physically assaulted in intimate relationships (including dating relationships) are often psychologically abused and/or sexually assaulted by their partners as well (Krug et al., 2002).

Reported rates of *sexual violence* vary between countries, and range from less than 2 percent in Bolivia, China, and the Philippines to 16 percent in the United States. In various countries around the world, approximately 25 percent of adult women report sexual assault by an intimate partner and up to 33 percent of teenaged girls report that their first sexual experience was forced (Krug et al., 2002). Fifty percent of Canadian women have experienced at least one incident of physical or sexual violence after age 16 (Johnson, 2005).

Childhood sexual abuse is documented in many countries, and this form of childhood abuse is associated with a wide variety of long-term adverse effects. The mean lifetime prevalence of childhood sexual abuse (involving contact forms of abuse) is estimated at 20 percent for females and 5–10 percent for males (Krug et al., 2002).

Although the best-known forms of sexual violence against women include sexual assault and child sexual abuse, other forms include violence against sex-trade workers, genital mutilation, forced virginity examinations, war-related rape, forced marriage (including marriage of children as young as seven years of age), forced abortion, and sexual trafficking. In many countries, violence against women is institutionalized, with little to no recourse for victims (Brack, 2006).

The World Health Organization (WHO) notes that hundreds of thousands of women are bought and sold each year for the purposes of prostitution and sexual slavery (Krug et al., 2002). About half of global sexual trafficking occurs in Asia (Huda, 2006); more than 200,000 Bangladeshi women are reported to have been trafficked during a seven-year period in the 1990s. The special rapporteur on trafficking in persons reports that approximately 30 million Asian woman and children have been trafficked over the past 30 years (Huda, 2006) and it has been estimated that approximately 120,000 women and children are trafficked to Europe each year (Bremer, 2001).

North America is not exempt from this problem: The WHO estimated that 45,000 to 50,000 women and children are trafficked annually to the United States (Krug et al., 2002); however, other estimates are lower, with estimates of 17,500 persons trafficked annually to the United States (Cicero-Dominguez, 2005) The accuracy of estimates is not clear, given various methodological issues in terms of obtaining accurate statistics from various countries. Statistics on sexual trafficking to Canada have not been systematically collected by the Canadian government to date; however, the Royal Canadian Mounted Police (RCMP) estimate that 600–800 persons are trafficked to Canada each year (Human Trafficking and Modern Day Slavery). It is also estimated that from 16,000 to 20,000 Mexican and Central American children are trafficked for the sexual purposes (Cicero-Domínguez, 2005). (The escalation in global human trafficking may be largely attributed to the ease of trafficking using the Internet.)

A certain proportion of victims may respond to sexual or physical violence by harming themselves (e.g., self-mutilation), attempting suicide, or committing suicide. As such, the violence does not necessarily stop for the victim when the traumatic event stops. Moreover, women who have previous histories of abuse are at increased risk of various forms of revictimization (Cloitre, 1998; Dietrich, in press; Messman-Moore & Long, 2000). In a study of adults who were maltreated as children, gender differences were reported for rates of revictimization, with women significantly more likely to experience physical revictimization, sexual revictimization, and various forms of abuse by an intimate partner than males. The only form of revictimization that was higher for males in this study was physical assault by strangers (Dietrich, in press). These results are consistent with a recent survey conducted by Goldberg and Freyd (2006) in the United States, which found that women are more often victimized by persons known to them than are men.

This chapter includes a brief overview of violence against women and an in-depth discussion of three of the most common forms of violence against females:

rape, childhood sexual abuse, and intimate partner violence. The psychological effects of violence against women are discussed and exemplified through three case studies, followed by recommendations for public policy.

Overview of Violence against Women in Relationships

When thinking of violence against women in intimate relationships, *battering* often comes to mind. Battering refers to repeated physical assault of a partner on a cyclical basis; however, in some relationships the abuse may occur occasionally rather than repeatedly, with anger and frustration sporadically erupting into violence. The more severe (battering) type of violence is seen most commonly in clinical samples (i.e., samples of women who seek treatment), whereas the occasional form of violence is found more often in general population studies (Kantor & Jasinski, 1998). In addition to the physical violence, women are often emotionally or psychologically abused and frequently sexually abused and/or stalked within the context of intimate relationships.

Although women from the middle and upper social classes can and do experience partner violence, research shows that women who live in poverty are disproportionately affected by domestic violence (Krug et al., 2002). There is no one "type" of perpetrator of domestic violence, and research suggests the existence of several different types among men who commit intimate partner violence. Violent behavior may result from loss of control, dependency, fears, anxieties, frustrations, and threats to self-esteem. Personality disorders (especially borderline and antisocial) are often common to batterers, and many have a history of attachment disorders that originate within their own families of origin (Kantor & Jasinski, 1998). Males who perpetrate violence against their female partners tend to hold traditional beliefs regarding gender roles (Krug et al., 2002); however, partner violence also occurs in same-sex relationships. The dynamics and patterns of abuse in same-sex relationships are similar to those seen in abusive heterosexual relationships (Harway et al., 2001).

Although research indicates that some women engage in partner violence against males, they do not engage in the same form of severe, escalating violence that is seen in clinical samples of battered women. Moreover, women who are victimized by male partners are more likely to be injured, require medical attention, and fear for their lives than are men who are abused by female partners. Women who do engage in aggressive behavior within intimate relationships often do so in order to defend themselves (Kantor & Jasinski, 1998; Krug et al., 2002).

When women remain in abusive relationships, people may question why they do not leave. The reasons why women remain in abusive relationships are complex, and often involve *traumatic bonding* (Dutton & Painter, 1981). *Traumatic bonding* refers to a particularly strong attachment bond that develops between victims and perpetrators in abusive relationships. The victim often feels quite ambivalent, knowing that the relationship is unhealthy but unable to break the attachment due to the traumatic bond. Many women leave and return to the relationship, only to permanently leave after many such trials. They may be financially dependent on their partners; ongoing abuse may affect their psychological state and functioning (e.g., denial, self-blame, impaired self-esteem, major depression, posttraumatic stress disorder), which may impact on their ability to end the relationship; they may have concerns for their children if they leave, may lack social support or have fears of being ostracized by their loved ones or communities, may hope that their partner will change, and/or may be terrified to leave the relationship out of fear of what their partner will do. Abusers often threaten to hurt the woman, the children, and/or pets should she try to leave, and may carry out those threats. Canadian, American, and Australian women in particular who leave abusive relationships are at a high risk of death at the hands of their partner (Krug et al., 2002).

Older battered women may face additional difficulties that may not be faced by younger women, which prevent them from leaving an abusive relationship. They may lack skills to seek and maintain employment, may have mobility problems due to health issues, and may have grown up in an era where divorce was unacceptable. Additionally, they may be caregivers to abusive partners and stay due to a sense of loyalty. Those who have health or mobility problems may stay as the abusive partner also functions as their caregiver. Older battered women may have less social support through death or isolation from family and friends; they may have no experience dealing with financial or legal matters, may be resigned to a pattern of living that has existed for decades, and may not be aware that choices exist. Moreover, transition houses are not always suitable for older women. As such, older battered women may be less likely to be seen in mental health settings, police settings, and community agencies that provide services for battered women, and many of them suffer in silence (Wolf, 2000).

Children Who Witness Domestic Violence

Between 6 and 15 percent of women surveyed in Canada, the United States, Chile, Egypt, and Nicaragua report that they were physically or sexually abused when pregnant, often with serious effects on the mother (including death) and the developing child, such as miscarriage, injury, stillbirth, and low birth weight (Krug, et al., 2002). Girls who witness domestic violence are more likely to become involved with abusive partners when they grow up, and boys are more likely to perpetrate domestic violence. This may be due to modeling (i.e., children learn how to behave in relationships through observing their parents and internalizing their relationship dynamics), due to the effects of witnessing on the child's sense of self or identity, and/or due to disrupted attachments with caregivers. Bowlby's (1988) empirically informed attachment theory posits that young children develop "maps" or "internal working models" (IWMs) of attachment relationships, which are formed through the quality and type of attachment the child has with his or her caregiver. When insecure attachments are formed during childhood and persist into adulthood, the adult tends to choose an intimate partner in accordance with those IWMs. From the perspective of attachment theory, it is through these IWMs and insecure attachment styles that the cycle of violence may be repeated. It should be noted that attachment styles and IWMs can change with subsequent relationships; for example, an insecure style may change to a secure style with psychotherapy or with healthy attachment relationships with significant other persons.

Although not all children who witness domestic violence evidence problems, many are at higher risk of various difficulties, including emotional, cognitive, physical, social, and behavioral problems. These children may experience excessive anxiety and depression, with low self-esteem and angry outbursts. They may withdraw from family members and from social contact. Children who witness partner violence may have difficulties at school and may have lags in language development. They often have problems with sleep and eating patterns (e.g., eating disorders), may have impaired motor skills, and may regress to behaviors of a younger age (e.g., a five-year-old child may soil his or her pants). These children may also report physical symptoms that have no medical cause. Behavioral difficulties such as aggression, tantrums, acting out, immaturity, truancy, and delinquency have been observed with samples of children who witness abuse. They may have problems interacting with their peers due to poor social skills and an inability to empathize with others, which may lead to rejection by their peers. It is not clear whether these difficulties stem directly from witnessing parental abuse or if they are associated with additional problems found in families with partner violence. Not all children will have these problems, and most children who are adversely affected will not experience all of the above problems (Jasinski & Williams, 1998). Women who are unable to escape the abusive relationship and who are aware of how the abuse affects the children are likely to experience significant guilt feelings, which will exacerbate their psychological distress.

Overview of Sexual Violence

Sexual assault includes any act of unwanted sexual contact, including being pressured or coerced into engaging in sexual activities when the victim does not want to do so. According to this definition, overt physical force is not required for sexual assault to have occurred. Perpetrators of sexual assault may engage in various behaviors. Women may experience males rubbing their genitals against them, especially in crowded places (*frotteurism*) and can be spied on unknowingly (*voyeurism*) when the women are getting undressed or engaging in sexual activity. Some women and girls experience males "flashing" or exposing their genitals (*exhibitionism*). Other forms of sexual assault include coerced or forced sexual molestation, masturbation of self or of the perpetrator, oral sex, attempted rape, and completed rape. When there are two or more perpetrators during a rape, it is called *gang rape*. Some women are subjected to particularly cruel or humiliating acts during sexual assault, such as being raped with objects or otherwise tortured, with the perpetrator feeling pleasure from humiliating or hurting his victim (*sexual sadism*). Perpetrator(s) of any of these types of sexual offense may be unknown to the victim or may be known to her. Sexual assault may or may not involve violence and bodily harm. These perverse forms of sexual offending are referred to as *paraphilias* (*DSM–IV–TR*; American Psychiatric Association, 2000).

Sexual Abuse of Children

Childhood sexual abuse occurs when a perpetrator touches a child sexually or has the child touch him/her sexually, and may include oral-genital contact and penetration. Children are often "groomed"—the perpetrator will befriend the child, treat him or her as special, and gradually gain the child's trust. Physical contact frequently begins in the form of "games," such as tickling the child, and progresses to sexual contact. *Pedophilia* (a paraphilia) refers to an adult having repeated fantasies and/or sexual contact with pre-pubescent children that persists for at least six months (*DSM–IV–TR*), whereas *Hebephilia* or *Ephebophilia* (not an official diagnosis) refers to sexual attraction to adolescent children (see Wikipedia, n.d.).

There is variation in the literature as to the upper age cut-off when defining childhood sexual abuse. Many researchers use 16 as the upper age limit provided the perpetrator is at least five years older than the child; however, there may be instances where this definition is not suitable. When the perpetrator is a family member or a person in a position of trust and/or authority, a 16-year old would be more vulnerable to sexual exploitation than if the perpetrator was not known to the child. Adolescent children who have experienced the actual or psychological loss of a father may be at increased risk of sexual exploitation, as perpetrators may provide the child with attention and feelings of being loved that the father is not there to provide. Children who are raised in environments where there is neglect are at increased risk of abuse outside of the family (Gold, 2000). Similarly, children of any age with an intellectual disability do not have the ability to consent to sexual activity. Moreover, the neurological development of late teenagers is not complete and is associated with deficits in higher cognitive functions, including judgment, decision making, and impulse control, particularly when the teen is under stress (Sabbagh, 2006). Thus, even though late teens look like adults and in many ways behave as such, under certain conditions they do not have mature cognitive skills. Therefore, their ability to consent to sexual activity with older adults is questionable. If they have histories of maltreatment, their ability to consent is further impaired.

Sexual violence against teenaged girls may result in pregnancies, and rates vary between countries. Approximately 5 percent of rape victims in the United States become pregnant, compared to up to 18 percent in Ethiopia and Mexico (Krug et al., 2002). Sexual exploitation at a young age often results in a woman's reduced ability to perceive herself as having control over her sexuality, thereby increasing risk of sexual revictimization (Zurbriggen & Freyd, 2004). Gynecological problems and sexually transmitted diseases may also ensue from childhood sexual abuse. In addition, there are serious psychological effects of violence against women and children.

Additional Forms of Violence against Women

There are additional forms of violence against women that occur internationally. Three of these forms include, but are not limited to, sexual trafficking of women, female genital mutilation, and rape as an instrument of war. This section includes a brief overview of these disturbing forms of violence, which occur on a massive scale.

Sexual Trafficking

Trafficking refers to the organized movement of persons between countries or within countries for the purpose of exploitation. It is estimated that 2 million persons are trafficked each year (United Nations Educational, Scientific and Cultural Organization, n.d.) and women and children are often trafficked for the purpose of sex work. They are made to believe that they will work in a domestic capacity, and later find themselves confined, sometimes beaten, with their passports and papers confiscated. They are forced into prostitution to pay for their purchase price, travel costs, and visa costs (Krug et al., 2002).

Female Genital Mutilation

Millions of girls (as young as three years of age) and women are subjected to female genital mutilation (FGM), usually in the form of female circumcision and often as a religious ritual. This practice is found in the Middle East and Asia, and is widespread in Africa. It is also found among immigrant populations in Europe, the United Kingdom, Australia, Canada, and the United States. It is estimated that between 100 and 140 million females worldwide have undergone FGM (Krug et al., 2002). Female genital mutilation varies from stretching of the clitoris and/or labia to *infibulation*, which involves the removal of the clitoris and labia and the joining together of the vulva across the vagina with thread. FGM is often done under unsanitary conditions by a midwife and may result in the transmission of HIV and other infections. Death may also ensue due to shock or hemorrhage. Long-term effects include sexual dysfunction, genital malformations, delayed onset of menstruation, chronic pelvic complications, and urinary and obstetric complications. Although FGM may be perceived by some as a rite of passage with little negative effect, it has also been reported to result in significant physical and emotional damage (World Health Organization, 2000).

Rape as an Instrument of War

Rape of women and children during armed conflict has been noted as far back as ancient Greek, Hebrew, and Roman times (Ward & Marsh, 2006). In 2002, the secretary-general of the United Nations reported that women and children have become the main targets of armed conflict and they constitute the majority of victims (United Nations Security Council, 2002). High proportions of women in Bosnia, Rwanda, Kosovo, Liberia, the Congo, Burundi, Colombia, Afghanistan, and the Sudan have been raped during armed conflict (Krug et al., 2002). One woman who survived the Rwandan genocide of 1994 was raped by over 500 men while her children were confined in the next room. Amazingly, she lived through the horror.

Rape may be the by-product of social collapse during wartime; however, it is often used as a deliberate form of attack on the enemy. It may be used to instill shame and humiliation, thereby undermining and collapsing social bonds within communities and families. It is used to instill fear and stop resistance by the enemy and has also been used for "ethnic cleansing" (altering the gene pool of the enemy via forced impregnation, genital mutilation, and intentional HIV transmission). In Bosnia, for example, Muslim women who were raped and impregnated were held captive until their pregnancies came to full term so as to prevent abortion. These women were required to raise their children in ignominy (a state of shame or dishonor within the community); some committed infanticide. Women and girls may be abducted and used as sexual slaves for soldiers, and "voluntary" child and women soldiers are often sexually abused by the males. Female refugees are also at high risk of rape as they flee their countries. Many of these adult and child victims of war-related sexual violence end up in the sex trade as the only means to support themselves, given the fact that they are often rejected and abandoned by their communities and families during the war and after it ends (Ward & Marsh, 2006).

Traumatic Effects of Violence against Women

Violence against women and girls can have a wide range of adverse effects, including but not limited to depression, anxiety disorders (including posttraumatic stress disorder), substance-related disorders, dissociative disorders, and somatoform disorders. Chronic maltreatment may affect physical health through direct injury or as mediated by the effects of chronic stress on physiological processes (Schnurr & Green, 2004). Chronic abuse during childhood may also result in various behaviors that increase risk of physical illness, including use of drugs and alcohol, smoking, risky sexual behaviors, and lack of appropriate self-care (e.g., see Felitti et al., 1998). As such, reduced quality of life and life expectancy due to effects on physical health are two significant long-term adverse effects of violence against women and girls.

Posttraumatic Stress Disorder

Individuals who have experienced or witnessed severe traumatic events may experience a constellation of symptoms that result in clinically significant distress or functional impairment. These symptom clusters and the associated dysfunction are called posttraumatic stress disorder (PTSD) (DSM–IV–TR).

The symptom clusters of PTSD include the following: Reexperiencing symptoms, such as intrusive distressing memories of the traumatic event, nightmares, and flashbacks; avoidance and numbing symptoms, such as avoiding talking about the event, not wanting to think about the event, feeling emotionally numb or cut off from other people; and hyperarousal symptoms, such as being hyperalert for danger, irritability, problems concentrating, and jumpiness.

According to the *Diagnostic and Statistical Manual of Mental Disorders*, fourth edition, text revision *(DSM–IV–TR)*, for an event to constitute a traumatic stressor event, it must involve actual or threatened death, physical injury, or threat to physical integrity and must also involve intense fear, helplessness, or horror. Ongoing psychological or emotional abuse does not constitute a traumatic event according to these criteria for PTSD, which is a limitation of the *DSM* system. There is accumulating evidence that childhood psychological abuse is significantly correlated with the symptom criteria, distress, and impaired functioning of PTSD (Teicher et al., 2006). Similarly, physical abuse that does not result in death or a threat to physical integrity would not constitute a traumatic stressor event in the *DSM* system, although it may be experienced as terrifying. An exception to the physical damage criterion is childhood sexual abuse (CSA). Children who are sexually molested without threat of or actual physical injury or death meet the traumatic event criterion for PTSD insofar as the physical invasion of the body by the perpetrator is a threat to physical integrity. In short, the *DSM* emphasizes physical injury over psychological injury when defining traumatic events, and many experts in the trauma field view this as a significant limitation.

Depression is highly correlated with PTSD (Kessler, Sonnega, Bromet, Hughes, & Nelson, 1995). Many women who have had violence perpetrated against them also suffer from at least one major depressive episode and frequently suffer from recurrent episodes or chronic depression. Substance use and PTSD are also correlated (Kessler et al., 1995). Traumatized persons may engage in substance abuse in an attempt to control their symptoms (e.g., become intoxicated in order to sleep or to numb their distress; regularly use tranquilizers in order to calm themselves), and may develop substance dependence disorders (Bremner, Southwick, Darnell, & Charney, 1996; Stewart et al., 2000). The coexistence of two or more psychological disorders is referred to as *comorbidity*.

We should also mention "Complex PTSD" or "Disorders of Extreme Stress Not Otherwise Specified." In the 1980s to early 1990s, many clinicians observed that individuals who had experienced chronic trauma in their lives (e.g., chronic domestic violence survivors, childhood abuse survivors, war survivors) evidenced a cluster of symptoms that went beyond those seen with PTSD. As part of the field trial on PTSD for the *DSM–IV*, several of these clinicians/clinical researchers conducted empirical research on this phenomenon. The symptoms include the following: difficulties in managing affective arousal (e.g., not able to calm oneself down, engaging in self-harm or high-risk behaviors in order to feel better), memory disturbances and dissociation, impaired identity or sense of self, impaired relationships with others, somatic symptoms (physical symptoms with no known medical cause), and altered belief systems (e.g., intense despair and hopelessness).

Psychiatrist Judith Herman (1992a) termed this symptom constellation "Complex PTSD" and others (e.g., Pelcovitz, et al., 1997) independently termed it "Disorders of Extreme Stress Not Otherwise Specified" or "DESNOS." In spite of research evidence documenting the relationship between chronic trauma and complex PTSD/DESNOS, the proposed diagnosis was not included in the *DSM–IV* and will not likely be included in the *DSM–V.* Although complex PTSD or DESNOS was not included in the *DSM–IV* as a distinct diagnosis, the symptoms are included as part of the associated features to PTSD, which are not required for a diagnosis of PTSD. It should also be noted that the gold standard for assessment of PTSD, the Clinician Administered PTSD Scale (CAPS) (Blake et al., 1998) does not assess for the majority of the associated features.

Herman's perspective, based on clinical and empirical data, is that the vast majority of women who meet the criteria for borderline personality disorder (BPD) have histories of childhood sexual abuse. Herman notes that BPD tends to be a pejorative diagnosis and downplays the traumatic underpinnings of the symptoms and behaviors. Her thesis is that complex PTSD, as an alternative to BPD, places more emphasis on the traumatic origins of the problems these women face and should result in more compassionate and effective treatment of survivors. Others have taken exception to this point of view, based on the finding that not all adults with diagnoses of BPD have reported CSA histories. However, it is not clear whether these individuals have histories of other forms of childhood maltreatment or other trauma. Further research is warranted.

In the next section I will describe three case studies of different traumatic events, and describe the preferred course of treatment for the symptoms and associated difficulties as presented by the individuals. These cases will include single-event sexual assault, chronic childhood sexual abuse, and partner violence. These are offered as snapshot views of potential assessment and treatment applications, but are not meant to be exhaustive with regard to the many treatment strategies available to clinicians. Nor are they intended as the best choice of treatment for a given client or patient. Choice of treatment method involves the consideration of many factors, which is beyond the scope of this chapter. Readers who are interested in a review of empirical studies on effective treatments for PTSD are referred to the text edited by Foa, Keane, and Friedman (2000), and for complex PTSD readers are referred to Cloitre, Cohen and Koenen (2006).

Case Studies

SEXUAL ASSAULT: SINGLE EVENT WITH POSTTRAUMATIC STRESS DISORDER AND DEPRESSION

Shelley is a 25-year-old woman who works as a waitress at a nightclub. One night after work, she was sexually assaulted by a man who had followed her to her apartment. The perpetrator held a knife to her throat during the assault and threatened that he would kill her if she screamed or otherwise resisted him. Shelley felt terrified during the attack, and because she feared for her life, she did not try to fight back or scream. When he left her apartment, she dialed 911 and was taken to hospital, where she was interviewed, examined medically, and treated.

That night when she returned to her apartment, she could not sleep. She kept hearing noises and was unable to relax—she lay awake all night with the lights on in her apartment and a knife under her pillow. She was terrified that the perpetrator would return. During the day, she felt a bit better, but not much. During the rape, she had felt detached from her body and as if time was slowed down (dissociation). These symptoms persisted over the next several weeks. When she was able to fall asleep, she would awaken through the night having "night sweats," and she would sit up in bed, terrified from nightmares of getting raped or otherwise attacked. When her friends and family asked her to talk about what happened, she would not do so. She tried to push all thoughts and memories of the rape out of her mind. She could not face going back to work and so she quit her job. The mere thought of the assault brought forth much anxiety and distress. Shelley found that she was jumpy—the slightest noise would make her jump out of her seat. Usually an avid reader, she found she could not concentrate enough to read even the newspaper each day. She was always on "red alert"—paying very close attention to her surroundings. After a month of these symptoms, Shelley decided to see a therapist who specialized in treating the traumatic effects of sexual assault.

Treatment of Acute PTSD and Major Depression

Treatment for single-incident traumatic events often includes psychoeducation and exposure therapy, such as cognitive processing therapy (Resick & Schnike, 1997), prolonged exposure (Foa, Dancu, & Hembree, 1998), or eye movement desensitization and reprocessing (Shapiro & Forrest, 1998). During the initial phases of treatment, clients undergo a thorough assessment with a focus specifically on PTSD and possible comorbid difficulties, such as major depression.

During the initial assessment process, Shelley was diagnosed with PTSD and major depression. When conducting assessments with traumatized persons, there are specific issues that require the clinician's attention, such as possible exacerbation of symptoms when discussing the event. These issues are beyond the scope of this chapter; however, the interested reader is referred to Briere (1997), Carlson (1997), or Wilson and Keane (2004). Shelley was referred to her physician to discuss whether medication would be useful for the depressive symptoms and also to rule out possible medical reasons for her symptoms.

Psychoeducation forms a significant part of the initial sessions for treatment of PTSD and complex PTSD—the client is provided with information on the index traumatic event (in Shelley's case, sexual assault), PTSD or complex PTSD, any comorbid problems, coping strategies for dealing with symptoms, and the theoretical rationale for the proposed treatment. It is important to provide as much choice as possible for trauma survivors in terms of treatment. Guided relaxation exercises may be incorporated into treatment sessions and/or assigned as "homework" to assist with reduction of hyperarousal.

Exposure therapy is one of the treatments of choice for PTSD with strong empirical support, and involves techniques that help clients face stimuli that they fear, including memories, thoughts, and images. Imaginal exposure to the trauma narrative is conducted within sessions, and in vivo ("real world") exposure activities are assigned as homework between sessions. The theoretical rationale behind exposure therapy is that avoidance of trauma-related stimuli prevents processing of the traumatic event and concomitant emotions, thereby interfering with recovery. Trauma memories are composed of stimuli that were present during the event, physiological and/or behavioral responses at the time of the traumatic event, and meanings that are associated with the event (Foa et al., 1998). These memories are highly distressing to the individual. With repeated imaginal exposure to the feared memories and painful emotions, clients learn to tolerate the negative affect and soon become habituated to the emotions. This is analogous to jumping into a swimming pool. When the individual first jumps in, the water feels cold; however, when the swimmer remains in the pool long enough, the water begins to feel warm and comfortable. The individual has habituated to the temperature of the water. With imaginal exposure, the individual learns to tolerate the emotions and habituates to them. With in vivo exposure exercises (facing safe yet feared stimuli in the individual's environment), clients learn corrective information through absence of harm, and maladaptive cognitions (e.g., "I am incompetent") are modified. High levels of emotional arousal also interfere with cognitions: individuals do not think clearly when they are in extremely emotionally aroused states. With habituation, thinking becomes clearer and cognitive distortions are more easily examined and replaced with healthy cognitions. Shelley showed improvement as sessions progressed—her narrative of the rape was initially fragmented and incoherent; however, by the ninth treatment session it was coherent and fluid, with a clear story line.

Shelley was taught to identify her cognitive distortions (CDs) related to the rape (e.g., "I caused the rape by walking home alone," and "It is my fault because I did not scream or fight back") and to replace the CDs with more accurate beliefs (e.g., "I could not possibly have fought back or screamed. The man held a knife to my throat. If I had screamed or fought, he could have killed me. I was smart to keep quiet"). Success in dealing with feared stimuli in her daily life also assisted her with forming more effective beliefs (e.g., "I am competent and can handle this"). Identifying and challenging certain CDs is also an important aspect of treating major depression, as are increasing the amount of daily activities, increasing social interactions or activities, increasing pleasurable experiences, and promotion of physical well-being through diet and exercise. Clients are assisted with developing goals related to improving depressive symptoms. For example, depressed persons tend to isolate themselves (as do traumatized persons), they stop engaging in pleasurable activities, and they may let their physical health falter. These interventions were incorporated into Shelley's treatment plan.

By the end of treatment, Shelley's symptoms of PTSD and depression had been reduced to subclinical levels (i.e., she no longer met the diagnostic criteria), her CDs had been successfully replaced with more effective cognitions, and her functioning had improved. She contacted her former boss and was able to return to work, where she functioned effectively.

COMPLEX PTSD BASED IN CHRONIC CHILDHOOD SEXUAL ABUSE

When Bonnie was six years of age, her mother met a man (Joe) whom she later married. Joe gave Bonnie a lot of attention from the start. He would buy her special gifts and take her to fun places, like the carnival. Joe liked to tickle Bonnie. She loved the attention, and she learned to trust Joe. Bonnie hadn't seen her birth father in years, and Joe made her feel important and wanted. It wasn't until Joe started to touch her genitals that Bonnie began to feel afraid and very confused. Joe told her it was their special secret and that if she told anyone that they would take Joe away from her. She had developed a strong attachment to Joe and by the age of seven when the molestation started, she couldn't bear losing her new father figure. So she remained silent. Bonnie was confused because in a way it felt nice to be touched[1] but she was also scared. There was something that felt bad about it, too. When the abuse progressed to more invasive activities, Bonnie would dissociate. At these times, she would feel as though she was floating on the ceiling, and could see Joe raping her on the bed below. These memories were so threatening to Bonnie that many of them remained out of her conscious awareness for years. Bonnie, once an excellent student, began to have behavioral problems and began to fail at school. She could not pay attention in class. She became depressed and withdrawn, had nightmares, and began to urinate in bed when sleeping. She also felt very angry and would "hurt" her dolls in the same way that Joe hurt her (behavioral reenactment through play). Bonnie became fearful of adult males and shied away from them, including her teacher. When he tried to find out what was wrong, she could not trust him enough to tell him. Bonnie kept the abuse a secret for decades.

Bonnie attended therapy in her early 30s after her marriage of five years ended. She found that she was always having problems in her relationships with men—she was unable to trust them, always fearing that they would betray her or hurt her in some way. Bonnie's relationship with her husband had been highly conflicted—they were always arguing. Bonnie had a hard time calming herself down when she was angry or upset. She would yell and scream, sometimes throwing things. When her emotional arousal became too high, she would binge on food or harm herself in some other manner (e.g., she would pinch her legs to the point where they bruised). Bonnie had problems with dissociation when she and her husband had sex. She would feel as though she was "floating" on the ceiling in the bedroom in the same way she had done when Joe abused her many years before. These symptoms of *depersonalization* or "out of body" experiences occurred whenever she felt threatened. Bonnie also experienced a lot of physical problems, including chronic pain, various gynecological symptoms, difficulties with her digestive system, and symptoms suggestive of lung disease. She underwent a lot of medical testing, but the doctors would tell her that they could find nothing medically wrong with her. Bonnie was severely depressed, and was terrified of being alone. Her symptoms of depression worsened when her husband decided to leave, and she started to have ideas about killing herself. Her despondency increased and one night, when she overdosed on sleeping pills, her neighbor found her and called an ambulance.

Treatment of Complex PTSD Based in Childhood Sexual Abuse

When Bonnie attended her first session with a psychologist she told the therapist that her main presenting problem was depression based in the breakup of her marriage. With chronic childhood abuse, relationship difficulties are often the triggering event that leads clients to treatment. Some clients do not have much knowledge about abuse and may not realize that what they experienced was abusive, believing that all families engage in abusive behaviors. Clinicians should therefore ask direct questions during the intake process about possible abuse, and questions should be phrased using behavioral descriptors.

Results of Bonnie's assessment indicated that Bonnie met the criteria for a diagnosis of PTSD, with problems of affect regulation, identity, relationship functioning, dissociation, somatization, and altered belief systems. Bonnie reported that she would reduce emotional distress or tension by binging and purging and by self-harming. She reported considerable interpersonal conflict, abandonment concerns, and idealization-devaluation dynamics in her relationships. She and her husband always fought; she was terrified of being abandoned and totally alone, and tended to have quick affective swings in which she would adore her husband one minute and hate him the next. Bonnie reported that she would often space out and lose track of her surroundings (*disengagement*), had out of body experiences, especially during sex (*depersonalization*), and significant amnesia (memory impairments). She reported several physical symptoms with no known medical cause (*somatization*), and she suffered from prolonged despair and hopelessness. Treatment for complex PTSD often occurs in phases and generally is a lengthy process, and therapy may last for several years, depending on client presentation.

Stabilization

When treating single-incident, adult-onset trauma, the course of therapy tends to be brief and straightforward, as with Shelley. With complex PTSD, the clients must be stabilized before any processing of the trauma can ensue. If this is not done, the symptoms will intensify and the client will be at increased risk of regression, significant self-harm, and suicide. If clients are in unsafe situations (e.g., in a battering relationship, living on the streets) they need to find safe housing; if they are addicted to substances and living a risky lifestyle, they should receive treatment for the addiction and reduce risk-taking behaviors; if they are highly suicidal and make frequent attempts and/or are highly dissociative, they need to learn skills to manage their emotions (Herman, 1992b).

An excellent and empirically validated treatment for childhood sexual abuse is an approach developed by Cloitre, Cohen, and Koenen (2006), termed STAIR/NST. This is a two-phase approach that includes stabilization via learning affect regulation and interpersonal relatedness skills in phase 1 (STAIR), and processing the trauma narrative in phase 2 (NST). Linehan's *Dialectical Behavior Therapy* (DBT) (1993) and Cloitre, Cohen, and Koenen's (2006) approach are very useful for stabilization. During the first phase of treatment with STAIR/NST, the client is introduced to treatment and learns skills for emotion regulation and effective interpersonal relating. Examples of skills learned during the first phase include exploring how feelings were managed in the client's/patient's family of origin, how abuse influences feelings, identifying and labeling feeling states, skills for managing emotional states, skills for tolerating emotional distress, and assertiveness skills. As with the prolonged exposure diagnosis, homework forms a significant part of the treatment.

During phase 2, processing of the trauma occurs using narrative storytelling (NST; imaginal exposure). The process of phase 2 work is similar to that of prolonged exposure; however, there are many modifications that are important with complex PTSD. In essence, as the clients tell their story of what happened, the clinician helps the client regulate her affective state by putting into practice the interventions of phase 1, and the client continues with the homework exercises of phase 1. With single-event trauma, only one memory is processed. With ongoing trauma, there are typically several memories and it would be impossible to conduct exposure for each memory. As such, the client identifies five of the most important memories to process, beginning with the least disturbing. The five memories chosen are those that have the most influence on the client's current functioning. As Bonnie listened to the tapes over the duration of treatment, she learned that the memory was just a memory and had no real power over her current life, and as her memories became more organized, she had a reduction in her PTSD symptoms. In addition, as her memories became more organized she was able to identify abuse-related interpersonal schemas and distinguish between current and past life circumstances. During the final session, Bonnie's therapist asked her about her experience of change and progress. They identified plans for Bonnie, reviewed risks for relapse, and reviewed strategies to recover from relapse. The therapist provided Bonnie with a list or community resources, and they said goodbye.

A Note on Amnesia

When clients have gaps in their memories of events, it is not advisable to use hypnosis as a memory retrieval technique. Sound research shows that individuals may create new memories when they are in a susceptible state of mind, such as hypnosis, and the veracity of the products of hypnosis may be suspect. Clients may remember more details or incidents when not hypnotized as they become psychologically stronger; however, the clinician should never tell a client that s/he was sexually abused when the client has no memories of the abuse and when there is no independent documentation that abuse occurred. If a client with no known abuse history and no memories of abuse asks a therapist if s/he was sexually abused, a reasonable response would be along the lines of "It is possible that you were abused; however, I cannot know whether you were abused because I was not there." The therapist is encouraged to adopt a stance of "reflective belief" (Van der Hart & Nijenuis, 1999), and the focus of treatment would be on resolution or management of the symptoms with which the client presents.

PTSD, MAJOR DEPRESSION, AND SUBSTANCE DEPENDENCE BASED IN CHRONIC PARTNER VIOLENCE

Kim met Phillip when she was 18. She thought he was okay at first, although he did like to control what she did and where she went, and he was extremely jealous of other men. Phillip would tell her that he did not like her friends, especially her closest friend Sylvia, and he tried to prevent Kim from spending time with Sylvia. Yet he was also very attentive and engaged in caring behaviors, so Kim decided to ignore his controlling actions. They had been dating for a year when the couple decided to get married.

After the wedding, Phillip's controlling behaviors escalated, especially when Kim became defiant. He would take Kim's car keys from her to prevent her visiting her friends and family. He became increasingly psychologically abusive and would criticize everything she did. If she did not have dinner on the table on time, he would erupt into a rage and break dishes. Kim became increasingly terrified of his rages, and was constantly on edge. When Phillip had problems at work, he would come home and take it out on Kim. Once when she was six months pregnant, he grabbed her by the arm and pushed her into the wall, resulting in several bruises. The next day he was highly apologetic and brought her some roses. Kim had been seriously considering leaving and moving to her parents' home, but when he apologized and promised to change, she wanted to believe him. So she stayed, and the abuse continued. When she was eight months pregnant, she awakened in the middle of the night to find an intoxicated Phillip choking her and screaming at her for not ironing his clothes properly. He threatened to punch her in the stomach unless she promised to do everything "right." Following the birth of their first baby, Phillip's abusive behaviors continued. Two more children were born. Kim was not working outside of the home and had no money to support herself and the three children. She could not relax and was always in a state of high anxiety. As the abuse continued she became severely depressed, became increasingly hopeless, and felt totally helpless. She started to believe many of the things that Phillip said to her and blamed herself when he beat her. She was even more terrified to leave, especially since Phillip told her that if she ever tried to do so, he would find her and kill her and the children. Kim knew that he was capable of it.

Kim started to drink excessively and smoked marijuana as it seemed as if the drugs and alcohol would help her to relax and sleep. The alcohol helped to dull the pain and helped her to temporarily "forget" the misery she was in. She stayed with Phillip until her aunt came to visit and got a glimpse of how Phillip was treating her. Her aunt asked Kim if Phillip was hitting her, and Kim started to cry. She was too terrified to speak; however, her nonverbal reaction was enough to let her aunt know that Phillip was indeed hitting her. Kim's aunt told the rest of the family what she had learned. A few months later, Kim and the children fled from the house and went to stay with Kim's parents.

Treatment of Intimate Partner Violence

Kim was diagnosed with chronic PTSD, major depressive disorder, alcohol dependence and cannabis abuse. She agreed to attend an inpatient alcohol dependence program and successfully stopped drinking. During the program she learned some affect regulation skills but continued to have much difficulty with depressed mood, PTSD symptoms, conflicted relationships, poor self-esteem, and some marijuana use, although on a lesser scale. During her individual therapy, her therapist provided psychoeducation, stress reduction and relaxation techniques, and cognitive behavioral therapy for depression (as was done with Shelley in case 1; however, the CDs in this case were not in relation to sexual assault but in relation to partner violence).

Kim started to make some significant progress in treatment; however, during a subsequent session she told her therapist that Phillip was contacting her and he had really changed this time. Kim and the children returned to live with Phillip against the therapist's advice. Soon thereafter, the abuse began again and Kim relapsed into alcohol use. She continued with therapy (which she kept secret from Philip) and she and her therapist developed a safety plan. Kim put together a suitcase with necessary items for herself and the children if she had to suddenly get away from Phillip. The suitcase was well hidden in a location in the house that Phillip never found. Kim had a list of emergency contact numbers for ransition houses, crisis centers, and family and friends who were supportive of her. She contacted the police and made sure they were fully aware of the situation, and she programmed emergency numbers into the phone. She let a trusted neighbor know what was happening so that she could keep an eye on Kim and the children, and she called the local transition house and informed them of her current situation. In addition, she hid some money away and talked to the children so they would know whom to call and which neighbor's house they should go to in case of an emergency. She began a nonresidential rehabilitation program for alcohol dependence and managed to stop drinking. She boosted the program with regular AA meetings during the day when the children were in school and Phillip was at work. She had a plan prepared, outlining what she would do if she ever had to leave Phillip.

Kim continued with her work in therapy, and learned a great deal about how witnessing partner violence affects children. She noticed many of these effects in her own children and this knowledge helped to strengthen her resolve to eventually leave her husband. One day Phillip followed Kim to her therapist's office. He waited until her session was over and then followed her to the elementary school, where she picked up the children. As soon as Kim and the children were inside the front door of their home, Phillip burst into the house in a rage. He beat Kim and, for the first time, he hit the oldest boy when the boy tried to protect Kim. Kim knew that this was it. She was finished with her husband. Phillip finished off a bottle of vodka and passed out downstairs in the family room. Kim grabbed the suitcase from its hidden location, called a taxi, and she and the children went to a local transition house. She contacted the police the next day and had an officer accompany her to her home to obtain more personal items for herself and the children. She also visited a lawyer, had a legal separation agreement prepared, filed for custody of the children, and applied to raise the children in the family home (i.e., Phillip would be required to move out if she was successful).

After one month at the transition house, Kim and the children moved into her parents' home. Phillip began stalking her, and she obtained a restraining order against him. Kim and her therapist focused on reframing her self-blame in such a way that Kim could learn to take responsibility for her own behaviors and learn to place the responsibility for the abuse squarely on Phillip's shoulders. Kim's substance dependence/abuse was well managed and she was actively practicing relapse prevention: she identified high-risk situations for use, avoided those situations, and learned new strategies for managing her distress. Kim continued to work on identifying and challenging CDs, particularly as they related to her role as a wife. She had internalized Phillip's beliefs about how she should act as a wife, but now she replaced those CDs with healthy cognitions that were empowering and that honored her individuality. Once Kim's self-esteem had improved and she was successfully abstinent for several months, she and her therapist engaged in prolonged exposure therapy for her PTSD. Kim found employment. The judge awarded full custody of the children to Kim, and ruled that she and the children were to reside in the family home.

Recommendations for Public Policy

Preventing and stopping violence against women can be approached from many levels, including international, national, regional, community, family, and individual levels. In the United States, the Violence against Women Act (VAWA) was signed into law in 1994 and has since been revised and reauthorized in various forms. This landmark legislation paved the way for funding sources for programs to reduce domestic violence, rape, and stalking and also impacted federal criminal law to reduce violence against women. Various recommendations have been suggested by groups and agencies, many of which may be read in full in the National Advisory Council against Violence's (2001) *Toolkit to End Violence against Women.*

Internationally, the United Nations General Assembly approved the Declaration on the Elimination of Violence against Women in 1993. This was the signal for other international organizations and bodies, such as the World Health Organization, the United Nations Human Rights Council, and the United Nations Development Fund for Women (UNIFEM) (1996-2007) to work toward combating violence against women. In addition, the United Nations Human Rights Council has also prepared documents on recommendations for stopping violence against women.

While progress has been made in the last 15 years in combating violence against women more needs to be done in the areas of public policies that address government funding, public education, professional education and standards, legal practices, the media, and treatment of offenders.

Specifically, increased government funding is imperative for preventing and intervening in violence against women. Funding is required for the following: screening programs in schools to identify children who exhibit signs of abuse, programs aimed at identification of children who witness domestic violence followed by early intervention (after school hours), programs for women who live in poverty (who are at highest risk of domestic violence), outreach workers, modifications of transition homes such that they are suitable for elderly women and the disabled, provision of specialized staff for working with special populations (e.g., the elderly, immigrants/refugees), second-stage housing, crisis lines, sexual assault centers, women's centers, welfare programs, job training programs and educational opportunities for women leaving abusive relationships, and access to medical care and mental health treatment.

Public education may be one of the most effective ways of empowering women and children who are at risk. Examples of such programs include education on the dynamics of intimate partner violence, the effects of intimate partner violence on women and children, actions that abused women can take for the safety of themselves and their children, and information on community resources available to them. For example, women who receive information on traumatic bonding may gain a better understanding of why they stay in the relationship. This information may assist them to stop blaming themselves for the abuse and increase their sense of control through taking action. Education about gender roles and intimate partner violence should be part of the school curriculum to foster prevention.

The media play a significant role in terms of public education and also in shaping attitudes about violence against women. Ideally, the media would refrain from portraying women as sexual objects, and television would avoid programs that are inherently misogynistic and would provide balanced coverage of stories on sexual assault, childhood abuse, and domestic violence.

Training for health care professionals should include screening for domestic violence, as well as continuing education courses post licensure. Education of professionals, including legal professionals, should include information on the cognitive limitations of older teens and the way this may impact on their ability to consent to sexual activity with older adults under certain circumstances. Health programs and practices should meet the diverse needs of women in the community.

It is recommended that legal abortion should be made available for women and teens who have been raped and impregnated. This should include preabortion counseling and the option of postabortion counseling. Supervised access to abusive men's visits to children should be routinely available to families in which abuse has occurred and there is risk of harm to the woman or the children. Increased communication links should be established between child protective services, courts, and domestic violence agencies. Recommendations for perpetrators in terms of postvention should include funding for research and treatment and early identification.

Summary

Violence against women and children takes many forms and is widespread across the globe. Although some forms of violence against women are culture specific, domestic violence, childhood sexual abuse, and sexual assault occur across most cultures. Violence has significant and far-reaching effects on the physical and mental well-being of women and children, and violence within the family is frequently perpetuated through the generations.

One of the most crucial components of violence against women is the attitudes toward women that are inherent in society. Some countries are more enlightened than others in terms of implementing public policies with the aim of prevention; however, the persistence of the problem worldwide indicates that much more needs to be done. In this writer's opinion, viewing women as objects and as inferior to men is a major aspect of violence against women. This view is perpetuated by corporations who use women to sell goods (e.g., using sex to sell cars) and by those who perpetuate the trafficking of humans for financial gain. It is evident in domestic violence (women as subservient to men), and it is evident in sexual assault against both women and children (females as sexual objects or as objects of misogynistic beliefs). In industrialized countries, the media can play an important role in altering the view of women as objects. Equality in terms of educational and career opportunities, as well as salary and rights, also assists in reducing the perception of women as inferior. While much has been accomplished in efforts to eliminate violence against women, much more needs to be done.

Acknowledgments

I would like to thank Lyn Williams-Keeler and Denise Hawthorne for their helpful comments on this chapter.

Note

1. All children require physical touch to develop in a healthy manner. Sexual molestation, when not physically violent, may produce some pleasant sensations for children, for which they tend to feel significant shame and self-blame. The human body is structured to respond

to touch, and any pleasant sensations do *not* indicate that the child enjoyed the abuse or that there is anything "wrong" with the child.

References

American Psychiatric Association. (2000). *Diagnostic and statistical manual of mental disorders* (4th ed., text revision). Washington, DC: Author.

Blake, D. D., Weathers, F. W., Nagy, L. M., Kaloupek, D. G., Charney, D. S., & Keane, T. M. (1998). *Clinician Administered PTSD Scale for DSM–IV.* Department of Veterans Affairs. Retrieved April 3, 2007 from http://www.ntis.gov/products/pages/caps.asp

Bowlby, J. (1988). *Secure Base.* London: Routledge.

Braak, J. (2006, November). *Multidimensional aspects of advocacy for trauma and ISTSS at the United Nations.* Symposium held at the annual meeting of the International Society for Traumatic Stress Studies, Hollywood, CA.

Bremer, Hans-Hager (2001). *Trafficking in women reaches new heights in Europe.* Retrieved April 3, 2007, from http://www.freerepublic.com/forum/a3ad2b4951392.htm

Bremner, J. D., Southwick, S. M., Darnell, A., & Charney, D. S. (1996). Chronic PTSD in Vietnam combat veterans: Course of illness and substance abuse. *American Journal of Psychiatry, 153*(3), 369–375.

Briere, J. N. (1997). *Psychological assessment of adult posttraumatic states.* Washington, DC: American Psychological Association.

Carlson, E. (1997). *Trauma assessments: A clinician's guide.* New York: Guilford Press.

Cicero-Domininguez, S.A. (2005). Assessing the U.S.-Mexico Fight against Human Trafficking and Smuggling: Unintended Results of U.S. Immigration Policy, *Northwestern University Journal of International Human Rights, 2*(2), Retrieved April 3, 2007, from http://www.law.northwestern.edu/journals/jihr/v4/n2/2/.

Cloitre, M. (1998). Sexual revictimization: Risk factors and prevention. In V. M. Follette, J. I. Ruzek, & F. Abueg (Eds.), *Cognitive-behavioral therapies for trauma* (pp. 278–304). New York: Guilford Press.

Cloitre, M., Cohen, L. R., & Koenen, K. C. (2006). *Treating survivors of childhood abuse: Psychotherapy for the interrupted life.* New York: Guilford Press

Dietrich, A. M. (in press). Childhood maltreatment and revictimization: The role of affect dysregulation, interpersonal relatedness difficulties and posttraumatic stress disorder. *Journal of Trauma and Dissociation, 8.*

Dutton, D. G., & Painter, S. L. (1981). Traumatic bonding: The development of emotional attachments in battered women and other relationships of intermittent abuse. *Victimology: An International Journal, 1,* 139–155.

Felitti, V. J., Anda, R. F., Nordenberg, D. F., Williamson, D. F., Spitz, A. M., Edwards, V. K., et al. (1998). Relationship of childhood abuse and household dysfunction to many of the leading causes of death in adults: The Adverse Childhood Experiences (ACE) study. *American Journal of Preventive Medicine, 14*(4), 245–258.

Foa, E. B., Dancu, C., & Hembree, E. (1998). *Treating the trauma of rape: Cognitive-behavioral therapy for PTSD.* New York: Guilford Press.

Foa, E. B., Keane, T. M., & Friedman, M. J. (Eds.), (2000). *Effective treatments for PTSD: practice guidelines from the International Society for Traumatic Stress Studies* (pp. 1–17). New York: Guilford Press.

Gold, S. N. (2000). *Not trauma alone: Therapy for child abuse survivors in family and social context.* Philadelphia: Brunner/Routledge.

Goldberg, L. R., & Freyd, J. J. (2006). Self-reports of potentially traumatic experiences in an adult community sample. *Journal of Trauma and Dissociation, 7*(3), 39–63.

Harway, M., Geffner, R., Ivey, D., Koss, M. P., Murphy, B., Mio, J., et al. (2001). *Report of the Intimate Partner Abuse and Relationship Violence Working Group.* American Psychological Association. Retrieved April 3, 2007, from http://www.apa.org/pi/iparv.pdf

Herman, J. L. (1992a). Complex PTSD: A syndrome in survivors of prolonged and repeated trauma. *Journal of Traumatic Stress, 5*(3), 377–391.

Herman, J. L. (1992b). *Trauma and recovery.* New York: Guilford.

Huda, S. (2006). Sex trafficking in South Asia. *International Journal of Gynecology and Obstetrics, 94,* 374–381.

Human Trafficking and Modern Day Slavery (n.d.). Retrieved April 3, 2007 from http://www.gvnet.com/humantrafficking/Canada.htm

Jasinski, J. L., & Williams, L. M. (1998). *Partner violence: A comprehensive review of 20 years of research.* Thousand Oaks, CA: Sage Publications.

Johnson, H. (2005). *Assessing the prevalence of violence against women in Canada.* Report prepared for a meeting on violence against women: A statistical overview, challenges, and gaps in data collection and methodology and approaches for overcoming them. Geneva: Expert Group Meeting. Retrieved April 3, 2007, from http://www.un.org/womenwatch/daw/egm/vaw-stat-2005/docs/expert-papers/johnson.pdf

Kantor, G., & Jasinski, J. L. (1998). Dynamics and risk factors in partner violence. In J. L. Jasinski & L. M. Williams (Eds.), *Partner violence: A comprehensive review of 20 years of research.* Thousand Oaks CA: Sage Publications.

Kessler, R. C., Sonnega, A., Bromet, E. J., Hughes, M., & Nelson, C. B. (1995). Posttraumatic stress disorder in the National Comorbidity Survey. *Archives of General Psychiatry, 52*(12), 1048–1060.

Krug, E. G., Dahlberg, L. L., Mercy, J. A., Zwi, A. B., & Lozano, R. (Eds.). (2002). *World report on violence and health.* Geneva: World Health Organization. Retrieved April 3, 2007, from http://www.who.int/violence_injury_prevention/violence/world_report/en/full_en.pdf

Linehan, M. (1993). *Cognitive behavioral treatment of borderline personality disorder.* New York: Guilford Press.

Messman-Moore, T. L., & Long, P. J. (2000). Child sexual abuse and revictimization in the form of adult sexual abuse, adult physical abuse, and adult psychological maltreatment. *Journal of Interpersonal Violence, 15*(5), 489–502.

National Advisory Council against Violence (2001, October). *Toolkit to end violence against women.* Retrieved April 3, 2007 from http://toolkit.ncjrs.org/

Pelcovitz, D., van der Kolk, B. A., Roth, S. H., Mandel, F. S., Kaplan, S. J., & Resick, P. A. (1997). Development of a criteria set and a structured interview for disorders of extreme stress (SIDES). *Journal of Traumatic Stress, 10*(1), 3–16.

Resick, P. A., & Schnicke, M. K. (1993). *Cognitive processing therapy for rape victims: a treatment manual.* Newbury Park, CA: Sage Publications.

Sabbagh, L. (2006, August/September). The teen brain, hard at work. *Scientific American Mind,* 20–25.

Schnurr, P., & Green, B. (Eds.), (2004). *Physical consequences of exposure to extreme stress.* Washington, DC: American Psychiatric Association.

Shapiro, F., & Forrest, M. S. (1998). *EMDR: The breakthrough therapy for overcoming anxiety, stress, and trauma.* New York: Basic Books

Stewart, S. H, Conrod, P. J., Samoluk, S. B., Pihl, R. O., & Dongier, M. (2000). Posttraumatic stress disorder symptoms and situation-specific drinking in women substance abusers. *Alcoholism Treatment Quarterly, 18*(3), 31–47.

Teicher, M., Carryl, N., Samson, J., Polcari, A., McGreenery, C., Rabi, K., et al. (2006, November). *Is parental verbal abuse a traumatic childhood stressor?* Symposium held at the annual meeting of the International Society for Traumatic Stress Studies, Hollywood. CA.

United Nations Educational, Scientific and Cultural Organization (UNESCO) (n.d.). Retrieved April 3, 2007, from www. unesco.org

United Nations Human Rights Council (1996–2007). Retrieved April 3, 2007, from http://www.ohchr.org/english/issues/women/index.htm

United Nations Security Council (2002, October 16). *Report of the Secretary-General on women, peace and security.* Retrieved April 3, 2007, from http://www.peacewomen.org/un/UN1325/sgreport.pdf

Van der Hart, O., & Nijenhuis, E.R.S. (1999). Bearing witness to uncorroborated trauma: The clinician's development of reflective belief. *Professional Psychology Research and Practice, 30*(1), 37–44.

Ward, J. & Marsh, W. (2006). Sexual violence against women and girls in war and its aftermath: Realities, Responses, and Required Resources. A briefing paper prepared for *Symposium on sexual violence in conflict and beyond* in Brussels June 21–23. United Nations Population Fund (UNFPA). Retrieved April 3, 2007 from http://www.unfpa.org/emergencies/symposium06/docs/finalbrusselsbriefingpaper.pdf

Wikipedia (n.d.). *Ephebophila.* Retrieved April 3, 2007, from http://en.wikipedia.org/wiki/Ephebophilia

Wilson, J. P., & Keane, T. M. (2004) (Eds.). *Assessing psychological trauma and PTSD.* New York: Guilford Press.

Wolf, R. S. (2000). The older battered woman. Published by the Institute on Aging, University of Massachusetts, Memorial Health Care. Retrieved April 3, 2007, from http://www.musc.edu/vawprevention/

World Health Organization (2000, June). *Female Genital Mutliation Fact Sheet.* Retrieved April 3, 2007, from http://www.who.int/mediacentre/factsheets/fs241/en/

Zurbriggen, E. L., & Freyd, J. J. (2004). The link between childhood sexual abuse and risky sexual behavior: The role of dissociative tendencies, information-processing effects, and consensual sex decision mechanisms. In L. J. Koenig, L. S. Doll, A. O'Leary, & W. Pequegnat (Eds.), *From child sexual abuse to adult sexual risk: Trauma, revictimization, and intervention* (pp. 135–158). Washington, DC: American Psychological Association.

CHAPTER 12

The Integration of Psychopharmacology and Psychotherapy in PTSD Treatment: A Biopsychosocial Model of Care

Elaine S. LeVine and Elaine Orabona Mantell

The serious symptoms of posttraumatic stress disorder (PTSD) often require intensive intervention. Interdisciplinary care, which combines an understanding of physical/psychological symptoms and social systems deficits with appropriate therapeutic techniques, psychotropic intervention, and changes in the social environment, is often most effective. As the readers learn in many chapters in this book, the efficacy of a number of psychotherapeutic interventions has been documented to assist in ameliorating symptoms of PTSD (Brewin & Holmes, 2003; van der Kolk, McFarlane, & Weisaeth, 1996). In addition, current research has demonstrated a variety of psychotropic medications that can alleviate various symptoms of PTSD, symptoms of physiological stress arousal as well as anxiety, which in turn may lead to dissociation and memory loss as well as flashbacks, hypervigilance, and hyperexcitability (Albucher & Liberzon, 2002; Hageman, Andersen, & Jorgensen, 2001). Intervention in the social environment is, of course, helpful when support systems can be fortified or when significant others are educated about the course of PTSD and how they can best support the sufferer. While psychological, social, and psychotropic interventions can all be components of effective change, often these treatments are not well integrated for PTSD patients. The biopsychosocial model appears to be particularly well suited for treating PTSD, which is often most successfully ameliorated through the integration of biological concomitants, specific cognitive and behavioral techniques, ongoing education, and training for support in the social environment.

Within the last 10 years, a new specialization of prescribing/medical psychologists has emerged. Their identity originated with a Department of Defense congressional demonstration project, in which 10 psychologists were trained to prescribe. By 2004, laws were implemented in New Mexico and Louisiana so that psychologists could prescribe in the private as well as the public sector. Prescribing/medical psychologists are committed to a biopsychosocial and, as appropriate, spiritual model of care. Their expertise and approach is collaborative, with the focus upon a continuum of health rather than disease and with therapeutic relationship as the key to optimal therapeutic progress. As such, the biopsychosocial model appears to be particularly well suited for treating PTSD, which is often most successfully ameliorated through the integration of biological concomitants, specific cognitive and behavioral techniques, ongoing education, and training for support in the social environment.

Phases of Therapy in a Biopsychosocial Model for Treating PTSD

In order to better understand the integrative approach of such a biopsychosocial model, the authors would like to outline basic processes in this biopsychosocial model of care. It is well recognized that the therapy process flows through various phases. These phases are given somewhat different labels but generally refer to the following processes: initial and ongoing phase; active working phase; maintenance phase; and termination phase. Figure 12.1 is a schema of how a patient and psychologist move through these phases. In the sections that follow, this schema is employed to organize constructs of an integrated biopsychosocial model of care for PTSD.

Initial and Ongoing Phase

Practitioners, such as medical/prescribing psychologists, ascribing to a biopsychosocial model of care recognize the importance of building a relationship with a patient and deepening it throughout the therapeutic process. These practitioners use the well-established psychotherapeutic techniques that enhance trust, such as active, nonjudgmental listening, unconditional positive regard, and summarizing and reflecting the patient's comments with careful attention to clarifying statements or direct/indirect expressions of disagreement. This process, as explained in figure 12.2, continues throughout the therapy so that the relationship becomes deeper in understanding and trust over time.

As part of the biopsychosocial model for treating PTSD, practitioners consider holistic factors, such as the patient's desires for change as well as his/her coping and problem-solving skills, level of resiliency, and social support. In a traditional medical model, the most prominent symptoms, such as anxiety or sleeplessness, might be immediately addressed with certain medications. In contrast, those prescribing from a biopsychosocial model seek to clarify with the patient the symptoms that the patient finds most troubling. In addition to seeking an understanding of what the patient chooses to change, the therapist explores the changes that the patient is willing to tolerate, including the willingness to risk the potential side effects of treatment. For example, one patient of spousal abuse might want some psychotropic intervention to assist with underlying

Figure 12.1 Phases of the Therapeutic Process

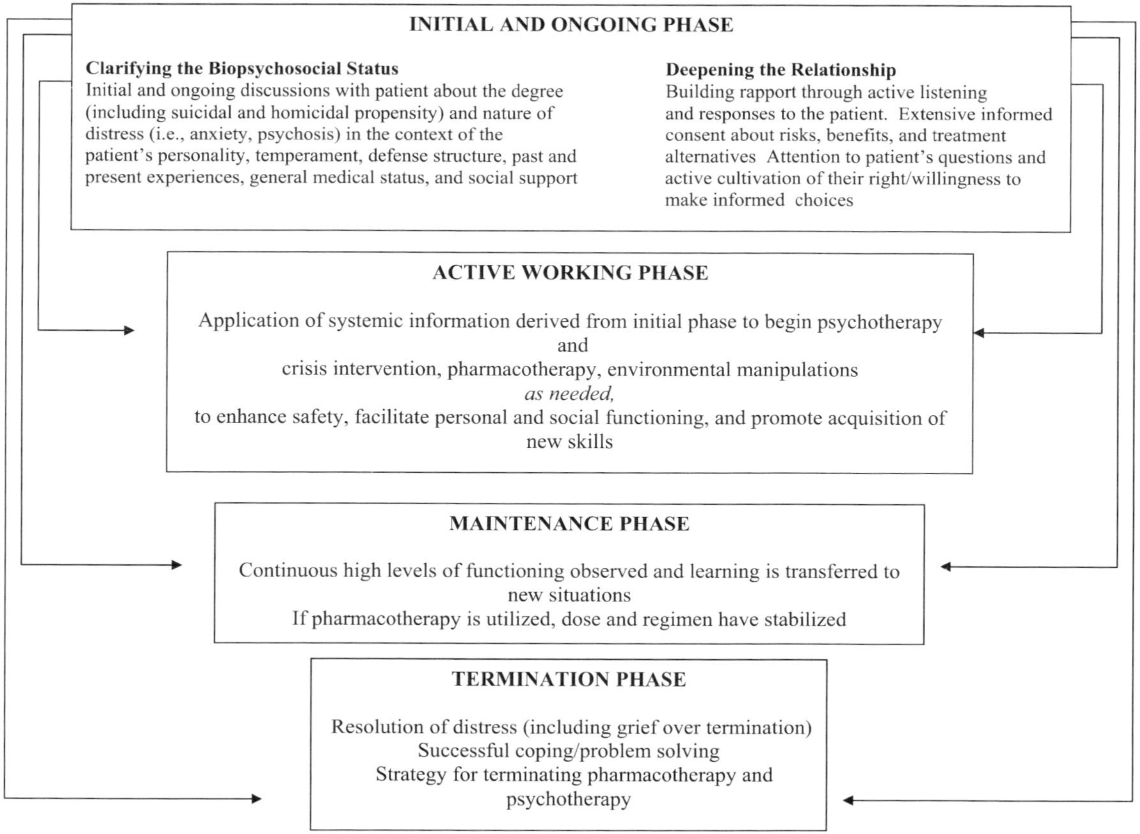

INITIAL AND ONGOING PHASE

Clarifying the Biopsychosocial Status
Initial and ongoing discussions with patient about the degree (including suicidal and homicidal propensity) and nature of distress (i.e., anxiety, psychosis) in the context of the patient's personality, temperament, defense structure, past and present experiences, general medical status, and social support

Deepening the Relationship
Building rapport through active listening and responses to the patient. Extensive informed consent about risks, benefits, and treatment alternatives Attention to patient's questions and active cultivation of their right/willingness to make informed choices

ACTIVE WORKING PHASE

Application of systemic information derived from initial phase to begin psychotherapy
and
crisis intervention, pharmacotherapy, environmental manipulations *as needed.*
to enhance safety, facilitate personal and social functioning, and promote acquisition of new skills

MAINTENANCE PHASE

Continuous high levels of functioning observed and learning is transferred to new situations
If pharmacotherapy is utilized, dose and regimen have stabilized

TERMINATION PHASE

Resolution of distress (including grief over termination)
Successful coping/problem solving
Strategy for terminating pharmacotherapy and psychotherapy

Figure 12.2 Initial and Ongoing Phase of Clarifying the Disorder and Deepening the Relationship

Clarifying the Biopsychosocial Nature of the PTSD and Comorbid Disorder(s)	Deepening the Relationship
Ongoing discussions w/patient about the degree (including suicidal and homicidal tendencies) and nature of distress (e.g., anxiety, substance abuse, mood instability) in the context of patient's personality, temperament, defense structure, cognitions, past/present experiences including traumatization, general medical status, and social support	**Building of trust and understanding through active listening and responses to the patient's concerns and extensive informed consent about risks, benefits, and alternative interventions in the context of the patient's goalsand gathered data**
• Differentiating symptoms of distress from identifiable psychological disorder(s), chronic and dysfunctional thoughts/ behaviors, reactions to the social environment	• Considering the patient's desires for change, the symptoms that are most problematic to the patient and the "side-effects" of behavior changes or medication that cannot be tolerated
• Assessing the patient's capacity to achieve goals by the most minimally invasive techniques	• Actively collaborating with the patient about risks, benefits, and alternative treatments such as:
• Differentiating symptoms of PTSD from underlying medical conditions	• Creating a protective environment through frequent sessions, social structures, or inpatient treatment
• Assessing if goals can be achieved first by psychotherapy alone	• Considering medication alternatives that have shown empirical support in the treatment of PTSD
• Ensuring that medication targets the core of the disorder rather than "chasing" symptoms	• Determining whether to initiate prompt versus long-term relief for symptoms
• Adjusting the psychotherapy and/or pharmacotherapy if the diagnosis changes and as patient improves	• Appropriateness of various forms of psychotherapeutic interventions (e.g., EMDR, Stress Inoculation Training (SIT), cognitive interventions, exposure therapy)
	• Appropriateness of uncovering (allowing patient to access own strengths) and using medication later in therapy

symptoms as long as the medication's side effects do not include weight gain. Another patient with the same presenting problem might want treatment but be unwilling to risk the "side-effect" of leaving the marriage.

Central to relationship building with patients is continual education about different forms of treatment and their efficacy. For example, in treating PTSD, the potential benefits of behavioral rehearsal in stressful situations, hypnosis, cognitive behavioral restructuring, stress inoculation training, or cathartic techniques may be reviewed with the patient. In addition to this discussion of costs and benefits, practitioners employing a biopsychosocial model will integrate a discussion of the potential benefits, risks, and alternatives to psychotropic interventions, as well as relevant allopathic remedies (e.g., yoga, acupuncture, dietary changes, herbal/vitamin supplements, reflexology, and therapeutic massage).

In these authors' clinical experiences, patients suffering from PTSD tend not to initially reveal details of traumatic events. Because the trauma is often associated with shame or secrecy (Holmes, Grey, & Young, 2005), individuals may initiate treatment or be referred because of some other presenting complaint, such as difficulty sleeping, problems with irritability, or substance abuse. In a traditional medical model, these symptoms may be treated with medication, with minimal and/or no attempt to integrate awareness of causal factors. In contrast, the biopsychosocial, collaborative model seeks to enhance the interaction between the patient's increasing insight, the practice of new skills, and the use of medication, when indicated, to maximize the opportunity for success by marshalling the patient's existing strengths to regain balance. In the integrated biopsychosocial model of care, medication may be used early in treatment to relieve acute symptoms that are incapacitating, or to address conditions for which pharmacotherapy is the treatment of choice (e.g., recurrent or treatment-resistant depression). Otherwise, empirically supported psychological interventions are preferred as a first-line approach to uncover and treat the underlying condition(s) so that the patient can achieve his or her goals with the most minimally invasive techniques and those least likely to incur potentially lethal or troubling side effects. The focus of a biopsychosocial model of care will be to determine if recovery can be achieved by psychotherapy alone or if medication is needed because of acute, disabling, recurring, or otherwise intractable symptoms.

A critical aspect of the initial and ongoing phase is the dynamic clarification of the diagnoses. While PTSD is characterized by a cluster of symptoms, as summarized in the (*DSM–IV–TR;* American Psychiatric Association, 2000), therapists operating from a biopsychosocial model of care recognize that the exact nature of symptoms and the type and degree of distress will reflect the patient's underlying personality, temperament, typical defense structures, cognitions, behaviors, past and present experiences, and degree of social support. For example, individuals with pretrauma rigid personality types are more likely to suffer PTSD than those who are more flexible. The rigid views could be positive views about the self as extremely competent and the world as extremely safe, which would contradict the traumatic event, or rigid negative views about the self as being extremely incompetent and the world as being extremely dangerous, which would be confirmed by the traumatic event (Foa & Rothbaum, 1998). Also, it is logical to postulate that patients with vulnerable temperaments before a trauma, such as highly anxious individuals, will be more likely to experience exacerbation of their premorbid vulnerable temperament traits. Patients whose coping mechanisms involve dissociation may be more vulnerable to PTSD. Dissociative symptoms include emotional numbing, derealization, depersonalization, and out of body experiences. It has been suggested that such reactions reflect a defensive response related to "freezing" in animals (Nijenhuis, Vanderlinden, & Spinhoven, 1998). A number of studies have indicated that dissociation shortly after a trauma is a good predictor of later PTSD (Engelhard, van den Hout, Kindt, Arntz, & Schouten, 2003; Holeva & Tarrier, 2001; and Murray, Ehlers, & Mayou, 2002). Very likely, individuals who have relied upon dissociation for dealing with stress in the past will experience more dissociation during a traumatic event and are more likely to experience PTSD after a traumatic event. Janoff-Bulman (1992) has suggested that previous trauma may be a risk factor for later PTSD after a second trauma, because the patient has not reestablished the sense of a stable and secure world. For these reasons and others, many disorders, such as anxiety, depression, and substance abuse, may accompany PTSD (Schnurr, Friedman, & Bernardy, 2002).

A practitioner operating from a biopsychosocial model of care is careful to differentiate the symptoms of PTSD from underlying medical conditions. Exposure to trauma increases the risk of poor physical health (Schnurr et al., 2002; Schnurr & Jankowski, 1999). Further, Boscarino (1997) reported a direct link between trauma and a broad spectrum of medical conditions in a 20-year follow-up of men initially exposed to severe stress. David, Woodward, Esquenazi, and Mellman (2004) compared male veterans admitted to a rehabilitation unit for PTSD or alcohol dependence; and the results indicated that PTSD subjects were more likely than were their substance abusing counterparts to have diabetes mellitus, heart disease, obesity, and osteoarthritis. Before diagnosing PTSD or other anxiety conditions as the primary diagnosis, it is important to rule out other medical conditions that present with anxiety. These include heart disease, angina, mitral valve prolapse, congestive heart failure, hyperthyroidism, systemic lupus erythematosus, anemia, asthma, chronic obstructive pulmonary disease, and pneumonia.

It is similarly important to differentiate symptoms of PTSD from reactions to or side effects of other medications. Many classes of drugs used for medical as well as psychiatric conditions can cause symptoms of anxiety (such as bronchodialators, psychostimulants, and corticosteroids). Further, rapid discontinuation of some medications may precipitate anxiety (e.g., benzodiazepines, sedative hypnotics). Psychological side effects of over-the-counter medications such as migraine, allergy, cold, pain, diuretic, and stimulant medicines (e.g. NoDoz, Vivarin, Excedrin Migraine, Midol, Aquaban, and Triaminicin) should also be considered. As part of the biopsychosocial approach to assessment and treatment, a nutritional evaluation of dietary factors that could promote or worsen anxiety is necessary. For instance, excessive consumption of foods rich in caffeine, such as coffee, soda, chocolate, and black tea, can be anxiogenic. Use of nicotine through smoking or smokeless intake and use of herbal/dietary supplements, such as products containing guarana, should also be considered as part of the assessment of diet, medications, and lifestyle.

Because the severity of the patient's PTSD or comorbid conditions may change over time, the therapist employing a biopsychosocial model of care constantly reevaluates the impact of psycho- and pharmacotherapeutic techniques, including the type and amount of the psychotropic intervention utilized, especially as it pertains to the patient's background experiences, underlying medical condition(s), and comorbid psychological conditions.

Active Working Phase

With the patient's unique strengths, vulnerabilities, and goals clearly in mind, the prescribing/medical psychologist and patient enter the active working phase of therapy. Aspects of the working phase are summarized in figure 12.3. Extensive research about PTSD indicates that attempts to suppress unwanted thoughts about the trauma usually do not work and, in fact, lead to the suppressed thoughts returning even more strongly (Dunmore, Clark, & Ehlers, 1999; Steil & Ehlers, 2000; and Wenzlaff & Wegner, 2000). Relatedly, Horowitz (1986), a pioneer in the field of PTSD, argues that when faced with the trauma, patients' initial response is "outcry and despair." Gradually, the victim of the trauma tries to assimilate the new traumatic information with previous conceptions of the self. Because of information overload, two opposing processes are at work: defending against the overload by suppression of the trauma and working through the traumatic material so that it can be integrated into self. A number of psychological techniques can reduce the denial and dissociation and thereby facilitate working through the trauma and integrating it into the perception of self. As mentioned previously, the deepening of the therapeutic relationship and discussion of the diagnoses with the patient help create a therapeutic environment in which the patient feels safer to allow the traumatic material to be expressed. Psychodynamic approaches, hypnosis, eye movement desensitization reprocessing (EMDR), stress inoculation therapy, exposure therapy, cognitive therapy, imagery rehearsal therapy, group psychoeducational treatments, and family sessions in which the family is encouraged to talk about the trauma are all therapies that have been used with varying levels of success to facilitate healthy expression of the traumatic experience. In more intractable cases, or when these psychological techniques alone are not sufficient to allow a balanced working through of the traumatic material, the treatment may be supplemented with psychopharmacological interventions.

Pharmacological Treatment of PTSD

While no specific drug or medication combination is known to cure or prevent PTSD, the selective serotonin reuptake inhibitors (SSRIs) have become the initial pharmacotherapeutic treatment of choice for this condition (see table 12.1).

Figure 12.3 Active Working Phase

Application of systemic information derived from initial phase to begin psychotherapy and—*as needed*—crisis intervention, pharmacotherapy, environmental manipulations, to enhance safety, facilitate personal, social functioning and promote acquisition of new skills

— Consider medication and psychotherapy to reduce dissociation and facilitate optimal function

— Therapist and medication as transference objects

— Deepening relationship (ongoing from phase 1)

— Informed consent about psychotherapeutic techniques and pharmacotherapeutic intervention in order to optimize the collaborative process

— Adherence to homework and medication regimen

Selective Serotonin Reuptake Inhibitors: The SSRIs are generally preferred because of their broad range of efficacy in the treatment of PTSD and its comorbid conditions, such as depression, substance abuse, and panic disorders, and because the SSRIs are relatively safe in comparison to the other antidepressants, such as tricyclic antidepressants (which can cause cardiac conduction problems and can be fatal in overdose). Also, a decrease in serotonin has been implicated in the symptomology associated with PTSD as evidenced by fewer paroxetine binding sites on platelets of subjects with PTSD (Fichtner, O'Connor, Yeoh, Aurora, & Crayton, 1995). Currently, sertraline (Zoloft) and paroxetine (Paxil) are the only two SSRIs with FDA indications for the treatment of PTSD. FDA approval is based on results of large, multisite, randomized, double-blind controlled studies. However, it is generally accepted that off-label use of any of the other SSRIs may be equally efficacious. Therefore, selection of a particular SSRI is based on factors such as patient and family history, personal patient preference, side effect profile as related to possible aggravation or amelioration of prominent/disabling symptoms, and factors affecting the likelihood of adherence. Importantly, the off-label use of an SSRI or any other medication, even if common practice, should be discussed with the patient as part of the informed consent process. Other SSRIs that may be considered for off-label use include citalopram (Celexa) and escitalopram (Lexapro). The mixed serotonin agonist/antagonist, m etachlorophenylpiperazine (mCPP), should be avoided because it has been shown to produce flashbacks in a subset of individuals suffering from PTSD (Southwick et al., 1993). Similarly, yohimbine, an alpha-2 antagonist, should also be avoided in patients with PTSD. For instance, in one noteworthy study, Southwick et al. (1997) administered yohimbine intravenously to PTSD subjects and found that 70 percent experienced panic attacks and 40 percent experienced dissociative symptoms, such as flashbacks, while placebo demonstrated no panic attacks and only one flashback.

Table 12.1 Selective Serotonin Reuptake Inhibitors for the Treatment of Posttraumatic Stress Disorder

Chemical Name	Trade Name	Dosage	PTSD Symptom Benefits			
			Global Improvement	Reexperiencing	Avoidance	Hyperarousal
Fluoxetine	Prozac	20–60 mg/d	Yes	Yes	Yes	Yes
*Sertraline	Zoloft	50–200 mg/d	No	Yes	Yes	Yes
*Paroxetine	Paxil	20–60 mg/d	Yes	Yes	Yes	Yes

*FDA approved for treatment of PTSD

Source: VA/DOD Clinical Practice Guidelines Working Group, 2003.

Second Generation Antidepressants: The results of efficacy studies of the second generation antidepressants, also known as "novel" antidepressants, are mixed so that these antidepressants are typically considered second-line agents (see table 12.2). However, a recent 12-week, double-blind, multicenter trial compared the effectiveness of the novel antidepressant, venlafaxine ER (Effexor ER), to the SSRI, sertraline (Zoloft), and to placebo in the short-term treatment of PTSD. Venlafaxine ER (Effexor ER) demonstrated the highest remission rate. The rates of remission reported at week 12 were as follows: 19.6 percent for placebo, 24.3 percent for sertraline, and 30.2 percent for venlafaxine ER (Davidson, 2006). It is possible that the other serotonin norepinephrine reuptake inhibitor, duloxetine (Cymbalta), could have similar benefits, but there are no current data to support this assumption. Of all of the novel antidepressants, buproprion (Wellbutrin) has demonstrated the least efficacy and, according to several anecdotal reports, may even increase symptoms of PTSD (Asnis, Kohn, Henderson, & Brown (2004).

Other Antidepressants: Tricyclic antidepressants (TCAs), such as amitriptyline (Elavil) and imipramine (Tofranil) may be considered third-line agents in the treatment of PTSD (Davidson, 1990, 1993; Kosten, Frank, Dan, McDougle, & Giller El, Jr. (2003) because their characteristic, and sometimes fatal, side effect profile reduces both safety and tolerability (see table 12.3).

Thus, TCAs should be considered after safer and more easily tolerated alternative agents have failed. The monoamine oxidase inhibitors (MAOIs) are also

Table 12.2 Novel Antidepressants for the Treatment of Posttraumatic Stress Disorder

Buproprion	Canive et al., 1998	No change in total CAPS score
Nefazodone	Davis et al., 2000	Significant improvement in CAPS[a], HAM-D[b]
	Garfield et al., 2001	Significant improvement in CAPS, anxiety
	Gillin et al., 2001	Significant improvement in sleep, CAPS
	Hertzberg et al., 1998	CGI scores were "much improved"
	Hidalgo et al., 1999	High response rate; pooled data, 6 studies
	Zisook et al., 2000	PTSD symptoms lessened, CAPS
Trazadone	Hertzberg et al., 1996	Four patients "much improved"
	Warner et al., 2001	Reduction in nightmares; 9 reports priapism
Venlafaxine	Hamner et al., 1998	Case report of positive response
	Smajkic et al., 2001	Significant improvement, Bosnian refugees
Mirtazapine	Bahk et al., 2002	Significant improvement in IES[c], MADRS[d]
	Connor et al., 1999	Clinical improvement in > 50% of patients

Source: VA/DOD Clinical Practice Guidelines Working Group, 2003.
[a]CAPS is Clinician Administered PTSD Scale (1995)
[b]HAM-D is the Hamilton Rating Scale for Depression (1960)
[c]IES is the Impact of Event Scale (1979)
[d]MADRS is the Montgomery Åsberg Depression Rating Scale (1979)

Table 12.3 Tricyclic Antidepressants for the Treatment of Posttraumatic Stress Disorder

Amitriptyline	Elavil	Davidson et al., 1990	Effective for core symptoms of PTSD
		Davidson et al., 1993	Significant improvement: IES, CGI, HAM-D
		Cavaljuga et al., 2003	Significant improvement in acute symptoms of PTSD
Clomipramine	Anafranil	Muraoka et al., 1996	One case report
Desipramine	Norpramin	Reist et al., 1989	Did not show efficacy; no statistics
Imipramine	Tofranil	Kosten et al., 1991	Significant improvement, CAPS-2, IES
Nortriptyline	Pamelor	Zygmont et al., 1998 Dow et al., 1997	Effective for traumatic grief symptoms Improvement in CGE for dual diagnosis
Protriptyline	Vivactil	No studies, 1990–2006	

Source: VA/DOD Clinical Practice Guidelines Working Group, 2003.

considered third-line agents because of the potentially life-threatening side effect of hypertensive crisis when combined with foods containing tyramine or when taken in combination with drugs that increase sympathetic transmission, as well as the serious side effect of serotonin syndrome when taken with serotonergic agents. While two of the newer reversible inhibitors of monoamine oxidase type A (RIMAs), meclobemide (Manerix) and brofaromine (Consonar), have shown greater safety than the MAOIs and significant efficacy in the treatment of PTSD (Katz et al., 1994), they are currently not available in the United States.

Antiandrenergic Agents: Because autonomic hyperarousal is one of the common core symptoms of PTSD, medications that decrease sympathetic reactions have been utilized to dampen the response commonly known as "fight or flight." The four most commonly utilized agents are prazosin (Minipress), clonidine (Catapres), propanolol (Inderal), and guanfacine (Tenex). These agents can be beneficial in reducing nightmares, hypervigilance, hyperarousal, and rage (Simon & Gormon, 2004). The data for prazosin (Minipres), however, appear to be strongest. For example, Raskinde (2003) found this centrally acting, alpha1 adrenergic antagonist effective in reducing nightmares, sleep disturbance, and other PTSD symptoms. However, although these agents have held a theoretical attraction based on their sympatholytic properties, their clinical impact has been generally disappointing.

Table 12.4 The Use of Antiandrenergic Agents in the Treatment of Posttraumatic Stress Disorder

Clonidine	Catapres	.2 mg (three times/day)
Prazosin	Minipress	6-10 mg/d
Propranolol	Inderal	40 mg/d
Guanfacine	Tenex	.5 mg (three times/day)

Source: VA/DOD Clinical Practice Guidelines Working Group, 2003.

Further, data are emerging for the use of antiandrenergic agents to prevent the development of flashbacks if given soon after the traumatic event. Psychological theories of PTSD are built upon the concept that normal events are stored as verbally accessible memories (VAM) in which the temporal context is included so that the memories can be experienced as happening in the past. Conversely, it is theorized that highly traumatic events may be encoded in a more perceptual, automatic fashion, referred to as situationally accessible memories (SAM). These memories lack temporal context and thus are reexperienced in the present (Brewin & Holmes, 2003). It is hypothesized that beta-andrenergic stress hormones stimulate the amygdala, thereby increasing the storage of intense memories in the hippocampus. Beta-adrenergic blockade with antiandrenergic agents, especially propanalol, is theoretically believed to selectively impair memory for emotionally arousing material without impairment of long-term memory or memory for neutral stimuli (Strange & Dolan, 2004). The use of antiandrenergic agents to reduce the retention of emotionally charged memories is highly experimental, and there are no specific guidelines for their therapeutic use. In fact, there is much debate at this time regarding the advisability of prescribing these drugs for the suppression of memory, since the risks may outweigh the benefits given the current state of the evidence. When they are used in such an off-label manner, informed consent is essential, and thus far, most clinicians have not adopted these drugs in the treatment of PTSD, given the controversy and limited research. When used, however, these medications should be started at low doses and titrated slowly. Frequent monitoring of blood pressure is necessary, particularly in long-term use. Patients should be reminded not to discontinue any of these medications abruptly, to avoid the possibility of rebound hypertension (see table 12.4).

Benzodiazepines: Benzodiazepines may reduce anxiety and improve sleep in PTSD. However, they do not control or eliminate the core symptoms of PTSD. A significant limitation of this class of drugs is their addictive potential. Further, these drugs can cause or intensify depression and worsen anxiety by a phenomenon known as "rebound," which results as the drug wears off. Because of their tendency to produce cognitive blunting and problems with memory, benzodiazepines may also interfere with the therapeutic cognitive processing of the trauma. These drugs may be considered for short-term, adjunctive use but it is best to utilize them sparingly and only after considering or utilizing the first-line agents for long-term treatment of anxiety and sleep problems. As with any use of benzodiazepines, careful monitoring for sedation, abuse, depression, and mental clouding is essential.

Other Psychotropic Drugs: Psychotropic drugs other than antidepressants and antianxiety agents may be necessary to target residual PTSD symptoms and signs. Second generation (newer, atypical) antipsychotic drugs may relieve comorbid, psychotic-like features or anxiety refractory to other agents. These second-generation and third-generation antipsychotic agents include clozapine (Clozaril), risperidone (Risperdal), olanzapine (Zyprexa), quetiapine (Seroquel), ziprasidone (Geodon), and aripiprazole (Abilify). Because of the particularly serious side effects of leukopenia, seizures, and myocarditis/cardiomyopathy, clozapine (Clozaril) is not a first choice among the second-generation antipsychotic drugs. However, all second-generation antipsychotics carry a risk of metabolic syndrome and should therefore be used judiciously in patients with hyperlipdemia, diabetes, hypertension, obesity, and other vulnerable medical conditions. In addition to the risk of metabolic syndrome, first-generation (older, typical) antipsychotic drugs are more likely than second-generation drugs to produce significant motor side effects (tardive dyskinesia and the extrapyramidal syndromes of dystonic reactions, drug-induced Parkinsonism, and akathisia at clinically effective doses) and are also second-line choices to treat psychotic features in PTSD.

Therapist and Medication as Transference Objects

Therapists have long understood that patients may transfer their feelings about others onto the therapist. Therapeutic interpretation of this transference, rather than reaction to it, can facilitate patients' understanding of their underlying dynamics and the way they are approaching others in their world. Interpretation of transference may be particularly relevant for PTSD patients. Many victims of trauma develop altered worldviews with negative appraisals of the self and others (Ehlers & Clark, 2000). Thoughts that others are dangerous or cannot be trusted may perpetuate the PTSD patient's isolation and hypervigilance. The patient may project these feelings onto the therapist. The interpretation of the patient's anger or distrust created by the trauma may help the patient challenge his/her generalizations about an unsafe world. Thus, the interpretation can foster a more appropriate integration of the traumatic event into a productive worldview. In addition to interpreting possible transference to the therapist of the patient's anger and distress about the traumatic event, medication may also be viewed as a possible transference object. For example, a PTSD patient with significant hypervigilance and anxiety may express much anxiety about taking medication. A patient who is very angry because of a traumatic event may be quite pessimistic about a medication's potential value; or a patient who is denying much of the trauma may eschew medication, even though the symptoms appear overwhelming. Also, the tendency for many serotonergic agents to be experienced as anxiogenic, based on the side effect known as "activation," may be misinterpreted by the patient as a worsening of anxiety, and if not considered within the framework of a type of "inoculation" for this common side effect, may lead to further mistrust of the therapist and/or the medication. These scenarios can be predicted through enhanced education and addressed palliatively when necessary, thereby enhancing the therapeutic relationship and the opportunity for successful outcome.

Informed Consent about Psychotherapeutic Techniques and Pharmacotherapeutic Intervention in Order to Increase Patient Autonomy

In addition to offering support and interpretation, psychologists impart information to patients as a way of increasing autonomy. Educating patients may be particularly important in the treatment of PTSD. A requirement of the PTSD diagnosis, according to the *Diagnostic and Statistical Manual of Mental Disorders*, fourth edition, text revision *(DSM–IV–TR;* American Psychiatric Association, 2000), is the experience of intense helplessness as well as a sense of fear or horror. Related to the concept of helplessness, Ehlers and Clark (2000, p. 45) defined mental defeat as "the perceived loss of all autonomy, a state of giving up in one's own mind all efforts to retain one's identity as a human being with a will of one's own." The concept of mental defeat well reflects the statements of trauma victims who describe themselves as being destroyed, permanently damaged, or ceasing to care whether they live or die. When patients are offered information about PTSD or become educated about PTSD through bibliotherapy, their sense of autonomy is increased, thereby reducing their feelings of helplessness and mental defeat. When a therapist operating from a biopsychosocial model of care educates PTSD patients about the effects and side effects of medications and educates patients on how to monitor their own change, the medication becomes an integral part of the therapeutic process to build autonomy and optimize the collaborative process.

Maintenance Phase

When the major symptoms of PTSD have been ameliorated, the therapist and patient enter the maintenance phase of treatment, which is outlined in figure 12.4. In this important phase, patients are given an opportunity to solidify their learnings and to transfer their skills to new situations. The patient is encouraged to assume more independence in understanding himself or herself and interpreting his or her behavior. In this phase, the PTSD patient may, for example, be encouraged to approach environments and activities that are increasingly similar to the trauma and have previously triggered flashbacks, nightmares, and other symptoms of hyperarousal. For instance, a patient suffering PTSD following a car accident that occurred while driving in a night storm with limited visibility may become very fearful of driving. Seeing cars, hearing about car accidents, and watching them on television may trigger PTSD symptomology. During the action phase, this patient could practice a gradient of activities similar to those of the traumatic event, such as riding in a car in daytime, driving in the daytime, and then driving at night. By the maintenance phase, the patient's success in driving becomes routine, and this successful plateau is recognized and reinforced in the therapy.

During the maintenance phase, the therapist may begin to reduce both the number of sessions and, depending on the length of treatment and current dose, the amount of medication. In doing so, the patient becomes more confident that his or her gains in managing the PTSD have been internalized.

In addition to the potential for recurrence of PTSD symptoms, the PTSD diagnosis is often comorbid with other conditions, such as depression and substance abuse; therefore, it is necessary in the maintenance phase to talk about signs of relapse and how this would be approached. In other words, the patient is educated about symptoms to watch for and the kind of psychotherapeutic intervention and medication that may be helpful if he/she does relapse.

A special issue for the prescribing/medical psychologist employing a biopsychosocial model during this phase is that many patients will report that their medications seem to become less efficacious over time. This phenomenon is sometimes referred to as "SSRI poop out" or simply noted as a loss of effect (Barnhart, Makela, & Latocha, 2004; McGrath, Quitkin, & Klein, 1995; and Quitken, Stewart, McGrath, Nunes, Ocepek-Welikson, Tricamo, Rabkin, Ross, & Klein, 1993).

The causes of the reduced effectiveness, if present, can be varied and so signal a need to review current psychosocial circumstances, since this phenomenon is often observed during times of increased stress and social demands. The phenomenon may also prompt a need for changes in medication and/or psychotherapy. Further, the field of psychopharmacology is growing so rapidly that there may be more effective medications on the market than those prescribed for

Figure 12.4 Maintenance Phase

Gains are solidified and learning is transferred to new situations

- Patient assumes more independence in reinforcing the self
- Number of sessions are reduced
- Medications may be reduced
- May need relapse prevention and intervention
- May need to change medication if no longer effective or new medications are more efficacious
- Discussing long-term side-effects of changes in the psychosocial environment (i.e., divorce) as well as temporary and permanent medication effects (i.e., sexual side effects, tardive dyskinesia)

---

the patient initially. Therefore, during the maintenance phase, the patient is alerted to signs and symptoms that a medication may need to be changed; and, in some cases, medications may still need to be altered within this phase. The dosage may require adjustment or an alternate medication may need to be prescribed.

During the maintenance phase of therapy, the cost/benefit of personal changes as well as medication effects may need to be reevaluated. For example, a PTSD patient who is feeling very dependent may now be stronger and may need to change the nature of relationships. In other words, relationships formed when the patient suffered serious symptoms of PTSD and was feeling very helpless may no longer be functional. Similarly, as the patient improves, there may be certain side effects to medication (such as the sexual side effect or weight gain) that the patient is no longer willing to tolerate or that are no longer beneficial, as in the case of weight gain by an individual who had initially lost substantial weight due to loss of appetite. During the acute phase of treatment, the patient might have been willing to tolerate these side effects because of the potential gain in overcoming the PTSD symptoms. At a later point, with flashbacks under control, dissociative features resolved, appetite normalized, and relationships improved/discontinued, the patient may reassess the relative cost in terms of side effects in comparison to the benefits of the medication now that the symptoms are more manageable.

Termination Phase

As mentioned previously, a common aspect of PTSD is a shattering of one's assumptions that the world is stable and safe (Janoff-Bulman, 1992). Termination must be handled judiciously as outlined in figure 12.5 so that the patient does not reexperience a sense that the world is dangerously unpredictable and that the patient is alone in coping with difficulties. For the therapist employing a biopsychosocial model of care, the fears of stopping both the psychotherapy and the medication must be carefully addressed in the termination phase. In order to further build the patient's sense of autonomy, the therapist decides with the patient how rapidly this psychotherapy and medication should be discontinued. Information is shared with the patient regarding the recommended length of treatment on a particular medication and the speed with which the medication should be reduced. The patient's readiness for doing this will be integrated into the termination plan. The potential benefit of having periodic follow-up sessions will be decided collaboratively. In addition, if it is determined that it would be wise to continue on the medication for an extended time, the nature of the changing therapeutic relationship will be fully explored in this termination phase. More specifically, the follow-up sessions may involve less dynamic working through of psychological issues or less active cognitive behavioral exercises or exposure and more discussion of how the patient is responding to the medication. Typically, the time between sessions is extended when medications are maintained, and a timeline for tapering is instituted, if this is an option. In some cases, tapering is attempted and unsuccessful and medication is maintained over an extended time.

Figure 12.5 Termination

Successful resolution of reliance upon therapy and any grieving associated with ending the therapeutic relationship, with specific consideration of how quickly psychotherapy and medication should be discontinued

- Assessing how rapidly the psychotherapy and the medication should be terminated
- If changing to periodic medication checks, discussing the nature of the change in the relationship with the patient
- Dealing with fears about stopping psychotherapy or stopping the medication (which may include review of attachment issues and overreliance on pharmacological interventions)

CASE 1

Case 1 is an active duty soldier who served in Iraq and was treated by the second author. His case demonstrates some classic symptoms of a patient who presents with primary symptoms of PTSD, but who first required medication and a deepening of the therapeutic relationship before he could disclose the traumatic events he had experienced. The case exemplifies the importance of understanding various psychosocial stressors and noting how they can change during the therapy process. Psychotropic intervention alleviating primary anxiety symptoms was, of necessity, initiated early in therapy. This case also exemplifies how adopting a biopsychosocial model facilitates working with the adult patient in a collaborative fashion to help establish the type of medication and the type of psychotherapy and to set a course for the mutual monitoring of change.

Identifying Data and Reason for Referral

E.C. was a 30-year-old, white, married male, active duty enlisted airman with 10 years of continuous active duty service working as an aircraft specialist. He was referred to the second author by his primary care physician for assistance with anxiety management after unsuccessful attempts to treat his panic symptoms with paroxetine (Paxil) up to 20 mg/day, escitalopram (Lexapro) up to 10 mg/day and clonazepam (Klonopin) up to .5 mg twice a day. The patient's chief complaint at the time of intake was: "I feel something is wrong with my head.... I don't feel like I'm normal."

Initial and Ongoing Phase

The initial assessment involved determining the patient's biopsychosocial status. During the initial assessment, the patient presented with uncontrollable "anxiety attacks." He complained of unrelenting difficulty with nervousness (especially around crowds), irritability, which seemed to worsen in traffic, and difficulty sleeping. He often avoided going to malls, movie theaters, and restaurants, and was uncomfortable any place there were groups of people. He described frequent feelings of rage toward "slow" drivers because of his previous deployments to Iraq and Afghanistan: "if you slowed down, or worse yet, stopped on a convoy, you were an easy target for attack and could be dead in seconds." He further described difficulty concentrating and symptoms of panic: heart palpitations, gastrointestinal upset, sweating, feelings of unsteadiness, and a sense of impending doom, which occurred spontaneously, several times a day, with each episode lasting approximately 10 minutes. Concomitantly, he described generalized, low-grade anxiety in the form of an overall "keyed up" feeling. However, as is often the case with sufferers from PTSD, despite direct questioning about possible deployment-related traumatic events, he could not (or would not) elaborate on the stresses he had endured during any of his deployments. Other aspects of the biopsychosocial assessment revealed that E.C. had a history of self-mutilation starting at age 14. He was treated by a therapist for approximately one year from ages 15 to 16. He insisted that his cutting behaviors were never a reflection of suicidal or homicidal tendencies, and he had no history of suicide attempts or other self-destructive behaviors. His only other prior contact with mental health services was through military anger management classes that he had taken the year before, as a result of his labile reaction to his divorce from his wife of five years. His only significant medical or surgical history was a two-year diagnosis of hypertension. E.C.'s psychosocial family history revealed that both sisters suffered depression and anxiety. The paternal medical history was positive for myocardial infarction, hypercholesterolemia, and obstructive sleep apnea, while the maternal history revealed hypertension, rheumatoid arthritis and asthma.

His medication regimen at the time of intake consisted of escitalopram (Lexapro) 10 mg daily, hydrochlorothiazide/triamterene (Maxzide) 50–75 mg daily and loratadine (Claritin) 10 mg daily. He had no known drug allergies.

E.C. began drinking alcohol at age 18. He denied use of alcohol or cigarettes for the previous 12 months because he had decided to adopt a healthy lifestyle. He had no history of alcohol-related incidents, including DUIs/DWIs. His caffeine intake was moderate (three 12-oz cans of Mountain Dew per day). He did not take any herbal or diet supplements, over the counter medicines or illicit substances.

Significant social history centered on his middle and high school years, when he was ridiculed by peers for his short stature. E.C. believed that this humiliation was the source of his low self-esteem and self-mutilation. He denied any physical, emotional, or sexual abuse. His history revealed no conduct problems, suspensions, expulsions, or legal infractions throughout high school.

E.C.'s personality style was primarily avoidant, passive-dependent, and obsessive compulsive. He often hesitated in an effort to correct his speech so as not to offend, and he would apologize liberally for "wasting" the therapist's time. In addition to these individual personality dynamics, there were at least two cultural dynamics conspiring to place him in the role of subordinate: the medical culture's expectation that mental health treatments be "prescribed," and the military culture, which required E.C. (who was several grades below the second author in rank) to defer to senior officers. Special attention to the development of rapport and active discussion and explanation of the collaborative therapist-patient role was essential so that E.C. could become comfortable with his new roles as equal partner and esteemed expert on the subject of himself. The deepening of the therapeutic relationship in his case included fostering his risk-taking behaviors while in session (such as his use of "forbidden" language), his willingness to openly voice disagreement, and the practicing of other assertive behaviors directly with the therapist.

As a result of the information gathered during the first session, E.C. was given working diagnoses of panic attacks with agoraphobia and generalized anxiety disorder. He was informed about the diagnoses and the various treatments available for these conditions, both pharmacological and nonpharmacological. E.C. preferred individual psychotherapy, despite learning that group therapy could be utilized as a useful desensitization activity for his anxiety and agoraphobia, because he considered a group setting too intimidating, and he wished to continue utilizing medications to alleviate the disabling autonomic instability he felt on a daily basis. After some education about the pharmacologic treatment of anxiety, E.C. expressed an understanding of the value of incorporating a serotonergic agent in the pharmacological treatment of his anxiety and stated his preference for cognitive behavioral therapeutic (CBT) strategies (because of his natural proclivity to monitor and record his behaviors such as exercise, number of repetitions, amount of strength training during exercise, etc.).

Active Working Phase

As mentioned previously, E.C. had been placed on escitalopram by a previous healthcare provider. The possible benefits of increasing E.C.'s dosage of the escitalopram were discussed. E.C. did not experience any improvement on the 10 mg dose of escitalopram despite a three-month trial. Moreover, E.C. had a tendency to forget to take his medicine from time to time. Because of these factors, it was mutually elected to switch to fluoxetine (Prozac), a serotonergic agent with a long half-life that would be less likely to result in wide fluctuations of serum fluoxetine levels based on missed doses. E.C. was informed that one of the risks of fluoxetine use is a side effect known as activation, which can feel much like anxiety and therefore could initially appear to worsen his symptoms. E.C. creatively asked whether he could utilize the clonazepam already prescribed by his primary care doctor to alleviate these symptoms. E.C. was commended for his active participation in treatment planning by deducing a palliative strategy for the potential activation by the fluoxetine. The short term use of the benzodiazepine, clonazepam, was indeed incorporated into his treatment plan, and the value of his input in the collaborative process and learning to take increased responsibility for his care and well-being was reaffirmed.

Most of E.C.'s symptoms continued to improve over the following three months of his treatment, and he was able to participate in an anxiety-management psychoeducational group. As he improved, he began to accept more challenges. Also, he decided to remarry. About four months after beginning therapy, E.C.

complained that the fluoxetine was no longer effective, and he felt unable to use previously effective coping techniques to control his anxiety. Buspirone (BuSpar) 20 mg daily was added to his treatment regimen. E.C. showed only minimal response to this pharmacological intervention. He complained of anxiety and depression, worrisome irritability including "road rage," and disturbing night-mares. When the nightmares were probed therapeutically for recurring themes, E.C. was finally willing/able to introduce traumatic incidents that occurred dur-ing his first deployment; trauma he had denied during the initial data-gathering stage of therapy.

E.C. reported that he had deployed shortly after September 11, 2004, just two months after the World Trade Center terrorist attack, to a classified location in Iraq. His deployment activities were rapid paced and very stressful. Shortly after his arrival, he was assigned to clean up an aircraft that housed the dead, muti-lated bodies of fallen aircrew. "There was blood, and tissues, and bloody IV bags everywhere.... the bodies were taken off and then we had to clean the inside of the aircraft so that they [the air crew] could complete another mission that night." His stress was intensified because he had been participating in a classified mission and therefore could not discuss any of the events or activities of that traumatic event. The deepening of the therapeutic relationship and the experience of relief from pharmacotherapeutic treatment of his general anxiety symptoms allowed him to ultimately reveal this information in order to obtain further relief and targeted support for his PTSD symptoms. He explained that his persistent nightmares were the product of the images he saw during his deployment. Apart from the nightmares, he was amnesic for many of the events of that deployment except for other events in which "shots were being directly fired at [his crew]," requiring him to "take cover" on a frequent basis. E.C. later participated in two other Operation Iraqi Freedom (OIF) deployments, which he described as mili-tarily uneventful but emotionally charged because he received notice from his first wife during his third deployment that she had filed for divorce after their five years of marriage.

This therapeutic uncovering further revealed that in his dreams, he was reliving the ordeals that he had consciously repressed upon his return from deployment and that he had actively denied, despite specific questioning, during the initial assessment. Thus, he had reached a level of recovery in which he could cope with remembering and processing the events that were traumatic to him. At times, he attempted to utilize the old coping strategies and tried to convince the psychologist that "It really wasn't that bad.... there were other guys out there that had it worse than me.... I was just doing my job." In this new stage of treatment, work was done collaboratively with the patient to enable him to understand and agree to talk about these events as a means for treating his anxiety and nightmares. His recall and disclosure of traumatic events relatively late in the therapy process is not unusual for PTSD sufferers, who, as noted earlier, tend to withhold revealing traumatic events based on shame or secrecy , and illuminates why it is important for the diagnostic and rapport-building phase to continue throughout all stages of therapy. E.C.'s diagnostic formulation was appropriately modified to reflect these later emerging symptoms of PTSD.

The integrative, holistic approach to therapy within the context of a reliable, restorative therapeutic relationship allowed the therapist and patient to "piece together" the reasons for the resurgence/worsening of symptoms that went beyond the phenomenon commonly referred to as "SSRI poop out." At the time E.C. first revealed his history of traumatic events during deployment, he was also experiencing new stressors of increased work demands and wedding plans; but, also, he began to take energy supplements to assist his workout and in an effort to lose weight. E.C.'s blood pressure was unstable, and he was encouraged to discontinue the energy supplements based on their anxiogenic and hypertensive properties. The integrative approach included not only a focus on the updated diagnosis of PTSD but also consultation between his primary care physician and the therapist, which resulted in a decision by the primary care physician to add a long-acting form of propanolol (Inderal LA) to E.C.'s current antihypertensive regimen. It was believed that the antihypertensive would also add a palliative, sympatholytic effect in the management of the hyperarousal and rage symptoms E.C. was experiencing as part of his PTSD. Psychotherapy visits were increased in frequency and focused on relaxation and other cognitive behavioral responses to PTSD symptoms, such as controlled, imaginal reexposure. E.C. was instructed on the use of biofeedback techniques to be utilized at home and in the work setting for enhancing relaxation. Finally, a collaborative decision was made to switch from the selective serotonin reuptake inhibitor, fluoxetine (Prozac), 40 mg a day to the serotonin norepinephrine reuptake inhibitor, duloxetine (Cymbalta), 60 mg a day. The decision to switch from rather than increase Prozac was made as a result of the possible interaction effect between Prozac and propranolol, which can result in bradycardia at high doses due to cytochrome P-450 2D6 inhibition.

Maintenance Phase

The combination of psychotherapeutic, pharmacotherapeutic, and educational interventions resulted in overall improved functioning and health status for E.C. His blood pressure stabilized in the normal range, and he was once again able to exert control over his anxiety, although admittedly to a lesser extent with the PTSD symptoms than with the panic and worry. He invited his new wife to attend a therapy session in order to help her learn more about his battle with anxiety, and she was exceptionally supportive of his behavioral exercises and his occasional need to withdraw for private time to refocus his efforts in controlling his symptoms. E.C. was able to discontinue group treatment. His medication regimen remained stable with duloxetine as his only psychotropic agent, but he also continued use of antihypertensives, including propanolol, through his primary care physician. E.C.'s long-term treatment plan was to terminate treatment in three or four sessions, which would be set over an increasing time frame, and to continue with duoxetine, 60 mg, for at least another year. However, the provider was required to move prior to termination so that a therapist transfer was necessary.

Termination Phase

E.C.'s transfer was discussed openly, and the transition was accomplished uneventfully despite the therapist's and patient's mutual wish to have completed the journey together. Fortunately, at the time of transfer, E.C. achieved significant resolution of his most troubling symptoms, including nightmares, autonomic hyperarousal, panic attacks, obsessive worry, irritability, and road rage. He had generalized his relaxation and coping skills to the benefit of his work and home life. E.C. did not, however, believe he could tolerate future deployments, primarily because he feared that they would have a deleterious effect on his new marriage, as they had on his previous marriage. At the time of transfer, he was expected to separate from the Air Force through medical channels, specifically because of his inability to deploy.

CASE 2

Case 2 contrasts with Case 1 in several significant ways. First, the patient is a child who entered therapy with the first author. Second, this child suffered from significant neglect and probably also some biological deficits before incurring trauma from sexual abuse. In this dual diagnosis case, PTSD was secondary to other significant psychological and temperament problems; and progress in managing the patient's global, developmental, and adjustment difficulties needed to be addressed before the PTSD could be brought forth and worked through. Despite these differences, Case 2 is similar to Case 1 in several critical ways. In both cases, the patient (and in Case 2 also the mother of the patient) became active participants in selecting psychotherapy and medication treatment and became experts in analyzing the effectiveness of the treatment modalities. In both cases, medication as well as therapeutic techniques needed to be monitored and modified through the phases of the treatment process.

Identifying Data and Reason for Referral

J.W. was six years old when he was referred to the first author for therapy because of his overall adjustment difficulties. His performance in first grade was very poor. The teacher reported that he did not pay attention and did not complete tasks. The teacher and the child himself reported that he was not accepted by the other children. The teacher also observed that he often came to school "unkempt and smelly." When asked about his hygiene, the mother said that she tried to keep his clothes clean and statedthat he took baths; and she insisted that the smell was because "he had so much gas."

In addition to his school problems, his mother was concerned about his behavior at home. She explained that his tolerance for any frustration was low. He often seemed to not hear what she was saying and he would not follow instructions. He refused to clean up his room. He was often combative with his sister, who was three years old.

Initial and Ongoing Phase

As a part of the initial and ongoing phase of therapy, it was important to determine how J.W.'s presenting symptoms related to his biopsychosocial history. His kindergarten teacher was contacted to gain a better understanding of his earlier school performance. The kindergarten teacher reported that his skills seemed commensurate with the other children at that time. Further, he did turn in assignments. However, she had noted that it seemed he was not paying attention, even though he could complete the work requested of him. Moreover, the teacher also noted poor hygiene and rejection by his peers.

In terms of his psychosocial history, J.W.'s mother reported that she was using crack cocaine at the time of his birth. J.W.'s mother indicated that the father struggled with many learning difficulties and had trouble functioning independently. To the present, J.W.'s father is living with his own mother. The father calls J.W. occasionally but has not been an active part of his life since shortly after J.W.'s birth. The mother reported that she performed well throughout high school.

The mother's use of cocaine during pregnancy and the father's apparent difficulty with school highlighted the importance of considering whether J.W. might be struggling with developmental or learning deficits. Because of the possibility of such deficits, educational testing was implemented. Testing for educational level and attention deficit hyperactivity disorder (ADHD), reports from teachers, and behavioral checklists indicated average IQ and significant symptoms of ADHD.

In addition to this vulnerability from early history, the mother did acknowledge that she was negligent in caring for J.W. and his younger sister because of her earlier drug use. In fact, Human Services were called to the mother's apartment numerous times because neighbors complained that J.W. and his sister were wandering around in the neighborhood barefoot and without supervision. The Human Services reports indicate that the home was very dirty and in disarray. In fact, they had warned the mother on several occasions that the children would be put in foster care if she did not clean up the home. One time, a neighbor found J.W. curled up in a dryer in the laundry room. Towards the end of J.W.'s kindergarten year, a neighbor called Human Services because J.W. and his sister were wandering the neighborhood, and when she attempted to return the children to their apartment, no one was home. At this point, J.W. and his sister were taken into custody and remained in foster care for about six months.

Despite the mother's negligence, J.W. demonstrated a strong bond to his mother. For example, records indicate that when the authorities took him in to custody, J.W. announced, "Clean up that apartment, mother, so I can come home soon." His love for his mother was also evident in how close he sat to her and the warmth with which he responded to her before and after the play therapy session.

The mother did cooperate with Human Services. She attended parenting classes and gained control of her addiction. Unfortunately, during the six months that J.W. was in foster care, he was sexually abused by a 12-year-old boy who was the natural child of the foster parents. J.W. reported that he told the foster mother about these events, but no action was taken. On one visit with his mother, supervised by Human Services personnel, J.W. openly stated that he was upset that an older boy in the home had been touching his private parts. Several weeks passed before Human Services responded and removed J.W. from this foster home. Several incidences of sexual abuse were confirmed.

Therefore, initial assessment indicated that J.W. suffered neglect in the natural home and sexual abuse in the foster care home. The possibility of feelings of abandonment and depression from the lack of appropriate care needed to be explored. Testing and school records also indicated the presence of some developmental delays and ADHD. However, it was important to note that his year in kindergarten was more successful than his first-grade year. His academic performance in his first-grade year, following the sexual abuse, was fraught with adjustment and educational learning difficulties.

In the early play therapy sessions used to develop a relationship and to further clarify the diagnosis of this youngster, the therapist became aware of the strong smell of feces, suggesting encopresis: that the child was withholding his bowel, which would overflow when the sphincter could no longer maintain the feces, thereby soiling his pants with fecal matter. Upon inquiry, the mother did confirm that his underpants were often soiled.

Also during the earlier sessions, J.W. spoke briefly about his problems with his peers. He stated that many of them hit him and teased him at school. He appeared very sad and disillusioned.

The therapist attempted to discuss the sexual abuse with this young patient. Although he seemed to like to play and talk with the therapist, when the subject of the sexual abuse was raised, he spoke in the most cryptic terms. "It's gross. You don't wanna know." When the therapist insisted that she would like to know so that she could help him sort out his feelings, he stated it was just "too gross" to talk about, and he "want[ed] to forget it."

The patient did acknowledge restless sleep and nightmares. He thought that the nightmares were about being taken away from his mother and the sexual abuse but insisted that he could not remember anything specific about the bad dreams. When the patient was asked about any early neglect, he stated that there had not been any and that he loved his mother.

The patient seemed to be suppressing events regarding early neglect and sexual abuse. His problem of soiling seemed related to an overcontrolling personality style of trying to deal with matters, psychologically and biologically, by "holding in" his experiences. Thus, the patient seemed to rely upon a defense of suppressing painful events and dissociating from painful material. Content from this early therapy, particularly the nightmares, disturbed sleeping, and blocking of memories suggested that the patient was also suffering from PTSD. It was hypothesized that this tendency to "hold in" and dissociate from painful material about his early neglect and the abuse could be interfering with his concentration at school. This hypothesis seemed to be supported by the fact that he performed better in kindergarten, which preceded the sexual abuse, than in first grade.

The Active Working Phase

Since the patient could not or would not talk about the events of early neglect or sexual abuse, much of the trauma was initially worked out metaphorically through the play therapy modality. Issues of violence of one person against another as well as distrust of adults were frequent themes expressed in play. For example, when J.W. was the storekeeper, he refused to help the customer find what the customer needed, and the storekeeper cheated on giving change. In sandbox play, frequent themes of army men and animals overpowering others were played out and initially reflected and later interpreted as to what was happening in the play. Gradually, parallels were drawn to the young patient's life and his feelings of lack of support and distrust of others.

Early in the working stage, the benefits and side effects of medication were discussed with the mother. The therapist and mother agreed to intervene, initially, with psychotherapy alone. A goal was to provide a more protective environment for the youngster by involving the mother in individual sessions so that she would learn more effective parenting techniques. In particular, the therapist worked with the mother to educate her about the effects of sexual abuse and how to respond to J.W. if he indicated concerns about the abuse. In one session, the mother also brought in the maternal grandfather, who was living in the home, to discuss J.W.'s problems in standing up for himself when picked on by neighboring children or cousins. J.W. would allow other children to tease him or pick on him and then later, when alone, would have emotional outbursts or retaliate against his sister. Both the grandfather and mother were instructed in ways to shape J.W.'s behavior to be more assertive. In addition, the grandfather learned how to model appropriate assertive behavior for J.W. The mother and the therapist developed a behavioral program to control J.W.'s encopresis, which involved giving him additional fiber in his diet and putting him on the toilet on a regular schedule.

Over six months, the patient's behavior began to improve. He was less aggressive to his sister, more able to stand up appropriately to cousins and peers at school, and more willing to cooperate. He had managed his encopresis, and consequently, was more accepted by the children at school. However, the patient continued to look somewhat sad, to act in a discouraged manner, and to evidence a short attention span and low tolerance for frustration both at home and at school.

At this point, it was agreed that psychotropic intervention appeared appropriate. Because of his depression and PTSD as well as his ADHD, a trial of a norepinephrine reuptake inhibitor, atomoxetine (Strattera), was instituted. This medication has an FDA indication for ADHD. Because it is a norepinephrine reuptake inhibitor, it also has properties of a tricyclic antidepressant that could help with both mood and symptoms of PTSD. However, checklists completed at school and at home revealed the medication was not effective. The patient's attention at school did not improve; his nightmares did not decrease, and his frustration level at school and at home remained relatively high.

The possible benefits and side effects of a trial of the extended action methyl-phenidate preparation, Concerta, was discussed with the mother and with the patient. The mother had particular concerns about using a stimulant because of her own addiction to illicit drugs. However, after reviewing costs and benefits, she agreed that the use of the Concerta seemed appropriate. The patient was stabilized on 37.5 mg Concerta daily. One very noticeable change was that J.W. became not only willing but actually anxious to help clean at home (in some ways, the cleaning behavior seemed to be a metaphor for his wanting to make sure that he would not be separated again from his mother). His attention at school improved considerably. However, he was quite behind in academic skills, and this continued to be an impediment to his academic performance throughout his first-grade year.

After J.W. had been on medication for several months, his ability to communicate with the therapist improved. He was clear about the nature of his relationship problems at school, and it was possible to give him concrete suggestions for dealing with these difficulties. In addition, he began to remember some of his dreams. The grandfather, who was living at the home, stayed up very late. J.W. agreed that if he woke up in the night, he would try to tell his grandfather his dreams so that the grandfather could record them. J.W. was very pleased with himself when he was able to bring these dreams in to therapy for discussion. His first dream, as recorded by his grandfather, was as follows:

> This dream scared him. J.W. did not remember very much. He said there was a giant whirlpool. It would suck people into it. When they got out of the whirlpool, they would appear on the sand on the beach. When the people reappeared from being sucked into the whirlpool, they looked like monsters. The people looked horribly disfigured and grotesque. J.W. also mentioned that he got up from the beach and went looking for his mother, but he could not find his mother, and then he woke up.

The dream was processed with J.W. as possibly reflecting how he felt when he was put in to foster care and sexually abused, and it led to a very meaningful dialogue about how people who are sexually abused sometimes feel that they are "damaged goods." Working through the idea that he was damaged (and instead reconceptualizing that something bad had happened to him, but that he was not damaged or bad) was very important to J.W.'s recovery. Shortly after working through the issue, his behavior with other children became much more positive, and he began forming friendships.

About a month later, the mother ran out of medication for several days, and both mother and J.W. noted a quick deterioration in his behavior. J.W. and his grandfather recorded the following nightmare:

> J.W. thought he turned into a mean man/boy. He had had some pills, but his sister took the pills, not him. He dreamt he was hurting little kids. He was wearing all

black. He said he was between 32 and 38 years old. In his dream, he hit little kids with his hands or used a stick to hit them and scratch them. It scared him that he was hitting and hurting kids for no reason.

Over several sessions, this dream and other content were processed with J.W. as probably illustrating that he was very angry about past neglect and sexual abuse but afraid to express his anger. Relatedly, fears of being separated, again, from his mother and home were also explored. In addition, this dream served as an excellent context for helping J.W. better understand how the medication helped him. The possibility that J.W. might need medication over a long period of time and the fact that he could count on the medication and psychotherapy being available as long as he needed it were discussed. It was emphasized that as he worked through his trauma and learned new behaviors, J.W. might outgrow the need for medication. J.W. became active in discussing the medication effects and side effects. Thus, therapeutic intervention about his dream and about medication facilitated his self-understanding and the development of his autonomy. A critical aspect of the active working phase for J.W. was to focus on his school performance. This required a more systematic tutoring in academic areas in which he had fallen behind because of his previous difficulty focusing at school. The mother also received guidance so that she could be a more effective tutor and guide for J.W.

Maintenance Phase

During this phase, which began about two months into his second-grade year, J.W. began initiating more topics in therapy. Therapy involved more direct communication about what was working well and not well in his life versus working through his issues in a more indirect play therapy modality. The sessions were reduced to every other week.

J.W. had also upgraded his academic skills. While his grades in first grade had been unsatisfactory, in second grade, he achieved Bs in academic classes and "Satisfactory" in those subjects graded pass/fail. As sometimes occurs after medication has been stabilized, there was a necessity to change the medication because of a change in insurance coverage. J.W. was very clear in reporting effects and side effects. A change to dexmethyphenidate HCl (Focalin) was attempted, but the patient reported stomachaches and believed that the medication did not help him as much as the Concerta helped him. The patient was restabilized on methylphenidate, continuous release (Metadate CR).

The Termination Phase

At the time of this writing, J.W. has not terminated therapy because he continues to need assistance in adapting to new stressors and responsibilities. It is postulated that he will need sessions over years. Gradually, sessions will be phased out to longer intervals. Psychotherapy can be terminated when his relationships are age appropriate and he consistently performs successfully at school. Most likely, he will need continued monitoring of ADHD medication throughout his academic years and perhaps into adulthood.

Summary and Recommendations

The hallmark of the integrated biopsychosocial model of care in the treatment of PTSD as employed by prescribing/medical psychologists is the high level of collaboration between the treating therapist and patient. Throughout the therapy process, the therapist and patient work closely together to monitor patient needs and growth and to make appropriate changes in the psychotherapeutic techniques and psychotropic interventions. The therapist's goal is to educate patients about themselves and about the costs and benefits of various psychotherapeutic and drug treatment interventions. Information about human dynamics and psychotropic agents is shared with the patients as they are the ultimate, best experts about themselves. To be most effective, the therapist ascribing to a biopsychosocial model not only considers and talks about the biological effects and side effects of medications but also uses the medication as one more tool to help patients understand their reactions and learn to assess their well-being, thereby spurring a sense of competence in choosing how to overcome problems and to grow, and facilitating patients' hope and autonomy.

In an era of evidence- and effectiveness-based practice, we look increasingly to identify psychotherapeutic models and psychotropic medications that may be utilized for the treatment of PTSD. As explained in this chapter, many medications used to treat PTSD as well as other mental disorders are employed "off label." Drug companies' desires for financial gain do not encourage the research of novel uses of older drugs for which the companies no longer hold patents. Yet, documenting the efficacy of these uses is clearly essential in order to provide reliable, competent care. New research findings and perhaps legislative action may be needed to foster research for validating "off-label" uses that have evolved through clinical practice.

Research regarding the efficacy of combined psychotherapy/psychotropic intervention is mounting (Pampallona, Bollini, Tibaldi, Kupelnick, & Munizza, 2004; Riba & Babn, 2005). Case studies summarized in this chapter demonstrate the effectiveness of the biopsychosocial approach in the treatment of PTSD. Thus, both empirical research and case studies point to the importance of advocating for broader and integrative medical/psychotherapeutic coverage for trauma patients. The department of defense project, which trained psychologists to prescribe, and acts in New Mexico and Louisiana allowing properly trained psychologists to prescribe medication for their patients provide new opportunities for the application of an integrated psychotherapy/pharmacotherapy model. The passage of similar acts in other states will broaden the application of the biopsychosocial model for the treatment of PTSD and other disorders. In addition, third-party payers should recognize the potency of combination strategies and encourage integrative care through their payment and schedule.

While further funding for research and practice from a biopsychosocial model will enhance the treatment of PTSD patients, the biopsychosocial model of care also highlights the complex and unique nature of each patient as well as the "art" behind the science. What is known through science must be applied with wisdom and sensitivity with the greatest respect for patients' abilities to become the wise leaders of their own recovery and growth.

References

Albucher, R. C., & Liberzon, I. (2002). Psychopharmacological treatment in PTSD: A critical review. *Journal of Psychiatry Research, 6*, 355–367.

American Psychiatric Association. (2000). *Diagnostic and statistical manual of mental disorders* (4th ed., text revision). Washington, DC: Author.

Asnis, G. M., Kohn, S. R., Henderson, M., & Brown, N. L. (2004). SSRIs versus non-SSRIs in post-traumatic stress disorder: An update with recommendations. *Drugs, 64*, 383–404.

Bahk, W. M., Kim W., Pae C. U., Chae J. H., & Jun T. Y. (2005). Effects of mirtazapine in patients with post-traumatic stress disorder in Korea: A pilot study. *Psychiatry and Clinical Neurosciences, 59*(6), 743–747.

Barnhart, W. J., Makela, E. H., & Latocha, J. (2004). Selective serotonin reuptake inhibitor induced apathy syndrome: A clinical review. *Journal of Psychiatric Practice, 10*(3), 196–199.

Blake, D. D., Weathers, F. W., Nagy, L. M., Kaloupek, D. G., Gusman, F. D., Charney, D. S., et al. (1995). The development of a clinician-administered PTSD scale. *Journal of Traumatic Stress, 8*, 75–90.

Boscarino, J. A. (1997). Diseases among men 20 years after exposure to severe stress.Implications for clinical research and medical care. *Psychosomatic Medicine, 59*, 605–614.

Brewin, C., & Holmes, E. (2003). Psychological theories of posttraumatic stress disorder. *Clinical Psychology Review, 23*, 339–379.

Canive, J. M., Clark, R. D., Calais, L. A., Qualls, C., & Tuason, V. B. (1998). Buproprion treatment in veterans with posttraumatic stress disorder: An open study. *Clinical Psychopharmacology, 5*, 379–383.

Cavaljuga, S., Licanson, I., Malabegovic, N., & Petkoncate, D. (2004). Posttraumatic stress disorder among women after the war in Sarajevo: a rationale for genetic study. *Bosnian Journal of Basic Medical Science, 3*, 12–16.

Connor, K. M., Davidson, J. R., Weisler, R. H., et al. (1999). A pilot study of mirtazapine in post-traumatic stress disorder. *International Clinical Psychopharmacology; 14*(1), 29–31.

David D., Woodward C., Esquenazi C., & Mellman, T. A. (2004). Comparison of comorbid physical illnesses among veterans with PTSD and veterans with alcohol dependence. *Psychiatric Services, 55*, 82–85.

Davidson, J., Kudler, H., Smith, R., et al. (1990). Treatment of posttraumatic stress disorder with amitriptyline and placebo. *Arch Gen Psychiatry; 47*(3), 259–66.

Davidson, J., Kudler, H. S., Saunders, W. B., Erickson, L., Smith, R. D., Stein, R. M., et al. (1993). Predicting response to amitriptyline in posttraumatic stress disorder. *American Journal of Psychiatry, 150*(7), 1024–1029.

Davidson, J. (2006). Venlafaxine extended release in posttraumatic stress disorder; A sertraline- and placebo-controlled study. *Journal of Clinical Psychopharmacology, 3*, 259–267.

Davis, L. L., Nugent, A. L., Murray, J., Kramer, G. L., Petty, F., (2000). Nefazodone treatment for chronic posttraumatic stress disorder: an open trial. *Journal of Clinical Psychopharmacology, 20*(2), 159–164.

Dow, B. (1997). Antidepressant treatment of posttraumatic stress disorder and major depression in veterans. *Annals of Clinical Psychiatry, 9*(1), 1–5.

Dunmore, E., Clark, D. M., & Ehlers, A. (1999). Cognitive factors involved in the onset and maintenance of posttraumatic stress disorder (PTSD) after physical or sexual assault. *Behavior Research and Therapy, 37*, 809–829.

Ehlers, A., & Clark, D. M. (2000). A cognitive model of posttraumatic stress disorder. *Behavior Research and Therapy, 38*, 319–345.

Engelhard, I. M., van den Hout, M. A., Kindt, M., Arntz, A., & Schouten, E. (2003). Peritraumatic dissociation and posttraumatic stress after pregnancy loss: A prospective study. *Behavior Research and Therapy, 41*, 67–68.

Fichtner, C. G., O'Connor, F. L., Yeoh, H. C., Aurora, R. C., & Crayton, J. W. (1995). Hypodensity of platelet serotonin uptake sites in posttraumatic stress disorder: associated clinical features. *Life Science, 57*(2), 37–44.

Foa, E. B., & Rothbaum, B. O. (1998). *Treating the trauma of rape: Cognitive behavioral therapy for PTSD.* New York, Guilford Press.

Garfield, D. A., Fichtner, C. G., Leveroni, C., Mahableshwarkar, A., (2001). Open trial of nefazodone for combat veterans with posttraumatic stress disorder. *Journal of Traumatic Stress, 14*(3), 453–60.

Gillin, J. C., Smith-Vaniz, A., Schnierow, B., Rapaport, M. H., Kesloe, J. R., Raimo, E., et al. (2001). An open-label, 12-week clinical and sleep EEG study of Nefazodone in chronic combat-related posttraumatic stress disorder. *Journal of Clinical Psychiatr, 62*, 789–796.

Hageman, I., Anderson, H. S., & Jorgenson, M. B. (2001). Post traumatic stress disorder: A review of psychobiology and pharmacotherapy. *Acta Psychiatrica Scandinavia, 6*, 411–422.

Hamilton, M. (1960). A Rating Scale for Depression. *Journal of Neurology, Neurosurgery and Psychiatry, 23*, 56–62.

Hamner, M. B., & Frueh, B. C. (1998). Response to venlafaxine in a previously antidepressant treatment-resistant combat veteran with PTSD (Case report). *International Clinical Psychopharmacology, 13*, 233–234.

Hertzberg, M. A., Feldman, M. E., & Beckham, J. C. (1996). Trial of trazodone for posttraumatic stress disorder using a multiple baseline group design. *Journal of Clinical Psychopharmacology, 16*, 294–298.

Hidalgo, R., Hertzberg, M. A., Mellman, T., Mahableshwarkar, A. (1999). Nefazodone in posttraumatic stress disorder: results from six open-label trials. *International Clinical Psychopharmacology, 14*(2), 61–68.

Holeva, V., & Tarrier, N. (2001). Personality and peri-traumatic dissociation in the prediction of PTSD in victims of road traffic accidents. *Journal of Psychosomatic Research, 51*, 687–692.

Holmes, E., Grey, N., & Young, K. (2005). Intrusive images and "hotspots" of trauma memories in posttraumatic stress disorder: An exploratory investigation of emotions and cognitive themes. *Journal of Behavioral Therapy and Experimental Psychiatry, 36*(1), 3–17.

Horowitz, M. J. (1979). Impact of Event Scale: A measure of subjective stress. *Psychosomatic Medicine, 41*(3), 209–218.

Horowitz, M. J. (1986). *Stress response syndromes* (2nd ed.). Northvale, NJ: Jason Aronson.

Janoff-Bulman, R. (1992). *Shattered assumptions: Towards a new psychology of trauma.* New York: Free Press.

Katz, R. J., Lott, M. H., Arbus, P., Corcq, L., Herlobsen, P., Lingjaerde, O., et al. (1994). Pharmacotherapy of post-traumatic stress disorder with a novel psychotropic. *Anxiety, 1,* 169–174.

Kosten, T. R., Frank, J. B., Dan, E., McDougle, C. J., & Giller El, Jr. (2003). Pharmacotherapy for posttraumatic stress disorder using phenylzine and imipramine. *Journal of Nervous Mental Disorders, 179,* 366–370.

Marmar, C., Schoenfield, F., Weiss, D. S., Metzler, T., Zatzick, D., & Wu, R. (1996). Open trial of fluvoxamine treatment for combat-related posttraumatic stress disorder. *Journal of Clinical Psychiatry, 57*(Suppl..), 66–72.

McGrath, P. J., Quitkin, F. M., & Klein, D. F. (1995). Bromocriptine treatment of relapses seen during selective serotonin re-uptake inhibitor treatment of depression. *Journal of Clinical Psychopharmacology, 15*(4), 289–291.

Montgomery, S. A., & Åsberg, M. (1979). A new depression scale designed to be sensitive to change. *British Journal of Psychiatry, 134,* 382–389.

Muraoka, M., Komiyama, H., Hosoi, M., Mine, K., Kubo, C. (1996). Psychosomatic treatment of phantom limb pain with post-traumatic stress disorder: A case report. *Pain, 66*(2-3), 385–8.

Murray, J., Ehlers, A., & Mayou, R. (2002). Dissociation and posttraumatic stress disorder: Two prospective studies of motor vehicle accident survivors. *British Journal of Psychiatry, 180,* 363–368.

Nijenhuis, E.R.S., Vanderlinden, J., & Spinhoven, P. (1998). Animal defensive reactions as a model for trauma-induced dissociative reactions. *Journal of Traumatic Stress, 11,* 243–260.

Pampallona, S., Bollini, P., Tibalidi , G., Kupelnick, B., & Munizza, C. (2004). Combined pharmacotherapy and psychological treatment for depression: A systematic review. *Archives of General Psychiatry, 61*(7), 714–719.

Quitken, F. M., Stewart, J. W., McGrath, P. J., Nunes, E., Ocepek-Welikson, K., Tricamo, E., et al. (1993). Loss of drug effects during continuation therapy. *American Journal of Psychiatry, 150,* 562–5.

Raskind, M. A. (2003). Reduction of nightmares and other PTSD symptoms in combat veterans by prazosin: A placebo controlled study. *American Journal of Psychiatry, 160,* 371–373.

Reist C., Kauffmann, C. D., & Haier, R. J., (1989). A controlled trial of desipramine in 18 men with posttraumatic stress disorder. *American Journal of Psychiatry, 146,* 513–516.

Riba, M. B., & Babn, R. (2005). *Competency in combining pharmacotherapy and psychotherapy: Integrated and split treatment.* Washington, DC: American Psychiatric Publishing.

Schnurr, P. P., & Jankowski, M. K. (1999). Physical health and posttraumatic stress disorder: Review and synthesis. *Semlin Neuropsychiatry, 4,* 295–304.

Schnurr, P. P., Friedman, M. J., & Bernardy, N. C. (2002). Research on posttraumatic stress disorder epidemiology, pathophysiology, and assessment. *Journal of Clinical Psychology, 58,* 877–889.

Simon, A., & Gormon, J. (2004). Psychopharmacological possibilities in the acute disaster setting. *Psychiatric Clinics of North America, 27,* 425–58.

Smajkic, A. (2001). Sertraline, paroxetine, and venlafaxine in refugee posttraumatic stress disorder with depression symptoms. *Journal of Traumatic Stress, 14*(3), 445–452.

Southwick, S. M., Krystal, J. H., Bremer, J. D., Morgan, C. A., III, Nicolaou, A. L., & Nagy, L. M. (1997). Noradrenergic and serotonergic function in posttraumatic stress disorder. *Archives of General Psychiatry, 54,* 749–758.

Southwick, S. M., Krystal, J. H., Morgan, C. A., Johnson, D., Nagy, L. M., Nicolaou, A., et al. (1993). Abnormal noradrenergic function in post-traumatic stress disorder. *Archives of General Psychiatry, 50*(4), 266–274.

Steil, R., & Ehlers, A. (2000). Dysfunctional meaning of posttraumatic intrusions in chronic PTSD. *Behavior Research and Therapy, 38*, 537–558.

Strange, A., & Dolan, R. J. (2004). β-Adrenergic modulation of emotional memory-evoked human amygdala and hippocampal response. *National Academy of Sciences.*

VA/DOD Clinical Practice Guidelines Working Group. (2003). *Management of post traumatic stress.* Veterans Health Administration, Department of Veterans Affairs and Health Affairs, Department of Defense. Washington, D.C.: Office of Quality and Performance. Publication 102-CPG-PTSD-04.

Van der Kolk, B. A., McFarlane, A., & Weisaeth, L. (1996). *Traumatic stress: The effect of overwhelming experience on mind, body and society.* New York: Guilford Press.

Warner, M. D., Dorn, M. R., & Peabody, C. A. (2001). Survey on the usefulness of Trazodone in patients with PTSD with insomnia or nightmares. *Pharmacopsychiatry, 34,* 128–131.

Wenzlaff, E. M., & Wegner, D. M. (2000). Thought suppression. *Annual Review of Psychology, 51,* 59–91.

Zisook, S., Chentsova-Dutton, Y. E., Smith-Vaniz, A., Kline, N. A., Ellenor, G. L., Kodsi, A. B., Gillin, J. C. (2000). Nefazodone in patients with treatment-refractory posttraumatic stress disorder, *Journal of Clinical Psychiatry, 61*(3), 203-208.

Zygmont, M., Prigerson, H. G., Houck, P. R., Miller, M. D., Shear, M. K ., Jacobs, S., et al. (1998). A post hoc comparison of paroxetine and nortriptyline for symptoms of traumatic grief. *Journal of Clinical Psychiatry, 59*(5), 241–245.

INDEX

320 Index

Hospitalized children, 40–42
HPV. *See* Human papillomavirus
Human papillomavirus (HPV), 84
Hyperarousal, 208
Hypnosis: amnesia and, 273–74; for burn victims, 122; pain management and, 52–53
Hypnotic drugs, 63–64

Imagery, 159
Imaginal exposure therapy, 55
Immune system, stress and, 32
Infibulation, 265
Informed consent, 296
Injuries, caused by traffic accidents, 2
Inpatient rehabilitation, for spinal cord injury (SCI), 162–64
Internal working models (IWMs), 262–63
International Association for the Study of Pain, pain defined, 47
Internet-based interventions: for medically ill children and their parents, 36; for motor vehicle accidents (MVAs), 22
Interpersonal violence, 83–85
Intimate partner violence/domestic violence (IPV/DV), disclosure and, 170, 173, 175, 178–79, 181, 184–85. *See also* Violence against women
Intraoperative consciousness. *See* Anesthesia awareness
Intravenous drug users (IDUs), 91–93
Intrusion symptoms, 119
Intrusive thoughts, 207
IPV/DV. *See* Intimate partner violence/domestic violence
Iraq War veterans, screening for trauma, 173
IWMs. *See* Internal working models

JCAHO. *See* Joint Commission for Hospital Accreditation
Joint Commission for Hospital Accreditation (JCAHO), 49, 74–75
Juvenile fire setting prevention programs, 116

Litigation, pain and, 55
Losses, due to spinal cord injury (SCI), 142–47, 161

Maintenance stage, for change, 185
Major depressive disorder (MDD), 145
Massachusetts Burn Injury Reporting System (M-BIRS), 128
M-BIRS. *See* Massachusetts Burn Injury Reporting System
McKinney-Vento Homeless Assistance Act, 222
MDD. *See* Major depressive disorder
Medicaid, 163
Medically ill children and their parents, 27–45; acute stress disorder (ASD) and, 31; best practices, 38–40; family systems approach to treatment, 34, 39; hospitalized children and, 40–42; identification and early interventions to prevent PTSD, 35–36, 39; Medical Traumatic Stress Toolkit (National Child Traumatic Stress Network), 39; pain control and, 37, 41; pharmacological interventions, 36–37, 39; physiological consequences to PSTD, 32–33; play, drawing, and retelling of the event, 34; preventive group interventions, 35–36, 39; psycho-educational intervention, 35, 39; public policy and, 40–41; research in medical traumatic stress, 28–33; specialty children's' camps, 36, 39; trauma-focused cognitive behavioral therapy (CBT) and, 32, 34, 39
Medical Traumatic Stress Toolkit (National Child Traumatic Stress Network)
Medicare, 163
Memory: PTSD in children and, 33; situationally accessible, 294; verbally accessible, 294
Men, childhood sexual abuse and HIV/AIDS and, 86
Mentoring, 184
Men who have sex with men (MSM), 80, 83, 86, 88. *See also* HIV/AIDS
Mild traumatic brain injury (MTBI), 146

ABOUT THE EDITOR

Elizabeth K. Carll, PhD, is a clinical psychologist and author in private practice in Long Island, New York and also consults to organizations and corporations on crisis management, health and stress, trauma, and workplace violence. She is the author of *Violence in Our Lives: Impact on Workplace, Home, and Community*, and edited a special issue of the *American Behavioral Scientist*, "Psychology, News Media, and Public Policy: Promoting Social Change."

Dr. Carll has developed a variety of disaster intervention programs and has responded to many crises and violent incidents, including the Persian Gulf Crisis, 1993 WTC bombing, Long Island Railroad shooting, Oklahoma City bombing, TWA 800, and the 9/11 WTC disaster, and served on the American Psychological Association's National Disaster Response Advisory Task Force for 7 years. She founded (1990) the Disaster/Crisis Response Network of the New York State Psychological Association, the first statewide volunteer network in the nation, which she coordinated for 10 years.

A past president of the American Psychological Association's Media Psychology Division, Dr. Carll is a pioneer in working with the news media to help the public cope with the aftermath of crises and disaster. She is a representative to the United Nations for the International Society for Traumatic Stress Studies and vice-president of the Communications Coordination Committee for the United Nations, one of the oldest nongovernmental organizations (NGO) to work with the UN to promote civil society's role in developing solutions to global problems.

Dr. Elizabeth Carll can be contacted at Email: ecarll@optonline.net; Postal Mail: PO Box 246, Centerport, N.Y. 11721; and Telephone: 631-754-2424.

About the Contributors

James R. Alvarez, PhD, is founding CEO of Clarity Advisors Group Ltd., which provides consultation and training in hostage negotiations, kidnap management, crisis communications, psychological first aid, stress/trauma assessment and treatment. Dr. Alvarez is a clinical psychologist and the only consultant used by both Scotland Yard and NYPD's Hostage Negotiation Teams. He is an NYPD Honorary Police Surgeon.

Ellen Bassuk, MD, is founder and president of the National Center on Family Homelessness, the nation's preeminent authority on family homelessness. As a clinical researcher, psychiatrist, and advocate, she is at the forefront of research and evaluation, program design, and service delivery on behalf of homeless children and families. Dr. Bassuk is a board-certified psychiatrist and an associate professor of psychiatry at Harvard Medical School. She is a graduate of Brandeis University and Tufts University School of Medicine, and was awarded an honorary doctorate in public service from Northeastern University. She served as editor in chief of the *American Journal of Orthopsychiatry*.

Edward B. Blanchard, PhD, is currently a distinguished professor emeritus at the State University of New York–Albany. He has held numerous National Institutes of Health (NIH) grants in the assessment and cognitive behavioral treatments for headache, hypertension, and irritable bowel syndrome. His work with posttraumatic stress disorder began in the early 1980s, with an initial focus on Vietnam War veterans. Since 1989, he has collaborated with Edward Hickling on research with survivors of serious motor vehicle accidents. The work on this topic has been supported by grants from the National Institute of Mental Health.

Martha Bragin, PhD, LCSW, is on the faculty of the Department of Social Work, College of Social and Behavioral Science of California State University at San Bernardino, as well as the International Program on Refugee Trauma at Columbia University College of Physicians and Surgeons, and the Working Group on the Psychic Effects of Social Exclusion of the International Psychoanalytic Association. For the past 20 years, Dr. Bragin has consulted with governments, international and nongovernmental organizations in the design, monitoring, and evaluation of programs that mitigate the effects of all forms of violence on soldiers and civilians.

Fernando Chacón, PhD, is professor of social psychology at the Complutense University of Madrid, Spain. He is the coordinator of the research team in the Department of Social Psychology, focusing on longitudinal studies examining the psychosocial factors that influence the longevity of volunteer service and has published on community psychology, psychosocial intervention, volunteers' sustained helping, and other helping behavior in emergency situations. Following the 2004 Madrid terrorist attack, Dr. Chacon coordinated 948 volunteer psychologists to assist the wounded and their families He is also the president of the Association of Psychologists of Madrid in Spain.

Anne M. Dietrich, PhD, is a psychologist in private practice in Vancouver, British Columbia, Canada. She completed her studies at the University of British Columbia with a specialization in psychological trauma. In addition to trauma, she has training and experience with the assessment and treatment of individuals with eating disorders, personality disorders, substance-related disorders, mood and anxiety disorders, and physical and sexual offending. Dr. Dietrich is the recipient of several awards and fellowships and is currently the chair of the Disaster and Trauma section of the Canadian Psychological Association. She has published numerous articles, as well as book chapters on trauma.

Michael DiMarco, PsyD, is a health psychologist at Aurora Sinai Medical Center in Milwaukee, Wisconsin. He is also a consultant for Planned Parenthood of Wisconsin and Milwaukee Health Services, and is in private practice. His career focus is in the treatment of the psychological and behavioral aspects of physical illness including HIV/AIDS, an area in which he has published. Dr. DiMarco was granted the National Institute of Mental Health Service Award in HIV Prevention Research and trained as a postdoctoral fellow at the Center for AIDS Intervention Research (CAIR) with the Medical College of Wisconsin in the department of psychiatry and behavioral medicine.

Rona M. Fields, PhD, is a fellow of the American Psychological Association, president of the District of Columbia Psychological Association. She is author of *Martyrdom: The Psychology, Theology and Politics of Self Sacrifice,* and numerous articles, chapters, books on violence, torture, and social change. Dr. Fields has written for mainstream media and has been a broadcast journalist and professor abroad. She has served as senior research fellow in the Cyber-Security Policy and

Planning Institute at George Washington University, School of Engineering, Department of Computer Sciences. She served on the Amnesty International Medical Commission in the Campaign to Abolish Torture and was amnesty fellow at the Peace Research Institute of Oslo, Norway.

Cheryl Gore-Felton, PhD, is associate professor of psychiatry and behavioral sciences at Stanford University Medical Center. She has authored and co-authored more than 70 scientific articles, book chapters, and manuals on the biopsychosocial impact of chronic, life-threatening illnesses with particular focus on HIV/AIDS. A clinician, researcher, and teacher, she focuses on the amelioration of trauma-related symptoms and behaviors among culturally diverse populations.

Kathleen Guarino, LMHC, is a project manager at the National Center on Family Homelessness. She manages a project focused on the development and implementation of a self-assessment tool designed to facilitate the creation of trauma-informed shelter systems. She also works with service providers and school personnel in the Gulf region, to provide training on traumatic stress. Kathleen Guarino is a licensed mental health clinician who received her master's in counseling psychology from Boston College in 2001, and began her work as a clinician at a residential program for children aged 5–13, providing therapeutic services for children and families impacted by trauma.

James Halpern, PhD, is professor of psychology and director of the Institute for Disaster Mental Health at the State University of New York at New Paltz. Dr Halpern is author/co-author of numerous scholarly papers and four books, including *Disaster Mental Health: Theory and Practice.* He has given numerous presentations, trainings, and consultations in the field of disaster mental health and has been a regular expert guest on CNN television. He has served with the American Red Cross at both national and local disasters and was among the first mental health professionals to offer support in NYC on September 11.

Ronda Bresnick Hauss, LCSW, is a licensed clinical social worker and the founder of the Quiet Waters Center for Trauma, Stress and Resilience. Her expertise is in providing psychotherapy to people who have experienced severe trauma. Ms. Bresnick Hauss also worked for many years as a psychotherapist in a nonprofit mental health clinic. There, she assisted people from many different cultures, providing therapy to survivors of torture in a program funded by the United Nations and the U.S. government.

Edward J. Hickling, PsyD, is a clinical psychologist and principal partner of Capital Psychological Associates in Albany, New York. He holds adjunct faculty positions at the State University of New York–Albany and at Albany Medical College in the Department of Psychiatry. He has been senior research scientist at the Center for Stress and Anxiety Disorders since 1990, when he became co-principal investigator with Dr. Edward B. Blanchard on several National Institute of Mental Health (NIMH)-funded grants investigating the psychological impact of motor vehicle accidents (MVAs). He has published more than 80 papers and several books, and co-authored several with Dr. Blanchard on their work with MVA trauma survivors.

Allen Lebovits, PhD, is a licensed psychologist who has specialized in pain management for over 20 years. Dr. Lebovits was associate professor in the Departments of Anesthesiology and Psychiatry of the New York University (NYU) Medical Center and the NYU Pain Management Center. He is currently Director of Psychological Services, Neurology and Integrative Pain, Medicine, ProHealth Care Associates, New York and has a private practice in Lawrence, New York. Dr. Lebovits has authored nearly 40 scientific articles in peer-reviewed journals and is on the editorial board of *Pain Medicine* and the *Journal of Clinical Psychology.* He is co-editor of the 1996 book, *A Practical Approach to Pain Management.* He is a past president of the Eastern Pain Association.

Ruth Q. Leibowitz, PhD, received her doctorate in psychology from the University of Kansas, where she specialized in health and rehabilitation psychology. Her primary clinical and research interests are the associations between chronic physical illness and mental health (particularly posttraumatic stress disorder [PTSD] and depression). She is a health sciences research specialist at the Veterans Administration Medical Center in Portland, Oregon, where she conducts an interdisciplinary clinical research intervention for chronic pain in primary care. Prior to this she researched disclosure of trauma in the medical environment, as a VA Health Services Research postdoctoral fellow in South Texas.

Elaine S. LeVine, PhD, is a prescribing psychologist in private practice, treating adults and children in Las Cruces, New Mexico, and director of the Southwestern Institute for the Advancement of Psychotherapy (a collaborative program with New Mexico State University), which provides postdoctoral training in psychopharmacology for psychologists. Her professional articles and books consider aspects of child therapy, diversity issues, and psychopharmacotherapy.

Rachel M. MacNair, PhD, is the author of the textbook *The Psychology of Peace: An Introduction* and the monograph *Perpetration-Induced Traumatic Stress: The Psychological Consequences of Killing.* She is director of the Institute for Integrated Social Analysis, research arm of the nonprofit organization Consistent Life; she also coaches dissertation students on statistics. She graduated from Earlham College, a Quaker school, with a bachelor's in peace and conflict studies, and got her PhD in psychology and sociology from the University of Missouri at Kansas City.

Lieutenant Colonel Elaine Orabona Mantell, PhD, is a graduate of the Department of Defense's Psychopharmacology Demonstration Project. She has served as a prescribing psychologist in the United States Air Force since 1996. She currently serves on the medical staff of the 96th Medical Group, Eglin Air Force Base. She was awarded a presidential citation from the American Psychological Association (APA) for her pioneering efforts in the field of psychopharmacology. Dr. Orabona Mantell is a subject matter expert and item writer for the APA's Psychopharmacology Examination for Psychologists, and she has written several articles and book chapters on prescriptive authority and psychopharmacology.

Captain Robert J. Martin is a 28-year veteran of the Los Angeles Police Department and is currently vice president of Gavin de Becker and Associates. He is the founder of the LAPD Threat Management Unit, founding member of the Association of Threat Assessment Professionals, and the lead developer of threat assessment methods used by the CIA, the U.S. Supreme Court Police, the U.S. Capitol Police, the Federal Reserve Board, and others.

Donald M. Mathews, MD, is an anesthesiologist at St. Vincent's Hospital in Manhattan and associate professor of clinical anesthesiology at New York Medical College. At St. Vincent's, he is associate chairman for academic affairs, Department of Anesthesiology, and program director for residency training. He has a long-standing interest in preventing anesthesia awareness and is particularly interested in evaluating new technology that may decrease its incidence. He has given lectures on the topic at national meetings and published in peer-reviewed medical journals.

Jeffrey T. Mitchell, PhD, is a clinical professor of emergency health services, University of Maryland and president emeritus, International Critical Incident Stress Foundation. He is an adjunct faculty member, Federal Emergency Management Agency. He reviews for the *JAMA* and the *International Journal of Emergency Mental Health*. Dr. Mitchell, a recipient of the Austrian Red Cross Bronze Medal for his crisis intervention work, is on the Board of Scientific and Professional Advisors of the American Academy of Experts in Traumatic Stress. He is an expert consultant to the UN Department of Safety and Security Working Group on Stress.

Judy B. Okawa, PhD, is a clinical psychologist and founder of the Center for Traumatic Stress Studies in Washington, D.C. Dr. Okawa developed the first comprehensive treatment program for survivors of politically motivated torture and human trafficking in Washington, D.C. She is nationally recognized for her expertise in working with torture survivors and has trained many attorneys, medical, and mental health professionals. She has testified frequently before the U.S. Congress and has received a Human Rights Award for her work. Dr. Okawa has written on the cross-cultural assessment of refugees and asylum seekers and is currently collaborating on a book written by torture survivors.

Frank J. Padrone, PhD, is a clinical psychologist with extensive experience with spinal cord injury. He is director of the Inpatient Psychology Service at Rusk Institute of Rehabilitation Medicine, New York University Medical Center, and on the faculty of the New York University School of Medicine. He holds an ABPP in rehabilitation psychology and postdoctoral certification in psychotherapy and psychoanalysis from New York University. He has published in the areas of adjustment to spinal cord injury, sexuality and disability, and psychotherapy with family members of those with disabilities. His interests include psychotherapy, and the development of psychological and neuropsychological treatment approaches in rehabilitation, sexuality, and the treatment of psycho-physiological disorders.

Rhonda S. Robert, PhD, completed a doctorate in counseling psychology from the University of North Texas in Denton, Texas, and an internship at the University of Texas Medical Branch (UTMB). Dr. Robert's 10-year career in burn care culminated with her service as chief psychologist at Shriners Hospitals for Children, Galveston Unit, and associate professor at UTMB. Dr. Robert is currently associate professor at the Children's Cancer Hospital of the University of Texas M. D. Anderson Cancer Center.

Lenore Rubin, PhD, is at present consulting psychologist for Public Health Seattle King County Child Care Team. After completing her PhD in clinical psychology at Boston University, Dr. Rubin worked in community mental health settings serving children and families from economically disadvantaged communities. Dr. Rubin continues to work as a consultant to programs serving homeless families in Seattle.

Antoinette Collarini Schlossberg, PhD, is a psychologist and associate professor of criminal justice at St. John's University and has been in private practice in New York for 23 years. She has testified as an expert in court and has worked closely with her husband Dr. Harvey Schlossberg on issues related to forensic psychological issues. Dr. Collarini Schlossberg served in Westchester County government for 22 years, holding the position of executive director of the Youth Bureau. She has developed many educational programs dealing with police, corrections, and courts, and had hosted a weekly television program for 8 years. She has authored numerous articles, book chapters, and government monographs.

Harvey Schlossberg, PhD, is associate professor of criminal justice and director, Graduate Program for Criminal Justice Leadership, St. John's University. He is a pioneer of the hostage negotiation system and introduced the use of psychological screening for hiring of police. He developed early warning systems of police stress, critical incident debriefing of emergency responders, criminal profiling, and psychotherapy for criminal justice personnel, and has numerous publications. Dr Schlossberg served with the New York City Police Department (NYPD) from 1958 to 1978, retiring as the founder and director of the NYPD Psychological Services Unit. He later served as the chief psychologist for the Port Authority of New York and New Jersey.

Jakob Steinberg, PhD, is professor of psychology, Fairleigh Dickinson University, Madison, New Jersey, for 33 years and board certified in medical psychotherapy, certified expert in traumatic stress, and senior disability analyst. Dr. Steinberg maintains a private practice specializing in health psychology, anxiety disorders, and traumatic stress. He is on staff, Department of Psychiatry,

Morristown Memorial Hospital, a level-one trauma center, as the psychologist on the Multi-Disciplinary Trauma Service, Department of Surgery. He is president of Crisis Recovery Services LLC, a consulting firm specialized in managing the human impact of disaster and crisis for communities, companies, and corporate disaster recovery, business continuity/contingency planning services.

Margaret L. Stuber, MD, is the Jane and Marc Nathanson Professor of Psychiatry at the Semel Institute for Neuroscience and Human Behavior at University of California, Los Angeles. She has been a pioneer in research on posttraumatic stress in childhood cancer survivors, pediatric organ transplant recipients, and their families. She was the recipient of the Simon Weil Award from the American Academy of Child and Adolescent Psychiatry in 2001 for her work in pediatric consultation research.

Luc Taal, PhD, holds a doctorate in clinical psychology from the University of Utrecht, the Netherlands. He is the manager of special projects for the Trauma Center of the University Medical Center of Utrecht (UMCU) and has published extensively in various trauma-related areas and also in the application of online systems for disaster and trauma. He coordinated and was responsible for the development of the TISEI system, a Web platform for the victims of the 2004 tsunami. Dr. Taal is treasurer of ECHOES ONLINE, a nonprofit, nongovernmental organization dedicated to Web-based community building for large-scale disasters.

Sanna J. Thompson, PhD, is an associate professor of social work at the University of Texas at Austin. She has conducted multiple research projects and written extensively on homeless and runaway youth, focusing on their substance use and trauma responses. She is currently funded by the National Institute on Drug Abuse to conduct research aimed at understanding the engagement of high-risk youth and their families in the therapeutic process.

Mary Tramontin, PsyD, is the lead psychologist at the Traumatic Stress Studies Program of the James J. Peters VA Medical Center/Mt. Sinai School of Medicine. She is co-author of *Disaster Mental Health: Theory and Practice.* She has served on the Leadership Committee of the American Red Cross/Greater New York Chapter Mental Health Services function for more than 10 years and has been the mental health lead at multiple small- and large-scale disasters. Her disaster trauma expertise is informed by her professional work experience in local and federal law enforcement agencies and in the provision of specialized treatments for posttraumatic stress disorder.

Corine J. van Middelkoop, MSc, has studied psychology in the Netherlands. She is working on a European research project, "The Psychobiology of Post Traumatic Stress Disorder" at University Medical Center Utrecht. In this European-funded project, UMC Utrecht is working together with other Western European countries and former Yugoslavia countries. Her interests focus on the cross-cultural differences in various disciplines of psychology.

María Luisa Vecina, PhD, is assistant professor at the Complutense University of Madrid, Spain, where she teaches social psychology, community psychology, and group psychology. She is also a member of a research team in the Department of Social Psychology, focusing on longitudinal studies examining the psychosocial factors that influence the longevity of volunteer service and has published on volunteers' sustained helping and other behaviors of aid in emergency situations. She is the secretary of the board of directors of the Association of Psychologists of Madrid.

Eric Vermetten, MD, PhD, was trained as a psychiatrist in the Netherlands, and at Yale, Stanford and Emory Universities. He is interested in the long-term effects of trauma on the mind and body and has published extensively on PTSD, dissociation, and psychotherapy. He is president of the International Society of Hypnosis and president of ECHOES ONLINE, an NGO dedicated to Web-based community building for victims of large-scale disasters. Dr. Vermetten is head of research at the Military Mental Health Group in the Department of Defense and associate professor of psychiatry at the Neuroscience Division of the University Medical Center Utrecht.

Michael Wang, PhD, is professor of clinical psychology in the School of Psychology, Faculty of Medicine, University of Leicester, England. He is a former chair of the Division of Clinical Psychology of the British Psychological Society. He has worked as a clinical psychologist for more than 25 years, treating patients with PTSD, anxiety disorders, depression, obsessional compulsive disorder, and, in particular, psychological problems arising from unplanned anesthetic and surgical incidents. In 2004, he organized the 6th International Symposium on Memory and Awareness in Anesthesia and Intensive Care, and he has published numerous papers and book chapters on this topic.

About the Editorial Advisory Board

James R. Alvarez, PhD, is founding CEO of Clarity Advisors Group Ltd., which provides consultation and training in hostage negotiations, kidnap management, crisis communications, psychological first aid, stress/trauma assessment and treatment. Dr. Alvarez is a clinical psychologist and the only consultant used by both Scotland Yard and NYPD's Hostage Negotiation Teams. He is an NYPD Honorary Police Surgeon.

Jean Lau Chin, EdD, ABPP, is professor and dean of Derner Institute, Adelphi University. She is series editor, Race and Ethnicity Series for Praeger Press, and consulting editor for *Professional Psychology: Research and Practice.* Her leadership/management roles over the past 35 years include systemwide dean, California School of Professional Psychology at Alliant International University, and president, CEO Services.

Joan C. Chrisler, PhD, is professor of psychology at Connecticut College, where she teaches courses on the psychology of women and health psychology. She has edited or co-edited seven books, served a five-year term as editor of *Sex Roles: A Journal of Research,* and has been a consulting editor or an ad hoc reviewer for many other journals.

Patrick DeLeon, PhD, JD, is a former president of the American Psychological Association and is associate editor of the *American Psychologist,* editor of *Psychological Services* of the Public Service Division of APA, and served on other editorial boards. He has served on Capitol Hill for more than three decades, including as chief of staff for Senator Inouye.

Katherine DuHamel, PhD, is a psychologist in the Department of Psychiatry and Behavioral Sciences at Memorial Sloan-Kettering Cancer Center. Her practice focuses primarily on helping cancer patients and their loved ones cope with the distress associated with a devastating illness. She has published peer-reviewed articles on stress symptoms in medical populations, including posttraumatic stress disorder.

Cheryl Gore-Felton, PhD, is associate professor of psychiatry and behavioral sciences at Stanford University Medical Center. She has authored and co-authored more than 70 scientific articles, book chapters, and manuals on the biopsychosocial impact of chronic, life-threatening illnesses with particular focus on HIV/AIDS. A clinician, researcher, and teacher, she focuses on the amelioration of trauma-related symptoms and behaviors among culturally diverse populations.

Don M. Hartsough, PhD, is a retired clinical psychologist. He specialized in crisis intervention, critical incident stress, public safety, and disaster psychology. He directed Purdue's clinical psychology program, founded a crisis center, taught CISM, and was a pioneer disaster psychologist. In Indianapolis, he initiated CISM teams for public safety departments and was a hostage negotiator.

Harold Kudler, MD, is associate clinical professor of psychiatry at Duke University. He has led the Undersecretary for Veterans Affairs' (VA) Special Committee on PTSD, co-led development of VA/Department of Defense Joint Clinical Practice Guidelines on PTSD, and serves on the Board of the International Society for Traumatic Stress Studies.

Frederick J. Lanceley, MSAJ, is director of Crisis Negotiation Associates and author of *On-Scene Guide for Crisis Negotiators*. He retired from the Federal Bureau of Investigation as senior negotiator and program manager of its internationally recognized crisis negotiation training and participated in numerous hostage and kidnapping cases. He has trained law enforcement officers in the United States and in more than 50 countries.

Elana Newman, PhD, associate professor at the University of Tulsa, studies assessment and prevention of maladaptive traumatic responses, journalism and traumatic stress, and ethics of trauma-focused research. She is president of the International Society for Traumatic Stress Studies and has served on a number of editorial boards, including the *Journal of Traumatic Stress*.

Jeff Reiter, PhD, is co-director of the Primary Care Behavioral Health Consultation (BHC) services at Community Health Centers of King County (CHCKC) in Seattle, Washington. He frequently lectures about and co-authored a book on the BHC model. Dr. Reiter holds an ABPP in behavioral psychology and previously served as a psychologist in the Air Force for eight years.

Charles D. Spielberger, PhD, ABPP, is distinguished research professor and director, Center for Research in Behavioral Medicine and Health Psychology, University of South Florida. Author, co-author, or editor of more than 400 professional publications, Spielberger's research focuses on anxiety, curiosity, depression, job stress, and the experience, expression, and control of anger.

Beth Hudnall Stamm, PhD, is research professor, director of Telehealth, director of the National Child Traumatic Stress Center for Rural, Frontier, and Tribal Health, and director of the Idaho State University Institute of Rural Health. Dr. Stamm has more than 100 publications, including focus on health policy, cultural trauma, telehealth, and secondary traumatic stress among health care providers.

Jamie Talan is a science reporter with an expertise in brain and behavior. She has worked on staff for *Newsday* since 1985. She has also written for dozens of national magazines, including *Scientific American MIND* and *Psychology Today*. She co-wrote a book with her husband—*The Death of Innocents*, which won an Edgar Award for best nonfiction.

ABOUT THE SERIES

The Praeger Series in Contemporary Psychology

In this series, experts from various disciplines peer through the lens of psychology telling us answers they see for questions of human behavior. Their topics may range from humanity's psychological ills—addictions, abuse, suicide, murder and terrorism among them—to works focused on positive subjects including intelligence, creativity, athleticism and resilience. Regardless of the topic, the goal of this series remains constant—to offer innovative ideas, provocative considerations and useful beginnings to better understand human behavior.

Series Editor

Chris E. Stout, PsyD, MBA
University of Illinois College of Medicine, Department of Psychiatry

Advisory Board

Bruce E. Bonecutter, PhD
University of Illinois at Chicago
Director, Behavioral Services, Elgin Community Mental Health Center

Joseph A. Flaherty, MD
University of Illinois College of Medicine and College of Public Health
Chief of Psychiatry, University of Illinois Hospital

Michael Horowitz, PhD
Chicago School of Professional Psychology
President, Chicago School of Professional Psychology

Sheldon I. Miller, MD
Northwestern University
Director, Stone Institute of Psychiatry, Northwestern Memorial Hospital

Dennis P. Morrison, PhD
Chief Executive Officer, Center for Behavioral Health, Indiana
President, Board of Directors, Community Healthcare Foundation, Indiana

William H. Reid, MD
University of Texas Health Sciences Center
Chair, Scientific Advisory Board, Texas Depressive and Manic Depressive Association

Recent Titles in Contemporary Psychology

Helping Children Cope with the Death of a Parent: A Guide for the First Year
Paddy Greenwall Lewis and Jessica G. Lippman

Martyrdom: The Psychology, Theology, and Politics of Self-Sacrifice
Rona M. Fields, with Contributions from Cóilín Owens, Valérie Rosoux, Michael Berenbaum, and Reuven Firestone

Redressing the Emperor: Improving Our Children's Public Mental Health System
John S. Lyons

Havens: Stories of True Community Healing
Leonard Jason and Martin Perdoux

Psychology of Terrorism, Condensed Edition: Coping with the Continuing Threat
Chris E. Stout, editor

Handbook of International Disaster Psychology, Volumes I–IV
Gilbert Reyes and Gerard A. Jacobs, editors

The Psychology of Resolving Global Conflicts: From War to Peace, Volumes 1–3
Mari Fitzduff and Chris E. Stout, editors

The Myth of Depression as Disease: Limitations and Alternatives to Drug Treatment
Allan M. Leventhal and Christopher R. Martell

Preventing Teen Violence: A Guide for Parents and Professionals
Sherri N. McCarthy and Claudio Simon Hutz

Making Enemies Unwittingly: Humiliation and International Conflict
Evelin Gerda Lindner

Collateral Damage: The Psychological Consequences of America's War on Terrorism
Paul R. Kimmel and Chris E. Stout, editors

Terror in the Promised Land: Inside the Anguish of the Israeli-Palestinian Conflict
Judy Kuriansky, editor